Management Education

Management Education in the New Europe

Edited by **Monica Lee,**
Director of Human Resource Development Pathway Unit
Lancaster University

Hugo Letiche,
Professor of International Business and Research Methodology
Keele University

Robert Crawshaw
Lecturer in Modern Languages
Lancaster University

Michael Thomas
Professor of Marketing
Strathclyde University

INTERNATIONAL THOMSON BUSINESS PRESS
I ⓣ P An International Thomson Publishing Company

London • Bonn • Boston • Johannesburg • Madrid • Melbourne • Mexico City • New York • Paris
Singapore • Tokyo • Toronto • Albany, NY • Belmont, CA • Cincinnati, OH • Detroit, MI

Management Education in the New Europe

First published by International Thomson Business Press

I(T)P   A division of International Thomson Publishing Inc.
        The ITP logo is a trademark under licence

British Library Cataloguing-in-Publication Data
A catalogue record for this book is available from the British Library

First edition 1996

Typeset in th UK by J&L Composition Ltd, Filey, North Yorkshire
Printed in the UK by Clays Ltd, St Ives plc

ISBN 0-415-100135

International Thomson Business Press   International Thomson Business Press
Berkshire House   20 Park Plaza
168–173 High Holborn   13th Floor
London WC1V 7AA   Boston MA 02116
UK   USA

http://www.itbp.com

Contents

Figures

Tables

Notes on contributors

Professor Emeritus Francis Aguilar is Executive Director of the Management Education Alliance, comprising 21 corporations and business schools dedicated to improving management education for minority business students. He had served as Deputy Director, Central and Eastern European Teachers Program, Chairman, International Teachers Program, and Faculty Chairman, International Senior Managers Program in Switzerland. He recently authored *Managing Corporate Ethics* (Oxford University Press, 1994) and *General Managers in Action*, 2nd ed.(OUP, 1992). He received an honorary D.Ec.Sc. from Janus Pannonius University in 1995.

Address: Professor Francis Aguilar, Graduate School of Business Administration, Soldiers Field, Harvard University, Boston, MA 02163, USA.

Robert Crawshaw is a lecturer in Modern Languages at Lancaster University. Formerly Director of International Relations in the Management School at Lancaster and adviser on higher education to the European Commission, he is joint editor of the series *European Business Environments* and author of the EC study *The European Dimension in Management Education*, as well as of books and articles on language and management.

Address: Mr Robert Crawshaw, French Studies, Lancaster University, Lancaster LA1 4YX, UK.

Steve Crawshaw was born in 1955. He studied Russian and German at Oxford and Leningrad Universities and lived in Poland from 1978 to 1980. He worked for the *Economist* and for Granada Television before joining *The Independent* on its launch in 1986. From 1988 to 1992 he was East Europe Editor of *The Independent*, covering the revolutions of 1989, the collapse of the Soviet Union and the wars in Yugoslavia. From 1992 to 1995 he was the Germany correspondent. He has been Chief Foreign Correspondent of *The Independent* since 1995, and is author of *Goodbye to the USSR* (1992, 1993, Bloomsbury).

Address: Mr Steve Crawshaw, Chief Foreign Correspondent, The Independent, 69 Huddleston Road, London N7 0AE, UK.

Professor Edward Cyrson is Professor of Economics and Marketing in the School of Law and Administration at Adam Mickiewicz University, Poznań. He graduated in Law from Adam Mickiewicz University, Poznań (1965), and in Economics from the University of Warsaw (1966). He obtained his PhD in Economics and Post-doctoral Habilitation in International Economics at the College of Foreign Trade, Main School of Commerce, Warsaw. He teaches marketing at graduate and doctoral levels and serves as a marketing consultant to several non-profit institutions and business companies. He has twice been Chair of the Department of Economic Sciences, has had two appointments as External Professor in the USA (1981–7), and is an alumnus of Harvard Business School (ISMP). He carries out research in International Economics, Business and Marketing, and has published extensively in this field. Recent publications include *Multinational Corporations: Patterns of Foreign Expansion* (1981, Warsaw: PWN) and *Fundamentals in Economics and Business* (co-author and ed., 1996, Warsaw: PWN).

Address: Professor Edward Cyrson, Adam Mickiewicz University, School of Law and Administration, Department of Management and Marketing, 90 Sw. Marcin Street, 60–809 Poznań, Poland.

Professor Jerzy Dietl was born in Poland in 1927. From 1950 until 1968 he was Assistant Professor and Associate Professor at Poznań School of Economics. Since 1968 he has been Associate Professor and Full Professor at the Department of Marketing at the University of Łódź, and was Visiting Professor in Finland in 1975. He was also Director of the Marketing Institute. Between 1989 and 1991 he was Senator of the Republic of Poland and Chairman of the Extraordinary Committee for Economic Legislation. He has been President of the Educational Enterprise Foundation since 1991. He is still a member of a number of international editorial boards and boards of directors of different research institutions and other organizations. He has lectured at over forty different universities in Poland and abroad. His main area of interest is business administration and marketing. He is author of over 400 publications in Poland and abroad.

Address: Professor Jerzy Dietl, President of Foundation Council, Educational Enterprise Foundation, ul. Piotrkowska 86, 90–103 Łódź, Poland.

Ms Kristina Genell is a PhD candidate at the Department of Business Administration, Lund University, Sweden. She is presently completing her thesis, which is about changes in education in business administration and management at Polish and Russian universities. The study is based on an institutional perspective and the ongoing change processes are interpreted as processes of de-institutionalization, re-institutionalization and translation.

Address: Ms Kristina Genell, Department of Business Administration, Lund University, PO Box 7080, S–220 07 Lund, Sweden.
E-mail: Kristina.Genell@fek.lu.se

Dr Devi Jankowicz is Reader in Management, and Director of the Central & Eastern European Unit (CEEU) at Teesside Business School, University of Teesside. His interests in the occupational applications of Personal Construct Psychology and Repertory Grid technique inform his research in organizational behaviour and development. He maintains an uneasy, busy, but hopefully fruitful, balance between these interests and the more administrative duties involved in leading the CEEU's management development programmes in Bulgaria, Poland, Romania, Slovakia, the Ukraine and the Far-Eastern CIS. His main teaching involvement is with research methods at MBA and professional personnel management programme level, and he is the author of a successful basic text in this field.

Address: Dr Devi Jancowicz, Reader in Management, Teesside Business School, University of Teesside, Flatts Lane, Normanby, Middlesbrough, Cleveland TS6 0QS, UK.
E-mail: devi@Tees.ac.uk or anima@devi.demon.co.uk

Associate Professor Monika Kostera is currently at the Faculty of Management at Warsaw University, and teaches Organizational Sociology and the Anthropology of Organizing. Her fields of interest are the poetics of organization, organizational impressionism and expressionism, and the social anthropology of change. Recent publications in English can be found in the *Scandinavian Journal of Management, Organisation Studies and Management Learning.* Recent publications in Polish include *Postmodernizm w zarzadzaniu* (Warsaw: PWE, 1996).

Address: Monika Kostera, Warsaw School of Management, Szturmowa 3, 026 78 Warsaw, Poland.

Professor Dr Andrej K. Kozminski is Professor of Management at Warsaw University in Poland, Director of the International Postgraduate Management Centre and Rector of the College of Entrepreneurship and Management. Since 1990 he has been Visiting Professor at the University of California, Los Angeles. He is Vice-President of the Central and East European Management Development Association (CEEMAN) and a member of the European Foundation for Management Development (EFMD) Board. He specializes in management and enterprise restructuring in the economies in transition and international and comparative management. He has published seventeen books and over 250 articles in all major languages. Recent publications include: *Catching Up? Organisational and Management Change in the Ex-Socialist Block* (1993) and *Winning: Continuous Improvement Theory in High Performance Organisations* (1995), both published by the State University of New York Press.

Address: Professor Andrzej Kozminski, Director & Professor, International Postgraduate Management Center, Warsaw University, ul Nowy Swiat 4, 00–497 Warsaw, Poland.

Dr Monica Lee is Director of the Human Resource Development Pathway Unit, Lancaster University, UK. She came to academe from the business world, where she was managing director of a development consultancy. She has worked extensively in Central Europe and the CIS coordinating and collaborating in research and teaching initiatives, each of which have confused her attempts to make sense out of life. She believes that organizations are a function of the people within them, and therefore that most management disciplines are really just subsets of HRD. Her controversial approach can be seen in her recent publications in *Management Learning* (26, 2, 1995), *Personnel Review* (24, 6, 1995) and *Human Resource Development* (J. Stewart and J. McGoldrick (eds), 1996, London: Pitman).

Address: Dr Monica Lee, Director, The HRD Pathway Unit, Department of Management Learning, The Management School, Lancaster University, Lancaster LA1 4YX, UK.
E-mail: m.lee@lancaster.ac.uk

Professor Hugo Letiche is Professor of International Business and Research Methodology at Keele University, UK, and lectures in Research Methodology at Rotterdam School of Management, Erasmus University, The Netherlands. His research interests centre on postmodernism, knowledge work/management and the ethnography of work. Via TEMPUS and ACE projects he has been active, principally in Poland and Slovakia, in the process of redirecting management education in Central Europe. Recent publications are in *Studies in Organisations and Cultures* (vol. 1, no. 1, 1995), *Understanding Management* (S. Linstead, R. Grafton-Small and P. Jeffcutt (eds), 1996, London: Sage) and *Organisational Behaviour and Change in Europe* (F. Chevalier and M. Segella (eds), 1996, London: Sage).

Address: Professor Hugo Letiche, Rotterdam School of Management, Erasmus University, Burg Oudlaan 50, PO Box 1738, 3000 Dr Rotterdam, The Netherlands.
E-mail: H.Letiche@fac.fbk.EUR.NL

Dr Slawomir Magala acquired a PhD in Philosophy of Science at the Poznań University and followed this with post-PhD research as a Humboldt Fellow at the Goethe University in Frankfurt-am-Main, specializing in sociology of culture and organizations. He is a co-founder of a research committee on social movements and change of the International Sociological Association, a member of the International Academy of Business Disciplines in the USA and an expert of the United Nations International Development Organisation (UNIDO) for assistance and development programmes in business management education in the post-Communist countries. He has travelled and lectured in the United States, Denmark, France and Switzerland. Since 1995 he has been teaching cross-cultural management, theories of organizational change and problems of transition to the market economies at the Department of Business Management of Erasmus University in the Netherlands and participates in management development programmes of the EC in China, Singapore, Poland, Hungary, the Czech Republic, Russia, Slovakia and Slovenia. He has written a number of books reflecting his research interests, including cross-cultural studies of India, China, Russia, Poland and Hungary, the role of the critical theory in the sciences of management and the problem of sociocultural and economic transformation processes.

Address: Dr Slawomir Magala, Associate Professor of Cultural Anthropology, Rotterdam School of Management, Erasmus University, Burg Oudlaan 50, PO Box 1738, 3000 Dr Rotterdam, The Netherlands.
E-mail: s.magala@fac.fbk.EUR.NL

Dr Urszula Ornarowicz is Vice-Dean of Elementary Studies at Warsaw School of Economics. She specializes in Operational Management and teaches in the Department of Management Theory. She works with the management of big and small companies, the management of human resources and management education, and publishes extensively in these areas.

Address: Dr Urszula Ornarowicz, Vice-Dean of Elementary Studies, Warsaw School of Economics, Leonidasa 33, 02–239 Warsaw, Poland.

Professor Charles Gordon Shenton is 60 years old and is of French and British nationality. He obtained his MA at Oxford in 1959 and his PhD at Harvard University in 1968. He has been Professor of French Literature at Harvard University, USA (1968–75); Head of Studies at ISIGC (Institut Supérieur de Gestion Commerciale, Saint Étienne, France; 1976–80); Head of the Language Department at Groupe ESC Lyon, France (1980–7); and Dean of ESC Lyon, France, since 1987. His publications include *The Fictions of the Self, The Early Works of Maurice Barrès* (1979, Chapel Hall); *Le Robert & Collins du management*, co-authored with Michael Péron (1992, Dictionnaires Le Robert); and *L'Europe interculturelle, mythe ou réalité* (1991, Éditions d'Organisation).

Address: Professor Gordon Shenton, ESC Lyon, 23 avenue Guy de Collongue, BP 174, 69132 Écully Cédex, France, or 4 rue de Villeneuve, 69130 Écully, France.

Professor Marianna Strzyżewska-Kaminska is Professor of Economics at the Department of Marketing in the Warsaw School of Economics. She is a member of the Scientific Board for the Institute of Management, Polish Academy of Sciences and is Director of Doctoral Studies of the Collegium of Enterprise Sciences. She is also a member of the Interregional Network on Privatisation (UNDP) and Adviser to the Minister of Finance. She is the author of several books and articles, and her recent interests include marketing in small businesses and marketing orientation in Polish enterprises.

Address: Professor dr hab. Marianna Strzyżewska Kaminska, Szkola Glowna Handlowa (Warsaw School of Economics), Al. Niepodleglosci 162, 02–554 Warsaw, Poland.

Professor Michael J. Thomas is Professor of Marketing at Strathclyde University. During 1995 he was Chairman of the Chartered Institute of Marketing. He has been involved in Poland and Eastern Europe since 1977. He founded the Gdańsk Managers' Training Foundation (Know-How Fund) and is on the Board of Directors of the Alliance of Universities for Democracy. The President of Poland, Lech Walesa, awarded him the Commanders Cross of the Polish Order of Merit in November 1994 for his services to the Polish economic transformation. He has published a number of books and journal articles, and his *Handbook of Marketing* (Gower Press, 4th edn) is now translated into Polish. He travels abroad regularly as a visiting professor (Indiana University Graduate Business School, Georgetown University Business School, University of Tennessee, Rochester Institute of Technology, University of Malta, University of Karlstad). He believes only in the efficacy of ornithology as a means to saving souls.

Address: Professor Michael Thomas, University of Strathclyde, Stenhouse Building, 173 Cathedral Street, Glasgow G4 0RQ, UK.
E-mail: michaelt@market.strath.ac.uk

Professor Bogdan Wawrzyniak is Business Administration Professor with the Institute of Organisation and Management in Industry, Chairman of the Polish Foundation for Management Promotion and Vice-President of the Committee of Organisation and Management Sciences, Polish Academy of Sciences. He is the author of several books and over 200 articles on business management. His special interests include the development of strategies and current operations management of business enterprises in crisis.

Address: Professor Bogdan Wawrzyniak, Warsaw Central School of Commerce, Warsaw, Poland.

Acknowledgements

With many thanks to Charles Lee and Maria Letiche for putting up with their spouses during the creation of this book, but especially during the turmoil surrounding the activities described in the book.

Thank you, also, to Carole Elliott (Administrator of the HRD Pathway Unit at Lancaster) for her unfailing efficiency and support during the aforementioned turmoil.

Last, but not least, there are many people from across the world who contributed significantly to the projects described here, and who go unnamed. To mention everybody would be a book in itself. Thank you for your effort and your involvement. You are remembered with fondness.

Introduction

This book exists because a group of authors agreed that they had to address the questions and doubts, surprises and successes, ideals and restrictions they had met with while working in management education in post-Communist Central Europe. The editors are faculty in the UK and the Netherlands who have been 'purveyors' of 'management knowledge' from the western capitalist countries to the Central European states in transition. The 'recipients', for want of a better word, were Central European (predominantly Polish) academics. The outcomes of our educational project were almost impossible to foresee, given the rapidly evolving and unpredictable economic and political developments in the recipients' culture(s). Nevertheless we voluntarily engaged in a ritual contract, in which the providers offered a 'model of good practice' to recipients who may very well have been less interested in the model itself than in the insights and experience which participation in the project might afford. Likewise, the 'purveyors' hoped to create a 'learning community' where the 'model' would be (re)negotiated on the basis of local needs, i.e. they wanted something else to happen than what they 'contracted' for.

The economic and symbolic value of what we did was unpredictable to us all. Would the workshops and seminars, business visits and research periods be marketable in the context of Brussels (or London, New York, etc.) decision-makers; and also prove marketable in a Central Europe in the midst of economic transition? If the myth of western 'management knowledge' reigned supreme in Central Europe, would potential participants value our emphasis on local circumstances and contexts? And if our plans proved 'marketable'; would we, the 'purveyors', still be able to look at ourselves in a mirror, after the fact? Voiced less cynically, were we effective 'change agents'? Did we develop key 'competencies' needed in a market economy? Could we provide a 'valid model' for management training?

How far did we truly want to 'sell' a model of management education which we believed in; and how far were we really willing 'to go local'? How much of what actually happened came from the western visitors; and how much from the Central Europeans themselves? What were the links really like between the two groups? For fifty years the perceptions which Western and Eastern Europeans have had of one another have been saturated with ideology. During the last five years we have been able to rediscover that we actually live on the same continent. On both sides there have been surprises, but they are often to be found in small everyday things. For 'westerners', being a 'Zloty millionaire' seemed very strange; for the Poles, the size of their hosts' houses in England, Scotland or Holland was extraordinary. As we got to know one another we went through different phases of 'strangeness' and 'familiarity'. The shock of a first (Spring 1990) visit to Warsaw and Poznań was the discovery that the people seemed to be so similar to those at home. Later visits revealed that Polish academics got along with one another in very different ways from ourselves. They seemed to accept authority and hierarchy, as well as inefficiency and needless waste, more than we do; and to enjoy a level of camaraderie including song and fun-making as well as toasts and speeches, unknown to us. But later we discovered that they find it just as hard to change, to live with anxiety and to deal with constant reorganization as we do. But they do hold down as many as five jobs per person and are entrepreneurial to a degree that we don't even have nightmares about!

For many of us, emerging from the Cold War, working in Central Europe was exotic. A Polish colleague described an American academic who had come on sabbatical to Gdańsk because it was more strange and foreign than going to his other possibility, Peru. The Pole was filled with disbelief, and was not quite sure whether the idea angered or amused him. The experiences described and analysed in the book bear witness to the fact that the process of learning in the unusual, even unique, conditions of the new Europe is a dual one. Through their engagement in the different projects presented in *Management Education in the New Europe*, the Central European academics became yet more adept at turning western management thought to their own ends. The 'providers' for their part found it necessary to question, still further than had hitherto been the case, the rationale on which their own educational models are based. Hence there were changes on both sides.

On the side of the 'providers', the degree of 'certainty' or belief in the validity of the type of programme and the nature of the knowledge propagated differed at times markedly. What was 'on offer' started from very different socio-economic and pedagogical presuppositions. At one extreme there was the American-style MBA, in which learning was based on an a priori view of corporate reality supported by existing case-study material; at the other extreme the principle of 'action learning' in which the responsibility for understanding the process of learning and of applying knowledge was deemed a matter for the 'learners/educators'. In reviewing the range of experiences, which fall at different points on this scale, the book considers the educational challenges which face the 'western' educator attempting to 'empower' Polish learners to make changes within their own institutional environments. The book is, therefore, wide-ranging in its implications; it explores an educational *problématique* rather than attempting to offer ready-made solutions to a clearly defined problem. Above all, it does not express a partisan point of view but presents readers with a variety of information and approaches which have to be evaluated according to their own terms of reference.

In the period following the fall of the Berlin wall, Central European countries and Poland in particular, because of its readiness for change were a rich terrain for misunderstanding bred of excessive optimism. Expectations were often much too high. The utopian vision of capitalism, as a social panacea, was a consequence of the Communist years. It is not a complete caricature to say that an MBA from the west was viewed by many as the key to immediate personal prosperity in the new economic and political world. The fact that organizations in which the MBA's management principles could be implemented did not yet exist was of secondary consideration. If they did not exist, then they could be created. The writers contributing here have avoided both the extreme optimism of championing unrealistic instantaneous change and the subsequent excessive pessimism resulting from thrashing gradual step-for-step transition.

Fuelled by support from international funding agencies, both parties in the learning experience voluntarily stepped into a common adventure. There was the hope that investment in educational human resources would bring about institutional change from within, and that it would do so at a rate which was noteworthy. Despite the apparent eagerness for change, apart from the Polish sense of tradition and independence of spirit, it was naive to suppose that Communist institutional networks could be instantly dismantled with foreign 'help'. Some individuals involved with the programmes of educational reconstruction described in this book were still so closely bound up with the structures of the previous regime that it was impossible, whatever their intentions, for them to free themselves from their continuing responsibilities and internal allegiances. There was an inevitable tension between the idealism of 'providers' and 'recipients', and the bureaucratic realities. Continued existence of state monopolies, the unchanging assumptions of senior managers, educationalists and politicians who could not immediately be replaced and the economic and organizational difficulties of effecting bottom-up change all restricted what was possible.

Former members of the *nomenclatura*, younger more enthusiastic innovators, the naturally entrepreneurial, have developed alternative enterprises in the fields of consulting, sales and distribution. Such operations led to the growth of para-educational institutions offering independent 'management' qualifications. The activities of these 'knowledge workers', which have led to a broad range of degrees of varying pedigree, may well be undermining the state monopoly on education. There is little public money to support the university system and to introduce the changes which would be necessary if fresh and reinvigorated programmes of learning are to be implemented. The main consequence of the western-funded programmes described in this book has, therefore, been to excite the imagination and entrepreneurial initiative of individuals. They are only now beginning to effect real institutional reform often from without rather than within. The fact that the state institutions have been resistant to change while individual enterprise has flourished has led to a blurring of the boundaries in all spheres of educational activity related to management: between the public and private, education and training, consulting and post-experience learning. It has become clear that the concept of the university, and hence of higher education as a whole, has been partly 'disestablished' or – literally – 'mobilised' (see Chapter 16, by Kristina Gennell and Monika Kostera). The availability of courses of different types, to different recipients, in different contexts, for different purposes, offered by a range of different people and leading to different qualifications has meant that management education has become a commodity whose quality standards, conditions of packaging and delivery, purposes and goals are now very variable.

Against this fluid and flexible environment, the reference points of the 'providers' were inevitably called into question. To bring western management principles to bear in such an unfamiliar, yet responsive, context amounted to holding a mirror to one's own shortcomings and diversity. It became clear, if it was not known already, that despite the emphasis on European unity, western 'models' of management education were more culture-specific than had 'traditionally' been supposed. Western management knowledge did not transplant easily to an environment where market share, competition and product quality were more or less alien concepts at the corporate level but operated ruthlessly at the level of the individual entrepreneur. The existence of a new and burgeoning capitalist community on the doorstep of old nationalized industrial mammoths generates uncertainties to which western management educators have no unequivocal answers.

Furthermore, during the last thirty years western researchers have pretty much concluded that no 'standard science' of management, grounded in a general theoretical framework, capable of producing universal propositions holding for all organizations is possible. At least three key sources of uncertainty make any such general theoretical framework problematic: (1) how cultural conditions influence business, (2) how relevant socio-technical domain(s) impact on it, and (3) how interdependencies between the various operational sub-units effect it (Thompson 1967). We lack a trustworthy cause–effect understanding of the culture at large, of socio-technical systems and of the interdependencies between organizational sub-components. No closed-system approach, predicated on formal rationality, is truly workable. At best, management thought can achieve 'bounded rationality'; i.e., a way of attuning organizational structure to its cultural environment while respecting relevant socio-technical parameters. For instance, Thompson, in effect, calls for a process of political bargaining and negotiation to create a 'dominant coalition' which can 'cope' with managerial uncertainty.

Open-systems thinking leads to the 'bounded rationality' of 'good enough' decisions (Simon 1947; March and Simon 1958). Faced with durable macro-economic problems to which there are no evident solutions, the debate in Western Europe focuses more on different possible responses by management education and training than on 'certainties'. Essentially, current debate is linked to the extent to which state regulation and the protection of social welfare is thought desirable in a modern capitalist economy, and whether the state ought to have an industrial policy which encourages the development of a high-tech/high-value-added economy. The debate raises questions of how best to strike a balance between socio-technical, political-economic and personal skills in educating a managerial elite capable of handling the complexity of organizational leadership. Thus, management education involves much more than widespread training in basic business skills. The encounter, in the post-Communist societies, with an emerging capitalism, whose future form is still uncertain, only increases the uncertainty about what form of 'management knowledge' might be relevant. It is clear that in an environment where the focus is on practical skills and immediate outcomes, issues of social desirability and cultural balance can all too easily take second place. Yet it is precisely in a transitional social context of this kind that open-ended, developmental forms of learning are potentially most relevant. This, too, is a question which the book explores.

The Central European academics and entrepreneurs involved in the projects described in *Management Education in the New Europe* are not so much 'recipients' of a body of knowledge or beneficiaries of 'good educational practice', as active participants in a debate. While avid for insight and experience, they did not stop there. Whatever ingredients of 'knowledge' were provided were immediately translated into the 'know-how' most appropriate to their circumstances. The outcome has been the potential disestablishment of educational provision, coupled with a continual renegotiation of roles and boundaries. It is possible that educational initiatives, such as those described in this book in the field of management training in central Europe, will merely benefit the multinational (consulting) corporations who will redefine the field in terms of their own commercial and cultural goals. The entrepreneurial energy and commitment of younger academics and consultants may, thus, not reach students at all.

The accounts given in this book illustrate that Management Education is a complex and situated activity that defies easy analysis and facile prescription of 'right' solutions. Even the distinction between 'recipients' and 'providers' has become blurred; the key questions have had to be addressed to all participants. Often it is the seemingly simple, childlike, question that is the hardest to answer: what are we doing here? The authors attempt to account for their 'doing' in their own terms, and so have presented us with a complex conceptual web of very differing material. To what extent do we want to untangle this web? The accounts include everything from history to the future; they span theory and practice; they arise from different discipline-, political-, cultural- and gender-based perspectives. The authors hold up for view a gamut of different interpretations that can be placed upon management education and its relevance to change in the new Central Europe. To impose any regimented discipline upon this tangle of viewpoints would be to sanitize its complexity and to deny its reality.

The aspect that unites each of these accounts is the notion of change. Almost all the authors have been involved in some sort of western-funded management education change programme in central Europe.[1] These programmes assume that higher education (policies, structures, staff and provision) can have a deep-seated influence upon national development. Most were designed to help faculty from universities across Central Europe to evaluate critically (and redesign if necessary) their management teaching provision in the light of a range of different western experiences, within an atmosphere of open academic investigation and sharing. The editors believe that the more successful programmes have been based upon some variant of 'action learning'. Resultant change projects have focused upon the generation of alternative approaches to existing provision or the creation of new provision; and range across the full spectrum of management education. Some immediate results: increased inter-university networking; publication of home-grown teaching materials (for instance, a book which contained a variety of Polish case studies springing directly from a change programme; Bednarski 1991); and implementation of new or renewed curriculum.

Within the 'action learning'-based programmes a critical evaluation of a wide range of opinion and practice occurs; it is noticeable that the actors and institutions within these programmes adopt differing logics towards the 'reality' of change: i.e., 'closed', 'patterned' and 'goal-oriented'. These logics were not pushed upon the 'recipients', who tended to shift from one to the other. But, at the risk of over-categorization, the 'assumptions' about 'change' can be seen as follows. In extreme terms, a 'closed logic' of change refers to the view that each system is a fixed whole, and thus 'change' is about confrontation of systems and choices between apparently mutually exclusive alternatives. The titans clash and the best one wins all. In 'patterned logic' life is thought of as a succession of circumstances with change an inherent part of the structure. Any apparent coherence in the 'pattern' is a product of the presenting system(s) employed and depends upon the observer's perspective. A change in perspective will cause the pattern to (seem to) alter; the elements of the pattern will regroup in (apparently) novel formation(s). Boundaries are continually transgressed as one changes perspectives. The third logic incorporates a strong view of 'agency' into the ordering activity. The required end result determines the framework chosen, which then generates the particular pattern of perception needed. Change is about sifting through possible frameworks in order to understand and utilize those elements that best suit the chosen way forward. Entrepreneurship emerges in this activity.

What differentiates the accounts of 'What are we doing here?'; is the focus adopted on the processes of change. All the writers grapple with the bounded logic of change in Central Europe. First, everyone acts on partial information about the current situation, possible courses of action and the likely results of (attempted) change. Second, in any given project one can only explore a few possible change strategies – especially given the impatience for action with which one is confronted. Third, it is very difficult to attach accurate judgements to outcomes – on what scale does one 'measure' change? The change projects discussed were concerned to make the transitions involved 'manageable', mostly without any delusion that 'change' is (really) under control.

The contributions to Part I of the book explore the relationship between management education for change, and the cultural, political and economic boundaries to (potential) action. At issue is how much change has occurred via management education in the post-Communist setting, and in what direction(s)? Limits to the current change programmes in management education are examined. In Part II of the book the writers investigate possibilities for going just a bit further than current boundaries to change permit. This section explores transgressing (more or less) established limits, and innovations leading to new initiatives or the adoption of new perspectives on the change process. The emphasis is more on the possible than the already realized. In Part III we examine proposals for change which try to break down current barriers and transcend the limits described in Part I. Thus, Part I evaluates known initiatives; Part II explores innovative possibilities for breakthroughs and renewal; and Part III proposes logics for moving ahead transcending current limits. The logic of Part I is fairly tightly bound to events; the logic of Part II breaks down some of these boundaries; and the logic of Part III attends to best-case possibilities within the bounded rationality of concrete circumstance and context. Each section thus reflects a different underlying logic (though none of the contributors is as categorical as is implied here).

Each part also reflects a different stage in the development of the programmes described and is accompanied by a case derived from a relevant part of the in-practice experience. The first case illustrates how competing understandings of management education are highlighted when negotiating to establish (the goals of) a programme. The second illustrates the emergent complexity which manifests itself as the boundaries of models of management education are transgressed during the change effort. The third centres on a case, developed during a change programme, which has since been used as teaching material in both Central and Western European institutions. These cases are included in order to help contextualize the associated accounts and in order to emphasize the link between theory and practice evident throughout the book.

In essence, the book reflects the personal challenges, confusion and enjoyment associated with working alongside like-minded and dissimilar colleagues during times of rapid change. The book's writers share a common commitment to describing and analysing our role(s) in fostering management education in Central Europe since 1989. All of us have been directly involved in the processes described. The strength of the book is that its authors have earnt their way to the conclusions presented, by undertaking responsibility for working for change in Central Europe. This is a book from the field, written by authors who have tackled together the concrete problems of working to change management education. It brings the reader into direct contact with a large number of innovators who have been working on the ground to facilitate the new management education in the new Europe.

NOTE

1   Many were involved in a three-year regional TEMPUS programme funded by the EC and Austria that focused upon nascent management education in Central European universities. This programme involved an international partnership, has linked more than forty-five institutions across Europe, fourteen nationalities and 130 management academics (many of whom also held managerial positions in small and medium-sized enterprises). The programme was coordinated by Monica Lee at Lancaster University and was initially entitled East-European Management Teacher Development Programme (EEMTDP). The title was changed to CEMTDP in order to reflect the political changes in Europe that 'centralized' those countries that had previously been 'eastern'.

REFERENCES

Bednarski, A. (1991) *Materiały pomocznicze do cwiczen z organizacji i zaradzania*, (Teaching materials for organization and management courses) Torun: Torun Copernicus University..
March, J. and Simon, H. (1958) *Organisations*, New York: John Wiley.
Simon, H. (1947) *Administrative Behaviour*, New York: Macmillan.
Thompson, J.D. (1967) *Organisations in Action*, New York: McGraw-Hill.

Part I

Competing models of management education: bounded logic

Case 1: in the beginning there was a meeting with the Under Minister of Education

Hugo Letiche

I and two colleagues had an appointment at the Ministry of Education in Warsaw, on Saturday at 11 o'clock, to discuss the possible establishment of a collaborative management education programme for lecturers in Higher Education. We arrived with only a couple of minutes to spare. The taxi had taken longer to get from our hotel than we had predicted. Were we supposed to enter the Ministry at eleven or be somewhere down kilometres of corridors at that time? Was this already a false start?

We rushed up the stairs to the principal entrance. It was a stately building of neo-classical pomposity; just what you'd expect of a Ministry. The door was open; inside it was much darker than outside. The large entrance hall seemed to be deserted. Of course, civil servants do not work on Saturday. I should not have expected the building to be busy. I assumed that there must be somebody present as the heavy doors had not been locked. Indeed, a small concierge's cubicle off to one side was inhabited. Approaching it, I saw a man there, apparently in his late sixties, reading a newspaper. He looked up, unconcerned, seemingly all alone in this immense building. He responded with a couple of words in Polish and a smile. I asked my way in English, but was unable to make myself understood. Luckily I had the letter confirming our appointment, which I fished out of my briefcase. The concierge nodded in a friendly manner. He pointed to an enormous staircase and held up two fingers. Thus I assumed I had to walk up to the second floor. The concierge picked up a red plastic telephone and dialled. I assumed we had been announced and that someone would be waiting for us.

I felt isolated and exposed, walking across the enormous hallway to the immense granite staircase. The building was stuffy and over-heated; the warmth of my winter coat didn't help. Arriving dishevelled to my first ever appointment with a Polish Under Minister of Education seemed undignified if not downright improper. So, I climbed the stairs slowly, saving my breath, arriving calmly at the second floor. All my fears of being too late had been repressed by the new fear of arriving inappropriately. A young man in his mid-twenties was waiting for us on the second-floor landing. We shook hands and he introduced himself in such a manner that I had no idea where his name began or ended or what his function actually was. But his 'Please follow me' made it clear that I could once again make myself understood in English.

The sense of foreign space without an ability to make oneself understood was gone. High ceilings and broad corridors followed one another for several minutes as we navigated through the Ministry. A knock on a door and we had arrived. He ushered us into a large old-fashioned office decorated in the style of the late 1950s or early 1960s. A large light-wood table flanked by eight chairs stood between me and the Under Minister's desk, which was near the large windows. This was a world of 'former glory'. A thin, balding, grey-haired man was working at the desk in his shirtsleeves. Piles of cardboard-covered dossiers were evidently being examined one by one. Some of them seemed to have red ribbons in them. I briefly wondered what that might mean, but he was standing up to greet us. Evidently he worked under the light of a single old-fashioned desk lamp; an enormous office lit by 60 watts.

The Under Minister shuffled towards us, hand outstretched. This was evidently the Under Minister of Education. He looked much more like the Professor he had been, than like a politician. There was none of the charismatic emanation of power which I'd expected. The Under Minister welcomed us and offered to take my winter coat. I was very happy to be rid of it; the building was so over-heated that being enclosed in a winter coat was hard to bear. I could only guess why this enormous building was so warm on a Saturday. Were they not concerned about the energy loss? Was it all just for the few of us present; or couldn't they regulate the heat? Were we so important, or was the building management so inefficient? Meeting with such a key person had encouraged me to dress as well as I could, given the limited clothes I had brought with me. The Under Minister registered my tie and tweed jacket, and seemed just a bit ashamed of his shirtsleeves and loosely knotted tie. 'Hello, hello. Welcome' – he said as he walked back to his desk and put on his suit jacket. I felt rather silly about 'forcing' an Under Minister to put on his jacket. He seemed relieved and gestured us to sit at a large table in the middle of his office. The young man joined us, pen and pad in hand – he took notes throughout our conversation but did not join in.

'Please explain your project,' he said. I explained what we were proposing to do: 'initiate a cooperative management teacher development programme based on an action-learning model, whereby we facilitate curriculum development and programme renewal'. Was this too much jargon; how could I explain without seeming to talk down to my host? I continued, 'We propose a way of working together in which our role is not to lecture management (whatever is in the text books can be read easily enough by anyone interested), but to discuss how one sets up a new programme, teaches case material, organizes internships, combines consulting and research – in other words, how to facilitate in-practice learning'. I emphasized that we did not envision a programme of visiting management 'Guru's' who deliver their standard speeches, at enormous fees, to local bigwigs. We assumed that it was possible to effect a significant change in management education by helping ordinary university lecturers to change and adapt their teaching. This would be bottom-up work. The lecturers who are responsible for the undergraduate lecture courses would most likely not be the senior academics, but junior faculty. The elite, cosmopolitan, well-informed, international researchers are rarely burdened with the thankless routine of teaching large lecture courses on the introductory level (to management, to marketing, to organization, etc.). If we wanted the managers of the future to develop a post-Communist mindset, we needed to influence the basic undergraduate courses – those which introduce the greatest numbers of students to management and have the broadest general influence.

My host obviously agreed with what I had to say. He nodded repeatedly and often mumbled words of approval. After I finished, he explained his strong agreement with the change strategy I had described. He saw the everyday lecturer and not the elite professors as his concern. The top academics had their own networks and windows on the west. But most lecturers did not have good access to western know-how or the chance to discuss practice with outsiders. The Polish intellectual elite make too many trips and are too often outside the country. The lecturers who really taught the students were too limited in their experience and far too isolated in the pressures of their jobs. The 'foot soldiers' who did most of the work had not benefited from the opening to the West – if anything their bosses were now often absent and the 'juniors' had to stand in for them. Most of the previously proposed international programmes had been elitist. He was very happy at our alternative emphasis.

After a bit more conversation, he pledged his support for our proposal. It had been, really, an effortless and very natural conversation. The Under Minister had been modest in his mannerisms, and had acted more as a host than as an inquisitor. I thought back to my meeting with the Dutch Under Minister of Education; I found him to be an arrogant self-centred man who immediately let you know how privileged you should feel at being permitted to meet him. He had been a Social Democrat who looked at his visitors with an impatient gaze, as if asking 'are you really important enough for me to be talking to?' He had assumed that whatever we wanted we probably didn't deserve it and that we couldn't make it worth his while for him to help us. I was expecting the nasty arrogance of Dutch politicians, and was really very unprepared for the unimposing civility I received in Poland. This Under Minister was not focused on power or a champion of intrigues. Could an Under Minister be an honest individual who conducted a normal open conversation with his guests? I'd never dreamt of such a thing. This certainly was not 'politics as usual' – at least not if I took Holland as my norm.

The Under Minister had voiced opinions and given answers. He seemed quite willing to agree with me and not at all bothered to pretend that he'd had the idea already. His willingness to give direct answers was totally unexpected for me – in Holland politicians always have to consider matters, talk to colleagues and will get back to you. You assume that the politician checks if there's more in it for himself by working with someone else, doing some other project or stealing your idea and giving it to his followers. An alternative alliance or another deal might be better. A Dutch Under Minister wouldn't tell you what he wants and fears, what his criteria for judgement are or what he wants to achieve. By making his principles explicit the Polish Under Minister became accountable. I could come back to him later and argue that if he really believed in 'x' he would have to do 'y'. No Under Minister in Holland would ever get himself into such a position. He'd talk in clichés and generalities, if not riddles and paradoxes, so that he could retain the power to do whatever he wanted later. He would negotiate only from a position of strength; you want and need him, but he's free to choose.

Why was it so strange to have a normal conversation with a government official? Here I was in Warsaw, pretending to bring the 'west' to Poland; when I could not imagine the 'west' displaying the same level of integrity or openness I was encountering in Poland. Of course, I was very glad the meeting had been such a success. The blessing of the Ministry was really all we needed to have an excellent chance of being financed. But paradoxically our legitimacy was now under question. I pretended that we would bring valuable western know-how to Poland, when I doubted the value of what we supposed to import. In fact, I deeply disliked a lot of the 'managerialism' we were probably expected to bring with us. Did the Under Minister understand my duplicity? Did he realize that I'd rather bring a critique of the west to Poland than the 'real' way we did things? Could I maintain the double game; bringing (anti-) western practice to the new Europe funded by a West European government who want me to sell their ideology of success? Would the balancing act remain honest to the agreed goals? Would I betray the Under Minister's trust with what we could and would undertake to do?

In the five ensuing years of work in central Europe, that moment of ambivalence has never repeated itself. We were able to facilitate curriculum change and teaching innovation in management education. Our theoretical and practical know-how was more than up to the challenge. We needed to gain the personal trust of our central European colleagues if we were going to champion change and innovation effectively, but it demanded a lot from us. Of course, dialogue instead of a lecturer's monologue, questioning instead of obedience, and new ideas instead of old ones were all demanding and dangerous. Who were we to make these demands or to put our Polish colleagues into such dangerous situations? Our colleagues back home would never let us challenge their teaching practice (however ineffective) so deeply. But there was the excuse of inevitably – if we didn't challenge them, the market would. At least we offered to help them to change: the market merely demanded new products. The people we met understood that the market's sword of Damocles hung above their heads and were happy for assistance and support. They needed a discourse of western market know-how and management insights to survive. Of course, we would have no control over what they did with that discourse. We could decide to pick and choose which aspects of the western discourse we would present; leaving out the harmful and stressing the creative. Were we clever, merely manipulative, naive or much too arrogant? Did I keep my deal with the Under Minister?

I tried to bring a version of market society discourse to Poland which fitted the liberal democracy of the first post-Communist reform government. That government has long disappeared; who am I really addressing these days; what is the task?

QUESTIONS

1 If you were preparing yourself to present a management education proposal to assist in the development of post-Communist management education to a senior representative of a Central European government, what would be your assumptions about your audience? What would you expect the Central Europeans to want to hear?

2 The proposal made above was tilted to provide maximum funding to Central Europe but to keep intellectual control of the programme firmly in the hands of the providers. It explicitly addressed the theme of 'inequality of earning (wealth)' by subsidizing overhead costs in the new Europe and under-budgeting them in the west. It stressed maximum training value for the money by providing labour-intensive facilitation and project support. What would be the principles of your human resources policy in setting up such a programme?

3 The proposal tried to balance cultural sensitivities by having western staff offer support to Central European-run, and -led, projects. Thus the Central Europeans had to define their own change agendas and set local pragmatic change-goals which the western academics would then help them (as far as possible) to realize. The 'outsiders' were not telling the Central Europeans what to do. Would you follow a parallel or a different strategy?

4 If you were responsible for a comparable project proposal, what pressures and restrictions would you expect to encounter from administrators and politicians from your home country/institution? How would you handle these?

FOREWORD

In the chapters in Part I of this book the authors examine the baggage that western scholars took with them to the new Europe, and what the Central European (mainly Polish) academics supposed and hoped they would bring. This has been a process of 'translations', with each party trying to give and/or take what he or she wants to contribute/have. Everyone acts within their own assumptions and needs; expects their own definitions of the context to prevail; and tries to enrol as many others as possible into their version of change. The different claims are offered here as examples of a complex field of action. In order to be able to take action, each of the players is trying to impose his/her discourse on the others.

Chapter 2

Management education on the threshold level: a study of Polish business schools

Edward Cyrson and Urszula Ornarowicz

To paraphrase a proverb: 'one Polish management educator will be charming; a few Polish management educators will probably create unrest; and many Polish management educators will almost certainly form a "Polish problem"'. Since 1989 management education in Poland has graduated from the phase of 'unrest' to that of 'problematic'. Polish management education seems to be undergoing a cycle of 'boom then bust': numerous private business schools opened, then flourished briefly, but seem now to be floundering. They have been hampered by a severe absence of qualified instructors, a lack of resources to support research or curriculum development, and the inability to deliver managerial success to their graduates. The traditional university sector has seen a faculty which stayed on the payroll but lectured at the private schools to earn extra income, only later to turn their backs on the private schools and go into the much more lucrative activity of consulting. Prior to 1989 economic and management education in Poland was, in essence, realized by thirteen universities and institutes of economic studies. Now there are many times that number of players. But despite the clear institutional dynamism there has been little fundamental curricular renewal. In effect, the same teachers are delivering many more monologues than they used to. Few case studies, internships/fieldwork or practical applications of knowledge have found their way into higher management education. Even a clear division between the two fields of economics and management has not yet been realized at the university level. While a severe lack of professional management clearly forms one of the crucial problems of post-Communist societies, the effort to meet that need has been characterized more by increasing the quantity of the educational delivery than by adapting it radically to the new circumstances.

The transition from a state monopoly economy to market-driven economics has created an enormous gap between what Polish managers need to know and their previous training and/or experience. How can managers deal with profitability if fixed and variable costs are unknowable? Or act strategically if no SWOT[1] analyses have ever been made? How does one get good management if all decision-making is intuitively directed to short-term problems and production factors rather than to the logic of the market? Managerial careers used to depend on loyalty to the party, wherein subordination to superiors was much more important than taking initiative. Subservience, and not effectiveness, was rewarded. Prices, output levels and investment decisions were all determined by the higher ministerial echelons; and not by hands-on managers. While many people may have changed jobs since 1989, the vast majority of managers and management educators are still exactly the same people as before.

In this chapter we will indicate what has already been achieved to change management education since the fall of Communism; and we will try to open up discussion of what steps should follow. Our analysis of the current state of management education in Poland is based on research conducted between 1989 and 1995. First (phase one), we identified and globally characterized the institutions of management education. The term 'education' was interpreted broadly, to cover academic education, specialized instruction and vocational training of present, as well as potential, managers. The business schools studied are state-owned as well as private; university-based as well as entirely outside the university system. Provision includes vocational training and professional improvement, specialized instruction and academic degree-granting programmes. In fact, the university degree programmes and advanced specialized programmes are less popular than vocational training courses devoted to professional improvement. Student bodies seem more to be recruited from the pool of candidates for managerial positions than from actual managerial cadres, which certainly influences the nature of the demand.

Second (phase two), we have identified the nature of the educational activities undertaken by the various business schools, and analysed the internal and external factors influencing their choice of activities. Research was done by questionnaire; forty-three schools were polled in phase one and forty-five in phase two of the project. Eighty per cent of the schools taking part in phase one also took part in phase two. In phase two, nineteen universities participated and twenty-six non-universities. During phase two, a questionnaire was distributed amongst 155 students of business schools. The analysis of management education in Poland presented here is based on this research.

WHAT IS A 'MANAGER'?

Interpretation of the concepts 'management/managing/manager' are crucial to defining business school curricula. Is the quality of the 'manager's leadership', or the 'structure of management', or the 'processes of managing' (or whatever combination of these factors) considered to be the key to success? Differences between a faculty's concept of the 'manager' and the students can lead to conflict. Thus, it is important to know how the 'manager' is perceived by business school faculty and students. Our research showed that the two groups of respondents most frequently arrived at one of four meanings:

Definition 1 A person involved in leading and managing a company.
Definition 2 A person responsible for profit-making.
Definition 3 A person equipped with the knowledge and experience necessary to manage a company, who displays a propensity for business.
Definition 4 A person leading a group of employees, making decisions and responsible for team success.

As Figure 2.1 shows, the majority of both management school faculty (mostly Heads of Department and Deans) and students considered the 'manager' to be a person involved in leading and managing a company (definition 1). However, this response was more frequent among students than among business school faculty. Faculty ranked definition 2 second, emphasizing responsibility for profit-making. But this response was extremely rare among students. Less than 14% of surveyed business school faculty perceived knowledge and experience together with a propensity for doing business as the key features of a 'manager', and even fewer students chose definition 3 (almost 4%).

These outcomes indicate, we submit, that certain aspects of 'management' have been underestimated by students as well as business school faculty (though to a lesser degree). The underrated factors include: profit-making as a manager's basic responsibility and the mastery of theoretical knowledge, as well as practical skills, as a prerequisite to success. In other words, the features of becoming a 'manager' which contribute to the 'manager' being seen as a professional executive are severely undervalued. It is important to emphasize this, because the development of managerial professionals and professionalization was, in the era of the centrally planned economy in Poland and other Eastern/Central European countries, to a large degree blocked.

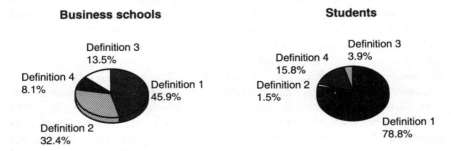

Business schools

Definition 3
13.5%

Definition 4
8.1%

Definition 1
45.9%

Definition 2
32.4%

Students

Definition 3
3.9%

Definition 4
15.8%

Definition 2
1.5%

Definition 1
78.8%

Figure 2.1 The structure of responses on the concept of 'manager'

There were executives, but very few professionals. Managers could neither establish nor control a 'jurisdictional domain' of their own. Line managers have not learnt to take responsibility; top management has not developed a sense of strategy. Occupational and organizational structures have favoured dependence, blind loyalty to superiors. Hard work and innovation have been discouraged or even punished. Managers were entrusted with supervisory functions because they were loyal to the Communist party and not because of their managerial skills. In the large state-owned companies which constituted a large part of Polish companies government administrators delegated management functions to those officials who would blindly carry out the central plan. There was no need for the professional education of executives, since managerial functions were divided up along non-professional criteria. Many managers still expect soft government loans and subsidies rather than having to run a client-oriented, market-aware organization.

The new social and economic conditions in Poland present us with the challenge of catching up with the EU countries in the realm of executive-managerial professionalism; but few managers, students or business school faculty have a clear idea of what a professional manager would look like. Such issues as product quality, value chain analysis, labour flexibility, effective distribution, sustainable growth and long-term strategy are little known and even less practised. The process of change has merely been inaugurated; the respondents to our research still do not perceive the executive as a professional manager. Bearing in mind that so many people underestimate the knowledge, professional experience and competencies demanded by a professional manager's function, the question impinges: can one teach the profession of 'manager' in today's Poland?

THE BUSINESS SCHOOLS

In response to the perceived need for post-Communist managers, many new business schools, primarily in the bigger cities, have been opened. Especially in 1990–91 there were numerous openings; at that time, 66% of the surveyed non-universities were established. As for the universities, slightly over half of their business schools (56%) were established in 1991. In 1993 a number of non-universities were transformed into universities. Our research conducted in 1992 at forty-three business schools showed that education and research took place at a mere 27% of the schools; 29% of them were exclusively involved in management education. A full 36% of them offered consulting services. Many schools (20%) organized conventions and seminars, and/or operated their own catering or lodgings. Quite a few produced and sold teaching materials. Fifteen per cent of the schools are involved in publishing.

At universities provision of management education dominates; whereas

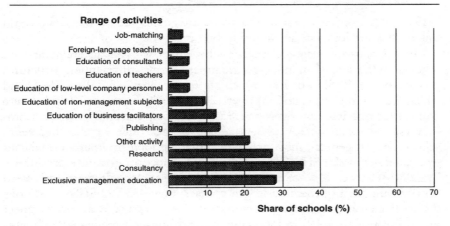

Figure 2.2 Types of activity undertaken by business schools, 1992

less than 25% of non-universities limit themselves to management education. Consultancy services, complementary to education, are prevalent at non-universities (40% of them offer consulting), but are increasingly present at universities (30%) as well. Research occurs at only 44% of the universities and 20% of the non-universities. In general, non-university business schools are more diversified than are the universities; activities independent of teaching play a bigger role at these institutions, whereas the universities limit themselves more or less to activities complementary to, and in support of, the teaching process.

If we examine the educative output of the business schools quantitatively, we discover that traditional three- and five-year university curricula dominate. We measured educative output in terms of 'student hours of study' (SHS), including contact hours, reading and preparation for class, studying for and taking of exams, researching and writing of assignments/papers/ essays. The number of students multiplied by the number of SHS gives us a quantitative measure of the activity level of business education. We assume that this purely quantitative measure has a qualitative correlation; i.e. over a longer period of time, the quantitative increase in the amount of management education will generate higher levels of learning. Forty-one of the forty-five schools surveyed (twenty-six non-universities and fifteen universities) provided us with quantitative data for 1993. The total number of SHS was 5.8 million, of which 51% was generated by universities and 49% by non-universities. Thus, the average quantity of educational activity undertaken by universities is larger than that of non-universities. The former generated 197,800 SHS and the latter 109,000; while the average SHS per institution was 141,500. If we divide the schools into those of (1) less than 100,000 SHS, (2) 100,000 to 300,000 SHS and (3) over 300,000

SHS, we discover that four of the six in category 3 are universities. Non-universities predominate in the other two categories.

Another, more pedagogic, criterion by which we can differentiate the schools is the length of their programmes: i.e. we differentiate between courses of (1) 60 SHS or less, which we term 'short'; (2) 60 to 120 SHS, which we call 'medium'; and (3) over 120 SHS, which are considered to be 'long'. One hundred and twenty SHS is roughly equivalent to one credit of university work at senior undergraduate or MA level. Polish business schools are, in general, most active in providing long programmes, which generated 4,550,200 SHS (78% of the total). Short programmes produced 795,200 SHS, i.e. 14% of total activity. Business schools were the least active in the field of medium-length courses; only 455,700 SHS, or 8% of the total educational output, occurred in this category. Universities produced 60% of the SHS in long courses, and non-universities 40%. Non-universities led in the provision of short (84%) and medium-length (75%) courses.

Thus, university business schools focus on long courses: 92% of their output is in this category (2,733,900 SHS). Education provided via medium and short courses plays an insignificant role (4% in each). This would seem to indicate that the universities have not adapted to the demand for the re-schooling of managers to function in a market economy, but have persisted in their traditional academic niche. Furthermore, and perhaps more startling, the non-universities are devoting a large part of their educational efforts to developing long courses of study: 65% of their total output (1,826,300 SHS) was in this category. The relatively low involvement of these schools in short and medium-length courses surprises us.

We have classified the forty-five business schools as follows:

1 general management schools offering courses in virtually all management disciplines,
2 schools offering courses in the major management disciplines,
3 schools offering courses in some management disciplines,
4 schools offering courses in a few (one to three) management disciplines.

Table 2.1 Educational activity measured in student hours of study (SHS) according to course length and type of business school, 1993

| Course length | Effects of educational work (volume in thousands of SHS) | | | | | |
| | Universities | | Non-universities | | Total | |
	Volume	% Share	Volume	% Share	Volume	% Share
Long	2723.9	59.86	1826.2	40.14	4550.2	100.0
Medium	113.3	24.87	342.4	75.13	455.7	100.0
Short	130.1	16.36	665.1	83.64	795.2	100.0

We found seventeen general management schools (38% of the total sample), 47% of which were university-based. University schools in categories 2, 3 and 4 made up 30%, 12% and 11%, respectively. Non-universities were spread quite evenly between categories 1 and 3 (32% general management, 29% major disciplines, 36% some disciplines). Only 3% of them offer only a few disciplines (category 4).

The educational programmes on offer are:

1 postgraduate programmes,
2 Master's and Bachelor's programmes (Magister, five-year university studies, and licentiate, three-year pre-professional; full and part time),
3 trade college programmes,
4 short courses, seminars, conferences,
5 training and workshops.

Most institutions (71%) offer short courses, seminars and conferences; 48% of the schools have postgraduate programmes. BA and MA pro-grammes (Magister and Licentiate) are provided only by the universities (37% of the sample). Trade college programmes and training/workshops are provided by only 20% of the surveyed business schools.

It is worth noting that the curriculum of the MA in Economics and Business is very controversial. Within Polish academic circles fierce discus-sion has occurred concerning the structure and content of the curricula. The pre-1989 MA (Magister) is characterized by the following division of subjects (paralleled by the structure of the sub-departments): (1) Econom-ics, (2) Finance and Banking, (3) Computer Science and Econometrics, (4) International Economic and Political Relations, (5) Management and Mar-keting, (6) Production. Some professors defend the old educational system and continue to support the status quo; others feel that economic and management studies should be divided into two different subjects along the lines of a more theoretical field of Economics and a more practical field of Business Administration. We believe that this alternative organization of the study much better corresponds to the present challenges and, hopefully, will be soon introduced at the Polish universities.

Analysis of business school curricula shows that between 1990–3 the courses most often offered were: Organization and Management, Market-ing, Finance and Banking, Business Law/Interpersonal Training.

Initially after the fall of the Berlin Wall a tremendous increase occurred in provision, which since 1991 has steadily decreased! After an initial surge in management education, there has been a steady decrease in demand. (This was discussed at the National Conference on Business Schools 'Their Achievements and Future Prospects', organized by Educational Enterprise Foundation, Łódź, 29 to 30 November 1993.) This is particularly true for non-university schools.

Courses provided

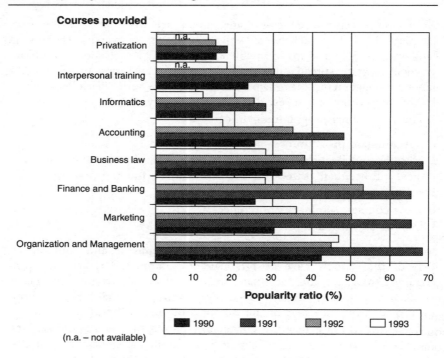

Figure 2.3 Popularity of courses provided by business schools, 1990–3

STUDENTS AND LECTURERS

The largest category of students (64%) are managers (50% from business and 14% from public administration). These students work mainly at lower and medium levels of management (31% of the total student population), whereas students representing senior executives (i.e. mainly company directors) constitute only 19% of the surveyed population. Representatives of higher levels of management in public administration are almost non-existent in the sample; lower and middle levels of management account for 7% each. Only 36% of the student body is pre-service, i.e. candidates for future managerial positions.

As Figure 2.4 shows, some university business schools are educating candidates exclusively for future managerial positions. There are also schools where representatives of higher levels of management in public administration constitute as much as 15% of the student body. Thus, Polish business schools attract primarily students who are out to become (future) professional managers, or low and middle-level managers who seek to be promoted. Few top-level managers, whose goal would be to expand or enrich their managerial knowledge, are present in the sample.

Student category

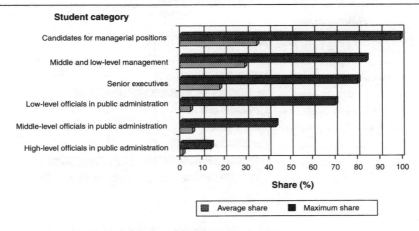

Figure 2.4 Structure of the student population, 1992

A large majority of the surveyed students (87%) report that they decided to start their management education studies on their own initiative; only 10% were sent to business school by their companies. The chief reason (stated by 29% of students) given for wanting to acquire a management education was to improve one's knowledge of, and ability to use, modern equipment. Other reasons included lack of professional experience, inexperience in organization (27% each), inability to speak foreign languages (20%) and the desire to learn to work in a team (10%). Students expressed the expectation that they would enrich their knowledge and master the practical application of that knowledge (65% and 64%, respectively). About 36% of surveyed students expected that they would obtain a higher salary, and about 29% a more challenging job. Acquiring skills in utilizing modern equipment and mastering organizational skills were only the fifth most popular expectation. Only 11% of students expected to be promoted.

There is asymmetry between the reasons stated for starting one's business education and the anticipated prospects after completion. The main reason for entering business school was a lack of technical/organizational skill, but expectations concerning actually mastering these skills were low. There is also asymmetry between the structure of the student body and the expectations for promotion. Almost one-third of the students come from the lower and middle levels of management, but as few as 11% of them stated that they desired and expected promotion. Are we confronted here with lack of personal ambition, very characteristic of the Communist period?

Faculty for the business schools have mostly been recruited from the universities. Nearly 70% of business school teachers are university faculty; only 9% are business practitioners, (6% are consultants and 4% work in

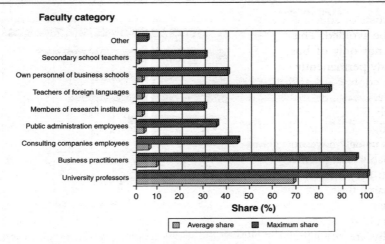

Figure 2.5 Structure of the faculty population, 1992

public administration). The remaining 10% are members of research institutions, 3% are teachers of foreign languages, 3% are made up of the schools' own personnel, and 3% are secondary school teachers. Some schools differ quite significantly from these averages: university business schools tend to employ only university faculty; there are schools where managers constitute as much as 95% of the faculty and schools recruiting as much as 30% of their staff from the secondary schools.

As many as 39% of the surveyed schools do not employ any professors on a permanent basis (either full time or part time). Both the number of schools employing part-time teachers and the number of teachers so employed are quite small. The largest number of schools hiring faculty on a permanent basis (42%) are schools employing only between one and ten staff members. Institutions with eleven to twenty permanent faculty constitute 17% of the group surveyed. One school employed over sixty professors on a permanent basis (i.e. 2% of the surveyed schools). The nature of employment contracts differs a great deal between the university and non-university sectors. In the former, nearly all professors are full-time employees. In 50% of the universities, the number of permanently employed faculty is between eleven and twenty; in 40%, between one and ten; and in 8%, between sixty and seventy. On the other hand, 60% of the non-universities do not employ any teachers on a permanent basis at all; and 40% of these schools do not employ more than ten. Their preferred form of employment is the temporary contract. There are two apparent underlying reasons for the pattern: (1) non-university administrators want to save on taxes. According to Polish tax law, permanent employment necessitates the employer paying social security, which, in turn, increases the costs of education; while in the case of temporary employment this cost can be avoided. This type of avoidance of social security costs is characteristic not only of business schools but also of private businesses. And (2) already permanently employed university professors do not want to change their contractual affiliation. This is because of the uncertain future of the non-universities. Another reason is the lack of an academic atmosphere, which brings permanent contacts with foreign universities as well as prestige. Teachers who decide to transfer from universities to non-universities usually have not been promoted by their university and, therefore, are probably less qualified. University faculty can, in effect, have their cake and eat it: they remain employed permanently by their university and work, at the same time, 'temporarily' at a non-university business school. Motivation is financial, i.e. to gain an extra source of income. In this situation it is very difficult for non-universities to achieve excellence. Their 'moonlighting' faculty are often insufficiently committed to curriculum development or to innovation. Less than 10% of those involved in curricula design and development at the non-universities are managers and less than 10% of their faculty are permanent members of staff. There is literally no one available to champion renewal and originality.

Our analysis of the teaching methods currently in use in the business schools shows lectures to be the most common teaching form. On average, at all surveyed business schools lecturing constituted 36% of all teaching. However, there are schools where 80% of in-class time is devoted to this method. The second most popular form of instruction was discussion groups (21%), followed by seminars (16%) and working in computer/ foreign language labs (13%). We note that at some schools this last method of teaching reached 70% of the total teaching time. Management simulation games took up, on average, 7% of the time available; however, business schools exist which specialize almost exclusively in this particular form of

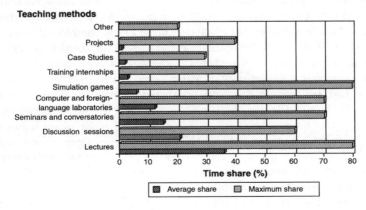

Figure 2.6 Time structure of teaching methods, 1992

education. Internships, fieldwork and case studies are found extremely infrequently among the teaching methods (2% each), and projects are nearly non-existent (1%).

Thus Polish business schools educate (future) managers primarily by means of the traditional university method of lecturing. This is not surprising, as 70% of all business school faculty are university professors. Clearly there has not been, since 1989, a radical renewal of teaching methods. It is not astounding, thus, that students claim to favour (60%) self-instruction, as they equate business education with having to organize one's own learning. Classes tend to take the form of a professor holding a monologue; active student participation is very limited, if not completely absent. At both universities and non-universities, teaching methods facilitating active learning, like action learning or group work, are non-existent. There are many reasons for this: teachers are reluctant to interact with students and students are afraid to ask questions. It is much easier for faculty to conceal their lack of knowledge during a monologue than in a dialogue. Likewise, students are afraid that by asking questions they will display their ignorance. Making matters worse, there is a chronic lack of teaching materials. Everything from textbooks focusing on the transition from a command to a market economy, to case studies of situations applicable to Poland, to relevant video material, to computer-assisted instruction, to articles readily accessible for student reading is wanting. Many mainstays of western teaching practice – photocopying, overhead projectors, VHS recorders, computer labs – are scarce. Yet another reason, and perhaps the most crucial one, for the lack of didactic change is the glaring lack of faculty awareness and knowledge of contemporary business and management teaching methods or techniques. It is very important that Polish business school faculty have the opportunity to observe and learn about western university teaching practices. This facet to management education cannot be mastered by reading alone (i.e. via self-study); training and seminars on business teaching methods organised by western universities in Poland are necessary. Good examples of this change strategy are the Eastern European Management Teacher Development Programme, organized by Lancaster University with Erasmus University, Copenhagen Business School and Vienna Economic University within the Tempus Programme; and Central and East Europe Teacher Program, organized by Harvard Business School.

EVALUATING THE SUCCESSES AND IMPEDIMENTS TO SUCCESS

The Deans and administrators of the business schools we have interviewed claimed that their schools' reputation and prestige depended primarily on the qualifications and skills of their faculty. An important secondary factor, they claimed, was a school's teaching equipment and facilities, including its buildings. The curriculum also played a role: the more popular courses offered (Organization and Management, Finance and Banking, Marketing), the better. Other success factors were the school's programmes and the quality of its students. According to the respondents, teaching methods were of minor importance. Perhaps surprisingly, virtually all schools (93%) had contacts with foreign business schools. But cooperation between the Polish business schools was very weak. A Polish business school association, to organize cooperation in curriculum design and development, as well as to monitor the quality of management education (certification?), has yet to be created.

Management education is, obviously, just beginning in Poland. In countries enjoying a long history of management education and where the academic and general business environments are supportive, a business school's reputation is determined by the attractiveness of its curriculum. This factor is only ranked third in Poland today. The quality of the student body was seen to have an even lower level of importance. In reality, the quality of the students most definitely (co-)determines the quality of the managers who emerge from the business school, and the professional achievements of the graduates influence a school's reputation. The business school's research record was totally omitted by the Polish Deans and administrators from their list of success factors! Certainly it is hard to imagine how one can sustain powerful business and management education without effective state-of-the-art (field) research. The attention given to such items as teaching equipment and facilities, which are taken for granted in western countries, highlights the poverty of the post-Communist context.

The Deans and administrators identified the following impediments to success: hiring competent faculty, recruitment of (good) students, profitability, acquiring teaching materials and equipment, obtaining adequate facilities. These barriers seem to be faced more by non-university business schools; however, not all university business schools have surmounted them. School profitability is likely to become the principal reason underlying the decline of many non-universities. This results from the decreasing demand for management education and from the schools' inability to hire qualified faculty members, which in turn hampers them from providing a quality product. These problems are worsening as potential faculty members discover that consulting pays much better than teaching.

As we have noted, the concept of the 'manager' is not clear in the current Polish context. Neither Deans/business school administrators nor students emphasize the professionalization of the role. We believe that the educational mission of business schools ought to be to prepare students for imaginative, responsible and effective professional leadership within the management of a business/organization. This mission cannot be accomplished by business schools whose Deans and chief administrators have not developed a concept of the 'manager' as professional. Furthermore, students with a poorly thought-through notion of the 'manager' will be unable to make effective demands of their teachers. We doubt that the new non-university business schools have identified a concept of the 'manager' which permits them to frame an educational mission statement, implement new programmes and/or develop curricula which answer to the challenges facing 'managers'. The hybrid non-university business school which organizes conferences, training, workshops and short to medium-length courses, as well as being active on many different markets such as consulting, head-hunting and out placement, is a new and virtually unique institution. Only the future can tell if these institutions can overcome their problems and prevail. The curriculum of the three- and five-year university programmes need to be redefined to meet the changed economic and political situation. New strategies have to be developed to overcome austerity conditions and to come up to international teaching and research standards. Schools will have to choose to provide (1) general management education and/or (2) specialist courses. A balance between up-market state-of-the-art programmes and more down-market generalist programmes (mostly for middle managers or students without any management experience) will have to be found. Some institutions will develop more towards the short to medium-length course market, while others will specialize in longer curriculum offerings. A shake-out seems inevitable, in which only the more successful schools/programmes will survive. For some schools, offering introductory courses in popular fields such as organization and management, marketing, finance and banking, and business law may be a viable strategy, but others will need to orient themselves to offering specialist courses. Universities will probably continue to train pre-experience students, while non-university institutions will dominate the post-experience market for lower and medium-level managers. Programmes for senior executives are still the least common sector. Perhaps this target group will go abroad; perhaps a market will develop later. Since business school students expect primarily to develop their managerial skills and knowledge, there is a danger that they will become disillusioned with what is now on offer. There is little tacit knowledge or competency-based training available. Most programmes are lectured by a staff with a minimum of practical business experience. Furthermore, if the chances of promotion after completing a business course are really as bad as the students say they think they are, then fading interest in management education has to be expected.

Currently, the business schools employ traditional teaching methods, i.e. mainly lecturing. Methods facilitating a more dynamic learning process and which stimulate creative and individual thinking are infrequently used. Students do not learn problem identification and solving skills. Casework and project-based courses amount to as little as 3% of the course offerings.

Action learning/research and group work are almost unknown. Thus western support is needed to help spread awareness of management educational techniques. Poland has no need to 'rediscover the wheel' of management education, when existing models could be adapted to the situation there much more efficiently.

At present Polish management education is extremely diverse and almost chaotic. On the one hand a myriad new institutions have appeared, and on the other there has been very little real change in the teacher–student relationship. Management education may seem to have been very fashionable in the 1990s, but the product offered has been much less innovative than one might have expected. Most unfortunately, a renewed vision of the 'professional manager' has not emerged to give substance to the development of the new management programmes. Too many people seem to be selling too much of the same. We feel that we have been too little able, as yet, to influence the business school agenda as we would like to, i.e. in the direction of genuine and fundamental change.

NOTE

1 SWOT refers to the identification of the Strengths, Weaknesses, Opportunities and Threats that the organization or individual faces.

Chapter 3

Management education models in Europe: diversity and integration

Gordon Shenton

The end of the Cold War and the renewed drive towards economic integration through the European Community's Single Market programme have brought about deep changes in geopolitical awareness and in the organization of business. The old system of closed competing nation states trading with each other at arm's length is slowly being replaced by a new, if still indeterminate, system of cooperation. In the west we are being forced to change our concept of the political space in which we live. In Central and Eastern Europe the movement is, in a sense, reversed, as the Soviet bloc has broken up into its constituent parts, restoring full sovereignty to newly independent countries. Increasingly, European managers have to take responsibility for decisions affecting operations in several countries, often in Central as well as Western Europe – a purely provincial (regional/ national) view of business more and more often provides inadequate grounds for action. How can one fill the gap between the transnational responsibility of the (future) European manager and the focus, all too often, of management on immediate, local problems? What is the best way to create transnational management awareness and skills? Can one universal form of management education, such as the MBA, fill the gap, or are different, potentially complementary, programmes needed, with participants attending several different ones? Central Europeans in transition towards a market economy have to ask themselves which model(s) they should look to. Who should they imitate in managing their 'reborn' business enterprises? And, thus, to whom should they turn for help as they tackle the immense task of retraining present managers and educating future ones.

I examine, in this chapter, the experience of Western European management education – faced with the need to look beyond national frontiers in order to identify what is relevant for Central Europe. What lessons can be drawn from attempts in Western Europe to adjust to the accelerating process of economic integration? How far is the debate about management and educational models in the west relevant to the problems of the Central European countries in transition?

THE CONTEXT OF MANAGEMENT EDUCATION

The debate about the comparative merits of different approaches to management education is symptomatic of the general tendency to compare institutions and national systems in the hope that we can identify the most successful model available. The primary meaning of the word 'model' is a representation of something on a reduced scale. Applied to human activity, it implies the description of the characteristic features of the activity through a process of simplification and generalization in such a way that it can be easily recognized and differentiated from other related forms of the same activity. By extension, the word 'model' also has the meaning of 'a standard to be imitated' (*Collins English dictionary, 2nd edn*). In the context of management, the 'standard' is the set of values, behavioural patterns and practices which characterize a particular management style. Using the term 'model' in this sense supposes that the management style to which it is applied can serve as a reference to be learnt from and imitated.

As the world becomes more interdependent and as Western Europe, in particular, ceases to be defined by its national differences, diversity is potentially becoming something to deal with. In the search for a successful model, attention is being paid to the structural and cultural factors influencing corporate performance in any given part of the world, on three interrelated levels: the level (1) of economic systems, (2) of different styles of management and (3) of management education.

ECONOMIC SYSTEMS

Awareness of profound differences in the way capitalism is practised around the world is, of course, not new; but the idea that different approaches may be in competition has come to the fore more strongly of late, under pressure of the increased competition arising from the European open market and the European Community's striving to draw up common policies (Maastricht). Each country is attempting, naturally enough, to project its own conception of capitalism on to the European Union (EU). France tries to create strong, centralized institutions of a bureaucratic nature, assigning an interventionist role to the powerful state. However much the French may be jealous of their own national sovereignty, they cannot help but imagine that strong, centralized, interventionist European policies ought to lead to a managed European economy. The Common Agricultural Policy, with its complicated machinery for regulating production and prices across Europe, is a reflection of the French approach. At the other extreme, there is the British dream of liberal deregulated free trade, with a minimum of interference from Brussels. What sort of a Europe are we preparing for; what sort of Europe will we need to manage? A liberal free-trade open Europe exposed to unhindered international competition? Or a more protectionist, interventionist Europe, with coordinated industrial, economic and social policies? Or will there be some synthesis of these antithetical conceptions, closer to the German model of a consensus-regulated balance between liberalism and 'social capitalism'?

Michel Albert has focused the counter-attack on hyper-liberalism in his book *Capitalism Against Capitalism*. He argues that capitalism is not monolithic and seeks to make sense of the diversity of national traditions. He identifies two major, opposing, forms of capitalism. On the one hand, there is neo-American capitalism, which he is tempted to call Anglo-Saxon capitalism because of the proximity of the British Conservative and American Republican policies; and, on the other hand, there is what he calls Rhineland capitalism, which is the central tradition of the continental European heartland, centring on Germany and stretching from the Benelux to include the Alpine countries and Scandinavia. In many respects Rhineland capitalism is considered to be close to Japanese practice, so much so that Albert is tempted to talk of a Germano-Nipponese model. Point by point, the German model is opposed to the liberal Anglo-Saxon one. Stable stakeholding structures, in which banks play a major role in corporate finance, are contrasted to the volatile situation in the USA, where companies are hostage to the stock market. The preference for savings is opposed to the preference for debt; productive investment is contrasted to speculation; the dogged pursuit of a strong stable Deutschmark contradicts the volatility of the pound/dollar; the long view of corporate strategy weighs in against short-termism. In the one model the business enterprise plays a wide social role in relation to employment, quality of life and national wealth; while in the other it is seen as a commodity with profit as its only objective. Albert, a French socialist and business leader, writes to defend Europe's distinctive postwar model: i.e. social justice and a free market economy, efficiency and participatory democracy, management cooperating with trade unions, government determining macro-economic policy but without excessive intervention in the firm. But that model has broken down in France, which currently suffers from too much structural unemployment and too little innovation, too much stagnation and too little entrepreneurship. Lester Thurow, in his recent book *Head to Head: The Coming Economic Battle among Japan, Europe and America*, develops an argument similar to Michel Albert's: 'The economic competition between communism and capitalism is over, but another competition between two different forms of capitalism is already under way. Using a distinction first made by George C. Lodge, a Harvard Business School professor, the individualistic Anglo-Saxon British–American form of capitalism is going to face off against the communitarian German and Japanese variants of capitalism' (Thurow 1993: 32). He links this distinction to the difference between consumer economics, which forms the base of the individualistic Anglo-Saxon model and producer economics which characterizes Japan and Germany.

There is a growing fear that no model works, and that job destruction at an unprecedented rate will progressively threaten the social fabric of the European countries. The danger of regressive competition between national economic systems, in which advantage is sought through lower wage-levels, less social security coverage, favourable tax structures and competitive currency devaluations, is considered to be real.

STYLES OF MANAGEMENT

The second level of Albert's analysis of corporate performance concerned itself with management style (EFMD 1992). European national styles clearly exist: one can talk of French, German or Italian styles of management. But these are not really 'models', since one cannot generalize in some way from French, German or Italian practice and apply it (i.e. the 'model') elsewhere. It is convincing to describe the German version of capitalism as a model, but it does not make much sense to talk about a German model of management. The only two national styles which have attained the status of becoming a 'model' are the American and Japanese. But I believe that Japanese management is not applicable outside Japan; at least not as a system. Given the reservations already stated about the functioning of American capitalism, American management no longer seems to me to be an especially attractive import.

Europe is characterized by a mosaic of highly diverse, culturally rooted approaches to management; without (many) clear common points of reference. Despite the differences, there are two forces at work in Europe bringing European managers closer together. One is a common process of modernization. There is a clear tendency for definitions of 'good practice' to converge as far as the basic (marketing, logistic, etc.) techniques are concerned. The second factor is the drive towards economic integration. A more unified European market for business is emerging. But can we speak of a model of European management? Given that Europe is moving closer together, are we not, then, witnessing with regards to management a converging path which is specifically European in attitudes, values, behavioural patterns, competencies and business practices? Or is any such convergence merely the result of the generalized process of modernization which is bringing all industrial societies closer together? Clearly, European management does not exist as an observable describable reality rooted in the cultural substratum of a collective identity in the way that American management is rooted in American culture or that German management is rooted in German culture. However, this negative answer does not settle the issue. Rephrased, the question might better be: do we *want* and/or *need* a European management model?

I believe we need a consensus in Europe on such things as the social responsibility of business; the limits that ought to be set to the market and the role of the state. The uniqueness of European management, in comparison to concepts such as 'international' or 'global' management may be defined merely as doing business across a particular set of cultural/political boarders. By referring to 'European management', one could be taking a closed, restricted view of 'Europe' as a separate, self-contained area. Successful strategy may, though, require an 'international' focus and not a Fortress Europe perspective. But the concept of 'international management' also evokes negative connotations. It brings to mind an Americanized, culturally insensitive, English-speaking style of doing things. Be this as it may, 'European management' exists only to the extent that it is a concrete behavioural response to a set of circumstances which are different from those of the specific national environments, and it is also different from other forms of 'international' cross-border business. The 'European model' is linked to the paradox of a Europe integrated beyond mere interdependence but still remaining culturally diverse. While 'Europe 1992' has undoubtedly brought increased market integration, regressive Euro-sceptical reactions are now common in many countries. There is a temptation to turn inward and to revert to adversarial relations rather than further develop collaborative relations. The issue of European management reflects the more general issue of one's commitment to the existence of a European identity. Thus, European management education cannot be merely instrumental and technical; it is, of necessity, relative to the other two levels described, i.e. that of management behaviour and of overall political economics.

MANAGEMENT EDUCATION: THE MBA IN EUROPE

The Single Market, launched in the mid-1980s, brought changes to the world of higher management education in Europe. Deans, directors and professors began crisscrossing Europe with substantial travel budgets, partially financed by the European Community, bent on overcoming the mental barriers which had isolated management educators within their own national space. The first stage was to learn how their neighbours' systems functioned. Cooperation and exchange developed rapidly. Joint programmes were launched, networks were set up and strategic alliances formed. As cooperation spread on a pan-European scale, perceptions began to change. Management and business schools no longer saw their strategic positioning only in national terms, but began to measure their strengths and weaknesses in relation to their European competitors. Cooperation among schools was accompanied by a growing spirit of competition; especially in the postgraduate segment of the market, where the feeling quickly arose that only a limited number of players would prevail.

Innovation was rife, the market was growing as demand for business graduates soared; new programmes mushroomed all around Europe. An article in the American business magazine *Fortune* (23 May 1988) entitled 'Europe's best business schools' seems to have sparked off media interest in European business education and to have intensified the rivalry among schools. The programmes cited in the *Fortune* article differed from the North American MBA model in a number of important ways. In fact they are described as a distinct variant, the international or sometimes even the European MBA. These programmes recruit internationally, bringing together a wide mix of nationalities; participants are young fast-trackers with an international outlook and with demonstrated management potential. In general, the programmes admit engineers or functional specialists and teach them in twelve to eighteen months how to manage. Because the programmes are shorter than the standard American length of two years, they are very intense and focus directly on the managerial functions of decision-making and leadership. Teaching relies on case studies, but emphasizes group work, (in-company) projects and consulting missions, in contrast to the individualistic, classroom-centred approach in the United States. The institutions offering these courses are mostly outside the university system. Many are quite small and limit their activity to the top end of the market. In addition to offering an MBA, most provide short courses for senior executives and do related consulting work. At their best, these schools are more entrepreneurial, more proactive, closer to their constituency and far more pragmatic than their American counterparts. Research is sometimes their weakest facet, but, at their best, their investigation is more relevant than the narrow, hyper-specialized work of too many American academics.

The media visibility of the 'European MBA' and the rising demand for such programmes prompted new entrants to try to penetrate the market. But too much ballyhoo has been made of the MBA market. It is self-limiting, to the extent that it is aimed at an elite market. Although the European/international MBA obviously has its place, it can hardly serve as a generalizable model to meet the demand for trained managers across Europe. A benchmark for quality and innovation it may be, but a model it is not. North American MBAs are embedded in the mainstream university structure, while European MBAs are atypical of the higher-education systems of their countries. Many of the European institutions granting an MBA could be established in any European country with no fundamental change in their programme. To the extent that these programmes are taught in English and the student body is of mixed nationalities, the schools are not rooted in any single national culture. It is implicitly assumed by these programmes that European and/or international management is a general form of professional behaviour, to which one accedes by transcending one's own national culture; that English is the language in which it is practised; and that large multinationals are the natural habit of its practitioners. There is a danger that such transnationalism will become a form of cultural illiteracy practised by managers who neither know their own nor any other culture in any depth.

It seems very unlikely that the MBA, either in a 'European' form or in a variety of national forms, will ever become a dominant model in Europe, where educational traditions and company recruiting practices mitigate against the development of postgraduate post-experience courses. In the United States, where there is no rigorous examination at the end of secondary education and where undergraduate programmes are in large part geared to general education, considerable weight is placed on postgraduate education. In contrast, continental European university systems tend to offer specialist degrees, combining upper-division and MA-level course work in a single diploma. The best students, whom companies are anxious to recruit, are to be found in the high-prestige university courses, i.e. a *Grande École* degree in France, the *Diplom Kaufmann* in Germany, the *Doctoraal* in the Netherlands. Penetration of the MBA concept beyond a small elite core of schools is weak and uneven. Britain is a special case, as it has a tradition of master's degrees and a conscious, even political, effort has been made to develop the MBA as a remedy to the weakness of management education in that country. But even in the UK, the prestige and corporate acceptance of the MBA is much lower than in North America. The MBA has been quite successful in Spain, no doubt because of the weakness there of management education in the mainstream university system. Purely national MBAs are either marginal or non-existent in Italy, Germany, France and the Benelux. Attempts are currently being made to introduce part-time and/or consortial (in-company) MBAs to Europe, with some apparent initial success.

The growth of the postgraduate market has had the effect that graduate management (business) schools have emerged. In France the *Grandes Écoles* had always been organized as free-standing, professional schools. After World War II the *écoles de commerce* were assimilated into the *Grandes Écoles* tradition and have begun more and more to resemble business schools as they have built up their faculties and diversified their activities. In Britain, management schools were founded in the 1960s at a number of universities, either as direct imitations of the US model (London Business School/Manchester Business School) or through a process of indigenous evolution wherein business studies were often fragmented in separate departments specializing in functional areas such as accounting, operations, behaviour in organizations and marketing. Quite recently some universities have federated these disciplines into schools of management, allowing for the development of an integrated approach in addition to the specialist one. In North West Europe one finds business schools more or less embedded in the school of commerce model, i.e. linked to a faculty of economics. In some cases the management school has separated itself from the faculty of economics and become more management directed (Benelux), but in many (Germany and Scandinavia) it has not. An additional barrier to the MBA is that there is strong financial resistance in Europe to high-cost postgraduate programmes. In many countries students pay little or no tuition for high-quality university programmes and are not inclined to pay high fees for a master's. Furthermore, fears born from widespread downscaling make the choice of leaving a job for post-experience training very painful indeed. There may still be room for expansion in the pre-experience postgraduate market in Europe, provided that the costs are not excessive. Due to the tight job market and because of a growing need for a relevant professional qualification students are interested in prolonging their studies.

Because diversity is increasing, the market for management education is becoming more confused. Germany is the most stable business environment, but also the one which generates the least educative innovation. The trend towards increasing diversity is particularly apparent in the MBA and executive education market, but it is also evident in the traditional university sector. Executive education, that is to say the training of managers within companies in non-degree courses, is an especially dynamic market. There is competition between traditional university providers, MBA management schools, training and consulting organizations and in-company training departments. Market trends have been driven by two related, factors: (1) human resource management has become increasingly strategic as downsizing and reorganization (in the wake of mergers, acquisitions and strategic alliances) have put pressure on companies to manage change more rationally; and (2) the popularity of the learning organization concept. Training has shifted to tailor-made programmes, linked less to upgrading individual skills and more to the pursuit of collective corporate objectives. Education and training have become more crucial to strategy implementation; the scope of some programmes has become so great that companies talk of corporate universities. Clearly there's an opportunity here for academic institutions, if they can design and deliver new programmes which shape managerial behaviour.

MANAGEMENT EDUCATION: EUROPEAN DIFFERENCE AND DIVERSITY

I believe that European managers must learn not only to transcend the limits of their own national culture, but also to immerse themselves in other culture(s). For instance, a Spanish student spending a year in a German university will not have the same experience as a Spanish student spending a year in an English-speaking international (MBA) programme. Implicitly, two quite different conceptions of transnational management are opposing one another. On the one hand, there is the model of 'international management as a universal form of practice' and on the other there is a multicultural multilinguistic concept of management as something necessarily different in each culture and which requires the ability to manage diversity and difference. Continental European university courses are supposed, on the one hand, to provide for the general cultural development of the student coupled to development of necessary basic intellectual skills and, on the other hand, to take care of their professional, career-oriented training. The North American distinction between undergraduate and graduate levels is non-existent. The university degrees which take five years in France (*Grandes Écoles*) and Spain, five and a half years in the Netherlands or six years in Germany lead to a professional qualification which is generally considered to be sufficient and normal to gain employment. There are four distinctive models of European university business education: the British universities, the French *Grandes Écoles*, the Northwestern European university system (Germany, Scandinavia, Austria, Switzerland, the Netherlands) and the Southern European university system (including the French universities).

In the German system[1] there are virtually no business schools and no MBA programmes. Management education has taken root in the dominant university system, where it has become fully integrated into the Humboldtian university tradition. The *Diplom Kaufmann* is awarded upon successful completion of the eight-semester BWL (*Betriebswirtschaftslehre*) curriculum, which students take on average six years to complete. The degree reflects the same values of science (*Wissenschaft*), theory and research as all other university degrees at the *Hochschule* level. The BWL programmes are housed in the economics faculties, where they constitute a separate major alongside economics. Because of their disciplinary affiliation, business studies in Germany include a rigorous core curriculum in economics. Their lack of institutional contact with the business world causes the university curriculum to be largely separated from praxis. The value system emphasizes very strongly *Wissenschaft*. University management education is to provide students with the scientific conceptual tools needed to tackle problems throughout their career. Hands-on managerial skills are to be acquired on the job. One might think that such a system would be severely criticized by the business community, on the grounds that it wasn't teaching students how to manage. This is not the case; German companies look to the universities to provide them with graduates with a solid scientific education. The development of managerial qualities is seen to be the companies' own responsibility. The emphasis on academic values is reflected in the fact that a doctorate, taken after the *Diplom Kaufmann*, is actually considered to be of further value to a business career. The teaching of management as an integrative, decision-oriented form of behaviour – in contradistinction to the study of economics and/or functional disciplines is not perceived to be necessary by German corporations. The concept of 'professional management' as a separate set of generalizable skills is unknown.

In Scandinavia, the Netherlands, Austria and Switzerland various degrees of 'impurity' have entered into the German commerce school tradition. The Dutch and Norwegians are quite Anglo-Saxon in their practice-oriented programmes; while the Danes are a bit less so; and the Swedes, Swiss and Austrians come closer to the German model. This German model assumes the need for initial preparatory scientific training, followed by a management career with a single company with an in-depth lifelong association with that company i.e., with its product(s) or service(s). German companies invest not in management education, but in the technical development of their personnel. They finance employee professional education to a much greater extent than occurs in the USA, Britain or France. To the extent that they look to the higher-education system for employees who have graduated from a professionally oriented programme of study, they turn to the *Fachhochschulen,* which provide a practical skill-based education for specific jobs within industry and commerce. Here praxis is legitimate and learning is not merely academic. *Fachhochschulen* are not designed to produce future top managers, even though nothing in the German tradition would prevent a *Fachhochschule* graduate from rising to a senior position on the strength of his/her performance within the company. The BWL programme, I submit, has worked well in Germany because it is coherent with the values of both the university and the corporate world.

French management education is also deeply embedded in that society's tradition of higher education. High-status management education took root not in the university system, but in the vocational Chamber of Commerce schools. After World War II these schools were assimilated into the *Grandes Écoles* system, whereby the best of them could recruit very high-calibre students through the *classes préparatoires* and the *concours* (a highly selective entrance examination). Graduates gain fast-track positions in France's top companies. The *Grandes Écoles* management degree has come to be seen as a passport to success. The schools have retained many of the values of their vocational school origins: proximity to the business world, a managerial skill orientation, preference for praxis above academic theory. Inclusion in the *Grandes Écoles* system brought with it high selectivity and a sense of belonging to a technocratic elite defined by a *diplôme.* The curriculum is far closer to the standard American MBA than it is to other, university-based, programmes in Europe. The schools have built up their faculties and introduced research with the American graduate school of business as an explicit model. The originality of the *Grandes Écoles* lies in their ability to transform cloistered *classe préparatoire* eggheads into dynamic hands-on managers within three years. In contrast to the situation in Germany, recruiters attach no importance to academic achievement while at the business school; it is assumed that students have demonstrated 'brilliance' by passing the difficult *concours* in order to get into the school. Graduates are expected to be rapidly operational in a functional position. Recruiters look for personal qualities of dynamism and leadership, attaching considerable importance to the validity of internships and extracurricular activities.

The German and the French systems are two examples of how management education has been successfully integrated into higher education in a manner coherent with the local culture. Integration of management education into the British higher-education system has been fraught with difficulty. Historically, the introduction of business studies into university education faced two major obstacles. The first was resistance within the business community to the idea that management can be taught in the classroom. Traditionally people were trained in the UK for work in business either on the job or within the professions. The second obstacle was the attitude towards higher education of an acutely class-conscious society which shunned science and commerce in favour of the classics and liberal arts. There is no equivalent in Britain of the technocratic *Grandes Écoles* tradition, which confers prestige on engineering and business education. In Britain engineering was something to be studied at the industrial provincial universities or at a technical college; business was not taught beyond the vocational college level. The prestigious career paths for university graduates were directed towards the civil service and the professions. With the exceptions of law, theology and medicine, university education was not expected to have direct professional relevance. Corporate recruiters did not expect graduates to have any knowledge of business or economics; anyway, graduates went directly into company trainee programmes. None the less, management education has been progressively introduced at the undergraduate level, at first in the lower-status, vocationally oriented polytechnics reinforcing prejudices against commerce and practicality. University educators claimed that management was not an appropriate subject to train minds and that it would undermine the humanistic ethos of the undergraduate programme. Successive waves of attempts at economic modernization since 1960 have brought business majors into the undergraduate university curriculum, though the leading management schools are still often not at the traditional high-status universities.

Thus management education has been integrated quite differently into higher education in the various European traditions. The form management education takes must be understood in relation to the dominant structure(s) of social reproduction; the relation between management education and corporate recruiting; in terms of the relation to prevailing values; and in relation to the national (regional) management style. Differences clearly are not superficial. The model which works in one context may well not work elsewhere without substantial institutional engineering to adapt it. To understand the diversity of European management education, one needs to understand the systemic nature of educational processes and to identify the value structures upon which the variety of practice is based.

From the point of view of each model of practice the other models seem 'strange' or 'alien'. German students invariably think that courses in French *Grandes Écoles* are not 'scientific', by which they mean that lectures are not systematically structured or ideas placed in a theoretical context. On the other hand, French students (professors and corporate recruiters alike) cannot understand why BWL programmes are not more 'concrete' and 'practical'. Why devote so much time to theory and economics? Anglo-Saxon and Northern European students, used to a more learner-centred and participative approach, are confounded by the passivity of French students, who do not read books before going to class or engage in an exchange of ideas among themselves. The French see it as the teacher's job to provide the input. The French have obvious difficulty as managers adapting to a participative, collaborative style of work. The staff–student relationship tends to reflect accurately the way in which people in a given country relate to authority. The Americans and British are usually at ease with an informal, high-trust relationship with their professors; whereas French students prefer to maintain hierarchical distance. These attitudes clearly carry over into the management styles prevalent in these countries. In the German university system the professor is not just hierarchically distant but also physically remote from students, who are more likely to see his assistants. Likewise, German managers show marked respect for the authority of scientific and technical expertise, a value which links the corporate world to the university.

Comparing the German and the French systems reveals fundamental differences in the attitude towards time and managerial work in these two countries. The French are educated in a system which stresses precociousness and the rapid completion of the *Grande École* curriculum. The qualities needed for success are intellectual brilliance and an ability to think quickly. The rapid pace of study in the *classe préparatoire* leaves little time to spend on any one problem. Students are impatient to get on to the next point as soon as they have understood the issue at hand. The German system could not be more different. Students take time out to work or travel before completing their degrees, and hardly anyone completes the *Diplom Kaufmann* course in the formally allotted four years. They are used to a slower rhythm than the French; thorough painstaking preparation for examinations is normal. These behavioural patterns continue into professional life; the French are quick with ideas and impatient to see things happen; the

Germans are slower and more careful in management. The Germans accuse French managers of lacking seriousness; the French see the Germans as plodding and dull. It is not my purpose to pursue these comparisons any further, but rather to make the point that there is a behavioural continuity between the way managers are educated and the management styles which prevail in each country. This continuity is based less on the content of what is studied than on the implicit values and deep-rooted attitudes implicit in the educational process itself. A number of problems arise from what has been observed: how do you establish successful educational joint ventures across these cultural differences? How can you introduce meaningful reform, when change is felt to be necessary, to a national management style? Can you import a foreign model of management education if it does not correspond at the deeper systemic level with the values and attitudes of the host country?

LEARNING TO WORK TOGETHER

If Europe is to function effectively as a single market, a significant level of managerial compatibility will be needed. But is this to be achieved via the path of harmonization (the European manager model) or via awareness of diversity (a model based on differing national traditions in dialogue with one another)? Obviously the answer is a bit of both, though I wish to emphasize the second element. The fear exists that in management education, as in so many other fields, Europe will be paralysed by cacophony. If each country remains entrenched in its own higher-education system, if management education is understood to mean so many different things, if companies recruit graduates with such different expectations how can we ever work effectively together, how can we envisage a common European model? To begin with, the illusion of uniformity has to be set aside and diversity recognized as an essential feature of European training which deserves to be defended as a value in itself.

There are several major trends working towards proactive diversity. The first is the wave of student and staff exchanges and programmes of cooperation which have swept Europe. The exchange of students has led to the spread of cooperative programmes involving joint degrees as well as courses and seminars taught by faculty from different institutions. Networking has proven very effective – management schools have gone beyond bilateral cooperation to enter into complex forms of multilateral educational provision. Schools are learning from each other, acknowledging their own shortcomings and recognizing their partner's strengths. Like business enterprises, educational institutions – confronted by the double imperative of international cooperation and international competition – have become 'learning organizations'. There is now a far greater openness to new ideas from outside and a far greater willingness to envisage major change in the values, structures and practices of the institutions than in the past.

European economic integration is the second major force towards convergence. It has become almost impossible to teach management subjects from an uniquely national perspective. European law overlays national legal systems; production, marketing and the distribution of goods and services defy separate national treatment; regulation is shifting, at least in part, to Brussels; corporate strategy, before it can be global, has to be coherent in terms of the 'home' European market; human resource management requires an understanding of European social policy.

A third factor towards convergence is the desire within the management education profession to strengthen its own position via cooperation. Competition with North American consulting and training institutions is growing in the up-market segments. There is a desire to regulate competition between European institutions and to strengthen their common position. Professionalization can be stimulated by cooperating in research projects, publication and conferences. Some form of accreditation to define minimum standards for management institutions might well be in the interest of all.

A fourth factor is the widespread, if still unfocused, interest in the concept of European management. Almost all management education institutions throughout Western Europe feel that they have a duty to train European managers or at least managers for Europe. This leads them to ask what specific skills are required for effective management in a hybrid Europe which is a mosaic of separate cultures and yet, at the same time, a partially integrated economy. In the context of increasing economic integration and extensive institutional collaboration, there is a demand for European management education. There is agreement on certain elements of the ideal profile: the future managers for Europe will have a thorough education in their own home country, they will have a working knowledge of the institutions and practices of European integration, will know several languages, will have immersed themselves in at least one European culture other than their own, and they will be 'at home' in the wider European environment. The European manager will not be an expatriate or rootless manager, but will need to be a good local (national) manager with an added European dimension of competencies. Of course, the educational challenge is huge and goes beyond the scope of management education in its narrowest sense. The learning of languages, particularly those other than English, requires a commitment of the entire educational system. The development of intercultural skills is only possible if it builds on a solid educational background in the humanities and in the social sciences. A purely technically oriented approach to management education will be less and less relevant. Management education in Europe needs to become value-driven by a consensus on the importance of making diversity work and of appropriating difference as an asset.

CONCLUSION

This chapter amounts to an argument against the extreme volunteerism of those who seem to have thought that one could quickly train a new management elite, with fundamentally altered attitudes, in Poland, Hungary or the Czech Republic. No such thing is possible. The best service western educators can render is to help Central Europeans to analyse the interrelated levels of the indigenous economic system, style of management and practice of management education in order to define educational goals which are realistically coherent for them. Obviously, educational systems cannot easily be transposed from one society to another. The wholesale import of western models must be viewed with deep suspicion. Thus, I believe that great care must be taken in importing the American model, both in terms of its cultural compatibility and its potential fit into the Central European university system. Admittedly, while the universities in Poland, Hungary and the Czech Republic are all, more or less, rooted in the German tradition, a great diversity of approach should none the less be expected. I believe that the situation I have described in Western Europe applies to a large extent in Central Europe. Poland, Hungary and the Czech Republic are part of a fragmented but economically interdependent European space, in which the values and skills of 'European management' are becoming essential. Every effort must be made to draw the educational institutions of these countries into the dynamic process of convergence. Thanks to EU subsidies and (cultural) programmes they have become players in the networking and integration game which has been so effective in bringing institutions closer together. But it is not enough to see the relationship between the central and western parts of our continent as a one-way transfer of educational and managerial know-how, with western institutions in the role of consultants bringing 'revealed truth'. Western respect for difference and acknowledgement of diversity will be enriched via successful cooperation with Central Europe.

NOTE

1 I am indebted to the work of Robert Locke and Peter Lawrence for the discussion of the German system in this chapter.

REFERENCES AND FURTHER READING

Albert, M. (1991) *Capitalisme contre capitalisme*, Paris: Éditions du Seuil.
Charkham, J. (1993) *Keeping Good Company: A Study of Corporate Governance in Five Countries*, Oxford: Oxford University Press.
EFMD (1992) Annual Conference, Vienna, *European Management Unlimited: Dynamics*

of an Emerging Process (see also 'Towards a definition of European management', *EFMD Quarterly Review* 92/2).

Gattaz, Y. (1993) *Le Modèle français*, Paris: Plon.

Hampden-Turner, C. and Trompenaars, A. (1993) *The Seven Cultures of Capitalism*, New York: Doubleday.

Keeble, S.P. (1992) *The Ability to Manage: A Study of British Management 1890–1990*, Manchester: Manchester University Press.

Lawrence, P. (1980) *Managers and Management in West Germany*, London: Croom Helm.

Locke, R.R. (1989) *Management and Higher Education since 1940: The Influence of America and Japan on West Germany, Great Britain and France*, Cambridge: Cambridge University Press.

Porter, L. and McKibben, L. (1988) *Management Education and Development: Drift or Thrust into the 21st Century*, New York: McGraw-Hill.

Thurow, L. (1993) *Head to Head: The Coming Economic Battle among Japan, Europe and America*, London: Nicholas Brealey Publishing.

Chapter 4

Management education in Central and Eastern Europe: creating relevant models for educational institutions

Francis J. Aguilar

In 1992, a Czech university faculty member gave the following description of the managerial environment in Czechoslovakia before the 'Velvet Revolution.'

> Company managements were absolutely dependent on state planners, who decided products, prices, quantities and delivery dates and allocated material, human, and financial resources. The decision criteria were influenced by political as well as economic considerations.
>
> The state plan was law; the managers' task was to meet the goals. Managers fulfilled the target quotas if possible, or pretended to do so if not. As a result, little attention was paid to product quality, customer satisfaction, profits, or costs. Companies were more likely to accumulate surplus inventories and labour force as a hedge against shortages.
>
> In general, industrial and business management in this environment was characterized by the following behaviour:
>
> - Managers avoided taking responsibility. Instead of looking for ways to solve problems, they concentrated on explaining why the problem could not be solved;
> - Top managers were servile towards government authorities, on whom their rewards and career possibilities depended;
> - Top managers spent more time and energy bargaining with the central bodies in setting targets and in obtaining resources than in paying attention to business operations or to the marketplace.

Collapse of the communist regimes in Central and Eastern Europe in 1989 and 1990 brought to an end a half century of *dirigiste* economic and political systems that underlay the management practices described above.[1] In their places emerged prospects of market-driven economies, private property, and democratic forms of government. Spurred on by the urgings of Western politicians, business practitioners, academicians, and other interested parties, the peoples of Central and Eastern Europe quickly initiated efforts to hold free elections, to introduce market prices, to liberalize trade and foreign exchange, to restore private ownership, and to establish the necessary supporting legal, financial and social structures. While opinions differed, often sharply, as to the appropriateness and effectiveness of the specific programmes that were being implemented to transform the political and economic systems, there was general agreement that political stability would depend on economic recovery and sustainability. On this point, the spectre of the Weimar Republic's collapse in the early 1930s and Germany's acceptance of fascism as a force to end the degradation of its economy and self-respect continues to haunt Western society.

A successful market economy requires people who know how to lead and manage manufacturing and service businesses in a competitive environment. The supply of business practitioners with such capabilities in Central and Eastern Europe, however, is severely limited, as noted in a 1993 United Nations study: 'While some managers from Eastern Europe possessed some basic knowledge of the fundamentals of market economies – profit, competition, price, etc. – there was a lack of understanding about what these concepts meant in practice: e.g. the function of profits, the reasons for pricing goods, the importance for an enterprise of developing its comparative advantage, etc.'[2] To help correct this problem, high quality management education is required quickly and on a large scale.

The purpose of this chapter is to provide information that can help Central and Eastern European business educators in considering their institutional strategies. While business people have been trained and developed in a variety of ways – such as on-the-job experiences, in-company training programmes and individual coaching – the following observation by Philip L. Smith, former chairman of the General Foods Corporation, points to the growing need for formal and rigorous management education in the years to come:

> Two decades ago, Peter Drucker observed that the corporation was the first social institution to learn how to bring together a diversity of knowledge in a common effort to pursue a coordinated series of goals. In doing so, it developed what he called 'an almost insatiable appetite for all kinds of knowledge and conceptual skill.'
>
> Now, as we approach the final decade of the 20th century, that appetite has grown more voracious than ever. Businesses of all types require more and more managers who have both the depth of business expertise to operate the complex mechanisms of finance and industry, and the breadth of knowledge to do so wisely and ethically, in accordance with the demands of the wider society.
>
> (Porter 1988: xvii)

Gordon and Howell, in their seminal study of business education, make this point while still recognizing the limits involved:

The new situation does not necessarily mean that all future businessmen should attend a business school. There is no disagreement that a variety of roads to a business career must be left open. But it does suggest that the educational requirements for the practice of business are becoming more rigorous and that some combination of a general and a professional education can make businessmen better businessmen, although no form of education, business or otherwise, can ever guarantee business success.

(Gordon 1959: 12–13)

This chapter's focus on educational institutions also reflects the current state of management education in Central and Eastern Europe.[3]

THE CENTRAL AND EASTERN EUROPEAN TEACHERS PROGRAMME

While management education in 1991 differed from country to country, certain conditions were generally common throughout Central and Eastern Europe. State-run universities, institutes, or academies were the dominant providers of business education. Business training in these institutions focused primarily on first-degree programmes, almost always involving large numbers of students. The faculty was divided by a structure of professorial chairs that tended to compete with each other for resources and prestige. Relatedly, while curricula of the various chairs tended to be narrowly focused on specific techniques – such as those relating to accounting, information technology, international trade – they also often overlapped with each other in an effort to be comprehensive and to appeal to students. Courses emphasized theory rather than practice, and teaching was heavily dependent on lecturing. In general, faculty expertise was considerable with respect to computer science and quantitative analysis, and deficient for marketing, corporate finance, management control, and organizational behaviour. Despite heavy teaching loads, many faculty members had second jobs to supplement the low university pay. In the former DDR, faculty members also experienced uncertainty concerning employment as the government selected West German professors to fill many of the chairs in the East German universities.

Also relevant to management education in Central and Eastern Europe in 1991 were the various initiatives underway involving Western European and US business school faculties, the former in connection with the European Community Tempus and Phare programmes and the latter with US AID or other government funding. Examples would include Nottingham University's effort to help the Bratislava School of Economics to create a part time post-graduate MBA programme and a similar effort by the University of Washington at the Academy of Economic Studies in Bucharest, Romania.

It was in this setting that Harvard Business School, Kellogg Business School (Northwestern University), Sloan Business School (MIT), Stanford Business School, and Wharton (University of Pennsylvania) joined forces in 1991 to offer a training programme for teachers of management in Central and Eastern Europe. Experiences with the start up and development of management education over the years in countries around the world had provided these schools with a number of important lessons that would guide the consortium's efforts:

1 Long-term management training needs could best, and probably only, be met through the efforts of local educators. This premise recognizes that specific educational needs differ from country to country and would be markedly different from those in the United States (or even Western Europe). It also recognizes that the demand for widespread management training requires a large number of educators who can conduct classes in the native language.
2 Individual faculty member training must be guided by a cohesive and realistic institutional strategy.
3 Creation of a centre of excellence in management education requires a sustained effort over many years.
4 Management education must relate to practice as well as to theory and must reflect the particular circumstances in which it is to function.

With respect to this last point, the appropriate model for management education in any given country is largely determined by the interplay of three factors: (1) the business environment, (2) the knowledge and skills of business teachers, and (3) their values and attitudes. The business environment – involving such elements as the variety and importance of the specific business operations underway or planned, the condition of the existing industrial and commercial assets, a country's political structure, laws and regulations, money and banking, transportation and communications infrastructures, human and natural resources, and society's expectations – defines what *should* be done in the way of management education. The knowledge and skills of business teachers in turn delimits what they are *able* to do in the way of meeting such needs. And their attitudes and values determines what they are *willing* to do in this regard. While all three factors are subject to change over time, management education – whether in an academic or in-company setting – must accord with the realities of each as they exist.

The scope, complexity, and urgency of the management education challenge in Central and Eastern Europe coupled with resource limitations precluded the consortium from offering custom tailored training programmes for each institution, or even for each country. In consequence, the approach adopted was to offer a single, common programme that would expose the participating teachers to the thinking and practices of the five sponsoring business schools. The limits of this approach were openly acknowledged, and participants were advised of the need for them to pick and choose among the lessons offered, deciding what to adopt, what to adapt, and what to reject.

The Central and Eastern European Teachers Programme was designed to inform students in the following areas: current managerial concepts and practices in a global market economy, teaching and learning at the university and post graduate levels, the case method of instruction, research methodologies, and institutional strategies for management education.[4] Management education in the United States served as a starting point for the consideration and discussion of institutional strategies for meeting the management educational needs of the relevant business community (Aguilar: 1992).

THE MISSION OF MANAGEMENT EDUCATION

Business education, a term with many meanings, covers a wide spectrum of instruction. In one of the earliest conferences to address this subject, Robert Calkins identified three broad categories: (1) vocational training; (2) specialized instruction; and (3) preparation for the management and leadership of business affairs (Calkins 1948: 53). He argued that professional business schools should take on the third type as their primary task. Coming to the same conclusion, one of the subsequent defining studies of management education in the United States described this role for business schools in the following manner:

> The special province of higher education is to strengthen the individual's capacity to think for himself. In the context of business situations, this capacity involves the ability to relate basic skills and general knowledge to specific business decisions and the capacity to approach particular problems in an imaginatively intellectual manner. Both of these capacities are greatly prized at all levels of business, they are wholly in keeping with the highest traditions of college and university work, and they mark out an area in which business schools, working in close collaboration with various nonbusiness disciplines as well as with business organizations themselves, can assume a leadership role of the greatest importance.
>
> (Pierson 1959: 157)

Studies of this nature, coupled with the experiences of the premier institutions for management education around the world, point to the following broad educational mission for business schools that aspire to professional leadership: to prepare students for imaginative and responsible leadership roles in business and society; to contribute to the lifelong learning needs of managers; to advance the science and practice of business through research. The professional nature of business education requires that the learning process encompass the positive development of skills and attitudes as well as knowledge.[5]

CHARACTERISTICS OF SUCCESSFUL BUSINESS SCHOOLS

The above mission, with its primary focus on the preparation of business leaders, has implications for curriculum, students, faculty, teaching methods, research, and institutional relationships. Each is discussed in turn.

Curriculum

As Porter and McKibbin note, 'What business schools do with – and to – students is in large measure a function of the curriculum (Porter 1988: 47).' It reveals the educational objectives that a faculty thinks should be pursued. Gordon and Howell describe the basic skills and abilities that are most needed in the business world:

> The most important of these are analytical ability, judgement, skill in interpersonal relations, the ability to accept responsibility and make decisions, general administrative skills (including the capacity to lead others, to plan, to organize and delegate), breadth and flexibility of mind, imagination, facility in personal communication, and strong personal motivation. These qualities are not needed in precisely the same combination for every type of position and for all kinds of careers in business. But, particularly for the higher administrative positions, they seem to be the qualities that need most to be emphasized.
>
> (Gordon 1959: 100)

The trend over the past 25 years for business education at the university level has been to give increased attention to general management instruction, to offer two-year masters-level instruction, and to have a significant required core in the curriculum.[6] As Gordon and Howell note, 'In general, business courses can be taught with any one of three kinds of emphasis, which can be called the descriptive, and analytical, and the managerial-clinical'. Descriptive instruction presents fairly detailed subject matter 'to the student, who passively absorbs and then regurgitates it on examinations. What is needed is a combination of the analytical and the managerial-clinical, although some descriptive material cannot be avoided. The student needs to acquire a command of systematic knowledge at as high an analytical level as he can handle and then be made to put this knowledge to use in problem-solving situations that will help him develop the basic skills that he will need as a businessman' (Gordon 1959: 135).

Setting a balance between breadth and depth is an ongoing curriculum challenge for business schools. Porter and McKibbin frame the issue well:

> In concrete terms, the issue can be rephrased as follows: To what extent should graduates be prepared for the *first job* after graduation versus a longer-term career in business/management. If the former objective is emphasized, a student may do well when initially out of school but may falter somewhat on the way up the corporate ladder. If the latter is a programme's focus, a graduate may have a difficult time in early jobs and possibly never attain (or attain relatively late in his or her career) a job level which emphasizes broader responsibilities and skills. This is an issue with no absolute answers.
>
> (Porter 1988: 104)

Students

For business schools to prepare effective leaders for business, students must be of high quality. The measure of student quality is twofold: (1) intellectual aptitude; and (2) desirable motivation, interests, and other personal characteristics. To populate a programme with such students requires selective admissions.

The second set of traits points to older candidates who have had the time to gain maturity in their thinking and emotions and even some exposure to business practice. The grounds for scepticism regarding business education for young students (from 18 to 22 years of age) are several: they generally do not have the intellectual maturity and judgement that rigorous training aimed at developing problem-solving and organizational skills requires; many lack the necessary seriousness of purpose; and they lack the business experiences that give deeper meaning to formal training. This final point argues that formal business education should be preceded by responsible, full-time work experience.[7]

Faculty

According to Pierson, 'The most precious resource which any business school can possess is a highly qualified and highly motivated faculty' (Pierson 1959: 268). He goes on to describe the requisite qualities of individual faculty members: 'Some of the more important are personal and professional integrity, a sense of community responsibility, intellectual imagination, genuine interest in students, capacity to communicate ideas effectively in oral and/or written form, thorough grounding in at least one broad area of learning, understanding of background subjects most relevant to the individual's area of special competence, and close familiarity with and active participation in current research developments' (Pierson 1959: 269).

Collectively, a business school faculty 'needs to have sufficient familiarity with broad background subjects and the tools of the major disciplines in the humanities, sciences, and social sciences to be able to work with them effectively in different contexts', and to be versed in managerial decision making. Moreover, it should include persons who have a thorough grounding in the basic business subjects – accounting, statistics, economics – and persons with a special competence in the principal business functional areas – finance, marketing, production, personnel, managerial control (Pierson 1959: 270–1).

The challenge of providing high quality business education has led business schools to rely largely on full-time career faculty members who hold an earned doctorate. There is general agreement that most faculty members should have a significant amount of responsible business experience, whether obtained through an interlude of full-time business practice or through consulting activity (Gordon 1959: 352; and Porter 1988: 184).

Consulting

Consulting benefits faculty members by enabling them to gain valuable experience with business practice, to keep abreast of changes in business, and to earn additional compensation. Gordon and Howell point to the possible risk that such work 'consists of routine jobs that absorb the time and drain the energies of business school teachers without adding much if anything to their professional competence' (Gordon 1959: 435). A related risk is that faculty members devote a disproportionate amount of their attention to outside assignments to the disadvantage of school programmes. As a result of these risks, it is customary for business schools to attempt to control the amount and kind of faculty involvement in outside consulting. In this connection, Pierson concludes: 'The convention of limiting consulting to one day a week, for example, seems an appropriate one to apply in most cases. Limiting this type of activity to new issues as opposed to the familiar and repetitive is another useful criterion to keep in mind' (Pierson 1959: 279).

Teaching methods

The method of instruction is largely shaped by the educational objective of the individual school. The lecture method with heavy reliance on textbook recitations tends to predominate where the emphasis is on training for particular jobs. Schools stressing the managerial approach or preparation for general careers in business tend to put more emphasis on participation, discussion, and investigation by the individual student. The teaching method which has exerted more widespread influence than any other in this field is the case method (Pierson 1959: 286–7).

The case method of study may be characterized in the following terms: 'The student is placed in the position of the businessman who must act, who must before he acts weigh the bearing on his problem of a variety of different considerations, both short-run and long-run in character, but who must in any event make a decision and implement it' (David 1954: viii). Early advocates of the case method argued its merits as follows:

> The goal of business training by the case system, as it has been described by almost all who have written about it, is not to give the students the answers to questions, nor primarily to help them accumulate a store of knowledge, nor to acquaint them with best practices. Rather it is to help the students learn how to go about answering questions, to help them develop skills in discovering and defining the questions which ought to be answered, and to help them realize that in real life they frequently will have to take action before they can get all the facts which they would like to have in deciding what is the right action.
>
> (Culliton 1948: 86)

> The case system does not aim to give the student ready-made answers to the problems which it assumed his business life will present to him. Such an enterprise would be futile for the questions which he will have to answer have not yet been asked. The question that has not been asked cannot be answered.
>
> (Cabot 1931: 162)

The case method has its limitations. Some subject areas lend themselves to this form of instruction much better than others. As Pierson notes, its effectiveness 'largely depends on the amount of systematic knowledge already available and the amount which students have to master. In the human relations area, case analysis is apparently the most effective way to get at the principal issues involved. It seems quite otherwise in such an area as modern statistics. The difference lies in the fact that the formal content of the first subject is relatively small, whereas it is relatively large for the second' (Pierson 1959: 288). Other forms of active learning that can help business schools to avoid excessive emphasis on lectures and textbooks would include the use of exercises, analysis of current readings, field studies of actual business problems, and computer games.

Research

According to Pierson, 'The broad purpose of business research may be said to be to increase the fund of scientific knowledge about the operations of the individual firm. To this end business schools need to concentrate on developing a body of widely applicable generalizations which have been scientifically tested and can be used in developing still further knowledge in this area.[8] (Pierson 1959: 313.)

Porter and McKibbin admonish business schools to guard against an overemphasis on quantity of output (number of articles, etc.) in relation to quality and to encourage the inclusion of business practitioners as well as the academic community among the intended audiences of research.

Institutional relationships

There are at least two sets of 'publics' with which the typical business/ management school has relations: the university community in which the business school is housed, and the professional management/business community external to the university. Porter and McKibbin describe the many dimensions of the internal relationship:

> The business school, with rare exception, operates within the structure of a larger university community; it is strongly affected by the culture of that community and has only limited freedom to diverge from the mainstream of the formal as well as the informal norms and customs of the university. The wider institutional policies affect the selection, promotion, tenure, and salary decisions that pertain to business faculty, limit the degrees of freedom to set standards of admission and graduation, typically set limits on the extent to which the business school can engage in fund-raising, prescribe the amount of time a faculty member can devote to consulting, and often constrain the schools' non-degree-programme activities.
>
> (Porter 1988: 181)

While these relationships differ widely among institutions, depending on history and local circumstances as well as other factors, the leading business schools have gained considerable freedom of action, especially with respect to curriculum content, research, and the selection of faculty and students.

As Pierson notes, schools of business can make important contributions to professional training in other fields of study where some significant proportion of graduates are likely to manage organizations or to interact with business – such as engineering, law and government. Conversely, business schools can draw on other schools of the university – such as law, economics, and the behavioural sciences – for specialized support (Pierson 1959: 148, 158).

The business school also has important linkages to the business community. Among other things, business firms hire the graduates, are a source for part-time and visiting faculty, use faculty as teachers in executive development programmes and as consultants, utilize research findings, and make major financial contributions to the business school (Porter 1988: 182).

THE INSTITUTIONAL CHALLENGE

The institutional challenge of providing management education that best meets the needs of its relevant community is likely to require considerable soul-searching and effort. A clearcut mission must be defined, a strategy formulated, changes and innovations implemented, and the work of business education effectively carried out. In all this, great care must be taken to discover a realistic approach that fits the prevailing and prospective circumstances in which the institution finds itself. The special problems that a university faces in restructuring its business education are generally different from those facing an independent institution.

University

One of the most difficult problems in upgrading business education within a university structure is to gain the necessary freedom of action that will allow sufficient responsiveness to the distinctive educational requirements of the field. Pressures for conformity can inhibit the proper functioning of a business education in a variety of ways. For example, the strong bias toward theory over applications and practice that characterizes most universities in Central and Eastern Europe could adversely affect curriculum, teaching methods, research, and faculty evaluation. Likewise, the structure of independent departments or chairs in many universities can impede the coordinated instruction called for in business education. Other issues of concern are associated with faculty assignments and workloads, faculty promotion decisions, fund-raising, and executive education.

Faculty compensation can pose another difficulty. Talented management educators normally have attractive career opportunities in business that could lure them from teaching.[9] While academic life offers many attractions to faculty members, salary is not usually one of them. Consulting fees are one way to reduce the compensation gap. One problem with this arrangement is that any appreciable disparity between the incomes earned by faculty members in business and their peers in other parts of the university can be a source of friction leading to restrictions.

Independent business schools

One of the early challenges in founding an independent business school is to establish its legitimacy. Some kind of university affiliation, however loose, appears to be the most effective means of accomplishing this.[10] The support of the business community also plays an important role in gaining acceptance. Having business leaders serve actively on a board of advisers has proven valuable for many schools in obtaining such support. In some countries, active and open government support can also be of vital importance.

Financial considerations often dominate the start-up strategy of newly founded independent business schools, especially with respect to programme offerings and faculty manning. In many cases, the initial focus is exclusively, or heavily, on executive education in order to generate cash income. To attract participants, faculty members from prestigious business schools are engaged to teach in such programmes. To limit costs, faculty manning is likely to include practitioners for part-time teaching assignments. These practices, however, have their limitations. Part-time and visiting faculty members are less likely than full time career educators to devote the necessary time and energy to creating teaching materials and course offerings that are particularly responsive to the client business community.

Faculty formation is another critical consideration in establishing a strong business school. The requirements for faculty qualifications normally change over time. In the early years, faculty members might need to engage themselves almost exclusively in teaching and administration. For this purpose, MBA-level education, coupled with business experience, is likely to be the most suitable faculty preparation. Over time, as the institution develops its own teaching materials and begins to engage in business research, doctoral training becomes more appropriate. This kind of evolution can be seen at work as of 1994 in the following three business schools: at Instituto de Alta Dirección Empresarial (INALDE), founded eight years earlier in Bogotá, Colombia, none of four full-time and one of its 15 part-time faculty members had a Ph.D.; at Instituto Panamericano de Alta Dirección de Empresa (IPADE), in existence about 25 years ago in Mexico City, about 40% of its faculty of 35 total were so qualified; and at almost 40-year-old Instituto de Estudios Superiores de la Empresa (Universidad de Navarra)(IESE) in Barcelona, Spain, all of the approximately 70 faculty members had, or soon would have, doctorates.

INITIAL RESPONSES TO THE US MBA MODEL

Most participants of the Central and Eastern European Teachers Programme (CEETP) were generally in favour of adopting the following key features of the traditional US MBA model described above: (1) an emphasis on business-practice-related issues; (2) a programme that is multi-functional and integrated in its coverage; and (3) use of the case method (along with lectures and seminars). Of the approximately 100 teachers who had had no prior experience with cases (out of a total of 125 participants), about 25 taught one or more cases in their home institution during the 18 month training period, either as isolated experimental events or as part of an established course.

These sentiments pose several related issues for each participating university. One is whether to apply one or more of the above three pedagogical concepts to its offerings or to regard the training programme as only affecting what teachers might do in their individual courses and classes. If a university favours making structural changes to its offerings, it then typically must decide, in view of limited human resources, whether to start with university programmes or post graduate programmes. Finally, with respect to post graduate education, the university has to decide whether to offer such programmes through the established organizational structure or via a separate institution that has some degree of independence.

By the fall of 1993, twelve of the eighteen participating universities had taken initial steps to adopt the active learning, multifunctional coverage, and practice related precepts. Most favoured starting in the post graduate arena because of the reduced complexity of the smaller and more flexible activities involved. Even more important, this choice lowered the likelihood of university faculty resistance. A number of these schools were introducing part-time executive MBA programmes (e.g. Prague, Bucharest, Bratislava). Most participating universities are considering or have already established a separate institution for post-graduate education. This arrangement offers a greater freedom of action in curriculum and programme content and in compensating teachers. Both benefits are important if teachers are to be employed on a full-time basis. In a few cases (most notably Budapest), initial emphasis was on making changes to the university degree programmes. One concept under consideration in this latter realm is to create a special track in the last two years of a five year degree programme that would resemble a full-time MBA programme. This strategy would allow the participating faculty to focus on a limited number of bright and motivated students selected from among the normally large student body.

The experience of Rostock University is instructive as to the nature of the challenges involved in bringing about change. The need to await the German government's selection of professors to fill the vacant chairs coupled with severe budget cuts precluded the university leadership from taking any actions other than those required for sustaining normal operations. In light of this situation, the five CEETP participants from Rostock proposed to organize themselves as a working group (Arbeitsgruppe 'Case Teaching Method an der Universität Rostock') to develop case materials and to teach cases as part of their regular workload. The university agreed to this proposal and assigned an office room for their use. Professor Theodore Nebl, dean of faculty, described the university's strategy as follows: (1) to keep the CEETP teacher group intact and motivated during the time it takes the university to deal with the transition crisis that it faces; and (2) as soon as practical (in about two years time), to introduce case instruction into the university curriculum as well as ongoing executive training under the leadership of a chaired professor of management. If step two turns out not to be feasible, then the university would attempt to establish a separate centre for post graduate education.

FUTURE EVOLUTION

As the above account for Rostock University suggests, the management education situation in Central and Eastern Europe remains quite fluid as of 1994. For a university to develop high quality programmes that are suitable for the needs of its nation or region requires a process drawing on two sources of information to guide the way. One source is the local (or otherwise relevant) business community to help the university identify the training needs as they exist at the time and as they change over time. The other source is the academic community to help it to keep abreast of emerging business and teaching concepts. Each educational institution needs to cultivate such sources and to foster its abilities to perceive and act on useful inputs.[11]

The only predictions that one can make about management education in Central and Eastern Europe is that the needs in Sofia will be different from those in Warsaw and that they will change with time for any given institution. Not only does each institution have to find the right model of management education for its specific needs, but must also seek *institutional flexibility* so as to be as responsive as possible to changing needs (Porter 1988: 44).

Business education is a complex affair. As should be apparent, no single set of precepts for what to do exists. Pierson perhaps best captures the challenge for those intent on creating a centre of excellence in management education:

> The diversity and complexity of purposes served by business schools put chief responsibility on the individual institution to meet its obligations in its own way. Each school should accordingly approach its work in a bold and independent spirit, demonstrating the same qualities of vigorous, imaginative leadership which its graduates will be increasingly called on to display.
>
> (Pierson 1959: 122, 3)

EXHIBIT A-1
INSTITUTIONAL PARTICIPATION IN THE CENTRAL AND EASTERN EUROPEAN TEACHERS PROGRAMME

Bulgaria

University of National and World Economy (Sofia)

Czech Republic

Prague School of Economics
Czechoslovak Management Center, (Celakovice)

Germany

Humboldt University (Berlin)
Frederich Schiller University (Jena)
Rostock University
Technical University Otto von Guericke (Magdeburg)

Hungary

Budapest University of Economic Sciences
Janus Pannonius University (Pecs)

Latvia

University of Latvia

Poland

Adam Mickiewicz University (Poznan)
Jagiellonian University (Krakow)
Warsaw University
Warsaw University of Technology

Romania

Academy of Economic Studies (Bucharest)
University Babes-Bolyai (Napoca-Cluj)

Russia

International Business School, MGIMO (Moscow)
Academy of National Economy (Moscow)

Slovakia

Bratislava School of Economics

Slovenia

International Executive Development Centre

Ukraine

International Management Institute (Kiev)

NOTES

1 While this simple observation fails to take into account important aspects of the former business environment, it does capture the bureaucratic nature of the resulting managerial process.

2 The report listed the following management training needs as urgent (p. 28):

- General Management (in market economy)
- Strategic Management (planning, portfolio analysis, etc.)
- Restructuring (privatization, downsizing, business valuation, etc.)
- Marketing
- Financial Management (sources of funds, equity, capital markets, etc.)
- Accounting and Auditing
- Innovation, Technology Management, Product Design
- Human Resources Development and Motivation
- Information Management
- Productivity and Quality Management
- International Business, Globalization, Networking
- Negotiating Skills
- Business Law

3 An increasing number of Western companies are supplementing or replacing business school education with quality in-house programmes. In many cases, the courses are planned and taught by business school professors. In the author's opinion, the required conditions for this model of education are currently unmet in Central and Eastern Europe. These conditions would include ample human and financial resources to mount and sustain such programmes and the availability of qualified teachers.

4 The Central and Eastern European Teachers Programme included four major elements. The first was to have each participant attend an integrated general management executive programme. This experience had a variety of learning objectives: to become familiar with concepts relating to how business is conducted in a market economy; to grasp the interrelated nature of business administration; to experience the case method of instruction; to be exposed to a variety of teaching styles; and to sample a residential, full-time, extended executive development programme. Approximately half of the participants attended established executive programmes at one of the five sponsoring US universities. (These programmes were offered at different times during the year and lasted from 4 to 13 weeks in duration.) The remaining participants attended a special seven-week 'executive' programme offered at the Harvard Business School during the summer of 1992. While this special programme did not give the teachers an opportunity to mix and work with business practitioners, it did place greater emphasis on issues relevant to Central and Eastern Europe and also had less stringent language requirements than did the other executive programmes.

   The second element of the programme trained teachers to write case materials for their courses. Participants were instructed to work individually or in groups in preparing at least one case and teaching note during the 1992–93 school year. Workshops were held in each country during the fall and again in spring to provide instructions and to review field experiences and case outlines and drafts. US faculty members reviewed completed case drafts and made suggestions for improvement.

The third element was to further academic development in a participant's field of interest. A six-week programme for general management and organizational behaviour was offered during the summer of 1993 at Harvard, for marketing at Kellogg, for operations management at Sloan, and for finance and accounting at Wharton. Each programme dealt with curriculum design, research, and teaching issues for its field or fields.

Efforts to help each institution to develop a supportive environment for the newly trained teachers, the fourth element of the programme, were made at every opportunity over the entire period of time. 125 faculty members of 21 educational institutions from 11 countries participated in the programme.

5 Gordon and Howell specifically address the importance of developing proper attitudes as a function of business education:

As we have seen, business education must be concerned not only with competence but also with responsibility, not only with skills but also with the attitudes of businessmen. This means that business schools have an obligation to do what they can to develop a 'sense of social responsibility' and a high standard of business ethics in their graduates.

(Gordon 1959: 111)

As we use the term 'attitudes,' it means the whole set of values by which a person governs his conscious behaviour. Every person has a more or less consciously formulated philosophy, a scale of values, with which to weigh the alternatives that are open to him. In a private enterprise system, no group needs more to have a carefully thought out philosophy than do businessmen, and it is vitally important to society as a whole that their philosophy contribute to the viability of an economic and political system that depends on the unplanned cooperation of groups with partially conflicting goals.

(Gordon 1959: 84)

6 Gordon and Howell caution against going too far in emphasizing general principles:

While this is clearly the trend of the future in business education, it does present at least one danger against which business schools need to be on guard. A broad curriculum emphasizing general principles, fundamental knowledge, and breadth of view does not prepare the student for the routine and detail that are likely to characterize his early years in business. He must learn to accept the routine and to benefit from it. What he has learned must be elaborated by experience before he is ready for the higher levels of management. A frequent complaint by businessmen against the products of particularly the best known graduate schools is that 'they all want to be vice presidents tomorrow.' More and wiser counselling can help with this problem. A more plentiful use of cases and problems taken from the lower levels of management can also help.

(Gordon 1959: 102)

7 See (Gordon 1959: 112–113). The growing emphasis on prior business experience can be seen in the increased average age of students entering the Harvard Business School's MBA Programme, from $23\frac{1}{2}$ in 1959 to 26 in 1992 as the result of adding requirements for two to three years of relevant employment.

8 Pierson goes on to observe:

> To be widely applicable, research findings must go beyond description to analysis. Both hypothesis forming and hypothesis testing are essential. Finding out how businessmen behave under various circumstances and what practices exist in different areas is an important step but is not research in any serious sense of the term. Not until the data are embodied in principles or generalizations which can be said to 'explain the facts' can research attain general significance. Research in an applied field, as in any field, must consider why, not simply how, events occur.
>
> (Pierson 1959: 313)

9 This pressure is likely to be especially severe in Central and Eastern Europe during the next several years for educators trained in market economy business practices.

10 Many different arrangements for affiliation are possible. For example, Institute for Management Development (IMD) originally operated 'under the patronage' of the University of Lausanne, the Asian Institute of Management in Manila was founded under the sponsorship of three established Philippine universities, and Instituto Centroamericano de Administración de Empresas (INCAE) began in Nicaragua with an informal, but well publicized, connection with the Harvard Business School.

11 In this connection, contact with other Central and Eastern European university business schools is likely to provide invaluable information concerning transition experiences (attempts at change that worked or that did not work).

REFERENCES

Aguilar, F. J. (1992) 'Business Schools', unpublished paper, Harvard University.

Cabot, P. (1931) 'The preparation for tomorrow's problems', in C.E. Fraser (ed.) *The Case Method of Instruction*, New York: McGraw-Hill.

Calkins, R.D. (1948) 'Aims of business education', in *Education for Professional Responsibility*. A report of the proceedings of the inter-professions conference on Education for Professional Responsibility, Buck Hill Falls, April; Pittsburgh: Carnegie Press.

Culliton, J.W. (1948) 'The Question That Has Not Been Asked Cannot Be Answered', in *Education for Professional Responsibility*. A report of the proceedings of the inter-professions conference on Education for Professional Responsibility, Buck Hill Falls, April; Pittsburgh: Carnegie Press.

David, D.K. (1954) 'Foreword', in M.C. McNair (ed.) *The Case Method at the Harvard Business School*, New York: McGraw-Hill.

Gordon, R.A. and Howell, J.E. (1959) *Higher Education for Business*, New York: Columbia University Press.

Pierson, F.C. (1959) *The Education of American Businessmen*, New York: McGraw-Hill.

Porter, L.W. and McKibbin, L.F. (1988) *Management Education and Development*, New York: McGraw-Hill.

United Nations (1993) *Management Development in East–West Joint Ventures*, New York: United Nations.

Chapter 5

Case studies as a management learning tool

Michael J. Thomas

Elsewhere in this volume Gordon Shenton provides a splendid mosaic, which represents the diversity of approaches to management education in Western Europe. He concludes that 'the picture in Western Europe as regards management education is, then, one of extreme diversity, and of fairly rapid transformation . . . Diversity is the wealth of Europe!' (Chapter 3). Eastern Europe is making a dramatic transition from command economy to market-driven economy. This book reflects the great variety of approaches to management learning that are emerging at the present time. When examining the many approaches to management learning it is important not to overlook the value of the case.

The management case has its intellectual roots at the Harvard Business School in Boston, Massachusetts. That business school, still regarded as in the first rank of American business schools, depends upon the case study as the primary vehicle for learning. Over the course of a two-year degree, graduates on the programme spend virtually their entire first year analysing cases on a team basis. As graduates of the school will attest, when they graduate they have enormous confidence in their ability to solve managerial problems.

Although it cannot be assumed that it is easy to export the case study method, it is my view that in the circumstances of Eastern Europe the case study has particular importance. I say this because in the period of transition there is very little folk memory of successful management of organizations, particularly market-driven organizations. The economic history of organizations in the eastern bloc is a history of bureaucratic management and control, where managers in individual organizations and enterprises were given relatively little freedom of action. The national plan was the compass that guided virtually all managers. In the new environment managers have to try to understand what it is to survive in a market-driven environment. One way in which managers can develop an understanding of this new environment is to study the behaviour of managers in the market-driven environments in the west. There is a very large body of cases available from both the United States and Western Europe which will serve their purpose in the short term, although clearly the ideal situation would be to have access to case-study material derived from the experience of companies in Eastern Europe since 1990. That body of cases will no doubt emerge in the near future, although, in the meantime, resort to western cases may be necessary. It should be noted that in the United Kingdom cases are widely used and many of them are cases drawn from the North American environment. Though the economic and cultural background of these cases is often seen by students as somewhat foreign, it can be demonstrated none the less that they are effective tools for management learning.

My own experience in transferring management know-how to Poland reinforces my view that case study is a very valuable tool in the management teachers' and trainers' display of learning instruments. I believe that the process of case analysis is as important as the content, i.e. the facts in the case. There are no definitive solutions to any one case. The instructor can delineate the significant cultural, economic and social assumptions that may differentiate an American-based case and it's relevance to managers learning in Poland. Western trainers can transfer case-development methodology to Eastern Europe. It should be possible for some western resources to be invested in East European case development, since it is an expensive business if it is to be done well.

WHAT IS A CASE STUDY?

Quite simply, a case study is a record of a real-life situation that has been observed, documented and then written up. In order to clarify the situation, let me draw from material available from the Chartered Institute of Marketing (UK) of which I happen to be immediate past Chairman. The Chartered Institute of Marketing uses a case study as the final unit in its Diploma in Marketing course. The Chartered Institute uses a case study in order to 'extend the practice of candidates in the qualitative and quantitative analysis of marketing situations, both to develop their powers of diagnosis and as a contribution to the creation of firm bases for decision making'. Through this means it expects candidates to be able to: identify, define and rank the problems contained in marketing (management) case studies; formulate working hypotheses regarding the solutions to problems identified in marketing (management) case studies; assemble, order, analyse and interpret both qualitative and quantitative data relating to a marketing (management) case, using appropriate analytical procedures and models; describe and substantiate all working assumptions made regarding the case problem(s), working hypotheses and data; generate and evaluate the expected outcomes of alternate solutions to case problems; formulate recommendations for action and feedback on case problems; and prepare and present appropriate marketing (management) case reports.

Although this refers to marketing cases the points made can be extended to all management case studies. Cases can be used in a number of ways. It should be noted that the Harvard Business School approach to cases is to have students working in small groups prepare case solutions and then to have open discussion in class about those solutions. At the Strathclyde Business School and in many other British business schools it is more usual for groups to make individual presentations in class. These presentations may or may not be followed by a general discussion. One advantage of this method is that the preparation and presentation of case solutions develops presentation skills in the students. We can summarize the skills that are capable of development by the use of the case method under the following headings:

Analytical skills

Case studies normally present a variety of information, much of it factual and quantitative. The student, presented with a detailed case, is faced with a challenge of trying to understand the information and then handling that information – what is vital, what is not? Using the data in a case, a student begins to understand the problem inherent in the case. To do this requires clear and logical thinking.

Application skills

Though much of the energy devoted to case analysis is spent on finding solutions to the problems inherent in the case, one of the most important purposes is to frame the real problem in the case (see Building block 4 below). Defining the problem requires great skill. The case method is a key vehicle for applying concepts, techniques and principles learnt previously, which are then reinforced through reading and other means. Knowledge of techniques alone is useless. It is the knowledge of how to apply those techniques in a problem-solving situation that is the key to management learning.

Creative skills

Implicit in the case method is finding solutions to problems. If solutions could be programmed, then the computer would take over all management tasks. It is the creativity inherent in the task of management that makes the difference between success and failure. The case study is therefore a method whereby the student can bring creative skills to problem-solving.

Communication skills

Management is a task associated with group dynamics, and the articulation and communication of solutions is an essential part of the manager's job. The case study is a vehicle for honing these communication skills among students.

Social skills

Case work is normally done on the basis of group analysis and group presentation. Each individual benefits from the social interaction that takes place when a case is in the process of being solved by a group, though some individuals may hide within the group, failing to work things out for themselves. That point notwithstanding, there is much evidence that it is at this level that most students find in the case study a very valuable learning tool. It teaches them how to handle themselves and how to deal with group dynamics.

Self-analysis skills

It is normal when cases are presented for there to be some open discussion. Students can therefore expect to be challenged in respect of solutions and at that point the individual can no longer hide behind the group presentation. Then is the opportunity for the student to display his own self-analytical skills.

PREPARATION OF A CASE SOLUTION

There is no fixed format for presenting a case solution, but some guidelines can be given. A useful acronym is DECIDE (after Kerin and Peterson 1995: 32): **D**efine the problem; **E**numerate the decision factors; **C**onsider relevant information; **I**dentify the best alternative; **D**evelop a plan for implementing the chosen alternative; and **E**valuate the decision and the decision process. We will return to discuss this framework later, but before we do that an understanding of the basic building blocks of good case analysis is reviewed.

Building block 1: understanding the situation

A case contains a lot of information since its purpose is to portray in some detail the history of a problem in a real business. A case, by definition, is not an invention but a piece of documented history. If you are to begin to understand the issues that are to be analysed and the problems to be resolved, you must grasp all the facts provided in the case – you must understand the situation.

Building block 2: diagnosing the problem

Some case studies provide the student with a clear identification of the problem, others provide a narrative in which the student will find the problem. So, **D**efining and diagnosing the problem is a crucial step in the decision-making process, and is therefore the most essential building block of case-study analysis.

Building block 3: assembling management information

Information, data, market research, facts – these are the raw material of decision-making. In analysing a case, the student must make judgements about the reliability and relevance of the management information contained in the case. Students in Eastern Europe find themselves in an information culture very different from the one that existed before 1989. In a market-driven system, information is vital to understanding the market environment. Cases developed in the west are usually data-rich. Students will find that handling such data is a new and challenging experience. All data need, however, to be handled with care. Information needs to be checked for reliability – can the source and method of collection be identified? Is it trustworthy? And for relevance, are the data up to date? Most cases do not contain enough information, and the student is expected to seek out additional information. The question 'how much more information do I need' is one continually asked by managers. In analysing a case, the student should draw up a list of information requirements, always subjecting that list to two questions; namely, 'What do we want?' and 'How will we use it?'

A very useful tool for organizing information and for identifying information gaps is SWOT analysis. **S**trengths and **W**eaknesses is an inward looking analysis, an attempt to assess the state of the health of the organization. Remember that a case can be set within a business firm or a public-service organization. **O**pportunities and **T**hreats looks outwards at the external environment. A summary of the applications of SWOT analysis to a case is given in Figure 5.1. The application of SWOT analysis will certainly reveal the quality of the management information contained within the case. As an aid to evaluating information needs, the micro-economic and macro-economic analysis frameworks given in Figure 5.2 will constitute a useful checklist for those trying to analyse a case.

Building block 4: re-examine the problem

Building block 2 is reiterated and revised as necessary, once all the management information has been assembled and evaluated. It is a not unusual experience in the real world for problem definitions to be revised once information is analysed and assessed. At this point we must be convinced that we have properly identified the problem. It must be said that true problem-identification is a great skill, perhaps the greatest skill possessed by the truly great business leaders, for it is they who are most skilful in

Figure 5.1 Example of SWOT analysis

INTERNAL ANALYSIS (Strengths & Weaknesses)

POSITION ANALYSIS
- Financial structure (funds, profitability, risk)
- Performance related to planning

OPERATIONAL ANALYSIS
- Research & development
- Products
- Distribution
- Price

CAPABILITY ANALYSIS
- Product capability
- Human capability
- Financial capability
- Key success factors

TECHNIQUES
- Gap analysis
- Ratio analysis

EXTERNAL ANALYSIS (Opportunities & Threats)

CUSTOMER ANALYSIS
- Segmentation
- Consumer motivation
- Unmet needs

COMPETITOR ANALYSIS
- Strategic group activity
- Representatives from strategic groups

INDUSTRY ANALYSIS
- Industry
- Industry structure
- Cost structure
- Industry trends & developments
- Industry key success factors

ENVIRONMENTAL ANALYSIS
- Economic
- Government
- Cultural & social
- Demographic
- Financial
- Technology

anticipating and uncovering problems early enough to overcome them before they become unmanageable.

Building block 5: generating alternative solutions

This is the really creative part of management. If we have a thorough understanding of a management problem we have to find a solution to that

Figure 5.2 Example of environmental analysis

A Framework for Micro-Environmental Analysis

Customer analysis	Segmentation Purchase motivation Unmet needs	
Competitor analysis	Identification	– Present competitors – Potential competitors – Substitutes
	Understanding	– Cost structure – Past strategies – Culture – Strengths/weaknesses – Size/growth/profitability – Objectives
Market analysis	Actual & potential market size Market growth Market profitability Cost structure Distribution systems Trends and development Key success factors	

A Framework for Macro-Environmental Analysis

Economic environment	Changes in inflation Changes in unemployment Changes in economic growth Changes in the level of international trade	
Political/legal environment	Political	'Economic objectives' Policies European political dimension Statute law
	Legal	Common law Industry codes of practice
Technological environment	'Macro'	Relating to evolving customer needs Manufacturing
	'Micro'	Storage & distribution Order & payment processing
Demographic environment	Age Sex Lifestyles Occupation Regional distribution	
Social/cultural environment	Social	Family Reference Groups Class Values
	Cultural/ subcultural	Symbolism Rituals Language

problem. That is what we call strategic management. And creative managers rarely have single-route solutions available to them. Major strategic alternatives have to be outlined and then evaluated. Before we can do that however, there is an intervening stage.

Building block 6: predicting outcomes

Each alternative solution will have a particular outcome. An essential step is to define each outcome and attempt to predict the likelihood of its occurrence.

Building block 7: evaluating alternatives

One solution to a case lies in recommending a single well-argued and well-supported solution. Thus one of the alternatives, identified in 5, subject to the predictive analysis in 6, will emerge in 7.

Building block 8: communicating the recommendation

Whether you are producing a written or oral report, the effective communication of your recommendation with its supporting argument is the last stage.

We can now return to the DECIDE framework described earlier. The basic building blocks described above are clearly embodied in the DECIDE framework. Points 5 and 6 in that framework need some further elaboration. Point 5 reads 'Develop a plan for implementing the chosen alternative'. Students in Eastern Europe often have difficulty with the word 'plan', because it resonates with memories of the dead hand of central planning! Written reports of cases usually take the form of a plan for implementation. This is planning at the level of the organization, or a department within an organization, so it certainly is micro- rather than macro-oriented, which was one of the curses of central planning. If you want to use the term management report rather than plan, I would understand why. Business planning is, however, a perfectly valid management tool, and a solution that follows the routine form of a business plan is often very acceptable, since it is a good way to communicate to other managers. Point 6 of the DECIDE framework process is a reminder that case study is a learning tool. When it is used for the purposes of management education and training, it will be necessary for the trainer to be proactive at this stage. Having observed the solutions, having observed the group dynamics of case groups at work, it is the trainer's responsibility to counsel students, in respect of both the quality of their solution and the ways in which they arrived at that solution.

Cases used properly can be an effective management training tool. Because it can simulate real-life situations and problems, it is an effective way of providing students of management with insights into a variety of management scenarios. But much depends on the quality of the case, much depends on the skills of management trainer in using the case. The Harvard Business School, the home of case-study analysis, has many decades of experience in using the case method, and over the years has invested heavily in case-study preparation and writing. Used well the case method is a powerful tool, used badly it wastes time that could be put to better use. Trainers in Eastern Europe should be encouraged to develop case-teaching skills and given material help in developing East European case material. Meanwhile, judicious use of western case material is recommended.

REFERENCES

Bonoma, T.V. (1984) *Managing Market*, Boston, MA: Harvard Business School.
Easton, G. (1982) *Learning from Case Studies*, London: Prentice-Hall International.
Hatton, A., Roberts, P. and Worsam, M. (1992) *Solving the Management Case*, Oxford: Butterworth-Heinemann.
Kerin, R.A. and Peterson, R.A. (1993) *Strategic Marketing Problems – Cases and Comments*, 7th edn, Englewood Cliffs: Prentice Hall.
Montana, J. (ed.) (1993) *Marketing in Europe – Case Studies*, London: Sage Publications.

USEFUL ADDRESSES

Cranfield Case Clearing House, Cranfield Institute of Technology, Cranfield, Bedford MK43 0AL, UK.
Harvard Case Clearing House, Harvard Business School, Boston, MA 02163, USA.

Chapter 6

The Polish experience of foreign assistance in management training: effectiveness, dilemmas and needs

Jerzy Dietl

MANAGEMENT EDUCATION AND THE TRANSITION FROM A NON-MARKET TO A MARKET ECONOMY

It is self-evident that a gap exists between what higher education has on offer in the fields of management or business, as well as economics, in the post-Communist countries and what is normal in prosperous market societies. Furthermore, even the most advanced business faculty do not really know how to proceed, during the period of transition, from non-market to market structures. This knowledge gap, between what is on hand and what is needed, may jeopardize the efforts at radical reform. The resulting uncertainty can be exploited by the exponents of social passiveness to stymie change. Even in a 'best case scenario' the lack of entrepreneurship and the shortage of needed support specialists in fields which stimulate entrepreneurship, such as marketing, financial management and logistics, may 'trip up' the transitional process. The tradition of over-specialization in training, where students are trained from the outset for a specific job, has to be broken. A flexible labour market has to be created which rewards achievement. But the restructuring of university and college education in the field of management will not offer short-term solutions to all these problems. No matter how important it is to 'fine-tune' management training to the economy's needs, this activity cannot solve the above-mentioned gap. But without a 'new' programme of management education, market economics will not be sustainable in post-Communist Central Europe.

The system of management education and training has to be remodelled, turning away from collective and egalitarian values and embracing individualistic and competitive behaviours. Forty years of populism has to be overcome. Selective admissions and meritocratic advancement have to become the order of the day. Then the ethos of the university can be consistent with the development of entrepreneurial spirit. The form and methods of training cry out to be changed even more than does the content. Higher education needs to be de-bureaucratized, i.e. to be decentralized at all levels. The ability of management schools to make independent decisions has to be enhanced. Education for the future can best be achieved via competition and innovation. Hereby we have the best chance that the university management schools will assist in the crucial restoration of the work ethos.

Market forces should also motivate training institutions to provide much-needed programmes for lower and middle management. Poland is threatened with the nightmare of a few producing a few elite, highly trained top managers who cannot get anything done because there are insufficient competent middle and lower cadre to carry out orders. At the present, even the best-qualified top management cannot properly fulfil their tasks due to the absence of carry-through from middle echelons. Thus, university management education has to prepare graduates to perform a wide variety of functions successfully on a broad spectrum of levels.

At present, higher education in Poland reaches only 18% (1995) of the age cohort, as compared to 30% in OECD (Organisation for Economic Cooperation and Development) countries. In the last few years this percentage has increased rapidly, from 12.4% in 1992. General university-level education has to be further developed, preparing students to be adaptable on the labour market. University training has to provide the basic cognitive skills needed for graduates to be effective in a market economy; companies have to provide the specific skill training in their internship programmes that graduates' need to do their jobs.

There is a crippling lack of effective short, practically oriented programmes. Two or three year, post-secondary-level training programmes in management have to be created (actually restored) to fulfil the above mentioned generalist need. I note that foreign assistance is forthcoming in this field via TESSA (Training and Education in Strategically Significant Areas), which is being realized within the framework of TEMPUS. Furthermore, urgent demand exists for comparable short training programmes to re-qualify redundant employees and to stimulate the setting up of private businesses. Such programmes needed to be linked to the provision of advisory services, business consulting and appropriate credit lines.

An important role is already being played in Poland by the various private schools of business and foundations which offer management training courses. The number and scope of these initiatives should be expanded. Retraining and permanent education schemes sponsored by companies, as well as distance-learning systems, are desperately needed.

On the content level, 'pseudo-scientific' economic training, particularly in micro-economics and management, were a result of the Communist 'ideologization' of science. A rampant lack of empirical verification of theories – due, among other things, to non-market relationships and the resulting aversion to taking the risk of verification has led to far too much second-rate scholarship. The result is that at present we are plagued by terminological chaos and conceptual fuzziness.

If higher education is to meet the needs of business, more cooperation will have to be realized. Job-swapping and internships, jointly organized action-learning sets, guest lecturing by businessmen and consulting (in-practice research) by academics all need to be developed to bridge the gap between the two communities. On both sides much dead wood has to be eliminated if cooperation is to be purposeful. University management schools need to shape up and provide the state-of-the-art programmes which business needs. Competition between schools, especially on the post-experience executive programme market, will benefit quality. Competition between professors for research funding, consulting contracts and executive teaching slots is also needed. Critical customers can do a lot to improve university standards. For this reason, I believe that students should partly finance their own studies, supported in part by a selective system of grants.

To maximize student adaptability on the labour market, initial management training should provide more breadth than depth. All functional subjects (finance, marketing, production, human resource management/organizational behaviour) and necessary academic fields (economics, sociology, social psychology) should be introduced. The hitherto-existing system of specialized studies, starting in the first year of post-secondary education, needs to be replaced. A two-tier system of studies must be introduced. The most promising graduates from the generalist programme (possibly after a long internship of practical in-company training or a few years of employment) would be admitted to the second, more advanced, MBA-level course. More narrow, specialist knowledge of a particular sector or branch should be obtained through professional experience. A modern system of in-company training is needed which assumes that participants have already mastered a generalist university programme in business. Advanced university (MBA-level) courses should be relevant to business needs. Likewise, specialist courses (in informatics, logistics, industrial relations, accountancy, etc.) should meet business requirements. To ensure requisite variety and lasting possibilities for innovation, individual programmes of study including the free choice of subject and tutors should be promoted.

Present confusion between the fields of economics and management demands clarification. Economics should be firmly grounded in the international academic and research traditions of this field. Its course of study should take five years and be offered at only a few qualified universities. Management or business studies should develop a two-tier curriculum. The first three years of the course should be followed by a long internship or traineeship. Thereafter only the most successful students should continue their university education for another two years at the MBA level. The initial programme should be very broadly available and the MBA programmes made available only at some centres of excellence. The first two years of training should be generalist, including all the functional areas and supporting social sciences, while in the third year specialization should be possible. The number of specializations should be restricted to the most relevant, e.g. to general management, banking, corporate finance, managerial accounting, human resources/organizational behaviour, marketing, industrial relations, international relations, etc. By comparing our curriculum to that of the OECD countries we should be able to locate any potential lacunae.

Obviously our university management education needs to undergo a major process of professionalization. We need to develop a system of academic review to examine programme standards and to justify the awarding of research grants. A national system of certification may be needed to make the two-tier system work effectively. Throughout, we need to develop systems consistent with current Western standards for business/management education. A major effort is needed to develop the new curricula and the appropriate teaching content. Suitable textbooks, student assignments, exams, field activities, etc. all need to be revamped. Virtually all business school teaching aids will need to be changed. 'Teaching software' (computer simulations, tools for strategic analysis, managerial and marketing games, audio-visual materials, etc.) must be developed. In normal times such an overhaul would require a major investment in time and effort. But in a period of transformation to market conditions, our problems are all the greater. Where do we find the theories and models to explain current business reality? No curriculum which is out of touch with what students see everyday outside the classroom can be credible. Our programmes in business and management are threatened by a crisis of legitimacy. The rapidly changing economic and technological environment may make business and management studies very relevant, but it also threatens to make them seem out of date or inadequate to the circumstances. And the universities are being crippled by an exodus of young and talented faculty members, shortages of specialists in key fields and a lack of cooperation with the new small and medium sized enterprises (SMEs). The SMEs simply are not interested in cooperating with the universities; their priorities are fairly immediate and commercial. The large state-owned companies remain on the verge of bankruptcy and/or reorganization. No dynamism can be expected from them. The universities need to get in touch with business immediately, and there is really next to no one from business for them to get in touch with.

Despite the numerous shortcomings in the university programmes in Business Administration and Management, the condition of the universities is probably better than that of economy itself. Business during the transition phase is not, in general, stimulating the development of state-of-the-art management education. There is, as yet, little actual demand for well-trained managers. Managers, under pressure of a rapidly changing economic environment and operating in conditions of uncertainty, simply make short-term decisions, which naturally enough does not promote investment in training. The state-owned companies do not have clear and consistent sets of goals or criteria for decision-making, which leads to ad hoc reactions and, again, little or no investment in personnel. Furthermore, many companies simply exploit accessible resources until they are completely depleted, with little or no eye for the future. All too often company management is not interested in the effectiveness of its actions but rather in defending its individual or group interests. Thus the sort of attention to long-term profitability which focuses on training needs is very scarce. But even with the best will in the world, management, confronted by erratic markets where future needs are very hard to predict, would find it difficult to know what sort of training one ought to invest in. The huge bureaucratic, state-owned companies are in the process of restructuring. The future role of privatized enterprises is not clear. The prospects for central and local government agencies are unsure. The small private firms, which are potentially a big market for training, remain overwhelmingly opportunist in their behaviour. The role of foreign companies and consulting firms in Poland is (too often) controversial.

Managers themselves do not display a pronounced desire for further training. Most are interested in practical and easy management methods – useful under the present conditions. Top management does not seem to be very interested in the sophisticated technical and economic information on which western business strategy is based. Nor are executive seminars or issue-driven forums very popular. Even advanced management techniques, such as computer-assisted cost and quality control, portfolio analysis techniques or network planning methods, are not really in much demand. As a result, the large (state) companies have to buy all these services from consulting firms at great cost. The main motive for managers from state companies to undertake training is a desire either to retain their present positions or to obtain a certificate enhancing their value on the labour market. In neither case is the interest of the company at the forefront. Meeting cognitive needs and/or upgrading one's professional skills plays little or no role in the decision to follow a course. It is highly paradoxical that the training of top management which is actually taking place is only strengthening the positions of the bureaucratic staff which constitute a barrier to the restructuring process.

Thus, present problems are not just a product of austerity conditions and our current material limits. Nor does the need to restructure management education into a two-tier system tell the whole story. Nor does the old elite's hold on too many key positions in society explain everything. Our lack of knowledge about the transition to a market economy is a crucial problem. We need to cooperate with western professors to do research and analyse the change process. Up to now, too many visiting Western Professors have preferred to give general lectures on business economics and management, rather than undertake the much more risky concrete and detailed analysis of the current change process which is needed. Furthermore, we will need help to translate state-of-the-art analysis of post-Communist change into effective teaching.

THE SCOPE OF THE ASSISTANCE RECEIVED

Since the end of 1989 Poland has been receiving foreign assistance to help facilitate the economic, social and political transformation. Education and training in the field of management and economics has, from the beginning, been targeted for assistance. The assistance has included bilateral projects, scholarships for Poles to attend training programmes in a donor country, multilateral training projects and expert missions of consultants. Grants are often provided over a period of a few years (generally three). The level of assistance has, if we assume that programming was spread across three years, amounted to roughly 3.3% of the annual Polish expenditure on training per annum. While the assistance has been very valuable, it must be admitted that in practice it plays a smaller role in the financing of training than the figures suggest. This is because the costs of the training programmes are often many times higher than similar training carried out by Polish institutions with Polish personnel. Furthermore, part of the training fund is earmarked for consulting and expert reports. All too often those responsible for carrying out the assistance schemes are more eager to write expert reports or do consulting than to become directly involved in training. Some sources do directly run training programmes or finance them, for example the Polish–American Enterprise Fund.

The resources which fall within the framework of bilateral assistance are fully controlled by the donor countries, which also decide how they are to be spent. In most cases, particular programmes are agreed to by both sides. Generally, bilateral assistance programmes are approved by ministries of both countries, mainly the Ministries of Foreign Affairs and of Education. Sometimes para-government organizations are involved. For example, the British Know-How Fund, created in 1989, is managed and controlled by the British Council from its office in Warsaw. While the allocation of funds is agreed with the Polish government, funding is provided almost solely in the form of services. Consequently, the costs of local training programmes, equipment, teaching materials and investments are excluded. It is difficult to estimate the amount of bilateral funding actually going to training, as consulting and expert advice is included in the same budgets. I would estimate that the amount has been US$180 to 200 million per year.

In addition to the Brits (Know-How Fund) several other Western European countries have their own national initiatives. France has financed more than ten projects of cooperation between French and Polish universities and business schools, mainly in the form of visiting lecturers. Traineeships for Polish managers in French companies, a programme of doctoral studies and the setting up of a branch of the French Institute of Management in Warsaw (SFG) have been realized. German assistance is directed primarily at practical and not at university-level training: 60% of it goes to business training. The Swedes have set up Management Training Centres attached to the Confederation of Polish Employers; provided courses spread throughout Poland; provided business school lecturers and supported an MBA programme in banking for over thirty participants. Norwegian aid has allowed the opening of a school of business at the Warsaw Polytechnic and supported the International School of Management in Gdańsk.

US assistance is very difficult to follow. It is entirely decentralized and based on direct contacts between American universities and Polish institutions. Some financial resources come from American government agencies United States Agency for International Development (US AID) and United States Information Agency (US IA), who provide grants to American universities to run training programmes in Poland or for Poles in the United States. In most cases the assistance only pays the salaries of the American professors who visit Poland or the costs of Poles attending training in the US. Within the framework of the US 'Technical Assistance' programmes, resources have been available – for instance to the Polish–American Enterprise Fund through the Educational Enterprise Foundation to finance training projects in Poland and to produce training materials and/or translate books into Polish. An alternative source of US funding comes from the various foundations, such as Mellon Foundation, German Marshall Foundation, Kosciuszko Foundation, Rockefeller and Rockefeller Brothers Foundations, Ford Foundation and others. These foundations support programmes in Poland and (amongst others) for Poles in the US. Finally, many American universities, consulting firms and non-profit organizations have developed their own initiatives. For instance, Junior Achievement has organized training for Polish school teachers. MUCIA (Midwest University Consortium for International Activity) and Alliance Universities for Democracy likewise have organized educative programmes in Poland. Canadian aid has had the same decentralized character as US aid. A consortium of thirty Canadian business schools is cooperating with the Warsaw Economic University.

Multilateral programmes have mainly been implemented by the EU, for instance within the framework of PHARE (Poland Hungary Assistance Restructuring of their Economies). TEMPUS, within PHARE, is mainly earmarked for academic education and allocated through the so-called Joint European Projects (JEPs). The main requirement is that at least two universities from the EU and at least one from Poland participate in a project (often other institutions, e.g. foundations or associations, also take part). Between 1989 and 1992 the programme included initiatives in several post-Communist countries at once (regional JEPs). At present the national governments have more influence in determining priorities, and programmes are more specifically targeted to national needs. Within TEMPUS one finds student exchanges and teaching traineeships (Mobility Grants).[1] The development of short-cycle programmes acting as a bridge between formal education and employment is strongly needed. The TEMPUS II Programme should further assist the universities in creating the programmes we need.

Via PHARE, specialized programmes have been developed targeted to skills development in the tax system, banks and the insurance sector. The focus has been on accounting and auditing regulations. The main task has been the education of highly qualified cadres for the banking sector, the provision of necessary consulting services and the popularization of financial reform. PHARE assistance also went to the introduction of the new tax system (Value Added Tax and Personal Income Tax) and to the restructuring of the banks.[2] Other sectors coming in for special attention have included businesses making export contacts, tourism, agriculture (land registration and ownership) and vocational training. PHARE initiatives have also combined training with the restructuring of the economy on a regional scale.

EVALUATING FOREIGN ASSISTANCE

Foreign assistance is important for encountering unexplored forms and methods of training, establishing stimulating contacts, gaining more insight into market economies, upgrading our socio-economic study of the business environment and transferring specialist knowledge, all of which help us in the task of restructuring management education in Poland. Existing institutions need to be strengthened and/or new institutions opened. Too often foreign assistance is not sufficiently directed at strengthening Polish institutions, but rather is focused on 'showing off' foreign expertise. Business education in Poland needs to be adapted to the requirements of the contemporary market economy. Assistance will achieve the much-coveted 'multiplier effect' when its trainees can provide the knowledge and services now having to be drawn in from western specialists. Unfortunately, the assistance now received only partly accomplishes this goal. With the prominent exception of TEMPUS, most assistance does not have the goal of strengthening Polish training *institutions*. At a minimum, assistance needs to be medium term to support institutional change. Curriculum change demands repeated visits and in-depth contact. Too few foreign partners have been able to invest enough in their Polish counterparts to be really able to play the role of change agents. Various institutions are receiving the needed continual structural support, i.e. the School of Banking in Katowice (USA), the University of Warsaw MBA (University of Illinois at Urbana-Champaign), the business programme at the Warsaw

Polytechnic (Norway), the business training centres in Gdańsk, Lublin, Łódź and Poznań (Know-How Fund), the TEMPUS programmes for different universities, the Post-Diploma School of Business at Nawojowa near Nowy Sacz (Sweden and USA). But these happy exceptions do not achieve a strong enough multiplier effect because there is too little networking between the institutions.

The content of programmes and courses provided via foreign assistance only partially meets their audiences' needs and expectations. The Polish trainees and participants complain that the knowledge transferred and skills taught are either too trivial or too sophisticated. Moreover, the lecturers and trainers too often provide knowledge and skills without paying attention to their applicability to Polish conditions. But too much attention to the immediate needs of the Polish economy will prompt short-term 'quick fix' solutions which form an inappropriate basis for future management education. Thus, anyone undertaking to provide foreign assistance is buffeted by the opposing winds of economic immediacy and academic rigour. Since there is no Polish consensus about what constitutes quality management education, any and all programmes are open to criticism. Because the various donors often function under comparable time pressures, with similar political obligations, and are subject to comparable bureaucratic procedures, they all find it difficult to match provision to needs. The donors function almost simultaneously, without much possibility to pay attention to what the other donors are doing. Furthermore, Polish beneficiaries are understandably happy to cooperate with whichever donor is willing to provide funds. The Poles often find it difficult to specify their needs, and at the same time donor organizations make general offers instead of developing concrete proposals. Polish partners need to display more initiative in specifying their needs. At present funding is much too piecemeal and a strategic overall plan for Polish business education and training is totally lacking. In addition, donors often have an eye on the needs of their home markets. Sometimes donor countries wish to use foreign assistance to support their own weaker universities or region(s) threatened with unemployment. As a result the appropriateness of the technical assistance or expertise offered is doubtful.

Some countries, for instance, only provide technical and/or expert assistance. Thus programmes realized with their cooperation are not self-sufficient. All overheads, then, have to be paid from Polish domestic funding. The common de facto demand of foreign assistance for Polish co-financing is rapidly becoming a major problem. Even the minimal funding of the past is, due to the budget deficit, no longer available. The budget pinch severely restricts the effectiveness of assistance. The Polish partners cannot pay for appropriate selection procedures for candidates applying for training abroad; travel expenses to meet and coordinate foreign-funded activities; translators' fees for lectures given by foreign professors; equipment needed by visiting teachers; visitors' accommodation; or the cost of publishing training materials produced by foreign-assisted programmes. Furthermore, foreign assistance tends to be highly bureaucratized, producing administrative costs for the recipients which under present conditions are much too high. Preparing the grant application, making preliminary visits and completing the negotiation process sometimes take more time than the training programmes themselves.

Too frequently insufficient allowances are made for the characteristics peculiar to post-Communist countries, which are inappropriately lumped together with the developing countries. Too many foreign partners do not realize that Polish contacts with western universities began to develop strongly in 1968; or that the Polish Communist system of the 1970s and 1980s was really quite liberal towards intellectuals. Hence Polish academics are confronted too often with comic situations where highly paid western lecturers deliver inappropriately introductory lectures in economics or management. What we need are specialized courses, with curricula clearly announced in advance and required preparatory reading made available to those registered. Better selection procedures are needed to ensure that those who can best profit from what is on offer actually get the chance to attend.

I believe that too much funding has not gone for the optimum goals. Unfortunately distance education has been disregarded. The Polish Ministry of National Education wants to encourage open and distance learning in business subjects, but effective assistance has not developed. Traineeships in banks, companies, etc. should play a major role in foreign assistance. Such experiential learning is absolutely necessary, and can only be provided by foreign sources. Pre-traineeship preparation is necessary to make sure that Polish participants benefit from their experience abroad.

The allocation of foreign assistance within Poland also gives some grounds for concern. Too much emphasis has been placed on training central government employees. The training of potential entrepreneurs should gain higher priority. Furthermore too much foreign assistance goes to Warsaw, Kraków, Gdańsk and Poznań. The institutions not located in the six biggest cities are deprived of help. We need to decentralize foreign assistance to avoid situations in which the same people are sent abroad several times while people in the regions most in need of support are completely neglected. Managers in smaller towns and the countryside, as well as middle management, feel that they are being totally forgotten in the provision of business education.

To be honest, I believe that foreign assistance has so far been more effective outside university than within. Unfortunately, university curricula have not been reformed to a sufficient extent. I note an inability, or even unwillingness, on the part of faculty to teach new content and a braking effect on change to rigid university structures. Furthermore, the universities are in a very difficult budgetary situation. The outflow of the most gifted young faculty to better-paid jobs hasn't helped. The effect of foreign assistance to the newly emerging (private) schools of business has been more significant than of that to the universities.

In my opinion, the experience of the most advanced economies with business and management education has not been utilized enough in programming the assistance provided. It would be very valuable to make use of a comparison between the US and European traditions in business education and training to identify possible scenarios and potential strategies. We can learn from the significant differences found between France, Germany and Great Britain. Could we not benefit from the Scandinavian experience of educating adults by *folkhog-skolor* (people's colleges) run by the local authorities? What can we learn from the Japanese experience, which places such a great emphasis on the role of the enterprise in managerial education and training? We do not need to reinvent the wheel; more knowledge of alternative systems elsewhere would be very valuable.

NOTES

1 Of the greatest importance are Management and Business Economics. In the year 1990–1991 16 projects in these fields were approved for Poland, which were next extended, and as many as 35 were approved in the year 1991/2. JEPs were allocated, among others, to general universities (19), technical universities (9) and economic universities (16) in the following cities: Białystok (3), Katowice (3), Kraków (6), Łódź (9), Poznań (3), Szczecin (2), Toruń (3), Warsaw (10), and Wroclaw (5). The allocations for TEMPUS training programmes amounted to 12.35 million ECU in 1990, 13.5 million ECU in 1991, and 26 million ECU in 1992. The allocations for the remaining training programmes of PHARE in the years 1990–2 reached *c.* 13 million ECU. At the end of 1992 the entire number of JEPs with participation of Polish institutions was 245. In 1992 142 Polish institutions in a total of 30 towns had been involved in JEPs .

2 Owing to this programme such training institutions as the following were established: Warsaw Banking School, the Insurance Training Centre (in cooperation with the École Nationale d'Assurances in France and the Chartered Insurance Institute in Great Britain), and the School of Tax Administration and Fiscal Control (in cooperation with the École Nationale des Impôts in France).

FURTHER READING

Beksiak, J., Chmielecka, E. and Grzelońska, U. (1992) Kierunki zmian w wyższym szkolnictwie ekonomicznym, Warszawa: Szkota Gtówna Handlowa. (*Directions of Changes in Higher Economic Education*, Warsaw: Central School of Commerce).

Dietl, J. (1992a) *Higher Education in the Period of Transformations in the Socio-Economic System*, International Conference 'The Strategy in Human Resources, Development and the Coordination of External Assistance', Miedzeszyn, Poland, 7–9 December, conference book, pp. 89–96.

Dietl, J. (1992b) *Report on Education and Training in Poland during the Transformation of the Socio-Economic System*, Conference on Education and Economy in Central and Eastern Europe, 29 June–1 July, Paris: OECD.

Dietl, J. (1992c) Business Administration w polskich uczelniach; Konferencja pt. Studia Akademickie przedsiębiorczość i zarządzanie. (*Business Administration in Polish Universities*, Conference on Academic Curricula Business Administration), 15–16 October, Łódź: Educational Enterprise Foundation.

Józerowicz, S. (1992) *Distance Learning in Adult Education*, International Conference 'The Strategy in Human Resources, Development and the Coordination of External Assistance', Miedzeszyn, Poland, 7–9 December, conference book, p. 55.

Kozek, T. (1992) Efektywność pomocy zagranicznej odnoszącej się do kształcenia akademickiego dla potrzeb bznesú, Konferencja pt. Studia Akademickie przedsiebiorczość i zarządzanie (*Effectiveness of Foreign Assistance to Academic Education for Business Needs*, Conference on Academic Curricula Business Administration) 15–16 October, Łódź: Educational Enterprise Foundation.

Kozminski, A. and Kwiatkowski, S. (1992) Konflikt pomiędzy teorią a praktyką zarządzania w perspektywie historyczneji Konferencja pt. Studia Akademickie przedsię biorczość i zarządzanie (*Conflict between Management Theory and Practice in Historical Perspective*, Conference on Academic Curricula Business Administration) 15–16 October 1992, Łódź: Educational Enterprise Foundation.

Maj, W. (1992) *Training Needs in Banking and Finance*, International Conference 'The Strategy in Human Resources, Development and the Coordination of External Assistance', Miedzeszyn, Poland, 7–9 December, conference book, pp. 12–35.

O'Sullivan, O. (1992) *Contribution of TEMPUS to Higher Education Reform*, International Conference 'The Strategy in Human Resources, Development and the Coordination of External Assistance', Miedzeszyn, Poland, 7–9 December, conference book, pp. 105–12.

Pladys, K. (1992) *Multilateral Co-operation in Vocational Education*, International Conference 'The Strategy in Human Resources, Development and the Coordination of External Assistance', Miedzeszyn, Poland, 7–9 December, conference book, pp. 47–52.

Samecki, P. (1992) *An Overview of G–24 Assistance Programmes in the Field of Education and Training*, International Conference 'The Strategy in Human Resources, Development and the Coordination of External Assistance', Miedzeszyn, Poland, 7–9 December, conference book, p. 92.

Chapter 7

System and actors: management development in Poland

Marianna Strzyżewska Kaminska and Bogdan Wawrzyniak

INTRODUCTION

The systematic transformation of Poland into a contemporary consumer society is very complicated and must be expected to last many years. No one knows exactly what a post-Communist society ought to look like or how the transition from a plan to a market economy ought to be organized. All too quickly one is confronted with the Catch 22 of the Polish situation; any top-down effort to change the 'system' only reproduces exactly the same dirigisme and inefficiencies which we are trying so hard to escape. We certainly need managers to 'reconstruct' Polish enterprises, but 'rationality' demands that these managers (i) must understand the nature of the desired change, (ii) will have to have the knowledge and skills to carry out the change programme, and (iii) ought to be highly motivated. The question is whether the demands of 'rationality' can be met in practice. But even without the 'counsel of perfection', we can commit ourselves to working for the betterment of human resources.

It is estimated that 4 million people have been involved in managing the transformation of Poland to a market economy. This encompasses, of course, a very diverse group: from politicians and members of government to civil servants, from regional and local administrators to managers in state as well as private enterprises. In addition, numerous members of the professional classes have taken part. Many enterprises have been privatized. The private sector has grown rapidly. There are now many more domestic companies than in the past. The amount of individual proprietorship has increased. Joint ventures have boomed. But the managers of all this activity, in private as well as state enterprises, have for the most part had very little practice at their new profession. New firms are very often managed by people who are just starting their business career. After 1989 the majority of directors in state enterprises were replaced for political reasons. It is evident that there's a huge task to be performed to develop the strategic human resources needed to run new/restructured enterprises. Only by meeting this challenge can we become a society which balances successfully its political aims and the development of its people.

Contemporary definitions of strategic resources prioritize information, knowledge and creativity above capital. Increasingly it is asserted than in a contemporary society human capital is more important than financial capital because the former determines the effective use of the latter (Naisbitt and Aburdance 1985). In the case of as sizeable a change as the transformation of the Polish economy and society with such an enormous number of stakeholders involved, the problems of human capital and especially those of finding people to manage the change is crucial. Well-prepared professionals are needed to staff the enterprises. In the very first place, managers are needed who can lead and accelerate change in the economic system. But the role of managers as opinion-makers also will be very important; managers must bring hands-on economic insight to the politicians if reform of the political institutions is to further the change process. We believe that the success of the transformation process is dependent on how far the managers, i.e. strategic human resources, will meet the challenges of the change situation. Three issues arise:

- What attitudes and skills do Polish managers need to have that are required to make a market economy successful? Are the managers motivated to develop these attitudes and to master these skills?
- What system now exists in Poland to meet the aforementioned needs?
- What conclusions can be drawn by confronting the training and development structure with these needs?

In this chapter we explore these issues, focusing on the managers from state and private enterprises.

THE ACTORS: THE TRAINING NEEDS OF POLISH MANAGERS

Very intensive training of Polish managers is needed:

- to upgrade their level of general and specialist knowledge of the functioning of a market economy in a (very) dynamic business environment
- to form the attitudes which are basic to creative management, with an emphasis on the ability to find opportunities and to minimize (competitive) threats
- to develop their skills in mobilizing available human resources, with an emphasis on group work and organizing effective teams
- to develop the skills of creating win–win relationships in an information society.

But do Polish managers acknowledge any such needs? Are they committed to self-development and, if so, how? Research carried out by the Polish Foundation of Management in cooperation with the Agency for Industrial Development provided rather disappointing results (Ludwiczynski 1992). In the first portion of the project, eleven specialists on management development were polled for their opinions; in the second, questionnaires were administered to top managers (114 CEOs, company directors and members of company boards). Research was undertaken in enterprises already involved in the restructuring process. These were fairly big enterprises which had contacts with foreign consulting firms, and they were aware of the need not only to restructure assets and commercial activities but also human resource policies. Research amongst small enterprises, often located in little towns or villages and in poorer regions, might have produced different results.

The experts thought that top managers would have very little motivation to be trained and/or towards self-development. They argued that the business environment does not motivate managers to learn and even discourages them from doing so. It was claimed that constant changes in government policy were a major negative factor. Frequent alteration in the economic line meant that, as a manager, you never really knew what the rules of the economic game were. Furthermore, managers were convinced that there is no reliable national industrial policy. Managers felt that they lacked reliable information about the government's economic plans, the process of restructuring, sectoral policy and regional development plans. The experts predicted that managers would find it difficult or even impossible to think in strategic terms about their enterprise's growth and their own future roles. How could you develop yourself if you never knew in what direction you might go next? The strong political influence on enterprises and their staffs – and especially the interface between politicians and top management created feelings of constant personal threat. The experts thought that managers would claim that knowledge and skills were less important for them than political astuteness. Management's highest priority would be maintaining good relations with the politically powerful and avoiding conflict.

The experts also thought that the lack of government subvention of management development would discourage human resource development. The passive attitude of the state matches that of enterprises, which give training a very low priority. Restructuring had brought downscaling and a profit focus; the influence of human resource departments had weakened. In general, personnel management with planning, selection, motivation and development of personnel did not exist. Thus, conditions were thought not to be supportive of top managers' defining or pursuing their own developmental needs.

The top managers answered via questionnaires that as many as 30% of them had not taken part in any training whatsoever in the previous twelve months. The sample group was all male and all those in it had university degrees; 66% were between 36 and 55 years old. Two-thirds (67%) had been directors no longer than three years, 59% no longer than two. While more than half of them had gained their position as a result of the post-1989 transformation and were relatively inexperienced as senior managers, they were not highly motivated to follow any form of management education. Those who had participated in some sort of management education had done so only once and then for a maximum of five days. The research showed that the respondents were reluctant to pay for training. Most were willing to pay from $100 to $300 for a five-day course. Only three people from the sample group were ready to pay $500. A significant minority of 17.5% of the investigated enterprises did not invest anything at all in senior management development; in 46% of the enterprises, the level of expense was lower than $2,000.

The research sample was drawn from top management in state enterprises. Lower-level management and management from private enterprises may be more training-minded. Our observations in training centres are that middle and low-level management are motivated to follow courses, and that only 2–3% of training participants come from top management. Thus, despite the dramatic managerial 'musical chairs' at the very senior level, the victors have not prioritized mastering market economy competencies via training or consulting. Furthermore, those subjects chosen for seminar attendance where more directed to current business 'hot items' than to depth-level learning. The actuality of 'enterprise liquidation' and 'privatization' made these into 'in' subjects. When asked to select the subjects they would most like to study, their answers were business diagnosis, marketing and business strategy. How much real commitment there was to studying any of these subjects in any real depth was not clear. When asked to identify skills they would most like to acquire, the managers indicated drafting a business plan, managing organizational restructuring, effective decision-making, negotiation. In comparison to western practice these are, of course, mostly rather basic managerial skills. Despite lagging so dramatically behind, there was no felt need to catch up quickly via crash management courses. An attitude of defensiveness or hostility to acknowledging what one does not know was more pronounced than an attitude of openness to new learning. Fully one half of the respondents said they wanted to learn to speak English fluently. In contrast, lower-level managers who do participate in training admit to lacking specialist knowledge and voice their desire to master western management techniques and to improve their analytical skills.

Not only is the demand less spectacular than one might hope, but also the supply tends to be pretty old-fashioned. The management development in which respondents had participated was dominated by traditional course and seminar forms (89% of all training attended). Only eight respondents had participated in postgraduate studies, two had followed a supervised internship in an enterprise and one had made use of consulting. The most popular form of management development was foreign study visits, followed by off-site consultant presentations and seminars. Conferences and part-time (work-related) courses were the least popular. The group's taste in teaching was very traditional: lectures came in first place! Practical problem-solving was valued. Independent study and studying management literature were unpopular. Those in top management positions were attracted to meeting other 'captains of industry' but did not want to participate in courses with managers from their own company. Small groups of no more than twenty-five were preferred. In general we note a very defensive attitude amongst the managers in the sample; they do not want to be confronted with what they do not know and they do not want to reveal their lack of knowledge in front of their colleagues. Safe, rather undemanding situations are preferred to challenging ones.

THE SYSTEM: HUMAN RESOURCE DEVELOPMENT (HRD) FOR MANAGERS[1]

From 1989 to 1992 the state system of management development was dismantled. This created favourable conditions for the rapid growth of alternative training organizations. As many as 450 to 600 training organizations are estimated to be operating now in Poland. Among them there are state universities, centres sponsored by government ministries, (private) business schools, private foundations, professional associations and consulting firms. Most of them are located in the big university towns and most operate autonomously. No institution collects information about them, accredits them or provides them with support. Researchers from Warsaw School of Economics (Kempisty 1992, 1993) and the Bureau for Coordinating Management Development (Wawrzyniak 1992a) have collected information from about seventy-eight such institutions. They looked at private and state universities which train students and organize postgraduate programmes for managers. The information collected gives us a picture of the current training situation, including the identity of the participants, the programmes on offer, the economic situation of the providers and the difficulties incurred by the HRD suppliers:

1   When the need to (re)train managers for the market economy emerged, university management schools quickly launched programmes for this target group. But the departments involved belong to the old university structure and have generally continued with traditional lecturing as their form of teaching.
2   Some universities set up new educational centres. They use university

buildings, make use of university facilities and hire in university teachers. Generally, cooperation with foreign organizations has helped these centres to modernize their teaching methods and programmes. In some cases, lecturers in these centres receive instruction abroad which permits them to catch up on western practice and creates good perspectives for the centre.

3   Some eight non-state business schools were set up before 1993. Students pay tuition for their education (at the state universities education is free). Mostly, these schools were set up in cooperation with foreign partners or on the basis of the foreign experience of their founders. These schools claim that their programmes meet American and/or Western European standards.

4   There are also many new schools which focus on management development. Sometimes they benefit from government or Chamber of Commerce support, but most of them are purely commercial enterprises.

5   Some foreign centres function as business schools. Independently or with Polish partners, they offer programmes originating in their countries (for example the French Institute of Management).

6   In addition to the organizations already described, various associations and foundations provide management education. Many Polish academic and professional associations have always seen knowledge dissemination as one of their tasks, but since 1989 they have become more active and have adjusted their programmes to actual needs. (Examples are the Association of Scientific Organization and Management, the Polish Economic Association, the Polish Marketing Association, the Polish Association of Accountants.)

7   Still to be mentioned are the consulting firms, which have been growing like mushrooms; many link consulting to training. Their number, significance and generated revenue are all increasing.

The universities and new business schools still have a dominant position in the management education market, but the universities have lost their monopoly. New market conditions mean that various contenders are competing especially for post-experience students. The new providers of management development are very often linked to foreign partners. The most numerous contacts are with German, French, British, Dutch and American partners; less numerous are Danish, Italian, Swedish, Norwegian or Canadian institutions. The para-university centres and professional associations have been able to staff their programmes with competent teachers; the new schools, which generally do not employ permanent lecturers, are having great difficulty finding good people. Most teaching is by university staff, though there are exceptions like the French Institute of Management, where 45% of teachers are consultants and 55% are managers.

Trainees come, first of all, from state enterprises, and then from the civil service and private firms. Medium and low-level managers predominate. Participants often want to change jobs, gain a promotion, upgrade their skills or enter into business for themselves. Competition on the training market is rife, while corporate willingness to finance employee training seems to be decreasing. There is a considerable variety of programmes on offer. Links to current business practice are common. Specialist as well as general management foci are to be found. While the traditional method of university teaching lecturing is still going strong, it has lost some ground. Methods such as computer simulation and case methodology, which demand active participation, are gaining ground. Unfortunately, courses on international business are still few and far between.

All in all, the biggest problem in provision is that the possibilities for lecturers to master state-of-the-art knowledge are too limited. Polish academics need to spend longer periods visiting Western management schools and studying Western business practices if they are to gain up-to-date insight into their field. Only then will textbooks, case materials and research both meet international theoretical standards and be truly adapted to local circumstances.

SYSTEMS AND NEEDS

Do Polish managers have the possibility to develop themselves profession-ally? – our answer is: 'Yes'. The educational system has reacted in a flexible way to the changes. The chief problems seem to be:

i)   stimulating top managers to professionalize their practice by participat-ing more in HRD;
ii) improving lecturer knowledge of management theory and mastery of relevant skills;
iii) up-dating and improving the relevance of management training programmes;
iv) redefining the role of the state in management development;
v)   gaining the cooperation of all players (especially business circles and educational organizations);
vi) maximizing the benefits of foreign help to management development.

Stimulating top managers to professionalize

Undoubtedly, transformation to a market economy creates the need for a better understanding of management techniques and practices. Further-more, managers are slowly becoming accountable for the results of their

Table 7.1 The relationship between self-development and external pressure

		External motivation	
		low	high
		A. HOBBY	D. UNDERSTANDING
Propensity to	high	I do not have to, but I want to	I have to, and I want to
self-development	low	I do not want to, and I do not have to	I do not want to, but I have to
		B. DISREGARD	C. PRESSURE

enterprises and will need managerial competencies to survive. But for the moment, the old skills of playing the 'clientist' game have prevailed above those of managerial professionalism in the struggle to survive. Privatization and the liberalization of foreign trade, foreign competition and the need to be profitable will produce especially strong needs for managers to adjust to new conditions. Stiff competition will force changes in the functioning of firms and of their managers. To meet the new situation new knowledge and skills will be necessary. But top managers are still saying, 'We know change must occur, but not just yet.' If we model the relationship between managers' propensity for self-development and the aggressiveness of external pressure we arrive at four different ways of operating as shown in Table 7.1.

At present the business environment acts on Polish managers mainly through economic factors – decreasing income, unemployment, increased competition between enterprises and open market conditions. Movement is from positions A and B to positions C and D. Managers may not easily be able to find the time or funding to engage in management development. But the business environment will increasingly demand increased professionalism. If the present generation of managers refuses to master market economy skills, a new generation of postgraduate-degree holders will emerge within a few years to threaten their position. The training needs of top managers in (ex-)state enterprises demands attention. The following steps are desperately needed:

● improvement of the financial situation and social status of managers in (ex-)state enterprises;
● diminishing of the political influence on state enterprises;
● (re)defining future perspectives for state enterprises and their top managers.

There is a real problem of management effectiveness throughout the Polish economy. Unprofessional and even unscrupulous management has often been the cause of bankruptcies.

Improving lecturer knowledge

The current educational market for management education and training resembles a 'bazaar' (Wawrzyniak 1992b). This is not an entirely negative description. In the bazaar one can find many of the goods needed to meet managers' wants during the process of economic transformation. From the bazaar serious educational institutions can and do emerge. The advantage of the bazaar is that apparent market anarchy permits a maximum of different educational products to emerge. The disadvantage is that what is on offer may be shoddy and a product of a 'fly-by-the-seat-of-your-pants' mentality. The lecturers may very well be only one chapter ahead of the participants. Faculty may not understand what they are lecturing about and have no practical experience at all of the content of the lecture. To improve the situation we need increased possibilities to carry on scientific research in Poland and increased possibilities for Polish faculty to learn abroad.

The first condition is presently limited by scarce funding for research and the near bankrupt position of Polish universities. In the long term, without rigorous research Poland will be forced to rely on foreign concepts, superficially adapted to Polish circumstances, without deep understanding of the concepts or a thoroughly researched knowledge of our own situation. Furthermore, Polish research needs stimulating to dare to tackle controversial hypotheses and to do innovative work. The second condition, if not fulfilled, dooms Polish academics to some sort of a provincial backwater. University careers will be attractive to the most gifted only if they can work at the forefront of intellectual activity. At present neither the Polish state nor foreign funding are meeting this need.

Updating and improving the relevance of programmes

Our analysis of the programmes offered by various educational providers has produced the following suggestions:

- Programmes at present focus far too much on fragmentary information, mainly connected with the immediate situation in Poland, or concepts which are suddenly fashionable in the west. Courses based on these agendas may be useful but are certainly not sufficient. Managers need a broad analytic interdisciplinary training covering all the functional areas, developing a so-called 'helicopter view' of organizing. Integrative themes such as crisis, change, and quality management should be stressed.
- Managers need to learn about different national and organizational cultures in order to facilitate communication and better performance in the global marketplace.
- The links between training and practice in Polish as well as foreign enterprises should be much tighter.
- Besides acquiring theoretical knowledge, participants should explore

attitudes and develop practical competencies. Attitudes allowing them to cope with a turbulent social and economic environment are desperately needed. Managers must be able to negotiate, to organize group work and to work as a team.

Redefining the role of the state

What should be the role of the state in management development; should it have (a) direct influence, (b) relinquish all responsibility, (c) create the necessary preconditions for a proactive HRD policy, (d) jointly manage HRD initiatives? Up until the 1980s the state had direct influence, deciding in effect what would happen and who could attend. We have shifted from one extreme to the other; the state has relinquished all responsibility for management development, leaving matters to market forces. The third option, whereby taxation, legislation and subsidies support HRD whilst the providers are essentially free, is the most attractive in our eyes. Most EU countries seem to have policies based on this approach. The last option has to be considered from the perspective of the current situation of human resource crisis, where investment in human resources, especially in managers, is crucial to the economic development of the nation. If one is convinced that the inadequate professionalism of management is defeating national goals and breaking economic growth, then one can choose, as government, to intervene actively.

It is to be hoped that, in the current transition phase, joint actions of state and business circles will, on the regional as well as national levels, be undertaken. It seems that in the highly developed, post-industrial countries this model is also gaining more and more acceptance as the crises of the information society deepen. In practice the state then enables and stimulates the coexistence of various training solutions. It does so in an effort to increase the effectiveness of the whole labour system and to generate synergy. The national goal is economic growth via 'smart production'; the hope is that a more creative management can generate high-value-added products and services which will stimulate the economy. The Polish state has virtually resigned from influencing management development and is relying solely on market forces. But, in our opinion, the period of transformation requires state activity in this field. Already foreign capital and (potential) aid cannot be put to maximum benefit because there are not enough managers able to 'pull the cart'. Foreign companies and governments, as well as international agencies, cannot find qualified partners to work with. Project negotiation, formulation, implementation and evaluation are possible only with qualified Polish input. If Polish management cannot fulfil these functions, interested parties can only go elsewhere. Also, we cannot evaluate the usefulness of potential (for instance foreign-proposed) projects to our own interests if we lack managerial project know-how. The status quo is not only breaking our economic development, it also extends the knowledge gap between ourselves and foreign practice.

Gaining the cooperation of all players

The links between Polish business circles and educational organizations are far too weak. Coordinated human resource planning is non-existent. Will we have the managers and skilled professionals in the future that we need? Of course we do not have them now, but that is no reason to keep things that way! We are stuck in a vicious circle; because we lack market-economy expertise we are doomed to improvise 'every-which-way'. We have kept the economy afloat, but it is not our intention to keep doing things this way indefinitely. No one has the time or the expertise right now to do the necessary planning for the future. We need to plan to meet the future needs of business in an environment where management cannot look beyond the immediate term. Thus, at present the best we can hope for is open communication and access to information in the anticipation that dialogue will lead to more clarity. The more the business community and management educators meet, the better the chance of cross fertilization.

Maximizing the benefits of foreign help

Since the second half of 1989, Poland has benefited from educational support offered by western countries. This support has come in two forms: programmes run in supporting countries attended by visiting Poles; or programmes run by western institutions in Poland. Certainly at the beginning, short term programmes dominated. Both parties – Poland and the foreign countries – were not prepared for the task and the results in most cases were not very satisfactory. Many programmes cost too much for the amount of training delivered. In some cases 90% of the funding went to covering the western institution's overheads and/or to paying the bills of their lecturers. Some Polish visitors to the West spent more time shopping or attending to private business than on the course they were supposed to be attending. More innocently, but just as frustrating, quite a few western courses assumed a more developed specialization of tasks/labour than exists in Poland, to such an extent that the course on offer was entirely inapplicable. In our opinion, four initiatives have proven the most positive and promise to have the best long term effects:

- Train the trainer initiatives have a strong multiplier effect – by professionalizing management development one (eventually) reaches a maximum number of managers. Not only university management teaching but also training and consulting need to be included in the focus. While the practical contents of much management practice can be studied in a fairly traditional manner (books, + lectures + assignments), the techniques of training/consulting (case methodology, use of group exercises, action learning) require an experiential introduction. While illustrative exploration of the techniques can best occur in Poland to achieve cost-effectiveness, foreign experience is needed to understand how the techniques fit into the human resource planning of western enterprises. One needs to understand training/consulting techniques in their context to see how advanced human resource systems really work. With this understanding we can adapt these systems insightfully to our Polish situation. The East European Management Teachers Development Programme (EEMTDP, financed by TEMPUS), organized by Lancaster University in cooperation with Copenhagen Business School, Erasmus University Rotterdam, Wirtschaftsuniversität Vienna and Adam Mickiewicz University Poznań, was just such a programme. The Synergy Programme, organized by the Polish Foundation for Management Promotion and Hanse Polytechnic Groningen (the Netherlands), is another one. Both integrated HRD, management teaching/training techniques, in-company analysis of western practice and current theoretical debate. The deliverables included company analyses (Synergy), new curriculum planning and new teaching materials (EEMTDP).

- Joint research on Polish management, the role of training and consulting in Poland and cross-cultural management/learning are a logical follow-up. Help in developing teaching materials (cases and simulations), learning to write textbooks and the introduction of multimedia (research by Internet, computer-assisted courseware) are still needed.
- Management training in Poland needs to be supported by experience abroad at managerial level. Much state-of-the-art management practice still has to be developed in Poland. Book mastery of principles is not enough; one has to see how management makes practical use of the ideas before one can adapt them to our circumstances. Furthermore, Polish managers need to develop a more international focus directed to long-term cooperation with western partners.
- We need to go beyond ad hoc initiatives, however effective they have been, and institutionalize cooperation in management development. A transnational clearing house for training techniques and materials is needed. Regular long-term contacts are needed to improve management education/training on an in-depth level. Recurring cycles of workshops, conferences and seminars are required. We no longer need short intensive courses, but rather long-term commitment to help facilitate and support the change process. Obviously, offices of western consulting firms have opened up and are offering western training; but they have their own profit-directed agendas. We need support from the west to bring our own (para-) university sector into line with international good practice. Establishing a journal focusing on management development in

Poland, jointly edited by Polish and foreign scholars, would be a helpful step in the right direction.

CONCLUSION

On the plus side, Polish management and management education have displayed enormous flexibility since 1989 to launch, in effect, an entirely new economy replacing the years of stagnation. Effective learning models and techniques of change-facilitation have been found and implemented. But three enormous problems remain: (i) the role of the state, (ii) the further professionalization of practice and (iii) the creation of a system of human resource development which matches Polish needs. The state must not abandon all responsibility for management education; to do so is to leave the identity of future Polish management to the whims of the marketplace. Obviously, training centres must attend to the 'bottom line'; short-term profit considerations have to be taken into account. But University management education has to maintain a long term perspective and develop the specialisms of the future as well as respond to immediate needs. Furthermore, preservation of our national integrity demands that the question be posed as to what is good for Poland, and not only what is profitable in the next 18 months.

Management education is too strongly linked to long-term social and political independence to be abandoned entirely to private initiative. But the state has to have a vision of the long-term national interest to fulfil its role in management education. Many fear that it has not always fulfilled this mission during the last years. The further professionalization of practice is a double-edged sword. It implies growth and learning, but, at the same time, the acknowledgement of what one does not know. Many in power refuse to do the latter and do whatever they can to deny their shortcomings. However pressing the need may be for professionalization, it is not easy to get those involved to acknowledge their learning needs and to take action to resolve them. Obviously fears of incompetence and of failing in future learning situations forms a real problem. Finally, Poland needs human resource development. Despite a good level of basic education the workforce has to adapt and change its skills in order to become competitive in the world marketplace. Human resources are the most important ones and we need to give them more opportunities to realize their potential. Training can offer a crucial bridge to becoming more effective in the workplace. We need to do all we can to let it do so.

NOTE

1 See Grzegorzewski, P. and Ornarowicz, U. *(1992) Informacje o osrodkach ksztalca-cych menedzerow,* (Information on centres for management training) Funds of Co-operation, Warsaw: unpublished.

REFERENCES

Kempisty, W. (1992) *Vademecum Szkoly Zarzadzania* (Biznesu), (Vademecum of Management Schools), Funds of Co-operation, Warsaw: unpublished.

Kempisty, W. (1993) *Niepanstwowe Wyzsze Szkoly Zarzadzania w Polsce,* (Private schools of management in Poland), Funds of Co-operation, Warsaw: unpublished.

Ludwiczynski, A. (1992) *Doksztalcanie i doslonalenie kadr kierowniczych w Polsce* (Raport z Badan), (Development of managers in Poland; Research Report), Warsaw: unpublished.

Naisbitt, J. and Aburdance, P. (1985) *Reinventing the Corporation: Transforming Your Job and Your Company For the New Information Society,* New York: Werner Books.

Wawrzyniak, W. (1992a) *Kierunki rozwiazywania problemow zwiazanych z przygotowaniem polskich kierownikow dia przyszlosci,* (Directions of solving the problems connected with adjustment of managers to the future) Warsaw: TNOiK.

Wawrzyniak, B. (1992b) 'The government role in the production of new managers', *Scandinavian Journal of Management* 8(3), special issue, guest ed. B. Wawrzyniak, Oxford: Pergamon Press.

Chapter 8

Competency and the 'new' manager in Central Europe

Monica Lee

INTRODUCTION

The views I express here are based upon research conducted whilst working with Central European teachers of management in higher education in a variety of roles and upon several different initiatives, but particularly as Coordinator of the Central European Management Teacher Development Programme (CEMTDP).[1] In essence this programme adhered to Prokopenko's assertion that 'A fundamental improvement in the quality of management is the key to a successful transition to a market economy and to dynamic technological and social change' (Prokopenko 1992: 2). The work I coordinated was designed by change agents to facilitate action steps and develop other change agents in the area of management teaching by offering the opportunity for collaborative learning and exploration whilst attempting to avoid some of the pitfalls of educational imperialism. In doing so the programme implicitly addressed issues of change (i) at the strategically related national and institutional level, (ii) at the structurally related institutional and departmental levels, (iii) at the design-related departmental and course levels and (iv) at the methodological and value-related course and individual levels.

Much debate, therefore, revolved around individual perceptions of the nature and roles of management and the manager in the current situation, potential ways of influencing these, and alternative views of an appropriate future. The intention of this chapter is to present my views, in so far as they address the implications of working as 'change agents' in transitional economies in which the understanding of 'competency' as adopted by such change agents is central to the product of change. In doing so, I am also presenting an unashamedly 'bounded' (see March and Simon 1958) viewpoint. I am suggesting that in 'creating' the future we need to step out of cultural relativism and proclaim, and actively work towards, the sort of future we want.

One of the driving forces behind the creation of CEMTDP was the belief that within a market economy the collective world-view of the managerial classes (and thus the forms of activity they are engaged in) has a profound effect upon the future of a nation. An additional belief was that the world-view of managers is likely to be strongly influenced by the form of management education that they receive. In other words, the form of management educational provision that is available to existing and nascent managers will influence the future of the nation. I explore these beliefs further in Chapter 17 on holistic learning in this volume.

I focus in this chapter on 'managerial competence' or 'what should a Central European manager be able to do?'; however, this cannot be adequately explored without addressing whose needs such 'doing' will be meeting and the implications of such 'doing' (for the manager, organizations, management education and the future of the nation). In order to contextualize the debate, I shall first paint a broad-brush picture of the effects of change in Central Europe (as if it were possible to talk of Central Europe as a unitary phenomenon). I suggest that Central Europe has looked to the west for its understanding of management and the managerial role; but the west itself is unclear in its 'understanding'. Attempts to define generic levels of management 'competency' have more challenged recipients, providers and structures alike than provided consensus. I then move on to explore the difference between opportunistic development and sustained development. I suggest that whilst there appears to be little difference between them in the implications they hold for managerial competency as defined by the 'doing', the difference between them is evident at the level of 'being'. I close by arguing that, globally, all nations are being challenged by the rhetoric of sustainable development, and that Central Europe, alongside the west, needs to be clear about which managerial attributes it wishes to foster, and thus which type of future it is working towards.

PERCEPTIONS OF MANAGEMENT IN CENTRAL EUROPE

Prior to the velvet revolution, Central Europe could be described as a centrally planned product-oriented command system, with economies heavily skewed towards smoke-stack industries. The focus on supply led to vertically integrated structures, with a large gap between supply and demand. Consumers had little market power, and this led to the production of low-quality products (Dubini and Cardini 1991). The reliance upon central planning led management of the state-owned companies to focus largely on 'scientific' management (work studies, time and motion, etc.) with 'development' linked to the reorganization of work, the redesigning of plant layouts, etc. There was no need, within the administered socialist economy, for strategic management skills such as marketing, financial management and personnel policy (Otta and Gorynia 1991). The Ministry of National Education defined educational requirements in central curricula, which tended to be normative and based upon theoretical model-oriented speculation. Management was not a discipline (these being natural science, engineering, medicine, law and social sciences), and teaching methods were traditional, i.e. lectures, seminars and classes based largely upon textbooks.

Under this system managers appear to have developed a limited entrepreneurial attitude, become strongly averse to risk, and to have valued knowledge more highly than skills (Jankowicz and Pettitt 1993), with a consequent valuing of expertise and the 'right' solution. There is evidence that this might be changing. Stachowicz (1991) found that in 1988 the orientation of organizational values within 789 large Polish enterprises was skewed towards 'power', with a diminishing focus upon 'roles', 'tasks' and 'people' (in that order). Repetition of the research in 1990 showed a strong shift towards a 'task' orientation. He cautions, however, that authoritarian cognitive orientations might well prove a strong barrier to change. Previously, successful innovation had low value to the individual the system benefited, whilst failure was focused on the individual. Trust and confidentiality were hard won and easy to lose, and self-motivation was an elusive concept. Beset by other difficulties, the government has now cut education and health care budgets dramatically, with much of the demand for management education being limited and specific (focusing on short courses with elements of problem-solving and crisis management). Central European governments can be accused of being unable to appreciate the long-term intangible effects of investment in education (Obloj 1991).

Initially, to 'Western' management educators Central European management education appears outdated and poorly developed; with some writers, such as Obloj, presenting a particularly gloomy picture. Others, such as McNulty (1992), argue that there exists an excellent management infrastructure, with managers at all levels holding university degrees and undergoing regular re-qualification. Assessment and education for promotion are well established. Senior posts are filled after open selection. Previously such appointments were also vetted by the Party. Now, the need for 'political' approval seems to be no greater than in the west. Equally, all management educators are highly qualified in aspects of management (or that which would be termed 'management' in the west) and are required to have had 'practical' experience – thus presenting some similarity with Japanese management education, which is seen as a formal adjunct to the processes that are already well rooted in organizations and in general education (Storey 1991). Although experience under the old system did little to prepare management educators for working with the market economy, the mandatory experiential element in the previous training of Central European management educators contrasts positively with the lack of practical experience in the training of many western management educators.

The process of re-educating Polish management teachers might, therefore, in part be about the provision of 'know-how': the acquisition of strategic, financial and marketing knowledge in particular. But, increasingly, writers are focusing upon the need for 'attitude change': the development of teachers/students and managers/workers who have the values appropriate for working in a capitalist system. The values thought to be missing, such as the shouldering of responsibility, self-motivation, initiative, resourcefulness, creativity and endurance, were present under the previous system amongst the reformers, cooperatives and small enterprises, many of which succeeded in 'illegal' entrepreneurial work. Lee (1995a) suggests that these values are evidenced once trust is gained, but are not apparent when the outsider is perceived to represent the 'system'. Thus, the command economy has left a heritage of particular sensitivity to authority, power, knowledge and the value of the 'expert'. Challenging this within the management educational process is both vital and very difficult.

This assertion is supported by evidence arising from CEMTDP, quoted here at length because of the relevance to the discussion. In the words of a participant on completing the programme:

Until recently I only had theoretical knowledge of successful motivation acquired from foreign literature. My students are in a similar position. They have very little practical experience and when they start to work in a business they meet people brought up in the socialist concept of motivation.

Nowadays people no longer believe that a manager can sit in seclusion and expect all members of his collective to carry out joyfully their allotted tasks for the benefit of society. We have been persuaded that activity, initiative and enthusiasm cannot be attained by force, nevertheless stereotyped phrases repeated for years have been deeply rooted in our people. . . . For years we were told that there was only one reality – the one proclaimed officially. We ceased to look at the world with our own eyes and thought that people with a different view of things were wrong, or even wanted to do us harm. Now we are surprised that one and the same thing can be seen by everybody in his own way and that a lot of so called indisputable facts were only presented as such. A precondition for understanding the needs and aspirations of other people is to realize that there also exist other realities which are to be taken into consideration. One should find out what the reality is for other people and be ready to accept that is a valid point of view – to accept diversity as a normal phenomenon. . . .

The existence of a discrepancy between the two groups (those who manage and those who are managed) was minimized or even denied for years. All of us had to work for the attainment of equal aims, the aims that were assigned for us. However, it was wrong to suppose that each employee would work to obtain the same objectives. We should not be surprised that some interests get into conflict with others. From economic and political points of view these discrepancies are a sign that the system is functioning. We have to get rid of the idea that only cooperation is normal and correct whereas conflicts and opposition are a pathological, incorrect phenomena. . . .

The most serious motivation problem is evidently unreadiness for self-motivation. We are used to waiting for somebody to come and bid us to work. If we intend to motivate other people, we have to establish our own positive attitudes, since today it is very important to do away with the barrier of negotiation based on anxiety, fear, and suspicion. Our overall life attitudes have been affected in a negative way under the former conditions and brought about resignation. Positive thinking means first of all putting emphasis on all positive aspects, and belief that success can be achieved and is desirable.

In CEMTDP it was evident that westerners were often seen as embodying a free-market philosophy. They were seen to be prosperous, entrepreneurial, free to speak and act, unhindered by bureaucratic or authoritarian structures, able to take risks and make mistakes, and to find employment enjoyable rather than working to live (Lee 1992). Westerners are often thought to be, and perceive themselves to be, further 'along the line' in some way, embodying a desirable culture in which personal worth, job satisfaction, quality of living and competitive advantage are causally related to the free market. Management education is perceived to contribute to all this by generating a well-qualified workforce that is frequently engaged in an educational process that is stimulating, uses a wide range of methods and technologies, is essentially creative and relevant, and which also contains a discrete and accepted body of knowledge. That knowledge supposedly creates competent managers within the capitalist system, is transferable and provides the 'right' way of doing things. These perceptions are unfortunate for several reasons.

PROBLEMS WITH PERCEPTIONS

First, Perica (1993) shows that, if anything, western management education is being forced to move away from flexible needs-related provision. She found that whilst there is an increasing demand (from organizations and individuals) for such provision (human resource skills, strategy, systems, short modular/in-company courses, and retraining) at the expense of generic knowledge-based qualifications, a reduction in education budgets and an increase in student numbers is leading to a focus upon the formal transfer of knowledge. Traditional didactic methodology seems to be expanding at the expense of other forms of learning. Second, there is little agreement in the west about what 'management' and the nature of managerial work really are (Darmer 1991). This lack of agreement is reflected by the furious and at times vitriolic debates about the identification, development and assessment of 'competency'. Finally, Nikolajew (1992) suggests that the development of transitional economies presents unique issues that can not be addressed appropriately within traditional paradigms. At the same time, post-Communism offers the opportunity for such economies to move to a new stage of development namely one of higher social awareness and ecological sustainability. If so, however, it follows that the west is not in a position to offer advice in so far as it is tied to traditional paradigms, and would thus be better seen as a co-learner/ developer. In the following sections I shall address the second and third points in turn. Before that, however, I shall take a few paragraphs to explore briefly the 'competency' debate.

Standardization and competency

Working towards competency is a politically sensitive notion in the west, where attempts have been made to assess competent behaviour, as measured against national standards developed by an understanding of the existing managerial role (Stead and Lee 1996). This process leads to a strong focus on the accreditation of prior achievement and hence the recognition of experience, work-based learning and flexible forms of assessment. Theoretically, the manager becomes a stakeholder in his or her own education and development, alongside both the organization and the provider. The problems come with the political and practical implications of the theory.

The focus on measurable outcomes (i.e. the assessment of being able to 'do') forces standardization and this can be seen as a 'good' thing. The construction of uni-focused multidisciplinary provision, such as centrally supported competency-based training with measurable outcomes, might appear to be the best way to meet the widely differing needs of the stakeholders (Binsted 1988; Constable and McCormick 1987; Handy et al. 1987: 12; Powers 1983). In practice (as evidenced by Smithers 1993), it is hard to reconcile the underlying value systems of the different stakeholders. The elements that appear most threatening to providers of higher education are those linked to access (the extent to which skills-based experience is seen as both necessary and sufficient for access), assessment (raising issues of how to accredit prior experience for entrance and how to assess development on experientially based provision) and provision (in which potential providers are assessed for their suitability and accredited as providers under a system that is separate and potentially inimical to that of higher education). An optimistic view would encourage the belief that with flexibility and communication these problems are surmountable; however, there are other issues that are even less easily resolved.

Deep concern is focused on the drive for standardization, which is seen as reducing diversity at a time when flexible structures are required to meet changing needs and shifts of national policy (Porter and McKibbin 1988). The nature of the assessment processes which seem to threaten the ideal of holism and do not reflect the variable nature of the managerial role (Burgoyne 1989, 1990) also gives concern. The cultural and political ramifications of choosing the membership of a 'standardizing body' (Nespor 1988) are also critical.

It is possible to sidestep the need for national standardization, and thus the seductive force of centralization, whilst sticking to the principle of a 'competency' point of view. Theoretically, the development of a multi-focused programme might defend individuality by working across different management and educational paradigms. However, Morgan (1993) noted that cooperation between proponents of different approaches was rare, and the supremacy of one view over another is more a product of internal politics between academic departments than of disinterested debate. However, evidence from the UK (Swan et al. 1993) and from Western and Central European nations (Lee 1996; Ryder and Easterby-Smith 1992) indicates that programmes designed to bring together those who would normally have little contact with each other (crossing disciplines and institutional barriers) are successful in helping participants acknowledge, understand and build upon diversity. The participants learn to locate their own approach and adopt what they see as 'good practice' drawn from other approaches.

Such programmes provide 'breathing space' for debate, but in doing so they challenge us to become interdisciplinary (Mudroch 1992). Implicitly, they question whether the business school environment is the most appropriate setting for managers to learn in, and challenge the assumed expertise of the management teacher. They are complex and politically sensitive. They form a bridge between the stakeholders and thus need to be established within the macro-structure, but in so far as they question and challenge they cannot easily be institutionalized.

The nature of the managerial role

The centralized/standardized/predictable vs. decentralized/free-market/chaotic debate is also evident in discussions about the nature of the managerial role in the west. At a time when western nations are moving towards the standardization of educational provision, and thus towards an internationally acceptable generic cross-sector understanding of levels of managerial 'competence', the literature is increasingly focusing upon difficulties associated with specifying the nature of the managerial role.

Freedman (1992) suggests that managerial problems are irredeemably complex and unpredictable, and that economic advantage will come to those who are best able to spot opportunities, to learn rapidly and to create appropriate commitment amongst colleagues. This notion of complexity, tied to that of the interdependent nature of organizations situated in a universe that is itself a massively integrated self-organizing system (Jantsch 1980), is a fundamental part of the holistic systematic co-evolutionary view propounded in recent publications (Davis 1990; Lessem 1990, 1991; Lievegood 1991; Norgaard 1988; Senge 1990). These ideas are being developed in new areas of research such as soft-system methodology (Checkland 1981). They entail a shifting view of organizations (Clegg 1990) and the nature of management (Dobson *et al.* 1992; Dumain 1990) and have implications for the managerial role. For example, Handy (1985: 335) states that 'organization theory would suggest that more trust and less control, more diversity and less uniformity, more differentiation and less systematization might be the ways that organizations should move'.

A suite of research projects conducted in the UK[2] show that organizations are becoming 'aware of the importance of developing their most important asset people'. Organizations are spending more on management training and development, and there is an increasing focus upon management development as lifelong learning (as opposed to periodic training). The research found that in order to survive in the changing world, managers of the future will need key skills, but the most important 'competencies' will be attitudinal. Managers will need organizational sensitivity as well as an holistic sense of the external environment; task skills (such as problem analysis, prioritizing and bench-marking) as well as process skills (such as empathy, facilitation, influencing, coaching and counselling skills). Managers will need to be able to act and think on their feet, as well as to be able to reflect and think strategically and in the long term, and to be able to take on responsibility for their own development whilst collaborating in teams and with people from a wide range of disciplines in temporary and non-hierarchical teams.

The competent manager (in these terms) is one who can create a business environment in which people can flourish spiritually and emotionally. Such managers nourish creative tension by maintaining a balance between a focus on human resources and personal wellbeing on the one hand and clear, hard, management practices on the other (Pascale 1990). Thus, management needs to involve the 'knowledge and acceptance of a wider repertoire of ways of being' (Kinsman 1990), one in which individuals are continually reanalysing their role in the creation and development of the processes they are part of. In doing so, managers confront their own ideas, unsurfaced assumptions, biases and fears (Argyris 1990), thereby addressing the development of themselves and others from an ethical standpoint. The competent manager, in these terms, must BE as well as DO. This repertoire of 'being' includes awareness of the impact of cross-cultural, ethical, environmental, race and gender issues upon the role of the manager, as well as a reflective and holistic understanding of self-development and the empowerment of others. Education takes the form of multidisciplinary flexible pathways of development and life long learning that benefit all stakeholders. Together, the stakeholders shape a 'learning organization' (Pedlar *et al.* 1991) that is able to adapt and change in response to a changing environment. Learning is a new form of labour and knowledge its key resource (Drucker 1993). Distinctions between managers and managed are eroded, with organizations structured around human beings and the relationships between them (Zuboff 1989).

These concepts do not deny the use of directive power under appropriate circumstances, but recognize the dilemmas faced by 'leaders' who hold a position of responsibility and at the same time wish to encourage individual action and maximize individual strengths while maintaining a group focus (Lee 1991; 1994). These concepts do not deny the manager's need for expertise and 'know-how', nor the necessity for 'street-wise' social skills (Lee 1995b). Competent managing can be likened to politically wise behaviour shown by the individual who is able to balance integrity and political awareness who is able to 'read' or understand the machinations of the external world, and to utilize skills appropriate for working in that world, whilst also working towards 'true cooperation' and demonstrating a lack of 'game-playing' (Baddeley and James 1987; Harris 1973). This approach strengthens the role of the manager as an agent of change, development and organizational commitment, who works in a holistic manner in which all aspects of the individual are combined (i.e. the human side of attitudes and values as well as expert knowledge or skill).

COMPETENCE AND SOCIETAL ASPIRATION

There is increasing agreement that in order for the competent manager to perform well he or she needs additional personal qualities or attributes that, for the sake of simplicity, can be classed as 'being'. Thus, competency takes on a wider meaning, one that incorporates the managers way of 'being' as a contributing factor in the 'doing'. The way in which managerial 'competency' is understood at present, and thus the way in which preferred forms of competence are supported, effects what managers are able to 'do' in the future. Similarly, the form of future we envision will effect what we consider to be acceptable 'competencies' at the present time (see Chapter 22 for a more detailed examination of possible futures). If we accept Nikolajew's assertion that the opportunity is now present in Central Europe to move to a further stage of development, we need to step out of the standard reactive cycle in an informed manner. Therefore, any discussion of competency needs, at some level, to acknowledge the strategic implications of choosing to promote any particular way of 'doing' and 'being'. In looking to the west for precedents in the delineation of managerial competencies, and for precedents in the design and delivery of provision that will foster the chosen competencies, Central European management educators (along with those from the rest of the globe) are embracing fundamental decisions about the future they wish to create.

As indicated at the start of this chapter and elsewhere in this book, Central European nations – their economies, the media, and the rhetoric – are becoming increasingly focused upon small and medium-sized enterprises, the free market and the notion that the world is an oyster for those with the talent for pearl-fishing. In addition, there is evidence, both from the UK (Bate 1990) and the Slovak Republic (Papula 1993), that societal aspiration is not necessarily indicative of organizational form. Both studies found that whilst, individually, members of an organization preferred a culture that met 'human' needs, the organizations were moving, in reality, from a hierarchical centrally planned system towards an uneasy integration of specializations, typified by interdependence and the embracing of change, but also by a lack of concern for the nourishment of the individual. Regardless of possible academic and governmental concerns to establish a sustainable and environmentally aware economy, individual members are searching for the skills and competencies associated with the entrepreneur – and the nouveau riche can afford to pay for those who offer the magic formula.

COMPETENCIES OF THE 'NEW' MANAGER

I suggest that, in reality, the social aspiration of the 'new' manager, the entrepreneur, is working upon a model of short-term opportunistic development, whilst a longer-term rational view might favour sustainable development. These two points of view lead to two different notions of what appropriate 'competencies' might be, as illustrated in Figure 8.1, and demonstrate some of the complexity of the competency debate.

The things that the Central European manager needs to be able to do to act effectively in a quasi-free-market economy are strikingly different from the activities previously required under central planning. There is, however, little difference between opportunistic development and sustainable development in terms of measurable action, apart from the ability to make use of different forms of power and channels of communication. If translated into the 'doing' form of competency-based training, in which assessment is linked to evidence of the ability to perform certain skills, the forms of management educational provision and assessment would be very similar.

As discussed above, however, there is a growing recognition that the demonstrable ability to 'DO' offers a particularly limited view of managerial competence, and that managerial action is also influenced by the manager's ability to 'BE'. Educational systems that focus upon the development on clearly defined, skills-based competencies (i.e. the narrow definition of the ability to 'DO') also focus, by necessity, upon the delineation, standardization and assessment of measurable outcomes. This leads, again by necessity, to standardizing bodies, centralization and a reduction in the ability of individuals and organizations to recognize their unique (and sector-specific) notions of 'competence'. Provision that adopts a wider view of competence (i.e. one that incorporates the less measurable aspects of doing, such as ways of thinking and personal resources) necessitates reduced standardization, as well as alternative and more flexible forms of provision and assessment. The wider view of competence addresses the individual's 'value base'. Such notions lead to a very different form of educational provision from that normally associated with 'competence'. These notions also lead to forms of educational provision that are at odds with the ex-cathedra heritage of Central and (to a slightly lesser extent) Western Europe; and are at odds with the drive for 'cost-effectiveness', larger classes and mass provision fostered by the reduced educational budgets of a free-market economy.

Formal education is well geared to providing knowledge and expertise, whilst skills can be fostered by training and work-shadowing. However, in talking about the need for change, Prokopenko, Jankowicz and Pettitt, Stachowicz, and Nikolajew, amongst others, have all singled out the need for a reappraisal of the attitudes and values prevalent in Central Europe and the implementation of ways of influencing these. Unfortunately (as noted above), the command economy has left a heritage of particular sensitivity to authority, power, knowledge and expertise, such that challenging these within the educational process is both vital and very difficult. The fostering of development in these areas necessitates a collaborative and facilatitive approach – one in which individuals define their own needs and goals, and work towards these by making use of external support as required.

Central to this discussion is the notion that long-term and stable change cannot be imposed, but must be whole-heartedly championed by those it effects. Thus, following on from Nickolajew's assertion, the west is not in a position to offer advice but is better seen as a co-learner/developer. This does not deny the existence of specific short-term areas of educational need and updating that can be supported by the west (in particular, the acquisition of strategic marketing, financial and legal knowledge; the establishment of small and medium-sized enterprises, entrepreneurship and the complexities of public administration; and the up-dating of technical skills and retraining to meet the needs of a changing market). However, the longer-term implication for management education in Central Europe is the need for Central European *self*-development, taking the Rogerian (1959) view that true development is fostered by helping individuals to help themselves.

In conclusion, it has been argued that whilst there are specific short-term needs in Central European management education that can be addressed by

Figure 8.1 Changes in the nature of management

MOVING TO OPPORTUNISTIC DEVELOPMENT:	MOVING FROM:	MOVING TO SUSTAINABLE DEVELOPMENT:
The charismatic manager:	All-knowing, all-powerful manager:	Manager as learner, developer and mentor:

COMPETENT TO DO	COMPETENT TO DO	COMPETENT TO DO
● design and function in flexible organizational structures; ● use charisma and resource power to maximize informal channels of power and communication; ● create islands of order amidst chaos and combine elements in new ways that embrace transition; ● turn ideas into action, take risks and experiment and work with stress and ambiguity;	● follow set routines and work within a fixed and stable organizational structure; ● use formal channels of power and communication; ● delegate responsibility for acting on ideas, defray responsibility for risks and look for precedent before experimenting; ● systemize, reduce ambiguity and maintain simplified order;	● design and function in flexible organisational structures; ● use personal power and facilitation skills to relate to others and use both informal and formal channels of communication; ● accept paradox of order amidst chaos and combine elements in new ways that embrace transition; ● turn ideas into action, take risks and experiment and work with stress and ambiguity;

ABLE TO BE	ABLE TO BE	ABLE TO BE
APPROACH TO ETHICALITY	APPROACH TO ETHICALITY	APPROACH TO ETHICALITY
● manipulate ethics to meet task-related needs; ● question profit and achieving the 'best solution';	● devolve ethical responsibility to superiors; ● operate as if believing the organizational rhetoric;	● operate with a high degree of personal integrity and honesty; ● question implications and ethicality of decisions;
ATTITUDE TOWARDS OTHERS	ATTITUDE TOWARDS OTHERS	ATTITUDE TOWARDS OTHERS
● care for close associates and the task, but remain alone; ● be competitive, but collaborate with others when necessary;	● care for institution and the role; ● be competitive and remain alone at top;	● care for, develop and contribute to institutions, groups and individuals; ● enter into trusting alliances;
APPROACH TO LEARNING	APPROACH TO LEARNING	APPROACH TO LEARNING
● learn in a reactive and task-focused manner, and transmit knowledge sporadically;	● use knowledge as power, and transmit it on a need-to-know basis;	● learn through others and self, and transfer knowledge openly within the organization;

STRATEGIC APPROACH	STRATEGIC APPROACH	STRATEGIC APPROACH
• intuit the short-term future; • identify problems and possible solutions; • maintain short-term goal-oriented vision and influence others to accept own vision;	• predict future from the past; • dictate goals and methods; • maintain domestic vision and impose own vision on subordinates, accept vision of superiors;	• intuit the long-term future; • specify and work with process; • envision and implement the strategy of thinking globally, acting locally, and facilitate vision of others;
PSYCHOLOGICAL FLEXIBILITY	PSYCHOLOGICAL FLEXIBILITY	PSYCHOLOGICAL FLEXIBILITY
• accommodate cultural diversity in so far as it meets organisational aims; • make self understood in other languages; • maintain both high mobility and an ethno-centric approach;	• reject cultural diversity in that it challenges stability, order and accepted values; • remain monolingual; • maintain low mobility and an ethno-centric view;	• manage cultural diversity, and be adept with cross-cultural influences; • be an excellent communicator, normally multilingual; • maintain high mobility

collaboration with the west and using traditional educational approaches, these do not meet the longer-term needs of Central European nations. Such longer-term needs are not unique to Central Europe they are shared by all nations, and are epitomized by the need to move towards an environmentally and societally aware scenario. It is also suggested that neither traditional educational approaches nor those associated with a limited notion of competence (that managers 'DO') can easily address these needs. Provision that embraces a wider notion of competence (that managers 'DO' and 'BE') is needed, but it is complex and challenges providers, recipients, professional bodies and governments to explore their motivations and the implications that their actions hold for the 'creation' of the future.

NOTES

1 This was jointly funded by the EC: TEMPUS and the Austrian Ministry of Education (see Lee 1992, 1993 for further details).
2 Conducted for the Institute of Management, and comprising the Cannon and Taylor Working Parties (Cannon 1994; Taylor 1994), and the Watson Consultation Document (Watson 1994).

REFERENCES

Argyris, C. (1990) *Overcoming Organisational Defences*, Boston, MA: Allyn & Bacon.
Baddeley, S. and James, K. (1987) 'Owl, fox, donkey or sheep: Political skills for managers', *Management Education and Development* 18, pp. 3–19.

Bate, P. (1990) 'Using the culture concept in an organisation development setting', *Journal of Applied Behavioural Science* 26, pp. 83–106.

Binsted, D. (1988) 'The development of interpersonal competencies', *Training Officer* 24(11), pp. 338–42.

Burgoyne, J.G. (1989) 'Creating the managerial portfolio: building on competency approaches to management development', *Management Education and Development* 20, pp. 56–61.

Burgoyne, J.G. (1990) 'Doubts about competency', In M. Devine (ed.) *The Photofit Manager in the 1990s*, pp, 20–7, London: Unwin Hyman.

Cannon, T. (1994) *Working Party Report: Developments since Handy and Constable, Management Development to the Millennium Research*, Corby, Northants: Institute of Management.

Checkland, P. (1981) *Systems Thinking, Systems Practice*, London: Wiley.

Clegg, S.R. (1990) *Modern Organisations: Organisation studies in the Postmodern World*, London: Sage.

Constable, J. and McCormick, R. (1987) *The Making of British Managers*, London: British Institute of Management & Federation of British Industry.

Darmer, P. (1991) *Deflating the Myth of European Management*, paper presented at the 17th Annual European International Business Association Conference, Copenhagen.

Davis, J. (1990) *Greening Business*, Oxford: Blackwell.

Dobson, S., Borucki, C.C. and Byosiere, P. (1992) *Changes in the Role of Middle Management: A European View*, paper presented at the 3rd International Personnel and Human Resource Management Conference, Ashridge, UK.

Drucker, P. (1993) *Post-Capitalist Society*, New York: Harper Business.

Dubini, P. and Cardini, A. (1991) 'Transition and management education in Eastern Europe', in H. Vestergaard (ed.) *An Enlarged Europe in the Global Economy*, pp. 383–409. European International Business Association.

Dumain, B. (1990) 'Creating a new company culture', *Fortune*, 15, pp. 5–58.

Freedman, D. (1992) 'Is management still a science?', *Harvard Business Review* (November), pp. 26–38.

Handy, C. (1985) *Understanding Organisations*, Harmondsworth: Penguin.

Handy, C., Gow, I., Gordon, C., Randlesome, C. and Moloney, M. (1987) *The Making of Managers*, London: National Economic Development Office.

Harris, T. (1973) *I'm OK – You're OK*, London: Pan Books.

Jankowicz, D. and Pettitt, S. (1993) 'Worlds in collusion: an analysis of an Eastern European management development initiative', *Management Education and Development* 24, pp. 93–104.

Jantsch, E. (1980) *The Self Organising Universe*, Oxford: Pergamon.

Kinsman, J. (1990) *Millennium: Towards Tomorrow's Society*, London: Allen & Co.

Lee, M.M. (1991) 'Playing the guru: inequality of power in interpersonal relationships', *Management Education and Development* 22, pp. 302–9.

Lee, M.M. (1992) 'Management education in Central Europe: problems, practicalities and potential', working paper for Conference: *The Role of Higher Education in the Reform Process of Central and Eastern Europe*, Brussels: Commission of the European Communities.

Lee, M.M. (1993) *Central European Management Teacher Development Programme: Final Report*, JEP–0183–89–93, Brussels: Commission of the European Communities.

Lee, M.M. (1994) 'The isolated manager: Walking the boundaries of the micro-culture', *Proceedings of the British Academy of Management Conference*, Lancaster, pp.112–36.

Lee, M.M. (1995a) 'Action learning: working with freedom of choice in Central Europe', *Management Learning*, 26(2) pp. 215–50.

Lee, M.M. (1995b) 'Learning for work: short term benefit or long term gain', *Personnel Review* 24(6) pp. 29–43.

Lee, M.M. (1996) 'Action Learning as a cross-cultural tool' in Stewart, J. and McGoldrick, J. (Eds.) *Human Resource Development: Perspectives, Strategies and practice*, London: Pitman. pp. 240–260.

Lessem, R. (1990) *Developmental Management*, Oxford: Blackwell.

Lessem, R. (1991) *Total Quality Learning*, Oxford: Blackwell.

Lievegood, B. (1991) *Managing the Developing Organisation*, Oxford: Blackwell.

March J. and Simon, H. (1958) *Organisations*, New York: John Wiley.

McNulty, N.G. (1992) 'Management education in Eastern Europe: 'fore and after', *Academy of Management Executive* 6(4), pp. 78–87.

Morgan, G. (1993) 'The challenges of management research', *Proceedings of the Crafting of Management Research*, British Academy of Management Conference, Milton Keynes, pp. 497–8.

Mudroch, V. (1992) 'The future of interdisciplinarity: the case of Swiss universities', *Studies in Higher Education* 17, pp. 43–54.

Nespor, J. (1988) 'Theoretical observations on applied behavioural science', *Journal of Applied Behavioural Science* 24, pp. 277–95.

Nikolajew, V. (1992) 'Transitional economies', *Futures* 24(6), pp. 635–52.

Norgaard, R. (1988) 'Sustainable development: a co-evolutionary view', *Futures* 20(6), pp. 606–20.

Obloj, K. (1991) 'Global systematic developments and East European economies: critical issues and challenges', in H. Vestergaard (ed.) *An Enlarged Europe in the Global Economy*, Copenhagen: European International Business Association.

Otta, W. and Gorynia, A. (1991) 'Business education and training in Poland: industrial structure and policy', in H. Vestergaard (ed.) *An Enlarged Europe in the Global Economy*, Copenhagen: European International Business Association.

Papula, J. (1993) *The Development of Management Education in Slovakia*, paper presented at TEMPUS: Central European Management Development Programme, Vienna.

Pascale, R. (1990) *Managing on the Edge*, London: Penguin.

Pedlar, M., Burgoyne, J. and Boydell, T. (1991) *The Learning Company: A Strategy for Sustainable Growth*, London: McGraw-Hill.

Perica, L. (1993) *Management Development to the Millennium*, Institute of Management Survey, an interim report, Lancaster: Lancaster University.

Porter, L.W. and McKibbin, L.E. (1988) *Management Education and Development: Drift or Thrust into the 21st Century?*, New York: McGraw-Hill.

Powers, E.A. (1983) 'The AMA management competency programmes: A developmental process', *Exchange* 8(2), pp. 16–20.

Prokopenko, J. (1992) *Human Resources Management in Economies in Transition: The East European Case*, Man Dev/66, Geneva: International Labour Office.

Rogers, C.R. (1959) 'A theory of therapy, personality, and interpersonal relationships as developed in the client-centred framework', in S. Koch, (ed.) *Psychology: A Study of a Science*, vol. 3, New York: McGraw-Hill.

Ryder, J. and Easterby-Smith, M. (1992) 'Working together in Europe: the case of the European Management Teacher Programme', *Journal of European Industrial Training* 12(2), pp. 12–16.

Senge, P. (1990) *The Fifth Discipline*, New York: Doubleday.

Smithers, A. (1993) *All Our Futures – Britain's Education Revolution*, Manchester: Centre for Education and Employment Research, University of Manchester.

Stachowicz, J. (1991) *Management Culture in Large Polish Enterprises of Heavy Industry: Diagnosing the State and Identifying the Need for Changes*, Poland: Polish Academy of Sciences, Centre for Industrial Management, Bythom Branch.

Stead, V. and Lee, M.M. (1996) 'Inter-cultural perspectives on HRD' in Stewart, J. and McGoldrick, J. (eds.) *Human Resource Development: Perspectives, strategies and practice*, London: Pitman. pp. 47–70.

Storey, J. (1991) 'Do the Japanese make better managers?', *Personnel Management* (August), pp. 24–8.

Swan, J., Aspin, T., Holloway, J., Lee, M.M. and Perica, L. (1993) 'The future of management education and development: an evaluation of the ESRC Management Teacher Fellowship Scheme in the UK', *The Crafting of Management Research: Proceedings of British Academy of Management Annual Conference*, Milton Keynes.

Taylor, F.J.W. (1994) *Working Party Report: The Way Ahead 1994–2001*, Management Development to the Millennium Research, Corby, Northants: Institute of Management.

Watson, J. (1994) *The New Challenges*, Management Development to the Millennium Research, Corby, Northants: Institute of Management.

Zuboff, S. (1989) *In the Age of the Smart Machine*, Oxford: Heinemann.

Part II

Categorizing change: identifying boundaries and transgressions

Chapter 9

Case 2: from clarity of purpose to situated complexity

Monica Lee

REFLEXIVITY

I am going to present to you an evolving picture that starts at a time in my life when I was filled with idealism and complacency (my ideas must be good, as they had been awarded funding), a time when I started to encounter the reality of what had previously been a matter of theorizing, politicizing and 'polite' discussion. I found myself walking a series of uncomfortable boundaries – I felt driven from my idealistic values about how people 'should' work together and about the processes of learning and education by the expectations of others. As discussed elsewhere (Lee 1993, 1995) the outcomes of the programme and the vast majority of 'student' evaluations were highly positive, yet I felt forced into compromise and chaos.

Any picture I can give of what happened is inevitably biased. It is painted from my perspective. I have chosen the form and descriptors, and have done so for the purposes of illustration. I am constrained by the meaning I wish to extract and have taken liberty with 'facts'. This picture is really a composite of my experiences over several years and of several peoples' experiences about the same situations – we have discussed these situations (sometimes ad nauseam) and I attempt to represent their views here, but, ultimately, their view is filtered through my perceptions; thus, this can be nothing more or less than a personal picture.

BACKGROUND

Depending upon your perspective you might call me visionary, uncomfor- tably evangelical or naively optimistic about such things as holism, open- ness, the sharing of experiences, the breaking down of barriers and the meeting of equals. The Velvet Revolution enthused me and I wished to engage with it. In viewing education as a form of social determinism in a world in which words such as 'culture' are given spuriously well-defined meaning, and in viewing management as an equally ill-defined term that gave the appearance of control and predictability and thus denied the 'reality' of complexity, I was inevitably drawn to the challenges of exploring the multiple roles of management education under rapidly changing circumstances.

It was important to me that the focus would be upon participants defining their own needs and that the provision would support them in this and in working towards ways of meeting these needs. It was also important to me that the programme would be designed to cascade, so that participants would be supported in passing it on to colleagues, and I wished to avoid (if possible) reinforcing the elites, instead working with a wide range of higher education institutions across Central Europe, mediated through Central European partners who coordinated the subsidiary partners. I developed my ideas into a proposal for funding and sought the partners necessary to support me in this. In keeping with my views on working collaboratively through the meeting of equals I attempted to achieve a working consensus (trying to move with my partners towards this, without acknowledging to them or to myself the level of ownership that I felt about the proposal, which in turn was driven by the sanctity that I bestowed upon my basal values). We largely ignored values and instead concentrated on ways of working. We agreed that we would call ourselves 'Tutors', that the 'students' would be called 'Fellows', that some Fellows would become 'Co-tutors' as part of the cascading process, and that the programme and the progress of the Fellows would be followed by 'Researchers' (research students from partner institutions). We agreed that when the Brits talked of a core tutor they meant the equivalent of a Danish specialist tutor, and that we all supported the use of action learning and case study.

The proposal became a practical reality and I gained TEMPUS funding. The funding was backdated and we were required to start immediately. We knew we hadn't prepared as well as we might, but there was no alternative – we would have to make final preparations when we met.

SCENE 1: ARRIVAL IN POZNAŃ, POLAND

The team from Western Europe arrive at the hotel – 7 lecturers, each an expert in her/his own field. The tutor team included one woman (myself as coordinator) and the rest were male. Their acolytes (i.e. two researchers for each nation) were also present, as were two non-tutors (representing Poland and Austria administratively). We met for an ice cream, but couldn't understand the menu so we ordered one of each variety. They were enormous, we were outfaced, but one of the researchers saved the day – he ate them all and earnt the nickname 'Bert the dustbin'.

We met at the hotel to iron out details and finalise plans for the first workshop. The Central European coordinator told us that, as planned, there were thirty academics ready to start the programme. They ranged from pro-rectors through ex-Party activists; some were senior staff, others were 'bright young things'. They had been chosen from higher education institutions across the country. The tutors began to develop a feeling of solidarity. We hadn't worked together before, but this was just another start to a new programme. It would have some odd quirks but would be similar to others we had taught.

We asked to see the teaching facilities and were taken across town to look at them. Although the coordinator appeared bemused that we might wish to do this prior to starting the course, it was clear that we were guests and ought to be humoured. We walked into a vast ex-Communist building – past an old lady and her (smelly) cat who was sitting in what looked like a telephone kiosk inside an echoing hall. We were taken down long corridors to a cavernous cellar and were told that it was the only space available for a group as big as ours. We learnt that under the cellar were the old dungeons and torture chambers of the local Communist party. We stood lost in an enormous space, seized by feelings of oppression.

The desks were joined together in rows and great pillars were dotted regularly around the room, cutting off vision. There were no flip-charts or AVA – the overhead projector the Brits had brought had been broken during the plane journey. A large blackboard was wheeled in at our insistence, and then the Danes produced some serious equipment: photocopiers, projectors, personal computers and a wild tangle of wires – but no paper. A tutor dashed to the student shop and bought a ream – their entire stock. We tried to do something about the seating, creating little islands. We left quietly, talking late into the night how could we act as normal in such an unusual setting? We agreed that this supported our belief in the need for lots of small group work, and the researchers were primed to work with subgroups.

SCENE 2: THE FIRST FEW DAYS

We start. Long introductions. We adapt (by necessity) to the apparent Central European need for monologues. Finally the floor is ours. The western experts sweep to the front and (cowed by the environment) follow the pattern – a series of monologues. We take turns, we lecture about learning from each other, action learning and equality. The Fellows sit and listen. We have a quick conference at lunch-time – how can we be more active?

The next session involves drawing our visions of the world we would like. This is fun (and very strange to some) and everyone gets involved. Lots of buzz and comparisons – but surprisingly little overall difference. Everyone wants to be valued – to be happy and healthy. The details are more revealing. Nearly every Fellow includes a dog in the picture – yet it is extremely rare to see them in the streets. The westerners learn that dogs are important status symbols – they imply a large apartment and an income sufficient to buy non-essential items such as dog food. We talk to each other about cultural differences.

Partners and researchers go back to the hotel and the discussions start. We should be doing this or that – it becomes heated at times and shifting political alliances are formed. I try to follow my belief in working towards collaborative agreement – I won't take sides, instead I stick to my ideology. Each person from the team buttonholes me (in corridors or wherever). The message from each is that I should lead from the front and make clear decisions that are (of course) in their favour. I refuse, it is against my view of life and instead attempt to facilitate. The Central European coordinator tries to help me by starting the catch phrase 'Monica's the Boss', without perhaps fully appreciating the reasons why I was refusing to lead, and neither of us realized (until later) the divisive impact it had upon the other tutors. (Incidentally, the catch phrase remained in use throughout the three years of the programme, but changed in nature – increasingly becoming a joking reference back to more tumultuous times.) I remind them that the programme is based around action learning and the sharing of information – that there is no 'right' way but that we just face different choices and need to think through the implications of each choice. I get verbal agreement to this, but the behaviour doesn't change. Each still competes to provide the dominant view.

It starts to become highly emotive. We are all deeply committed and are intensely engaged with the programme – we just can't easily agree on how it should be enacted. We act as if we are attempting to defend our fundamental principles about life. Some make it into a male–female issue. They form shifting splinter groups and use a mixture of charm and bullying in an attempt to take over. Another person uses his influence (skilfully and with short-term success) with my home institution in an attempt to destabilize me. It is not overtly hostile; instead it feels to me like a mixture of 'little boys behaving badly in order to get attention from Mummy' and of being patronized.

The difference of opinion starts to show in the classroom. We still maintain a pretence of solidarity – but one tutor falls asleep at the back whilst another is talking; one runs over by an hour, preventing another saying anything, and so on. It is much less noticeable (initially) when we work in case-study groups. These are managed by individual tutors and supported by cross-national pairs of researchers. We are working with real issues and towards an (apparently) clearly defined end-product (the written case and the transference of case-writing and case-teaching skills). The grail of a prescriptive 'solution' intrudes. The majority of Fellows want answers to their real issues and want to be able to transfer this recipe of success to those they will be using the case with. They want to use cases in their examination-based assessment procedures and mark their students on the extent to which they have identified the 'right' answer. They find the blithe western assurances that there is no 'right answer' to be facile, to indicate lack of expertise and to illustrate a lack of understanding of the world in which the Fellows have to operate.

Problems of language intrude. It becomes apparent that what the tutors had thought was agreement and understanding of the lectures was, in some cases, the behaviour that the Fellows would expect from their own students – lack of challenge, because to challenge the tutor is to challenge the power hierarchy. Through working in small groups on a wide range of multi-dimensional issues the Fellows are given the power to drive the discussion, but several are hampered by a lack of the detailed knowledge of English necessitated by the depth of debate. In one group a British researcher translates into German and an Austrian researcher translates onwards. Any reply follows the same route back again. In another group, French is used as a mediating language. Many of the concepts used are culturally specific and cannot easily be transferred without detailed discussion of their meanings and implications. The situation becomes messy – and we are out of paper again – we have emptied the local shops and now have to search the wider area for supplies.

SCENE 3: THE NEXT FEW DAYS

The disagreements continue. Situational issues intrude. The westerners are seen to be Zloty millionaires. They stay in the hotel whilst researchers and Fellows are (in many cases) in extremely impoverished accommodation. The tutors unwittingly flaunt their buying power. The westerners also flaunt other unspoken, but powerful, customs. They fail to hand in their hotel keys each morning, and ignore the customary leaving of coats and bags in the ubiquitous 'check-in' facilities when entering a building. They fail to pay when going to the toilet (leading, in one case, to much retrospective humour as an extremely irate attendant chased a fleet-footed researcher along the corridors). One person has his clothes stolen from his hotel room, and an Indian researcher suffers strong racial prejudice in a restaurant. The researchers run covert campaigns to sway preferred Central European Fellows to come to their home institution during the second workshop – the planned visit to the west. Through shared experiences, tutors and researchers begin to understand each other more clearly. Friendships become more intense and disagreements greater. They start to challenge each other on points of theory and practice within the workshop, and these patterns widen to include the Fellows.

In fighting amongst each other we (the tutors) had colluded in classing Fellows together as 'students' – quiescent recipients of our wisdom. They start to take sides, become vocal individuals/subgroups, real people. They shift from being polite hosts who tried hard to ignore the badly behaved guests towards expressing their individuality and needs. It becomes clear that some are political choices, others are attracted by a visit to the west, and others by the possibility of being part of a new and potentially exciting development. Their motivations and level of engagement differ, as do their institutional loyalties, their identification with different discipline roots, and their wider political allegiances and views on power. We are operating on 'first-name terms', but some Fellows still refer to more senior Fellows by their title, and the recipients of such deference are becoming increasingly annoyed by what they see as a lack of respect on behalf of the western students. This is exacerbated by the idea that they might 'learn' from students, albeit from the west. Many were new to each other at the start of the programme but have been working and socializing late into the evenings and understand each other better. Working in small groups on constructing local case studies, they become vocal in their newly found sense of communality.

Each case group is to present their work in plenary. We run out of paper again and are now driving to the other side of Poznań to search for more. The case studies are exciting and very good (several are later published). As planned, we use this opportunity to cover feedback and debriefing skills. People start to shift from moralistic and long-winded statements of view to supportive and challenging exploration. We move into evaluation groups and the whole process incites intense discussion and raises a host of issues (pedagogical, theoretical, structural, political and personal). The change is surrealistic, as cultural difference and power relations are forgotten in the fascination with complexity. We talk late into the night – barriers and boundaries have been temporarily forgotten.

SCENE 4: THE DENOUEMENT?

The next morning we gather with renewed lighthearted energy (so far the pace has been frenetic and we are all flagging), but this disperses as we get to the serious business of reaching decisions about who goes where in the west for workshop 2. National difference and specialist preferences re-emerge as each institution puts its 'goods' on show. Power difference, political and theoretical allegiances, and 'exclusive' friendship groupings re-emerge as the Fellows make their choices. The decisions are made, but the process has reopened previous issues. Individually and collectively they make it clear that the evident disagreement between the 'experts' is highly unsettling – that what they want is to learn from western experts, and that the stated philosophy of the programme is to meet their individual needs. They agree that working together on cases has helped towards this, but cannot agree theoretically and practically, or on how they would like to be treated and how they might treat their students. The different tutor/researcher factions link up with like-minded Fellows and together they find additional strength and justification for pressing for their preferred approaches. I am now tackled by gangs in corridors, all of whom wish me to lend credence to their particular view of the world.

I decide, once again, to attempt to address this directly – and am described by one tutor as a schoolmarm as I do so. I talk to everybody circled around me (seated in rows on benches, clustered around pillars – my words echoing in the far reaches of the cavern) about the need to engage in different views of the world, that there is no right answer – the 'west' can only offer a range of alternatives, each with their situation-dependent consequences. I suggest that what is occuring is a 'live case' of the tension inherent in working with multiple world-views, and that tension between views can be liberating, that conflict can be valued. I suggest that the Fellows pick the brains of tutors and researchers, seek out the problems within the tentative situated responses offered from the west and create their own 'solutions'. I suggest that after coffee we move into action-learning sets as planned and continue to air these issues in more depth in these groups. We break for coffee, surrounded by a thoughtful and relatively positive atmosphere, talking in mobile and dynamic clumps, and then go into action-learning sets.

I do not have a set – instead, I observe. All starts well – the sets are dotted around the room – a gentle hum of discussion pervades the place. One group breaks out laughing – people look round. Another group starts arguing – people look round. In the third, the western tutor is holding forth . . . gradually people start to lose focus on their own set and instead covertly compare what is happening in the others. The buzz of voices becomes sharper as it dawns on Fellows, researchers, and tutors alike, that (despite having discussed action learning extensively throughout the work-shop, and despite a generalized agreement between all participants about the processes of action learning and the ways in which sets operate) each set has, in practice, adopted a different model of action learning – that disagreement abounds even within the central tenet of the programme.

QUESTIONS

- Would this inter- and intra-group conflict have been avoidable if different actions had been taken; and, if so, what might those actions have been?
- What positive and negative outcomes would you anticipate from this scenario, and for whom?
- Who do you identify with and what would you do next?

THE COMMENTARY

I present the picture as a seemingly inevitable chain of events from which emerge inter- and intra-group conflict and shifting allegiances. I describe how the 'reality' of short-term situationally dependant factors (day-to-day existence) replaced the anticipatory preconceptions – the ideals – that I started out with. I recount how I struggled to maintain my 'ideals' despite the fact that all other participants (partners, tutors, researchers and Fellows) clearly wanted me to be more directive. I struggled against the increasingly clear evidence that my desire for 'collaboration' was such that I would impose it upon others, either directly or through deliberate inaction.

I presented a rhetoric of cultural relativity, pluralism, complexity and facilitation; yet, in attempting to realize it, I employed the tightly bounded logic of imposition and manipulation. The message on the 'T-shirt' was 'THE WORLD IS RELATIVE – ALL VIEWS ARE EQUAL – UNDER-STAND THIS – AND USE IT TO PROMOTE YOUR OWN'. It is clear that I am uncomfortable in this role, but I had no option. The chain of events unfolded – there is no alternative (see Hugo Letiche on action research/learning in Section 3). In presenting it like this I have exaggerated the role I played by lessening the contribution that others made to the process, but I have done so for two, contradictory, reasons. I wish to emphasize the minimization of agency that follows from viewing life as a pattern and oneself as a thread within the tapestry (all is relative, the cloth is predetermined and there is no option). At the same time I wish to emphasize the level of individual agency inherent in operating from a relativistic perspective: the end justifies the means. I manipulated others – and assuaged my conscience by telling myself that all interaction is influence, and all influence is manipulation. Whether we wished it or not (whatever we privately told ourselves) our every interaction would influence, and thus I chose to influence things in my preferred direction.

Both can be seen as justification for cultural imperialism, a position that is unnoticed if you believe the message – and very hard to challenge if you are a 'recipient' and are therefore, by virtue of your presence, colluding with the rhetoric. As recipient one can point to the hypocrisy of the message but cannot easily refute it without shattering the provider/recipient relationship. In part, the case is about shifts in this relationship, and each of the chapters in Part II (and particularly that of Slawomir Magala, Chapter 15) questions the extent to which the concept of provider/recipient is misleadingly simplistic, and is unworkable in practice.

The case also illustrates the multiple forms of classification that we applied to each other whether on national-, discipline related-, functional-, or other grounds. These ways of creating meaning for ourselves do not disappear. As Devi Jankowicz (Chapter 11) and Monika Kostera (Chapter 14) indicate, many of the differences are rooted in our cultural constructs and cannot easily be reconciled through the direct translation of language. They are part of our cultural mythology and are recreated in the search for our identity. The whole of Part II, however, indicates that these forms of classification shift – with time, and with perspective. For example, Steve

Crawshaw offers a pattern of interacting forces and change that opens out our understanding of a unitary 'Central and Eastern Europe', whilst Andrzej Kozminski, Slawomir Magala and Hugo Letiche each offer patterns focused upon function, requirements, or world-view (respectively). Each author creates their classification for a reason: to indicate the differences between their chosen groupings, and (by implication) the different patterns of relationships and preferred outcomes associated with each group.

The case is written from my perspective and I have therefore applied my forms of classification, and, perhaps more importantly, I have applied my criteria for 'success'. Short-and long-term evaluations were positive. Cases were written, projects were designed and enacted. Knowledge was 'transferred'. Curricular and structural changes were enacted. All participants were affected. Friendships remain. When we meet, the intensity, enjoyment, pain and associated changes in world-view are revisited and savoured. All this is said with hindsight, and in the knowledge that ascribing positive outcomes to that time of complexity and confusion might well be a form of self-defence (of the form 'it has changed me and thus I must be better'); however, these long-term outcomes meet my criteria for success.

In the short term, where the case finishes, it is clear that many did not feel that their preferred outcomes were being met. Some wanted clarity and functional skills – they were being given complexity and discussions about process. Some wanted understanding of short-cycle post-experience provision, whilst others wished to consider long-cycle undergraduate qualifications. Some wanted to consider implications for institutional structure and national policy, whilst others wanted to focus on the classroom environment, and so on. None, including researchers and tutors, received exactly what they had expected – though many received other things. This, perhaps, is the crux of the matter: the difference between expectations and reality when both are a matter of perception and co-creation.

Each individual had her/his own 'home situation' to manage and return to. To some extent they were 'free agents', but they were still a product of their circumstances and 'culture' (see Monika Kostera for an examination of the pervasive way in which such culture is perpetuated through the media). As Kristina Genell and Monika Kostera indicate, the appearance of individual 'change' might well mask a deep-rooted structural cycle – one which is fundamentally stable. Individuals return to their previous lives and struggle to implement the changes they feel are necessary.

I suspect that each person who participated in the 'case' developed during that time, but, in so far as 'development' is an unbounded and non-predictable phenomenon, the form of that development cannot be described in terms of preferred outcomes. The dilemma, as indicated in the case and in each of the chapters, is that as the classificational boundaries are eroded and the preferred outcomes associated with each lose clarity, so the processes become more complex, challenging and developmental. They also become less amenable to 'control', cannot be planned, and lead to variable 'outcomes'. The encountering of other's world-views has much to offer personally, but challenges the system and is thus hard to reconcile with the parameters of 'normal' educational provision.

REFERENCES

Lee, M.M. (1993) 'Evaluation of the Central European Management Teacher Development Programme', *Report for the European Commission (No 0183)*, Brussels: Commission of European Communities.

Lee, M.M. (1995) 'Working with Freedom of Choice in Central Europe', *Management Learning*, 26(2) pp. 215–30.

Chapter 10

From Communists to capitalists

Steve Crawshaw

Western views of Central and Eastern Europe have swung violently from one extreme to another. First, during the Communist years, there was resigned pessimism. Then, during the *annus mirabilis* of 1989, there was overwhelming optimism, followed by a return to pessimism, with an emphasis on all the things that had gone badly wrong. Caution is appropriate when looking at the problems facing all of Central and Eastern Europe. But, especially when looking at Poland, Hungary and the Czech republic, the wealthiest and most efficient countries in the old Soviet bloc, measured optimism is appropriate, too. Few could seriously have predicted that the foundations of a new market economy would be laid within just a couple of years of the collapse of Communism, and many of today's assessments forget the starting point.

DIFFERENT STARTING POINTS

Each country started its journey towards the free market from a different point. The contrasts between Communist Poland, say, and Albania were as great as the contrasts between east and west. Even Russia was poorer than many of its satellites. In Poland, the story was told of the Russian who took a train to Paris and the Parisian who took a train to Moscow. Both got out in Warsaw, convinced that they had already arrived at their destination. The Frenchman saw the greyness and thought that this must be the USSR; the Russian saw that this was brighter than anything he had ever seen, and thought he must have arrived in the west.

Elsewhere, too, there were many differences. In Hungary, the anti-Communist uprising of 1956 was brutally suppressed. But, from the late 1960s onwards, political and economic changes were introduced, which made it (in the Hungarians' own description) 'the most cheerful barracks in the camp'. In Czechoslovakia the politics were severe, especially after the Soviet invasion of 1968, but the economy flourished, in Communist terms at least. In Poland, by contrast even, paradoxically, during martial law, imposed in 1981 following the ban on Solidarity politics remained permissive, while the economy was a constant mess. A popular Polish joke described how a Polish and a Czech dog met at the frontier between the two countries. 'Why are you crossing into Czechoslovakia?' asked the Czech dog. 'I want to taste some sausage at last,' came the reply. 'But why should *you* want to come to Poland?' 'Surely it's obvious,' said his Czech friend. 'I want to bark.' The contrast was real: in Prague, the shops were relatively full and there was little freedom of speech; in Warsaw, the shops were empty but people complained without fear of being locked up much more loudly than they would have dared to in Prague or Moscow. In many countries, theatre, cinema and satirical cabaret provided a political escape valve.

Attitudes to private enterprise varied enormously. Albania was the most rigidly Stalinist regime in Eastern Europe, and private trade of any kind was strictly prohibited there. In Poland, by contrast, private enterprise was tolerated, and sometimes almost encouraged, thereby providing an economic escape valve (Boyes 1990). Mieczyslaw Wilczek, Polish Industry Minister for the last government before the collapse of Communism, was himself a wealthy private entrepreneur.

The end of the Party

In June 1989, following Solidarity's overwhelming victory in the Polish elections, Eastern Europe moved into a new era. Even before the Poles had their elections, Hungary had promised multi-party elections for 1990. None the less, it was the Poles who really unleashed the avalanche. In August, Poland gained a non-Communist prime minister. Within the next few months all the nations of Eastern Europe leapt into the breach that had now been opened: following a succession of surrenders to the huge demonstrations in Leipzig and Berlin, the Berlin Wall broke open in November 1989; mass demonstrations in Prague forced the collapse of the Communist regime in Czechoslovakia; and a month later even the brutal regime of Nicolae Ceauşescu, in Romania, was overthrown.

In retrospect, it seemed clear cut. At the time of the Polish elections, however, many still feared that there could be a backlash. In the years after the changes took place, many harked back to the alleged 'time of optimism' of August 1989. In reality, one of the most startling things about those wondrous, historic days was how resolutely downbeat most Poles were. Typical was the woman who said to me, when I asked her if she felt pleased about Solidarity's victory in August 1989: 'How can you be pleased? You can never get pigs away from the trough.' Poles had achieved many victories in the past; each time, the Communists had managed to claw back some power. Many people assumed that this time it would be the same. As a Solidarity supporter asked me: 'How can I feel cheerful? Have you seen what's in the shops?'

In autumn 1989, although Poland had a new Solidarity prime minister, many Communists still hoped that the elections would merely be a kind of delaying tactic. Communist Party representatives in the factories complained bitterly when asked to vacate their special offices. A Polish diplomat in London complained indignantly to me that he and his comrades were no longer permitted to hold Communist Party meetings at the embassy, as they had always done. He refused to acknowledge that life had now moved on. Only gradually did the former rulers and the ruled both acknowledge that Communism had truly died.

Economic changes

In January 1990, four months after Solidarity took over the reins of government, Poland launched its Big Bang, a bold liberalization programme which was regarded by many in the west as suicidal because it was so painful. Many assumed that Poland would soon explode in protest against the changes. At this time, Lech Wałęsa was saying, in all seriousness, that his biggest mistake had been to ensure that Solidarity took power in 1989, before it was ready to do so. Poverty was real, and seemed certain only to increase. Despite acute social tensions, bitter complaints and a chaotic political situation accompanied by scattered strikes and demonstrations, unrest never broke out on a mass scale.

Leszek Balcerowicz, the Polish Finance Minister, was watched with fascination by the Soviet Communists, who still hoped they could cling to power in Moscow. As Leonid Abalkin, Gorbachev's deputy prime minister in charge of economic reform, noted enviously in 1990: 'Poland's government enjoys the people's trust, and can bring in very unpopular measures with the support of society.' (Crawshaw 1992).

Resentments

There were – and, to some extent, still are – several main sources of resentment: first, the continued privileges of the old bosses; second, the extent to which progress towards the free market seemed to overlap with the development of organized crime; third, the enormous divisions that have opened up throughout Eastern Europe, as the gap between the haves and the have-nots has reached almost Third World proportions. These three sources of bitterness overlap to some extent but can also be treated separately.

Throughout Eastern Europe, many were angry at the problem of the *nomenklatura* – Communism's privileged class. It was the *nomenklatura* who had run the factories and with privatiztion it was often they who remained in charge. They had the clout and they had the cash, with which they could quickly become the affluent new capitalists. This provided an impossible set of choices for the new democratic rulers. Sometimes the *nomenklatura* were unimaginative apparatchiks, unsuited to running a factory in a competitive environment – sometimes they were competent managers who could still make a positive contribution. In either case, there was popular resentment at the idea that the old ruling class should continue and that the same boss remained in the comfortable seat even now that times had changed.

In schools and universities, too, it was difficult to draw a dividing line, for the purposes of a latter-day 'de-Nazification' (a process which, crucially, was only carried out with such relative ease in Germany after 1945 because it was imposed by the Allies, and in which only the most senior and the most active were weeded out). Thus, the following questions arose: was a loyal party member always a bad teacher or professor? What should be construed as 'unacceptable' collaboration with the old regime? Should there be complete public exposure of secret-police links, or should sleeping dogs be allowed to lie?

Resentment was also caused by corruption and crime. Throughout the Communist bloc, corruption had always been part of the system. Everybody expected to offer bribes, and everybody who held power, however petty, expected to receive them: surgeons, town planners, telephone engineers, shop assistants, bureaucrats. Gifts, cash, or tit-for-tat inducements ('You give my daughter the operation she needs; I'll make sure your son gets his university place') everybody had something to offer – a peasant might bring fresh sausage, a worker might have access to unavailable building materials, fallen off the back of a state-owned lorry. Bribery was endemic. To get on to a waiting list for one's own apartment, for example, it was almost unthinkable not to offer incentives, all the way down the line. After Communism ended, it was difficult for that mentality to change. Officials still expected to take bribes.

Equally, the collapse of the police state helped to unleash a crime wave such as the Communist bloc had never seen. The worst and most violent crime came in the countries that had been most buttoned-up: in the former Soviet Union and in Albania, which sometimes seemed to teeter on the edge of violent anarchy. In Poland and other Central European countries, too, the crime rate soared in the new and apparently lawless jungle. Many 'businessmen' often turned out to be merely sharp operators, making money out of an unsuspecting public.

The first few years after Communism were filled with stories of those who sought to bend the system to their own ends. People opened banks and made millions before disappearing out of the country; or they promised unbelievable interest rates, which brought hordes of grateful customers, until the bubble burst. In Russia especially, the 'mafias' – used as a general term for all forms of organized crime – dominated much of the most flourishing business. Almost anybody whose business began to do well soon found the mafia knocking at the door, asking for payoffs – backed by threats of kidnap or murder.

Disillusion with the new order was deep. The mood was captured by the Cellar of the Rams cabaret in Poland, which ran a satirical performance called '*Komuno, wróć!*' – approximately, 'Commies, come back!', less than a year after the Communists were gone. In the Soviet Union, many believed that they had a better lifestyle than did the average worker in America or Western Europe, and rejected outright the concept of a market economy. Elsewhere, few had such illusions about the market economy, but the division of society into the haves and the have-nots seemed destined only to get worse. Nobody could feel comfortable when BMWs cruised the streets while so many could scarcely afford even to feed and clothe themselves.

Negative views

These divisions helped to create largely negative international media and diplomatic perceptions of the changes taking place. On the one hand, the journalist's *vox pop* – that basic tool of the reporter's trade, as s/he seeks to take the national temperature – provided an almost unanimously bleak impression. Talk to the 'voice of the people' – taxi driver, factory worker, housewife, whoever – and one heard only complaints about the prices, about rising unemployment and about the new uncertainties of life.

Equally, the international media were themselves much influenced by the tone of the newly free domestic press which – quite rightly, in many respects – constantly criticized the changes that were taking place. In any free country, journalists do not like to be seen as doing the government's work for them. Thus, the new agenda consisted, above all, of long catalogues of what was going wrong, and of the very real hardships that were being suffered: soup kitchens, redundancies, corruption, political chaos.

It was all true. But it was not the whole truth. The stripping away of the Communist status quo was – and is – a painful business. At the same time, however, the positive changes that were taking place were enormous. For the first time in decades, green-for-dollars was not the only colour that mattered. Until 1989, in much of Eastern Europe, no important transaction was calculated in the local currency; the dollar ruled. Now, gradually, the currencies edged their way toward economic health, and dollar-shops became irrelevant (those that stayed open accepted local currencies). By 1993, despite the continuing pain, even the statistics (always the last to catch up, in the twilight economic zone) reflected the fact that a turnaround of a kind had begun.

PROBLEMS OF TODAY

And what is left over? Where do the main problems lie? Above all, perhaps, with a denial of responsibility. In Communist Eastern Europe, few people ever showed interest in their jobs. A popular aphorism declared: 'They pretend to pay us – and we pretend to work.' It was accurate. The useless currency was matched only by the uselessness of people's work. Nobody was required to care about the quality of what they were doing. Many might argue that those in the west are too obsessed with the workplace. None the less, Eastern Europe reached the other extreme, where most people were mentally divorced from their jobs. Jobs came from the state – in other words, from the loathed Party. There was no reason to do more than the absolute minimum in order to pick up the pay packet at the end of the month. This mental distance is difficult to reverse.

In Communist Eastern Europe, people expected many basic decisions to be taken on their behalf. The curriculum vitae and enthusiastic letter of self-advertisement – a basic part of every graduate's experience in Western Europe – was almost unknown. At the workplace, too, it was generally considered inappropriate for an employee to use her/his head too much. Creative intelligence was for using at home, with friends, and not in the office. There was no point in wasting one's energy seeking ingenious solutions on behalf of the state. That has begun to change with startling speed. None the less, it is difficult to change the habits of a lifetime, particularly for one who has learnt from experience that the less responsibility taken the better.

The sense of Them and Us was always very strong – and has continued to be so, even after the collapse of the old regime. 'They' were an enormously powerful element in the way that Communist societies existed. This sense of alienation continued, even after 'they' were gone. Disillusion with the politicians – *Politikverdrossenheit*, to use a well-worn German phrase – is common in many European countries today. But it has been particularly strong in Eastern Europe, where it is assumed that politicians' motives for seeking power are almost entirely venal.

MARKET ECONOMY V. WILD WEST

In Western Europe we have become accustomed to the idea of a natural balance between the needs of the market economy and the needs of the welfare state. A worker does a day's work, and is paid a day's wage, for creating a useful product. If the product is of decent quality and sells at a sensible price which people can afford, then the company will remain in business and will prosper; and if enough such companies exist and prosper, then all citizens together will pay enough taxes in order that the state can afford to look after the old people, and to build decent schools, hospitals, and roads.

Few of us often consciously think through the cycle. But each of us accepts our place within a working economy, where all the cogs run together: whether helping to manufacture a product, or when buying or selling; when seeking or offering advice in the bank; when serving or being served in a restaurant. Everybody expects both to provide and to receive a decent service. We may frequently be disappointed, but there is an overall framework which we expect to slot into and without which there is a collective assumption that nothing can work. Nobody would expect a restaurant offering Communist-quality service or a factory making Communist-quality goods to survive for long. Certain minimal standards have to be met.

Eastern Europeans, however, have no such overall framework to slip into. Eastern Europe has the enormously difficult task of building up the market economy at a time when large parts of the infrastructure do not yet exist. Banking, insurance and many other essential parts of a market economy are still primitive, except in the former East Germany, which is an obvious economic case apart. Capitalism is now found in its most naked form. Greed is the most obvious (though by no means the only) motor of change. Understandably, this is yet another source of resentment. And yet it can well be argued that there is no other way. Only gradually can the checks and balances of a more sophisticated market economy be created. Only gradually, too, can the democratic state, fed by the taxes of its wealth-producing citizens, satisfactorily fill in the gaps.

LAYING THE FOUNDATIONS

Many insist that much of the new entrepreneurial money is 'dirty money': Communist-dirty, mafia-dirty, or both. In the first two years especially, that was no doubt true. Gradually, however, a more solid entrepreneurial class has begun to be created. The first immediate effect of economic reform was an explosion of prices – and an explosion of goods on the shelves. Those first months saw an abundance of trestle tables set up in squares and on pavements throughout the country. People sold goods often literally off the back of a lorry, especially lorry loads brought in from the nearest western city.

At first, the goods on sale from these improvised stalls were mostly products which you would be less likely to find inside, in the state shops: exotic fruit juices, or all sorts of tinned delights. Gradually, however, a pattern more familiar to the western customer emerged. The product range inside and outside was similar: but the stalls outside, with fewer overheads, charged a little less and were therefore popular. In the Communist era, the shops had been empty – and the prices were low. The markets were expensive – and relatively well supplied.

Now, the balance changed. Queues formed, not for unavailable items, as in the old days, but for the places offering basics like flour and butter at lower prices. Then, the trestle tables gradually gave way to more permanent wooden stalls. Then – two years or more after the changes had begun – new shops began to open up, and the stalls turned into recognizable corner shops, in the western sense. And, finally – the most important stage of all – those shops began selling not just imported western products, but home-manufactured goods, too, from newly created or newly revamped or privatized factories. The fly-by-night businessmen have gradually begun to be replaced by those who see their future in a longer-term commitment to customer satisfaction. Quality of service and of products has improved, often dramatically.

Understandably, the resentment of the new insecurity has continued to be strong – as reflected by the resurgence of Communist factions in Poland and Russia. In western terms, earnings are tiny. In many respects, the Communist East has turned into an economic version of the Wild West. People don't pay taxes; violent crime is sharply up; there is a sense of 'anything goes'. And yet, in most parts of Eastern Europe the important foundations of a market economy have already been laid. Gradually and steadily, earnings when calculated in hard currency have begun to rise.

Can't pay, won't pay

Many Eastern Europeans are still used to the fairyland economics of the past. People complain endlessly about high tax rates (still lower than those in the west). But it is notable that, despite all the complaining, mass protests never quite ignite. The scattered strikes and demonstrations, accompanied by countless government crises, seem to serve, first and foremost, as a release valve for tensions. Even with the Polish Communists partly back in power, a return to the past seems unthinkable, and the achievements are considerable. (Much more worrying for future stability and democracy may be not the pro-European Community reform leftists, as in Poland, but the scarcely reformed nationalists, like Vladimir Meciar in Slovakia, or Leonid Kravchuk in the Ukraine.)

A comparison with postwar Germany may help to make the point of how remarkable are the changes that have already been achieved. Underneath the rubble, postwar Germany had a working economy: it had the skills, the knowledge, the experience. With the Marshall Plan, it also received massive help to get back on its feet. And yet, we still – quite rightly – regard as an economic miracle the fact that, ten years after the war, Germany had once more achieved a kind of affluence. Eastern Europe has not had these advantages. Despite the folk memory of a working economy, people had no real experience of what a market economy might mean. The economic ruins of Communism were much worse than the ruins left by bombing raids.

By the end of the 1980s, it was possible to predict, with some confidence, that Communism was about to see its last bow (most western politicians failed to notice what was on the way, but that was only because they had become obsessed with idea of permanence for the status quo) (Crawshaw 1989a, 1989b). Nevertheless, even the most Utopian optimist would have gulped before predicting how much of a working economy would develop within just a few years – even in neglected and confused corners like Romania.

Foreigners in, foreigners out

Despite the rapidity of change, the west has sometimes been reluctant to pay much more than lip service towards the mammoth task of building an economy from scratch.

Attitudes towards foreign help are ambiguous. Russia is the only country in the former Communist bloc where simple xenophobia is widespread, and where foreign involvement is regarded by many people as mere 'anti-Russian' meddling. In much of east Central Europe, there has always been a desire to be seen as part of 'the west'. Thus, any western involvement today is generally seen as positive. But there is ambivalence, too. Partly, this is a reaction to perceived patronizing attitudes. It is irritating for Eastern Europeans to be treated as if they had not previously come across the fridge or the television. It is frustrating, too, for Eastern European professionals (on average, far better read than their Western European counterparts) to have westerners treat them as though they know nothing about (for example) modern cinema, foreign literature or fashion. In general, there is massive asymmetry: Eastern Europeans have always known far more about Western European culture and society than vice versa.

A further cause for ambivalence is caused by a genuine sense of being swamped by foreign capital. Foreigners arriving to buy up every corner of the country are bound to be treated with caution. There is an insoluble problem here: foreigners are the only ones who have the money to invest, and therefore to help a rebirth of the economy; and yet, understandably, many Eastern Europeans fear becoming a Third World-style client economy. It is easier to lose one's economic nationalism when one's country is rich enough to buy as well as to be bought. But the time has not yet come when Zloty- or Forint-wielding industrialists can take a stake in factories in Sheffield or Stuttgart. The flow, for the moment at least, is all one way. Amongst Eastern Europeans there is a widespread assumption that their country will be treated by foreign investors as a kind of milch cow.

In Europe, out of Europe

An enormous long-term problem is the continuing sense of uncertainty for Eastern Europe. The process of European unity is generally seen by the west in terms of its spin-off for Western European policies and economies. But the spin-off for Eastern Europe is equally great. A confidently united Europe looked set to draw the east in, both directly and indirectly, in the longer term. This was not just a matter of membership of the European Community, but also because the EC seemed set to provide a kind of sheet-anchor in the post-Communist storms. The opening up of Western European markets, on the one hand, and training and education, on the other, can be seen as elements necessary to demonstrate Western European commitment. If the process of European unity begins to backslide, however, then the member countries of the European Community are likely to become more inward-looking, and will have even less time for the political and economic concerns of the east than they do today. There is little doubt that this could create considerable instability in the longer term.

Meanwhile, whilst the economies of all the Central and Eastern European countries edge forward towards a kind of stability, enormous changes are still needed. The politics are still shaky, especially in parts of the region: the collapse of the Russian federation could still have incalculable consequences, and Russia–Ukraine tensions could easily explode; growing tensions between Slovakia and Hungary could flare up violently. But such explosions are by no means inevitable, especially if the economies improve. In the meantime, the roots have already been put down and there is no obvious reason why the economic plant should not continue to grow.

REFERENCES

Boyes, R. (1990) *The Hard Road to Market*, Secker & Warburg.
Crawshaw, S. (1989a) 'East Europe: region where goalposts are on the move', *Independent* (26 January).
Crawshaw, S. (1989b) 'Crumbling of an empire', *Independent* (11 April).
Crawshaw, S. (1992) *Goodbye to the USSR*, Bloomsbury.

Chapter 11

On 'resistance to change' in the post-command economies and elsewhere

Devi Jankowicz

INTRODUCTION

Bringing about change in the post-command economies is often viewed as involving the reversal of fifty years of state socialism. The development of a market economy is seen as the introduction of business practices through appropriate structural changes at the level of the economy and the individual enterprise, supported by appropriate training of the people involved.

This is an oversimplified view. Even an initial familiarization with the culture and history of the countries concerned will indicate that the scope for change involves 500 years of local culture rather than fifty years of Communist economies. The depth of change involved in training must address the level of attitudes and values, much more than the level of knowledge and skills, if the behaviour which gives rise to new business practices is to change.

Values are resistant to change, and for very good reasons. By examining the learning situation in which the training and development of Eastern European managers takes place, using a conceptual framework taken from the personal construct psychology of George Kelly, I wish to suggest that even the most trivial knowledge-based informational changes, on which behavioural change depends, are value-laden. The more problematic changes of attitudes which our challenge to Eastern European values involves are even more value-laden. In doing so, I am challenging some of the western assumptions involved in the concept of 'resistance to change'.

TWO METAPHORS FOR THE TRANSFER OF WESTERN EXPERTISE: 'SALES' VERSUS 'NEW-PRODUCT DEVELOPMENT'

Some six years ago, when the political changes in central and eastern Europe symbolized by the dismantling of the Berlin Wall occurred, substantial funding became available to western management developers from such sources as the EU TEMPUS programme and the British Council/ Foreign and Commonwealth Office (FCO) 'Know-How' Fund. A great variety of projects designed to prepare eastern managers and academics for operations within a market economy commenced. An increasing number of accounts in the literature testify to the scale and variety of effort involved. For example, a review of the journals covered by the ANBAR and DIALOG databases shows that the number of publications relating to issues of culture and cultural change in these regions stood at 36,991 in 1995, and that publications relating to just one topic of interest, the consequences for management and organizational development, have increased from a total of 182 items in the years prior to 1991, to 81 items in 1991 alone, to an annual average of 265 in the years 1992–4 inclusive. While some of this literature records substantial achievements (see, e.g., Hibbert 1990; Auerbach and Stone 1991; Holden and Cooper 1994), much of the work has been based on what Kwiatkowski and Sanders (1993) have called the 'turnkey approach'.

The assumption has been made that, while cultural differences between western providers and Eastern European clients exist, they can be handled as a matter of accurate linguistic translation and that fundamental differences of thinking and conceptualization are not involved. If one models the transfer of western expertise on a simple 'technology transfer' model (as, for example, in the case of the UK 'Know-How Fund' initiative), one is likely to construe the task in terms like 'knowledge transfer'. One sees the task as a process akin to scientific, technical or engineering transactions, and adopts an oversimplified definition of 'knowledge' restricted to the purely conceptual and propositional. The conveyance of ideas, practices and techniques is identified with instruction in subject matter, and only the adequacy of one's translation from a western language into the Central/ Eastern European (C/E European) language is in question. The metaphor is one of 'export sales', where one prepares and works with a technical sales brochure. By and large, the physical, engineering and quality principles are assumed to be universally understood across cultural boundaries. So long as a good technical translator can be found to transcribe the brochure, parts list and price list into the client language in question everything will be satisfactory. Having made the sale, stuck local-language labels on the controls and delivered the machinery, one provides a quick training course, a manual and perhaps a maintenance contract, before turning the key to switch it all on. This is the mark of a 'knowledge-package' delivery service.

However, the transfer of management expertise is more complex than this. I wonder about the usefulness of a 'technology transfer' model, since management 'knowledge' is not simply a matter of knowledge but also of skills and attitudes. The material involved is affective, experiential and value-laden as much as it is conceptual and propositional. Far from being dependent on universal scientific and technical principles that allow one to 'sell from a well-translated brochure', one is involved in a creative activity in which the metaphor is more of 'new-product development' than of 'sales'. When one teaches management subject matter one is engaged in changing behaviour. More than conveying bodies of knowledge, one is creating new understanding to guide behaviour. This involves the creation of mutual meaning through negotiation over concepts, values, attitudes and practices as they apply to the person (the manager) being trained and developed.

The mutual creation of meaning through which behaviour might change involves a confrontation with social norms and personal values which draw on centuries of culture and history as much as on a fifty-year interlude of a command economy based on, variously, socialist or Marxist principles. Kwiatkowski and Sanders (1993) are among a relatively small number of authors who have attempted to grapple with the variables involved in the provision of management development assistance, with particularly valuable contributions on cultural factors coming from Jaeger (1986); Johnson (1991); and Vlachoutsicos and Lawrence (1990); how such variables might impact on particular training events has been addressed by Lynch (1992); Millman and Randlesome (1993); and Yanotlzas and Boukis (1993).

KNOWLEDGE TRANSFER OR MEANING-CREATION?

Even such an apparently straightforward endeavour as simple knowledge-based instruction in western managerial procedures and techniques bereft of attitudinal and skills components (e.g., exposition of accounting conventions; International Standards Organization (ISO) and British Standards Institute (BSI) quality standards; banking and trading procedures and conventions) has its difficulties. Setting aside for the moment the fact that differing expectations of how knowledge is taught and put into practice exist (e.g. Jankowicz and Pettitt 1993; Lee 1995; Yanotlzas and Boukis 1993), and the more serious difficulty of differences in the pre-existing knowledge base (see, e.g., Otta 1994), the fundamental difficulty for the straightforward 'sales-brochure' metaphor lies in the lack of common linguistic terms for the transactions involved. The slightest consideration of the problems involved in translating market-economic practices and procedures reveals an immediate difficulty of vocabulary. For example, there are no indigenous words in the Slavonic languages for such basic terms as 'management', 'marketing' or 'learning' which convey sufficient associations for the western concepts to be transferable in full. Terms such as 'management' are understood to mean, simply, 'governance', bereft of such English-language associations as 'coping' or 'developing'. The word 'marketing' conveys associations related to the tactical and operational activities of bargaining and selling, and does not evoke the wealth of English-language associations relating to marketing as a strategic orientation within the organization (Jankowicz 1994a).

The obvious way to handle such differences is to view language as a communication system, and to worry about the adequacy of translations. But in no system of equals does meaning pass uni-directionally between two participants (Jankowicz 1995). Because knowledge is being transferred about the market economy by a 'western' expert to a partner located and experienced in a command or indicative economy, the latter is placed in a client relationship. The focus of attention shifts from the bi-directionality implicit in communication between two parties to the unidirectionality implicit in an expert–client relationship. Western terms have to be adopted (as is happening in spoken and written Polish for example, the words *markéting* and *menedżer* are increasingly used as literals) since the indigenous ones do not carry the conceptual weight associated with their use in a market economy. However, this does not guarantee that the associations which these terms carry in the west are thereby automatically evoked in the minds of their eastern users. One encounters frequent reports of confusion and misunderstanding unless two interpreters are used: one to carry out the translation and the other to monitor and feed back the extent to which the intended meaning has been conveyed (McNeill 1991).

Noticeably, the discourse of the latter interpreter is at a meta-level with respect to the discourse of the former. The latter talks about the reasons why the direct translation is successful or unsuccessful, and this level of interpretation demands both a detailed subject-based knowledge of the material to be translated from both a western and a C/E European conceptual perspective and knowledge of the objectives of the provider. This role has been characterized as one of 'cultural catalyst' by Lee (1995: 217), who suggests that someone of a bicultural background would be particularly adept at understanding both perspectives. In short, adequate linguistic translation is impossible without the pre-existence, at some superordinate level, of a precise conceptual mapping between differing representations of the same event or phenomenon in the two separate cultures. Where this does not exist, 'translation' may succeed in a dictionary sense but will fail at the level of the mutual meaning and understanding.

Perhaps a more useful way of viewing the difficulty is, rather, to view language as a symbol system used for encoding and modelling phenomena. This immediately directs one's attention to the structural and functional issues of representation and to the constraints on what it is possible to represent. This includes such issues as grammar and orthography (the limitations and constraints present within the symbol system and its articulation); idiom (the habitual way of expressing meaning preferred within a culture an issue relating to the social norms of the culture concerned); and metaphor (the associations which users find most useful in representing particular phenomena as perceived within a culture a matter, frequently, of shared personal values). Each of these influences the completeness with which representations of a particular phenomenon can be constructed in a particular culture.

For example, as regards orthography, one notices that the English manager or the external consultant addresses colleagues, customers, subordinates and clients with the same personal pronoun, 'you'; the French manager or consultant will use '*tu*' with intimates and '*vous*' when being more formal, but without any direct correlation with the authority relationship involved in dealing with a subordinate as opposed to a client. The Polish manager, while punctilious in the use of informal forms with intimates and colleagues and formal forms with clients and superiors, will usually use the informal form (second-person singular) with subordinates while expecting the subordinate to respond in the formal (third-person singular) to underline the power differential.

Idioms are, by definition, quite arbitrary and must be learnt case by case if one is to be effective in a different language to one's own. An American subordinate would be delighted to receive 'a fat cigar' from her/his manager but a German subordinate would be mortified on receiving '*eine dicke Zigarre*' (a reprimand). Guthrie (1991), who draws on the ideas of S.K. Langer, proposes the concept of 'presentational symbolism', to attend to the non-linguistic representation of events through the expression of feeling, emotion, ritual, myth and all the non-verbal, behavioural ways of communication particular to a given culture. Cultural difference can then be analysed in terms of the grammar, orthography, idiom and metaphor of behaviour, as well as in terms of language. One can explore the extent to which different cultures mould the expression of meaning differently because of the different behavioural grammars, idioms and metaphors (see Jankowicz in press).

The focus of attention needs to shift from communication and translation problems to a deeper consideration of the two systems for modelling or representing phenomena which must be articulated into some form of mutual relationship if a shared understanding of the knowledge involved is to be created between two parties. This redefinition concedes equality of status to both participants, with both having equal knowledge of the phenomena which they seek to explain. The westerner has knowledge of the market economy, and the easterner of the present eastern, post-command economy within which market-economic concepts must, if relevant and after appropriate adjustments, be made to work. The language of communication must become bi-directional rather than remain uni-directional. The process of 'transfer' is redefined as collaborative verbal and behavioural negotiation over the meanings to be created about a mutually experienced event.

Bi-directionality has its problems, not the least of which is the negotiation over role relationships that it involves. How is one to adopt a participative approach in teaching, for example, in a culture which seeks authoritative ex-cathedra exposition? For example:

What right have we to preach a doctrine of equality? . . . In practice, we were saying 'in our professional opinion, effective management is inter-disciplinary and based around experience, and effective management education occurs when you work creatively within the choices open to you. As experts we tell you that you will gain more benefit from finding your own routes than listening to experts.

(Lee 1995: 221)

I have expressed the same ambivalence elsewhere:

as 'meta'-level experts in training methods, when our eastern managers express their discomfort with our approach since they prefer an *ex-cathedra* didactic style, we are absolutist in our request that they accept our relativist techniques!

(Jankowicz 1994b: 10)

And so, even in the most straightforward transfer of conceptual and technical subject matter ('knowledge' as distinct from 'skills' or 'atti-tudes'), the attitudes, values and social norms pertinent to the creation of mutual understanding are all engaged.

WHICH NORMS AND VALUES: FIFTY YEARS OF COMMAND ECONOMY OR 500 YEARS OF HISTORY?

But, as mentioned previously, management development is a matter of skills, techniques and attitudes as well as simple knowledge. One cannot bring about change in practice without considering the pre-existing cultural milieu in which the skills and attitudes are embedded and the functions which they serve. Drawing on the work of theorists such as Bourdieu (1971) and empiricists such as Hofstede (1980, 1991), a number of authors have tried to describe the environmental barriers to management develop-ment assistance.

It is possible that some of the difficulties which these authors describe stem from a particular, and relatively recent, way of doing things. For example, the command economy of the last fifty to seventy years led naturally and inevitably to the centralized, top-down, authoritarian manage-ment style described by such authors as Hibbert (1990), and Millman and Randlesome (1993) in the case of Russia, or Maczynski (1987, 1991) in the case of Poland. Faced with the recent problems of overstaffing, irregularity of supplies, insufficient spare parts, localized corruption of 'nomenklatura capitalism', and the collapse of markets and distribution (Krysakowska-Budny and Jankowicz 1991), managers in Central European countries had to develop survival skills which make our western concern for personal responsibility, empowerment of staff and participation in decision-making seem entirely misplaced.

Alternatively, and more likely, the differences in management style which make our development work so problematic and the 'turnkey approach' so dangerous might stem from considerably deeper and more enduring cultural differences. The Russian style of management stems, so it is argued by Vlachoutsicos and Lawrence (1990), from the practices of a millennium. The leader in Russian culture defined issues top-down, involved everyone, including the most menial servant, in bottom-up debate, and thereby legitimized a subsequent individual and autocratic top-down definition of objectives to achieve and procedures to follow. The Polish authoritative management style stems, it has been argued by Jankowicz (1994a), from a style of governance which seeks to control and prevent operational and corporate fragmentation. This style arose as a result of a 500-year history of political fragmentation (where the *Liberum Veto* principle of governance meant that, since 1652, all parliamentary decisions had to be taken unanimously to pass into law, with the consequences which one might expect; and where, since 1573, monarchy was elective rather than inherited, with all the instability that that implies). Polish managers do not 'manage'; in Polish, they *zarządzaja* that is, they 'rule' or 'govern'.

In other words, the difficulties in changing the attitudes of Russian managers described in terms of ethnocentricity by such authors as Millman and Randlesome (1993), and Holden and Cooper (1994), and the differences in management values among Polish managers outlined by Jankowicz and Pettitt (1993) stem from deeply rooted cultural norms and personal values. Thus the introduction of western business practices cannot proceed from simple structural changes to the command economy followed by relevant knowledge inputs, without substantial work at the level of cultural norms and personal values. Given their embedding in an enduring cultural tradition, which is, itself, different in different post-command economies, such work is very difficult. At the very least, as Child and Markoczy (1994) have pointed out, even when one recognizes the importance of the fifty years of socialist polity one cannot understand managerial behaviour in the post-command economy without also considering the 450 years of local history and culture which preceded the Marxist experiment and gave it its particular character in the particular country in question.

ASSESSING AND CHANGING VALUES

If norms and values provide the fundamental constraints on what it is possible to change and how this change might be effected, it would appear that the change agent who seeks to create situations in which new meanings can be mutually negotiated must proceed from two fundamental assumptions.

The nature of the values themselves

Firstly, s/he must discover what the culture actually is: the content of the norms and values within which s/he is seeking to bring about change. One does not change culture without knowing something of the pre-existing culture to be changed. This knowledge must be at a sufficiently detailed level for decisions about influence to be exercised. Working within single organizations, organizational development (OD) specialists such as Beckhard (1967) have offered us models in which working groups engage in problem identification and resolution, working under an umbrella of support for the group's recommendations, negotiated on its behalf by the change agent, who creates sufficient political backing within the organization that the group's recommendations are taken seriously. If one is to apply this model of change to the individual Eastern European organization, (change at the level of organizational culture), or even use it as a metaphor to guide the business of change at the wider level of societal culture, one is immediately faced with the task of discovering the values and norms which govern polity within the organization or society.

In the case of the organizational culture, one can take advantage of the strong possibility (see, e.g., Czarniawska 1986) that Eastern European organizational cultures, unlike their western counterparts, may be relatively undifferentiated, which would allow the use of a single approach to intervention in many different organizations; but one must first discover what that useful approach might be. What is the position within the organization with regard to such factors as authority, delegation and participation in decision-making; and what particular values exist which would legitimize attempts to change the way in which these factors operate? How, for example, do western notions of equity ownership translate into C/E European practices which insist on company employees owning a proportion of the shares of a newly privatized company? How might the governance of an organization differ when a significant proportion of the shareholders are people who were once members of its Worker's Council and who, under new legislation, still retain involvement in the recruitment and selection of the senior managers of the company?

In the case of the broader social norms within which enterprises must operate, whilst we may know the general kinds of factors to be taken into account from the work of such authors as Inkeles and Levinson (1969), Hofstede (1980, 1991) and Tayeb (1988), and, in the case of leadership style, from the work of Smith et al. (1989), and Smith and Peterson (1988), we are faced with the need to discover the actual values for the variables in the case of the Eastern European countries involved. Hofstede's 1991 samples did not include the Eastern European economies, and the data which do exist on such variables as Power Distance, Individualism, Control and Masculinity–Femininity are based on the subjective judgements of researchers familiar with the societies in question, rather than on empirical studies (see Chapter 22 in this volume). Alternatively, we may have to rely on inferences made from more descriptive accounts such as those in the Butterworth-Heinemann Cultural Guides series, or the work of such authors as Randlesome *et al.* (1993), for Western European countries, or Moran and Johnson (1992), for all of Europe, Western and Eastern. Moreover, such empirical findings may not be simple to obtain. In the case of Poland, for example, one distinguished commentator, Mikulowski-Pomorski, has stated that, when asked where management in an unstable society should be headed, the eastern manager is likely to answer that s/he no longer knows!

Fragmentation, change and confusion in the economy, incomplete and inconstant legislative and administrative frameworks, fuzzy distinctions between legality and illegality, socio-political confusion and the lack of any predictable basis for personal responsibility are all involved in the anomic situation that has been called the 'Polish Reality' by Polish managers themselves. Writing of the consequences of the Polish political changes of the 1980s, Mikulowski-Pomorski offered the metaphor of the ship of state, which, freed from its moorings, was awaiting bearings so that a course could be set in the postmodernist world (Mikulowski-Pomorski 1991). Returning to the metaphor in 1993, he stated that 'the ship is now further from the shore but, instead of moving forward with a purpose, it is drifting aimlessly. Drifting is movement where a body is not subject to its own forces but responds to currents and other external influences. It involves an absence of spontaneous activity' (Mikulowski-Pomorski 1993: 287). Reviewing the various Polish social values since 1918, and pointing out that the implementation of any one value has required the suspension of previously held values, but that the whole set remains in the repertoire of national aspirations, he asserted that the current programme for values, that of a 'return to the standards of European civilization', is vague, and subject to definition by foreign states and interstate agencies (one thinks of eastern aspirations to a better economic existence in the teeth of western economic protectionism, of the defensive postponements to entry into the European Union, and the like): 'The post-communist countries have, as it were, lost their ability to create authentic values. This can be interpreted as another way of saying that they have suspended their national integrity' (Mikulowski-Pomorski 1993: 293). It may be that this situation cannot persist, as he says, and that the European myth may fragment in a clash between east and west over the values they seek to espouse (we in the west came close to fragmentation in the 1993 debate over the implementation of the Maastricht Treaty, and the issue still rumbles unresolved. At the time of writing, the Polish electorate has chosen a Communist president to steer the ship of state, a ship which has been powered since 1992 by a Communist parliamentary majority). It seems clear, therefore, that eastern managers cannot currently look to Eastern Europe for their definitions, and must look to themselves in order to operate, survive and resource the mission statements which we exhort them to write.

The depth of change which is required and is possible

Having ascertained, where possible, the particular values which are likely to constrain any change interventions being contemplated, the second issue arises: the depth of change which is likely to be necessary for lasting behavioural changes to be possible. Harrison (1970) has offered as a principle to OD practitioners that they seek to change the individual to the minimum level concordant with her/his professional effectiveness. Kelman provides us with a simple metric in his classification of depth of change into Compliance (behavioural conformity motivated by simple reinforcement), Identification (conformity of affect as well as of behaviour based on identification with a role model) and Internalization (in which the norms and values of the change agent have been fully internalized) (Kelman 1958, 1970).

It is arguable that the depth of change required in order to grapple with cultural differences at the level of national culture and values cannot be achieved, no matter how sophisticated one's training and OD techniques. The carefully judged, culturally specific training approach of change agents, such as Holden and Cooper (1994), who approach the Russian management student's expectations of very authoritarian, almost autocratic teaching styles by telling course participants, unmistakably and in writing, which beliefs and values they have got to subscribe to as a condition of effective learning would be foreign to a western management audience, but is specifically geared to a Russian one. Yet this strategy is, as I have argued elsewhere (Jankowicz 1994c), most probably limited to the level of Identification by its dependence on powerful western role models, whose presence is transitory during the duration of their course, as a source of reward. See Cooper (1982) for a rationale of the mechanism involved. This strategy is unlikely to achieve the level of Internalization at which enduring changes in personal values and social norms occur.

RESISTANCE TO CHANGE

In our western, mainly intra-organizational change activities, we are accustomed to tackle this class of problem by means of the concept of resistance to change. Any basic text aimed at undergraduates or practising managers (take, for example, Hellriegel et al., 1995: 662) lists such personal factors as 'Perceptions, Personality, Habits, Threats to Power and Influence, Fear of the Unknown, Economic Reasons' and organizational factors such as 'Organisational Design, Organisational Culture, Resource Limitations,

Fixed Investments, and Inter-organisational Agreements' as sources of resistance to change. At one level, these factors are clearly important in understanding the variables and issues which must be understood if change interventions are to be appropriately designed. They clearly form an important part of any organizational diagnosis which a putative change agent would wish to conduct.

At another level however, an examination of the way in which these factors are seen to operate suggests that they are deeply value-laden. In labelling them 'barriers to change', we indicate that we view them in some sense or other as illegitimate. In generally evaluating them negatively, we indicate that their existence is seen as an instance of irrationality and the motives underlying them are disparaged. Hellriegel *et al.* cite 'the perceptual error called perceptual defence' (Hellriegel *et al.* 1995: 662); in talking about 'Personality' (and quite rightly cautioning the reader against overemphasizing the importance of this factor) they nevertheless cite such traits as 'dogmatism . . . dependency . . . low self-esteem' (Hellriegel *et al.*, 1995: 663).

Clearly, when removed from its original laboratory context perceptual defence is a mechanism whose status and legitimacy depend on the perspective and intentions of people other than the perceiver, and the motives and intentions of those others are quite as important as the assumed motivational state of the perceiver. To speak of 'error' is an absurd oversimplification. Even within its strict usage in laboratory studies of the perceptual mechanism, the phenomena of defence are as likely to reflect the structure of a particular perceptual model or schema rather than some necessarily dysfunctional and emotionally laden defensive process (not to mention the studies which point to lowered, and hence more sensitive, perceptual thresholds on presentation of certain kinds of affect-laden stimuli rather than to raised, dysfunctional thresholds).

Similarly, one can object to the negative connotations of the 'Personality' traits involved. A trait is a bipolar attribute (personality theorists are really speaking of 'liberalism–dogmatism' rather than 'dogmatism', and of 'self-sufficiency–dependency' rather than 'dependency'). The importance of 'resistance to change' as a variable in accounting for an individual's reactions to change is trivialized if only the negatively evaluated pole is cited. Where is the empirical evidence that responses to change do indeed proceed from a position at the negative extreme of the distribution involved?

Indeed, one can make similar points about all but the last three factors usually cited as examples of 'resistance to change', and equally one can posit neutral terms which do not prejudge the position of the person facing-change, as I have done in Table 11.1.

In contrast, the 'resistance to change' literature construes 'change', the work of the change agent and the efforts which organizations make to develop their staff in the face of changes in the environment of the

Table 11.1 The terminology of 'resistance to change'

Factor	Biased examples	Neutral variables
Perceptions	the perceptual error called perceptual defence	cognitive mechanisms
Personality	dogmatism; dependency; low self-esteem	liberalism v. dogmatism; self-sufficiency v. dependency; low self-esteem v. high self-esteem
Habit	coping, comfort, security	coping skills; level of predictability,
Threats to power and influence	disempowerment, loss of control	level of authority incommensurate/commensurate with level of responsibility; degree of autonomy
Fear of the unknown	anxiety, insecurity, fear	caring, predictability, anticipated challenges to basic values
Economic reasons	threat to economic security	feelings of justice and equity
Organizational design	rigidity, hierarchy of authority	organizational structure
Organizational culture	lack of flexibility, rigid socialization	functionality of existing norms
Resource limitations	lack of time capital, or skills	–
Fixed investments	fixed assets, unmotivated or entrenched senior employees	–
Inter-organizational agreements	contractual obligations	–

organization as unproblematic: *necessarily* positive, justified and legitimate. Moreover, the distinction between environmental change and the changes introduced by the change agent when making her/his interventions are rarely clearly presented in discussions of this kind. There may be a legitimate and necessary need for people to change in the face of environmental change (such as competition, market shifts, customer base and the like), while the particular intervention used may be misguided, technically inefficient or problematic in its motivation, intentions or ethical base. To label the response to the intervention 'resistance to change' may conflate a legitimate response to an inept or unwarranted intervention.

We enter very deep waters indeed when this language of organizational 'resistance to change' is transferred to the discussion of change interventions at the level of societal or national (as opposed to organizational) culture, as it has been in discussions of reactions to the western knowledge transfer initiative. The position of the western change agent is seen as legitimate and the reactions of her/his clients as lacking legitimacy, quite independently of the functional nature of their response to the change interventions. As Kostera (1994, 1995a) has pointed out in her analysis of the media image of western-style management in Poland (see also Kostera 1995b), responses to environmental change which may be very functional in the Polish business culture are seen as illegitimate simply because they are traditional, reflecting enduring preferences and values – in a word, old-fashioned. This is quite independent of their success or otherwise, since they are assessed against a crude, journalistic stereotype of a preferred 'modern and fashionable', western-styled orientation to environmental change. Or, in the words of Bourdieu:

> Misunderstandings, borrowings removed from their context and reinterpreted, admiring initiation and disdainful aloofness – these are all signs familiar to specialists on the situations that arise when cultures meet – any action for the handing on of a culture necessarily implies an affirmation of the value of the culture imparted (and, correlatively, an implicit or explicit depreciation of other possible cultures).
>
> (Bourdieu 1971: 198)

A PERSONAL-CONSTRUCTIVIST APPROACH TO THE PROBLEM OF CHANGE

The idea that a concept like 'resistance to change' depends on one's viewpoint, and that the C/E European 'knowledge transfer' endeavour of the last few years has drawn on a model of the transfer process which predisposes one to understand knowledge transfer as a uni-directional activity in which the recipient is necessarily at a practical and moral disadvantage (in view of the importance of expert and legitimate power differentials; French and Raven 1959), suggests a desperate need for a neutral analytic system and language. This is not because of any belief one might have in a dispassionate, positivist epistemology as a basis for analysis and explanation (one's own culture and values will always inform one's stance), but rather because our present model of 'knowledge transfer' and 'resistance to change' are, as I have tried to argue, predicated on bias. At the very least, an approach which is open to argument and understanding from a C/E European perspective is needed.

Personal Construct Psychology (PCP) (Kelly 1955, 1991; see also Bannister and Fransella 1985 for a scholarly account; or the more populist Burr and Butt 1992) offers a descriptive and analytic system in which the content of an individual's personal understanding can be described by means of the constructs s/he typically uses to give personal meaning to events. The individual's constructs are seen as a system used to model and predict future events based on the experiences of the past, the whole being subject to revision in the light of personal experience in the ongoing present. The individual is said to engage in 'sociality' when s/he deliberately sets out to view the world through the constructs of another person whom s/he is trying to understand. 'Sociality' provides us with a terminology to describe cross-cultural activities such as the 'knowledge transfer' process and, significantly, gives us no privileged position as observers of this process. As researcher, I am simply another person trying to understand others. It is this reflexive property of PCP which provides us, pre-eminently, with the constructivist rather than positivist epistemology which we need in order to model 'knowledge transfer' and 'resistance to change' while remaining open to the possibility of bias on every side. Neither the Western nor the Eastern European is in a privileged position with respect to the other. Equally, we have no privileged position as observers of the process – it behoves us to be careful in choosing our moral viewpoint.

Returning to the Kellian analysis, the 'world out there' and the world of the observer are equally real. The world is to be understood through neither a realist nor an idealist metaphysics, but through the process in which the two worlds are mapped on to each other by an individual – one who is trying to make ever more accurate predictions about the outcomes of actions based on the mapping s/he creates. Neither the western 'provider' nor the C/E European manager has necessarily a better understanding of the knowledge, skills and attitudes which are likely to be effective in managing the C/E European enterprise. Both must cooperate to create a 'joint mapping' within which they can subsequently collaborate in transferring knowledge. In the management education process, this is an argument for simulations, role plays, live cases and in-company projects based on C/E European definitions of the management environment and its problems, rather than western ones. The development of localized case material (even for the demonstration of purely western, command-economy practices and techniques) is essential if the wisdoms, and limitations, of those practices are to be demonstrated.

Secondly, the mechanism of sociality, as defined within PCP, requires both westerner and C/E manager to make deliberate efforts to view the enterprise and its environment through one another's constructs, as well as their own, if they are to collaborate successfully.

The success of this endeavour is defined quite explicitly in Kelly's construct theory. The effectiveness of the individual's construct system as a map of her/his world is judged, not in absolute terms (realism, idealism and all of their variants are eschewed), but relativistically (in terms of its success in achieving the individual's operational, personal and ontological objectives as these are defined by the individual concerned). Provided that one understands the individual's objectives as s/he defines them, one is free to disagree with an individual's self-assessment, and thus solipsism (a problem for some individual-constructivist theories) is avoided. Kelly's concept of 'constructive alternativism' asserts that there are always alternative mappings possible, depending on the personal objectives involved. When two persons collaborate in creating a joint understanding, their essays in sociality require them to clarify their objectives to each other on three levels (operational, personal and ontological) prior to negotiating which conjoint set of objectives makes sense to them both.

There would appear to be little difficulty about their operational objectives: the models of teacher and learner, consultant and client, buyer and seller, and joint venture partnerships all include a phase of mutual goal-setting about the collaborative tasks being addressed. Similarly, the social sensitivity of the actors and the usual social processes involved in each of these forms of relationship provide a natural dynamic for gaining a greater acquaintance with each other's personal preferences and make for greater effectiveness. Where Kelly's concept of sociality is particularly useful, however, is in its emphasis on the ontological: unless we know something of the personal and cultural values which underlie an individual's goals, and unless we exchange information about those goals, we cannot even begin to devise a criterion by which the success of the collaborative venture can be judged.

PCP offers a convenient and powerful technique, the Repertory Grid, for identifying the constructs which a person uses (see Fransella and Bannister 1977 for rationale and details; Stewart and Stewart 1982 for a comprehensive manual aimed at management and business practitioners; and Jankowicz 1990 for a survey of the applications in personnel, human resource management, management training and development). Constructs, the basic bipolar expressions which make up the individual's construct system, can be readily identified, and the values which underlie those constructs specified (see Figures 11.1–11.4 for examples). The extent to which any two individuals' construct systems about a common topic overlap, permitting meaning to be shared, can be described in a variety of ways. The most convenient is the SOCIOGRIDS algorithm described in Shaw (1980) and operationalized in the REPGRID microcomputer package, one of several commonly available (see Sewell et al., 1992 for a review). Exchange grid exercises, in which two people explicitly talk about an issue of common interest using the other's constructs, are easily devised (see, for example, Jankowicz and Cooper 1982; Thomas and Harri-Augstein 1983, 1985). The meaning which a whole group of respondents share about a topic of common concern can be identified by a method of content analysis developed by Honey (1979), with which a very high degree of reliability can be obtained.

The two Repertory Grids illustrated in Figures 11.2 and 11.3, are

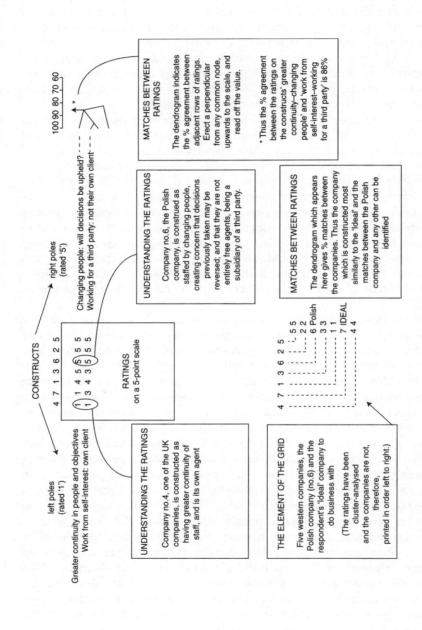

CONSTRUCTS

left poles
(rated '1')

Greater continuity in people and objectives
Work from self-interest: own client

right poles
(rated '5')

Changing people: will decisions be upheld? - - - -
Working for a third party: not their own client- - - -

100 90 80 70 60

RATINGS
on a 5-point scale

4 7 1 3 6 2 5
①1 1 4 5 ⑤ 5 5
①3 4 3 5 5 5

MATCHES BETWEEN RATINGS

The dendrogram indicates the % agreement between adjacent rows of ratings. Erect a perpendicular from any common node, upwards to the scale, and read off the value.

* Thus the % agreement between the ratings on the constructs' greater continuity–changing people' and 'work from self-interest–working for a third party' is 86%

UNDERSTANDING THE RATINGS

Company no.6, the Polish company, is construed as staffed by changing people, creating concern that decisions previously taken may be reversed; and that they are not entirely free agents, being a subsidiary of a third party.

UNDERSTANDING THE RATINGS

Company no.4, one of the UK companies, is constructed as having greater continuity of staff, and is its own agent

MATCHES BETWEEN RATINGS

The dendrogram which appears here gives % matches between the companies. Thus the company which is constructed most similarly to the 'Ideal' and the matches between the Polish company and any other can be identified

4 7 1 3 6 2 5
5 5
2 2   6 Polish
3 3
1 1   7 IDEAL
4 4

THE ELEMENT OF THE GRID

Five western companies, the Polish company (no.6) and the respondent's 'Ideal' company to do business with

(The ratings have been cluster-analysed and the companies are not, therefore, printed in order left to right.)

Figure 11.1 A key to the Repertory Grids shown as Figures 11.2 and 11.3

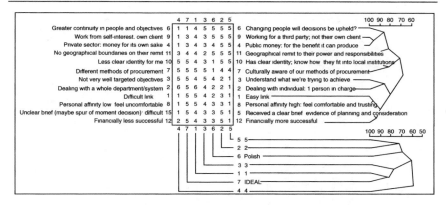

Figure 11.2 Constructs of the British companies about their Polish partners

interesting enough in themselves. One can discern important differences, as well as similarities, in the ways in which each partner construes the trading partnership with the other, in comparison to how the individual deals with partners in his own country. The status and position of a particular element in a construct system only takes on meaning by being compared with other elements. To understand the way the British partner thinks about the Polish company one must also see how he views other, western, companies since his constructs have been developed as a result of trading with western companies – and *mutatis mutandis* for the Polish partner. Clearly, one can also discern similarities in the two partners' constructs about trade.

It is more interesting to focus on Figure 11.4, which shows the values on which each partner draws. These have been derived in conformity with the Kellian idea of a construct system as comprising a hierarchy of constructs, each of the constructs (appearing in a Repertory Grid such as Figures 11.2 and 11.3) stemming from a smaller set of superordinate constructs. The technique used to derive this hierarchy of values has been described by Fransella and Bannister (1977) (see also Hinkle 1965). It proceeds by asking the individual which pole of a particular construct s/he prefers, followed by requesting the personal reason why this preference is important to the individual concerned. The two questions are repeated iteratively until no more superordinate construct can be derived. The most superordinate constructs are known as core constructs: they determine the fundamental meanings with which a person seeks to inform his or her constructs about the world as s/he understands it.

One sees in Figure 11.4, that similar values can be identified from rather different points of departure. We discover that two managers, one British and one Polish with concerns for personal affinity and for proper organizational procedures in the partner company, respectively reflect a value which

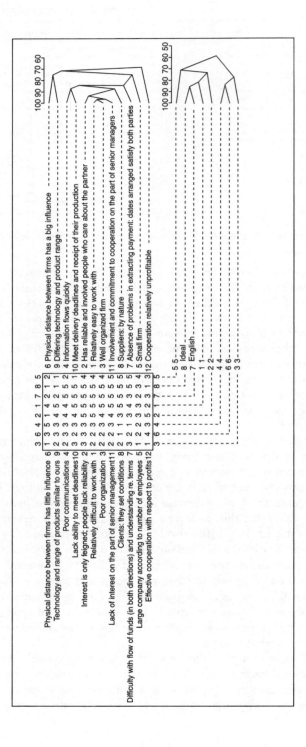

Figure 11.3 Constructs of the Polish companies about their British partners

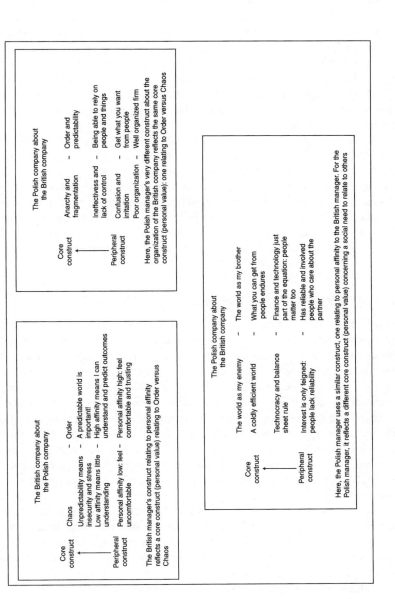

Figure 11.4 Examples of construct hierarchies identifying some of the values applied to the Polish company by the British company and vice versa

they both happen to share: a preference for order versus chaos – if they but knew it! There is also an example of the converse: the managers' basic constructs about personal affinity happen to reflect very different personal values: a value for order as opposed to chaos in the case of the British manager, but a value relating to the social need to relate to other people in the case of the Polish manager. Unless each understands these different values, and the different ways in which similar values gain expression in the peripheral constructs which guide their behaviour towards each other, their communications may founder.

The core constructs which PCP techniques identify have the nature of personal values and here is the key to my argument, personal values are resistant to change. Therapists and counsellors working with PCP never set out to change core constructs. Personal values are the bedrock on which the individual erects the edifice of her/his understanding of the world. The PCP counsellor will explore alternative peripheral constructs, encouraging the client to experiment with them in a search for new behavioural expressions of the enduring core constructs which are themselves resistant to change.

IN SUMMARY: WHY, THEN, RESIST CHANGE?

Viewed in this light, it becomes perfectly obvious why a manager in C/E Europe would resist the changes the westerners engaged in 'knowledge transfer' enjoin on that manager. Far from being a passive agent or a client of the western knowledge sales drive, s/he is a participant in a process in which a new 'knowledge product' is being developed. Knowledge is not being transferred, it is being mutually created. This process is constrained, not merely by the problems of translation from a western language into the C/E European language involved and vice versa, not only by the ortho- graphic, idiom- and metaphor- rules which govern the linguistic and presentational symbolism through which both parties model their mutual environment and their relationship within it, but also, and pre-eminently, by the values which each espouses.

Granted, it may be difficult to identify the values, particularly when confronted by the anomies which the post-command economies (the 'Polish Reality'; the Russian 'Mafia Capitalism' see, e.g., Copetas 1993) must grapple with and resolve; but the attempt must be made if our massive investment (the European Union's TEMPUS programme had a budget totalling 181.3 million ECU in 1991–4 alone) is to be fruitful.

At the level of the society in which each operates, the values involved take their provenance from 500 years of history and culture; at the level of the individual agent, they take their power from their function in providing a central direction and orientation to the most fundamental aspects of personal existence. It seems a massive trivialization to use models in cross-cultural collaboration which dismiss these fundamental historical, cultural and ontological factors as a matter of pathology, i.e. as 'resistance to change'.

The new ways of doing business which the westerner proposes may be resisted because the organization or the society still rewards the old way of doing things. For example, companies in C/E Europe had an important role as agents of welfare provision within their communities, providing the social, leisure, medical, child-rearing and retirement facilities which are provided by the state or the municipality in the west. This involvement presents a massive burden on a company which seeks to trade in open competition with western firms. Yet, until the state or the municipality can afford to take over the responsibilities involved, it is completely functional that the local manager will seek to 'resist' the implications of open competition in a market economy. Her/his values regarding personal security and social welfare are engaged.

Further, the checks and balances in our western polity that seek to constrain the extremes of social and economic Darwinism (anti-trust/ anti-cartel legislation, monopolies and mergers controls, legislation on insider dealing), and the existence of powerful industrial and social lobbies operating within and across the boundaries of nation states, do not, as has been pointed out by Auerbach and Stone (1991), exist in quite the same form in Central Europe. The behaviour which we might label 'resistance to change' and treat as irrational may be entirely wise and sensible as chaos is managed and, hopefully, mastered.

And what of ourselves in the west? If we really mean it about 'thriving on chaos' (Peters 1985) and 'mastering change' (Kanter 1984), perhaps we should consider the values involved. How do these values gain expression in action; give expression to our deepest ontological aspirations; and, most importantly, change over time?

REFERENCES

Auerbach, P. and Stone, M. (1991) 'Developing the new capitalism in eastern Europe: how the West can help', *Long Range Planning* 24(3), pp. 58–65.

Bannister, D. and Fransella, F. (1985) *Inquiring Man: Theory of Personal Constructs*, London: Croom Helm.

Beckhard, R. (1967) 'Optimising team-building efforts', *Journal of Contemporary Business* 1, pp. 23–32.

Bourdieu, P. (1971) 'Systems of education and systems of thought', in M.F.D. Young (ed.) *Knowledge and Control: New Directions for the Sociology of Education*, London: Collier Macmillan.

Burr, V. and Butt, T. (1992) *An Invitation to Personal Construct Psychology*, London: Whurr.

Child, J. and Markoczy, L. (1994) 'Host country managerial behaviour in Chinese and Hungarian joint ventures', in M. Boisot (ed.) *East–West Business Collaboration: The Challenge of Governance in Post-Socialist Enterprises*, London: Routledge.

Cooper, C.L. (1982) 'A theory of management learning: its implications for management education', in R. Freedman, C.L. Cooper and S.A. Stumpf (eds) *Management Education: Issues in Theory, Research and Practice*, Chichester: Wiley.

Copetas, A.C. (1993) *Bear-Hunting with the Politbureau*, New York: Touchstone, Simon & Schuster.

Czarniawska, B. (1986) 'The management of meaning in the Polish crisis', *Journal of Management Studies* 23(3), pp. 313–31.

Fransella, F. and Bannister, D. (1977) *A Manual of Repertory Grid Technique*, London: Academic Press.

French, J.R.P., Jnr., and Raven, B.H. (1959) 'The bases of social power', in D. Cartwright (ed.) *Studies in Social Power*, Ann Arbor, MI: University of Michigan Press.

Guthrie, A.F. (1991) 'Intuiting the process of another: symbolic, rational transformations of experience', *International Journal of Personal Construct Psychology* 4(3), pp. 273–9.

Harrison, R. (1970) 'Choosing the depth of organisational intervention', *Journal of Applied Behavioural Science* 6(2), pp. 181–202.

Hellriegel, D., Slocum, J.W.J. and Woodman, R.W. (1995) *Organisational Behaviour* (7th edn), Minneapolis: West Publishing Company.

Hibbert, N. (1990) 'Training Soviet managers: Coventry Polytechnic's pioneering courses', *Industry and Higher Education* 4(4), pp. 231–7.

Hinkle, D.N. (1965) *The Change in Personal Constructs from the Viewpoint of a Theory of Implications*, unpublished PhD dissertation, Ohio University.

Hofstede, G. (1980) *Culture's Consequences: International Differences in Work Related Values*, Beverley Hills: Sage.

Hofstede, G. (1991) *Cultures and Organisations: Software of the Mind*, London: McGraw-Hill.

Holden, N. and Cooper, C. (1994) 'Russian managers as learners and receivers of western know-how', *Management Learning* 25(4), pp. 503–22.

Honey, P. (1979) 'The repertory grid in action', *Industrial and Commercial Training* 11(11), pp. 452–9.

Inkeles, A. and Levinson, D.J. (1969) 'National character: the study of modal personality and sociocultural systems', in G. Lindsey and E. Aronson (eds) *The Handbook of Social Psychology*, Reading, MA: Addison-Wesley.

Jaeger, A.M. (1986) 'Organisation development and national culture: where's the fit?', *Academy of Management Review* 11(1), pp. 178–90.

Jankowicz, A.D. (1990) 'Applications of personal construct psychology in business practice', in G. Neimeyer and R. Neimeyer (eds) *Advances in Personal Construct Psychology*, Greenwich, CT: JAI Press.

Jankowicz, A.D. (1994a) 'The new journey to Jerusalem: mission and meaning in the managerial crusade to eastern Europe', *Organisation Studies* 15(4), pp. 479–507.

Jankowicz, A.D. (1994b) 'Parcels from abroad: the transfer of meaning to Eastern Europe', *Journal of European Business Education* 3(2), pp. 1–19.

Jankowicz, A.D. (1994c) 'Holden and Cooper's Russian managers as learners: a rejoinder', *Management Learning* 25(4), pp. 523–6.

Jankowicz, A.D. (1995) 'Knowledge transfer or meaning creation? Some issues for knowledge elicitation across cultural boundaries', paper given at the *Symposium on Cybernetics Factors for Social Economics and Management Frameworks*, 14th International Cybernetics Congress, Namur, Belgium, August.

Jankowicz, A.D. (in press) 'The stories hidden in the words which we use: a constructivist analysis of business language as a device for cultural encoding', in A. Ullmann and A. Lewis (eds) *Privatisation and Entrepreneurship: the Managerial Challenge in Central and Eastern Europe*, Binghampton, NY: Haworth Press.

Jankowicz, A.D. and Cooper, K. (1982) 'The use of focused repertory grids in counselling', *British Journal of Guidance and Counselling* 10, pp. 136–50.

Jankowicz, A.D. and Pettitt, S. (1993) 'Worlds in collusion: an analysis of an eastern European management development initiative', *Management Education and Development* 24(1), pp. 93–104.

Johnson, H. (1991) 'Cross-cultural differences: implications for management education and training', *Journal of European Industrial Training* 15(6), pp. 13–16.

Kanter, R.M. (1984) *The Change Masters: Corporate Entrepreneurs at Work*, London: George Allen & Unwin.

Kelly, G.A. (1955) *The Psychology of Personal Constructs* (1st edn), New York: Norton.

Kelly, G.A. (1991) *The Psychology of Personal Constructs* (2nd edn), London: Routledge.

Kelman, H.C. (1958) 'Compliance, identification, and internalisation: three processes of opinion change', *Journal of Conflict Resolution* 2, pp. 51–60.

Kelman, H.C. (1970) 'Processes of opinion change', in W.G. Bennis, K.D. Benne and R. Chin (eds) *The Planning of Change*, New York: Holt Rinehart.

Kostera, M. (1994) *Transfer tozsamosci w swiecie polskiego zarzadzania: krytyczna analiza kulturowa wizerunkow prasowych* [The transfer of identity in the Polish world of management: a critical cultural analysis of press images], working paper, School of Management, Warsaw University.

Kostera, M. (1995a) 'The modern crusade: the missionaries of management come to eastern Europe', *Management Learning* 26(3), pp. 330–52.

Kostera, M. (1995b) 'Differing managerial responses to change in Poland', *Organisation Studies* 16(4), pp. 673–97.

Krysakowska-Budny, E. and Jankowicz, A.D. (1991) Poland's road to capitalism, *Salisbury Review* 10(1), pp. 28–31.

Kwiatkowski, S. and Sanders, P. (1993) 'Management development assistance for Poland: a playground for Western consultants', *Journal of Management Development* 12(1), pp. 56–63.

Lee, M. (1995) 'Working with choice in Eastern Europe' *Management Learning* 26(2), 215–30.

Lynch, J.S. (1992) 'Training highly effective teams: an eastern European perspective', in D.S. Kirkbride, K. Rowland and B. Shaw (eds) *Proceedings of the Third Conference on International Personnel and Human Resources Management*, Ashridge, July.

Maczynski, J. (1987) *Efektywnosc asertywno-responsywnego kierowania ludzmi* [The effectiveness of assertive-responsive management style], Monografie 12, 43, Pracy Naukowe Instytutu Organizacji i Zarzadzania Politechniki Wroclawskiej, Wrocław, Poland.

Maczynski, J. (1991) *A Cross-cultural Comparison of Decision Participation Based on the Vroom-Yetton Model of Leadership*, monograph no. PRE 23, Institute of Management, Technical University of Wrocław, Wrocław, Poland.

McNeill, I. (1991) 'The reality of doing business in Poland', *The Intelligent Enterprise* 1(4), pp. 9–16.

Mikulowski-Pomorski, J. (1991) 'New challenge for a new Europe', in J. Hausner, B. Jessop and K. Nielsen (eds) *Markets, Politics and the Negotiated Economy: Scandinavian and Post-Socialist Perspectives*, Kraków, Poland: Academy of Economics Press.

Mikulowski-Pomorski, J. (1993) 'The drifting society', in R. Jessop, J. Hausner and K. Nielsen (eds) *Institutional Frameworks of Market Economies*, Aldershot: Avebury Press.

Millman, T. and Randlesome, C. (1993) 'Developing top Russian managers', *Management Education and Development* 24(1), pp. 83–92.

Moran, R.T. and Johnson, M. (1992) *Cultural Guide to Doing Business in Europe*, London: Butterworth-Heinemann.

Otta, W.J. (1994) 'Economic adjustment processes and policies: international applicability and transferability of national experiences', *Journal of European Business Education* 4(1), pp. 66–75.

Peters, T. (1985) *Thriving on Chaos*, London: Macmillan.

Randlesome, C., Brierley, B., Bruton, K., Gordon, C. and King, P. (1993) *Business Cultures in Europe* (2nd edn), London: Butterworth-Heinemann.

Sewell, K.W., Adams-Webber, J., Mitterer, J. and Cromwell, R.L. (1992) 'Computerised repertory grids: review of the literature', *International Journal of Personal Construct Psychology* 5(1), pp. 1–23.

Shaw, M.L.G. (1980) *On Becoming a Personal Scientist*, London: Academic Press.

Smith, P.B., Misumi, J., Tayeb, M., Peterson, M. and Bond, M. (1989) 'On the generality of leadership style measures across cultures', *Journal of Occupational Psychology* 62(2), pp. 97–109.

Smith, P.B. and Peterson, M.F. (1988) *Leadership, Organisations and Culture*, London: Sage.

Stewart, V. and Stewart, A. (1982) *Business Applications of Repertory Grid*, London: McGraw-Hill.

Tayeb, M. (1988) *Organisations and National Culture: A Comparative Analysis*, London: Sage.

Thomas, L.F. and Harri-Augstein, S. (1983) 'Learning conversations: a self-organised approach to management development', in T. Boydell (ed.) *Handbook of Management Self-Development*, Aldershot: Gower Press.

Thomas, L.F. and Harri-Augstein, S. (1985) *Self-Organised Learning*, London: Routledge & Kegan Paul.

Vlachoutsicos, C. and Lawrence, P. (1990) 'What we don't know about Soviet management', *Harvard Business Review* (November), pp. 50–63.

Yanotlzas, J.N. and Boukis, S.D. (1993) 'Transporting management training into Poland: some surprises and disappointments', *Journal of Management Development* 12(1), pp. 64–71.

Chapter 12

Management education in the transitional economies of Central and Eastern Europe

Andrzej K. Kozminski

INTRODUCTION

Since the fall of communism, management education has been consistently addressed as one of the key issues in the transition from the planned to the market economy. Countless educational initiatives have spread across Central and Eastern Europe, leading to a period of chaotic, spontaneous growth of management education programmes and institutions. In spite of all the enthusiasm shown, numerous and obvious shortcomings of management education in the post-Communist countries generated sharp criticisms from managers, government officials and management educators. The time has come to address these criticisms seriously, to reflect on past development and to identify options for the future.

The analysis presented below is an attempt to address the key issue – 'How management education was serving needs and how it can serve the needs of the economies in transition?' This analysis is based on nearly forty case studies of post-Communist enterprises (Kozminski 1993), the author's experiences in consulting and management education in Poland, surveys of management education in Central and Eastern Europe presented at the international conferences, and some opinion surveys and studies of managers and management educators (see Slay 1993 and other references throughout this chapter).

TRANSITION AS A MULTI-PHASE PROCESS

In order to make an inventory of real transition problems and to compare different countries in the region it is useful to visualize transition as a multi-phase process. A model of such a process proposed by Kozminski (1992) can be seen in Figure 12.1.

This model presents transition as a staged process and implies that the formulation of both 'premature' and 'delayed' policies causes complications and inhibits transition. For example, the first Hungarian stabilization plan (negotiated by the last Communist government with the International

Figure 12.1 Multi-phase transition model

Political	Early Marketization	Inflation Control	Institution Building	Anti-recession Policy	Growth Policy
Abolition of Communist political monopoly, resolution of conflicts, consolidation of democratic institutions	Lifting of price controls, internal convertibility of currency, lifting of private entrepreneur- ship barriers	Elimination of subsidies, reduction of budget deficit, restrictive monetary policies	Government restructuring, tax reform, banking reform, capital markets, privatization, social services reform	Modernization of infra- structure, agricultural policy, small businesses promotion, export promotion	Industrial policy of 'Asian type' (Korea, Taiwan)

Monetary Fund (IMF) and implemented in 1988) is a good demonstration of a 'premature' policy. It lacked political support because the Communists were still in power and the political phase of transition was just beginning. Similarly, the institution-building phase in Poland was far from completed by mid-1993 (banking reform, commercialization of the social services and a comprehensive privatization programme were still missing) and demonstrates a delay in transition policies.

Successful completion of one phase is dependent upon full implementation of the measures included in earlier transition phases. Privatization cannot really gain momentum without banking reform and start-up of the capital market. The capital market cannot function normally before inflation is under control. Foreign capital is not likely to come to economies hit by recession, where market institutions and a legal system that effectively protects property rights are not yet in place.

The model also implies that once one phase has been completed, the next one needs to be initiated without delay. Fixation on any one phase is due, in most cases, to only partial implementation – resulting in such policy mistakes as complete abolition of trade barriers without assessing the impact this might have upon jobs. Delays and lack of proper sequencing can easily lead to dangerous 'loops' in the transition process. Both unsuccessful inflation control (Russia 1992) and the lack of energetic and efficient anti-recession policy (Poland, Hungary 1992) can compromise political equilibrium and cause a return to the political phase.

The population of Central and Eastern European economies undergoing the transition process is highly diversified. Some countries are much more advanced than others. Some are facing the danger of temporary setbacks. Some failed to resolve political problems evident at the start of transition. The multi-phase transition model enables the identification of four categories of post-Communist countries:

1 Institutionally mature countries have completed the institution-building phase and succeeded in developing political and economic links with the West, because their business climate and infrastructure are largely compatible with western requirements. Such countries are capable of controlling inflation and are facing the problems of recession. Only Hungary and Slovenia seem to fall into this category;

2 Institution building countries are also capable of controlling inflation and were successful at 'early marketization', but have not yet completed the building of market institutions (especially within the creation and proper regulation of the financial markets). This is mainly due to political instability linked to unemployment and recession. Poland and the Czech and Slovak Republics demonstrate these characteristics;

3 Monetarily unstable countries are still in the 'early marketization' phase and are unable to control inflation and the 'corrective inflation' wave. Many former USSR republics as well as Romania seem to experience this problem, preventing them from taking further steps on the path of transition;

4 Politically unstable countries are still facing serious unresolved ethnic and political conflicts and are thus unable to complete the political phase prior to transition. These countries have to resolve all accumulated transition problems: political problem, early marketization, inflation control, institution building and recession. First of all, however, they need political stability and the firm establishment of democratic institutions. Russia is the most prominent representative of this category.

The ideal 'smooth journey' through all the phases of transition is unlikely to occur. It is certain, however, that some countries will go through transition in a more orderly way, thereby progressing more quickly and at less cost than others. The winners will be the ones who do not experiment with 'big leaps' but rely on consistent, comprehensive, well-focused and well-timed policies that are professionally implemented and adjusted to local conditions. Such pragmatic policies have to be eclectic in nature and not bounded by any specific economic theory. They are clearly contingent upon professional management both in the government and in the private sector and upon the ability of these people to cooperate harmoniously. Management education has a key role to play in providing for such cooperation.

MANAGEMENT PROBLEMS OF TRANSITION

Macro-level problems

The single most important inhibitor of the transition process is political instability resulting from an inability to resolve conflicts by the means of negotiated compromises, to cooperate and to accept common platforms. This leads to political paralysis, anarchy, violence or even genocide. Political instability is fuelled by ill-conceived and poorly implemented plans, by constantly changing official government policies, corruption, bureaucratic red tape, etc. It demonstrates the key role played by highly competent governments in the transition process and highlights the (often neglected) importance of the education, selection, training and development of a professional apolitical civil service.

In Central and Eastern Europe (even before Communism) civil servants were always perceived as political appointees and usually received training in administrative law and political economy. This tradition remains, largely because all attention has focused upon the training of private-sector managers, despite the fact that in most cases (especially in less advanced countries) the economies were not yet capable of absorbing such people. Such weakness within the civil service results in a failure to resolve key macro-level management problems (Abell 1992) and thus many post-Communist governments are not capable of managing the transition process. The following list exemplifies the managerial content of such problems and highlights their key importance:

- negotiation of long-standing agreements with the trades unions;
- formulation and implementation of industrial policies with sectoral and regional parameters, enabling gradual phasing out of the low-value-added smokestack industries and replacement by viable ones, conversion of defence industries, promotion of private entrepreneurship;
- putting in place modern infrastructure (transportation, telecommunication, energy, etc.), reducing transaction costs and attracting investment;
- coping with urgent environmental problems;
- formulation and implementation of agricultural policy;
- building banking institutions and financial markets, negotiating financial agreements with foreign banks and governments;
- selling government-owned assets to domestic and foreign investors, negotiating with multinationals and foreign trade partners;
- dismantling the Communist welfare state and partially commercializing social services, medical care, education and culture, without compromising budget equilibrium on the one hand or widening the 'civilization gap' on the other.

All these problems can be solved only by national governments and require a high degree of professional training in management skills and techniques such as negotiation, strategic management, expert systems, financial analysis, international finance, etc.

Micro-level problems

Identification of micro- (enterprise) level management problems calls for a typology of post-Communist enterprises. Five types of post-Communist enterprises (outside agriculture) were derived from an analysis of thirty-six cases of post-Communist enterprises in Poland, Hungary, Czechoslovakia and Russia (Kozminiski 1993). Each type has its own set of management problems and different types of enterprise gain key importance at different stages of transition, as can be seen in Figure 12.2.

'Dinosaurs'

These are huge and hopelessly overstaffed state-owned enterprises (SOEs) in the smokestack industries and in the military sector. Politically unstable and monetarily unstable economies are dominated by the fate of dinosaurs, which drain scarce resources, aggravate financial crisis and increase inflationary pressure. The problem is also important for institution-building economies, but it is less dramatic because new economic agents have already entered the game as result of successful early marketization.

All radical and simple solutions to the problems of big SOEs such as 'closing them all', 'instantly privatizing them' or 'giving them away' can be ruled out on the grounds of common sense and political consequence, as well as management theory and practice. Not all dinosaurs are hopeless. Some of them (especially, but not exclusively, in the military sector) have a relatively high level of technology, modern equipment and highly trained engineers and workers. Some dinosaurs can develop partnerships with market leaders. Some can be carved up and transformed into a number of smaller viable enterprises. Some have to be phased out in an orderly manner while alternative jobs are created in the region (low labour mobility has to be taken into consideration). In the case of huge industrial complexes mixtures of these measures can be developed.

Miraculous recipes simply do not exist. Restructuring of dinosaurs requires an individualized approach, meticulous programming, adequate financing and prolonged, extensive negotiations with unions and other worker's organizations (self-management), local governments, banks, clients, suppliers, etc. However, inherent weakness, instability, lack of consistent policy and lack of professionalism in post-Communist governments means that the leading role in the restructuring of the dinosaurs has to be played by their management.

Such restructuring requires market analysis and identification of viable products (in order to compete and develop in an open economy); sales projections (from which viable size and structure of the company can be determined); leading to programmed restructuring (which would indicate an orderly way of disposing of redundant human and material resources, and of acquiring new resources). These measures need to be backed by a financial package, resulting from negotiations with the banks and financial institutions and often requiring government guarantees. Access to markets, technology and financing can be also acquired through domestic and foreign business partnerships. The whole programme can be only imple-

Figure 12.2 Transition, management problems, management development

Characteristic types of countries	Transition phase	Dominating macro-economic problems	Enterprises with strongest impact	Dominating management problems	Forms of management development
Institutionally mature	Anti-recession policy	Recession	Growing 'sharks' foreign and mixed	International and domestic strategies, access to capital	MBA, Executive MBA, MSc
Institutions building	Institutions building	Institutional immaturity, recession	'Pretenders' 'dinosaurs'	Privatization and restructuring	Focused management development programmes
Monetarily unstable	Inflation control, early marketization	Inflation (repressed and open)	'Dinosaurs' 'mam & pap shops'	Restructuring, creation and development of private small businesses	In-house training + consulting, restructuring
Politically unstable	Political, early marketization	Inflation, restructuring, private business formation	'mam & pap shops'	Small privatization, legalization of the 'second economy'	MSc, entrepreneurship training

mented if it is negotiated with workers' organizations and accepted by them. New management systems need to be installed in areas such as information, selection, training and motivation of personnel, and production management in order to secure effective use of resources.

Whilst Aleksandrowicz's (1992) survey of Polish managers failed to confirm the stereotypical view that managers of the big state-owned enterprises are significantly more conservative than others, his data clearly indicate that post-Communist managers have a strong preference for an authoritarian style of management: 46 per cent of surveyed Polish managers prefer individual decision-making, 49 per cent admit some participation of close collaborators and only 5 per cent would consult workers' representatives. In Hungarian enterprises researched by Pearce (1991) traits inherited from Communist management practices still persist, such as weak performance, pressure and promotions through connections, and ambiguous responsibilities.

'Pretenders'

These are SOEs capable of turning out exportable products and maintaining domestic market but suffering from overemployment, lack of market access and marketing know-how, and inadequate technology and equipment. They are the most likely targets of the first wave of 'large privatization' (especially if based on public offerings of shares or negotiated sale of large portfolios), and are usually capable of doing relatively well during the political and early marketization phases of transition.

Pretenders are forced to revise their strategies and structures as the successful implementation of stabilization and anti-inflationary plans reduce aggregate domestic demand and expose domestic firms to foreign competition. The foundations for pretenders' adjustment and restructuring plans are laid by an analysis of market potential, identification of target markets, and the formulation of a new marketing strategy. In addition, self-analysis of the main sources of competitive advantage and the main weaknesses of the firm should enable the formulation of improvement programmes containing such elements as new production and quality management, a product development programme, inventory management, merchandise handling and service. Financing of the improvement programme should be linked to the chosen path for privatization.

'Mixed marriages'

These are joint ventures formed by SOEs or the State Treasury and foreign partners and play a more active role in 'institution building' and 'institutionally mature' economies as direct foreign investment becomes more important. Foreign capital involvement is directly influenced by the ability to initiate and implement successful anti-recession policies, in that whilst it is mainly tempted by the size and the rate of growth of the market, it also requires political and monetary stability and business-friendly environment which is (at least to some extent) compatible with western requirements.

Analysis of joint ventures with western capital participation operating in the post-Communist countries (Kozminski 1993) indicates that many of them fail because of short-term orientation, lack of serious commitment, partners' inability to spell out and communicate their objectives clearly to the other party, an unstable legal and fiscal framework, and incompetence and corruption of government administration. There are thus four management factors that determine the success or failure of such enterprises. The first of these is intercultural communication and intercultural management. This enables local and foreign managers to work together, to manage conflicts and intercultural clashes and to cope with the inevitable lack of compatibility between the foreign and local sections of the company. The second is joint strategy formulation which enables the company to cope with the post-Communist business environment. The third is the proper distribution of power within the company enabling 'local' (adjusted to local conditions) implementation of jointly decided strategy, and the fourth is the ability to finance operations and development on foreign financial markets, because of a lack of local financing.

It is evident that the first three of the four points presented above have one common denominator: the ability to attract and to develop local managerial talents. This seems to be the most important single factor conditioning the success or failure of the JVs operating in post-Communist countries once a viable common strategy is jointly decided.

'Growing sharks'

These are large, privately owned enterprises that emerge in institutionally mature and institution-building countries, and the problems they face are mainly strategic. They are often highly diversified and have to define and redefine their missions, their markets and their clients, and form adequate partnerships and alliances. First of all, they have to find sources of capital to support financial growth. The privatization process offers opportunities for acquisitions and mergers. However, post-Communist enterprises suffer from lack of capital, and restrictive monetary policies and budget deficits threaten to absorb all surplus, thereby aggravating the problems.

Kolvereid and Obloj (1992) compared Polish private entrepreneurs with those from Norway and New Zealand. They found that Polish entrepreneurs have a much stronger preference for 'bargain strategy': low price, low quality and a focus on a few products and market breadth. Such strategy favours increased sales, but does not provide for accumulated profits capable of financing future growth of production capability and upgrading of technology. Because of this, Polish entrepreneurs often fall into the trap of overextension by exceeding the maximum internally financable rate of growth (MIFROG). Such a mistake is especially deadly under conditions of extremely high interest rates and can be avoided if proper management training and advice are provided to the entrepreneurs and managers.

'Mam & pap shops'

These are small private businesses, and all the post-Communist economies share management problems related to the formation, development and morality of small businesses. It is important to remember, however, that 'mam & pap' shops play different roles at different stages of the transition process and in different types of post-Communist economies.

In politically unstable and monetarily unstable economies, small businesses make early marketization happen and create the market environment, enabling the achievement (relatively early) of the critical mass necessary for a systemic transformation from planned to market economy. Polish and Hungarian examples demonstrate that all private economic activities (even unregistered or illegal) can play such a positive role. In some cases, however, 'mafiazation' of the economy can prevent further changes because strong defensive coalitions between the state apparatus and the 'new entrepreneurs' are built and the parasitic image of private economic activity comes to dominate public opinion, as seems to be the case in Russia. In institution-building economies, legalization of the private small business and its full integration into the institutional framework of the market economy becomes a key issue. The banking system, taxation and government industrial policy promoting private entrepreneurship (in certain regions, sectors are created by certain actors) facilitate the process of integration. In institutionally mature economies, small businesses create employment and 'cushion' large manufacturers of final products against market fluctuations by a 'ring' or 'network' of small responsive suppliers, subcontractors, providers of services, etc.

A set of management problems encountered by small business is known by the common label of entrepreneurship. A standard list of such problems taken from textbooks and educational programmes includes such items as assessment of business opportunities, feasibility studies and forecasting of financial results, start-up procedures, simple production management and quality control techniques, and cash-flow analysis.

MANAGEMENT EDUCATION RESPONSE

In order to assess management education's response to the challenges of transition, key types of management education programme will be examined.

Executive MBA programmes

MBA programmes are perceived as the most prestigious. They are the most likely to attract high-profile foreign partners and are designed mainly for joint ventures, larger private enterprises and more successful 'pretenders'. Such programmes can be offered by universities (specialized postgraduate centres) or private business schools, and are often offered jointly by Central and Eastern European and western schools (for example Bocconi–Leningrad, Warsaw–Budapest–Prague–Rotterdam or Warsaw–University of Illinois) or by more advanced centres in the region alone (for example the International Management Centre in Budapest, the International Business School in Warsaw or the Executive Development Centre in Kranj, Slovenia). Participation by foreign professors and the use of foreign teaching aids and programmes are still necessary even in the most advanced institutions.

It has to be remembered, however, that especially in countries at the earlier stage of transition (politically and monetarily unstable) such programmes have limited impact: dinosaurs and the civil service are not likely to hire MBAs. Even in institutionally mature and institution-building countries, however, only a small number of large private enterprises are capable of using MBAs effectively, and foreign companies still prefer to hire foreign-trained MBAs. The market, therefore, is limited and demands high quality training involving both state-of-the-art management knowledge and a superior ability to perform in specific local conditions. Such high requirements and competition will probably eliminate the weaker institutions offering MBA degrees, particularly since the title of MBA does not yet have the same snobbish appeal in the post-Communist countries as it does in the USA and in some Western European countries. Executive and full-time MBA programmes should therefore be considered as 'the icing on the cake' and be developed mainly in more advanced countries, where the possibilities of employing MBAs in the private sector ('growing sharks') really emerge.

Masters programmes in management – (5 years or 4 years in some cases)

These are offered by a large number of universities in the post-Communist countries. Such programmes usually have high enrolment figures, which means that (potentially) they can have an important impact on transitional economies. Graduates fill junior positions in all types of post-Communist enterprises, start their own businesses (Poland) or quite often find employment in public administration, which is especially important in view of the key role of the civil service in the transition process.

However, the standards of these programmes are highly varied. In many cases old Communist 'economic studies' are now offered under the timely label of 'management' but are taught by the same professors from the same textbooks. Similarly, curricula are often structurally the same with some new buzzwords such as 'management accounting' or 'capital markets' added. This is not the rule, however, and many valuable programmes of that type can be identified in post-Communist countries (such as those taught at the Budapest University of Economics). They are normally located in the countries that were more 'open' under Communism and in the more prestigious and bigger institutions with a long-standing tradition of scholarship and contacts with western economic science.

Most of these programmes, however, require massive help in the form of doctoral studies or postdoctoral fellowships abroad, textbooks, cases, etc. MSc programmes also require proper targeting to meet the real needs of the government and the private sector. Unfortunately, these needs are not yet clear, are seldom articulated, and university professors are traditionally blind to signals from the marketplace. MSc programmes in management can play a very important role: for government, for state-owned enterprises and for the private sector. They require dramatic changes, massive help in training professors, in developing research programmes, preparing teaching materials, etc. Such radical changes are likely to be opposed by the old generation of professors formed under Communism.

Undergraduate, vocational programmes in management – (3 years)

These are offered in Poland by newly emerging private higher education institutions licensed by the Ministry of Education. Such schools seem to be geared toward the private sector. Their curricula put stress on practical skills such as marketing techniques but also include general education subjects. Professors usually come from the state universities and research institutes and teach in these institutions as part-timers. It is too early to evaluate the impact of these programmes.

In-house training programmes

These, combined with consulting and major restructuring projects, seem to be the most appropriate for the managers of the relatively large SOEs ('dinosaurs' and 'pretenders') which are undergoing radical change. Such programmes are often run by foreign experts (with a proven track record of practical achievements) in such fields as the restructuring of steel mills or coal mines, and seem to be ideal candidates for financing from foreign aid funds. They may be offered by domestic and foreign consulting firms or private business schools. Unfortunately, such programmes are rare and quite often they fail because of the lack of understanding of government bureaucrats who still supervise the state-owned enterprises.

Short, focused management development programmes

These exist in such fields as cost accounting, quality control, risk management, portfolio management, market research, inventory management, privatization techniques, etc. Such programmes can be offered to groups of managers from different industries or from one industry by private business schools or by specialized university centres. All kinds of enterprises can use this training vehicle for their specific needs in all the types of transitional economies presented above. The key to success is the selection of participants who are capable and motivated and a teaching methodology geared toward mastering skills, rather than a general education, which can at best make wiser but not necessarily better managers.

Seminars in entrepreneurship

These are open to large numbers of private entrepreneurs starting and/or running their own private businesses. Such programmes can be run on a commercial basis by private business schools or 'entrepreneurship centres' located in the universities. Foreign centres of education in entrepreneurship, such as Babson College in the USA, have an important role to play in developing curricula and training local teachers of entrepreneurship.

Such programmes, however, cannot just be copies of foreign ones. Local conditions should be taken into consideration, local cases prepared, etc. It is also important that such programmes should not only provide knowledge and understanding of entrepreneurship but also teach skills such as writing a business plan, cash-flow analysis, basic market analysis, basic accounting, etc. Seminars in entrepreneurship can play a key role in promoting small business, and so are important for all types of economies in transition. Even under Reagan in the USA and under Thatcher in the UK, such programmes were inspired and partially financed by government. Post-Communist governments do not realize yet that they have a leadership role to play here. Programmes in entrepreneurship are rather rare and are usually inspired by foreign sponsoring agencies. They are also not sufficiently practical and they seldom teach skills.

The above short outline of the management education programmes that are most commonly offered in the post-Communist countries of Central and Eastern Europe leads to the conclusion that management education is not responding adequately to the most urgent needs resulting from the transition process. This applies especially to the less advanced countries, where the needs are the most pressing. All countries, however, should redesign their university curricula in MSc programmes, develop specialized and postgraduate mass training of civil servants and establish different types of entrepreneurial studies geared toward practical skills. In politically unstable and monetarily unstable countries priority should be given to the training of the managers of the state-owned enterprises, especially through in-house training and focused, skills-oriented management development programmes.

COMMON NEEDS OF MANAGEMENT EDUCATION SYSTEMS

In order to undertake this formidable task, the common needs of management education systems in post-Communist countries should also be addressed, and these are categorized below.

The need for institution building

This should provide an institutional framework better adjusted to management development. The present framework is clearly chaotic, unstable and in most cases unable to generate, sustain and develop quality programmes. At the moment it is composed of very large numbers of small and weak ephemeral 'independent' business schools exploiting somebody else's limited human and material resources. It is also composed of traditional institutions, such as universities or institutes, which are only slowly adjusting to the new conditions. These two types of institutions develop different kinds of alliances and symbiotic relationships which western observers find difficult to understand.

In such a complex environment, institution building should consist of three types of actions or developments. First, some of the independent schools should be reinforced and upgraded to the status of 'centres of excellence'. Second, structural reform of the university system should be accelerated. This should enable business schools or research and training centres in management to emerge that are loosely connected to the universities and capable of rapid development and adjustment of curricula without administrative interference and with considerable financial independence. Third, quality standards for management development programmes and institutions should be developed and implemented through voluntarily agreed accreditation procedures.

The need for human resources development

The training of professors and teachers of management seems to be one of the most pressing needs. All provision is based on the same limited pool of management teachers and professors working on a contract or part-time basis and employed simultaneously in many institutions offering various management education programmes. In most cases their home institutions are universities and research institutes. Since demand, even for expensive programmes, is very high, the small number of high-quality professors (with extensive foreign experience and training abroad) cannot serve them all. As a consequence, management development programmes are often taught by the people with slight, often superficial, knowledge of the market economy and limited exposure to the modern practices of management.

Older professors are often unable to catch up because of a deficient working knowledge of western languages and the lack of a solid grounding in western economic science. Younger professors and teachers are often too busy making money on mediocre-quality training to learn and to do quality research and consulting. The relatively soft requirements of doctoral programmes and the financial crises of research institutions make faculty development even more difficult. Faculty development programmes are clearly the most critical factor in upgrading management development systems in the post-Communist countries, and management educators in post-Communist countries are starting to realize this. Out of twenty-seven Polish institutions surveyed by Kwiatkowski (1992), twenty-two expressed an interest in high-quality international doctoral programmes organized in cooperation with leading foreign schools. High-quality management education, management development and consulting are not possible in the long run without original research. Research programmes are needed, therefore, to assist the development of both faculty and teaching materials. A review of existing teaching materials points to the need to generate state-of-the-art aids, such as cases, games, textbooks, videos, etc., which should, to some extent, be developed locally and adjusted to local conditions.

The need for foreign know-how

This played, and still plays, a key role in the 'explosion' of management development in post-Communist countries. Many of the local management development institutions are totally dependent on foreign assistance and will collapse if the flow of western resources is terminated. Because of the lack of coordination and the weakness of the recipient structures, considerable financial resources have been wasted. Lots of poor-quality and over-priced foreign training was and still is provided. As demonstrated above, in most cases these programmes miss the target from the point of view of the real needs resulting from the specific conditions of transition. In many instances foreign assistance funds were and are used to assist low-quality training institutions from donor countries. At the same time, however, it is quite obvious that management development institutions in the post-Communist countries are not able to meet the challenges identified in previous sections of this paper without western know-how. Effective know-how transfer would require networking between mature institutions from the West and from Central and Eastern Europe.

The need for cooperation with the business community

This should provide feedback from the clients and the employers of graduates. Such feedback enables adequate structuring of programmes and curriculum development but is a novelty in the post-Communist environment. The emerging business community is just starting to become organized and educational institutions are not used to responding to market signals. Special networks or common platforms enabling close contacts between management educators and the business community need to be established. The Polish Management Development Association 'Forum' and the Central and Eastern European Management Development Association (CEEMAN) are examples of such emerging platforms.

ALTERNATIVE POLICIES

The key policy issues derived from this discussion are to satisfy the common needs of management education institutions in the post-Communist countries and to balance the challenges of transition with those of management development. Four major policy options can be envisaged.

Laissez faire

Laissez-faire policy means that in most countries of the region, the present state of affairs is allowed to continue in the hope that market forces will eliminate weaker institutions and ill-conceived programmes and provide for the development of the best. Such a policy option fits well with the general mood prevalent in post-Communist countries who have developed a real phobia of too much government intervention. It is also likely to occur because of budget deficits and resultant cuts in spending on education.

The outcome of such a policy is rather uncertain. Fragmentation of a management development system composed of a large number of weak institutions and programmes might very well persist for a long time due to imperfect information, the lack of 'hard' criteria for evaluation, the immaturity of the clients and continuing recession. Under a laissez-faire policy the necessary foundations for management education and development, such as strong academic centres capable of producing high-quality professors, educators and consultants, are not likely to emerge.

Government control policy

A government control policy would require a clear vision of the desired management development system, precise step-by-step programming and allocation of adequate resources. Government structures administering such a programme, evaluating, selecting and licensing institutions, allocating funds and closely monitoring the system would have to be put in place. The choice of such options by the post-Communist countries is very unlikely for obvious reasons: the instability and weakness of the governments and the lack of resources.

The Foreign domination model

This model implies that foreign governments, educational institutions funded by governments and private sources, or networks of these foreign actors would establish and practically run a number of management development programmes in post-Communist countries. Such long-term commitment, strongly financially backed, would require considerable western funding and consistent implementation of long-term strategic programmes. It is likely to produce low-quality Central and Eastern Europe replicas of western management education programmes and institutions which might eventually raise their standards in the future, following the example of some Western European business schools which were formed in the 1970s under the dominating influence of the most prestigious American business schools.

In the light of the growing controversy about western, and especially American, models of management education such an outcome might not seem desirable to many. It is also not very likely to occur given the drying-up of western aid funds and the lack of coordination between different western governments and agencies. This has resulted in underfunding and in uncoordinated policies that switch aid too quickly from one recipient to another and from one country to another.

Networking policy

This can provide a platform for innovative combinations of all the options mentioned above. It would require, however, some form of association between interested actors: business schools, universities, the business community, government agencies, foreign donors, professional organizations, business schools, international agencies, etc. Such loosely structured networks can enable interested parties to stay in touch and informed about each other's activities, interests, problems, etc. They can also make possible a large number of inter-institutional task forces, consortia and projects, mobilizing resources for various common purposes such as doctoral programmes, teaching materials clearing houses, curriculum development, etc. Finally, they can successfully lobby national governments, supranational institutions and donor agencies to allocate resources for effective management education and development thereby meeting the most pressing needs and initiating self-sustaining quality programmes.

The initiative to form and operate such networks should remain in local hands – Central and East European managers, management educators, consultants and governments. Under such a policy, western partners would provide 'requested assistance' and would participate in common problem-solving processes. The ability to identify and to articulate real needs and to compromise over the allocation of resources and resource pooling are key factors of success. Networks should help to develop original, innovative solutions in management development in the post-Communist countries, corresponding to their specific needs but based on state-of-the-art western science and know-how.

Networking seems by far the most promising and the most realistic of the policy options. It is contingent, however, upon the ability of the management education community in Eastern and Central Europe to organize itself and to develop working partnerships and alliances with other stakeholders in the management education system: business commu-nity, governments, foreign partners and students.

REFERENCES AND FURTHER READING

Abell, D. (1992) *Turnaround in Eastern Europe: In-Depth Studies, United Nations Development Programme*, Management Development Programme, New York: United Nations.

Aleksandrowicz, P. (1992) 'Polscy menedzerowie najwyzszych szczebli' [Polish top executives], *Rzeczposlpolita*, no. 171, 172, 173.

Fisher, B.J. 'Large Privatisation in Poland, Hungary and Czechoslovakia', *Radio Free Europe Radio Liberty Research Report* 1(44), , pp. 34–9.

Kolvereid, L. and Obloj, K. (1992) *Small Business Environment, Strategies and Aspira-tions: Cross National Comparison*, paper presented at the International Small Business Congress, Warsaw: October.

Kozminski, A.K. (1992) 'Transition from planned to market economy: Hungary and Poland compared', *Studies in Comparative Communism* XXV(4), pp. 315–33.

Kozminski, A.K. (1993) *Catching Up? Case Studies in Organisational and Management Change in the Former Socialist Block*, Albany, NY: Suny Press.

Kwiatkowski, S. (1992) *Sprawozdanie z sondazu opinii dotyczacych koncepcji i mozliwosci realizacji miedzynarodowego programu doktorskiego w dziedzinie zarzadzania* [Report from an opinion survey concerning possibilities of implementation of an inter-national doctoral programme in management], International Business School, Warsaw, December, (unpublished mimeo).

Pearce, J.L. (1991) 'From socialism to capitalism: the effects of Hungarian human resource practices', *Academy of Management Executive* V(4), pp. 75–88.

Slay, B. (1993) 'Poland: the role of managers in privatisation', *Radio Free Europe, Radio Liberty Research Report* II(12), pp. 52–6.

Chapter 13

From the rain to the gutter

Hugo Letiche

To explore the question 'what western management knowledge is worth transferring to Central Europe and why?' I will make use of my experience since 1989 in Poland, the Czech Republic and Slovakia, to characterize (potential) target group(s) and to identify probable forms of knowledge contextualization.

With the fall of Communism, it appeared that the most impossible dream of Central Europe had been realized and that it was time to turn to the enactment of possible dreams (such as creating a market economy). But when the peoples of Central and Eastern Europe shouted their opposition to Communism, they did so with one strong voice which appeared to come from a single mouth. Now there seem to be thousands and thousands of mouths, all apparently demanding to consume more and more! Chaos of purpose has replaced clarity; profiteering has risen its ugly head; demagogy has become part and parcel of the political landscape:

> The re-establishment of liberty has provoked such a state of shock that the populace has lost its points of reference. It finds itself without a clear hierarchy of values. It is a condition to be compared to that of a prisoner who has just been released. While incarcerated, the prisoner looks forward with joy to the moment of release. However, once liberated, prisoners feel lost and long to regain their cell, because while they know what they will find in their cell, they do not know what to expect from freedom. It is the same thing with a society that has been held prisoner, it does not know how to manage its own liberty.
>
> (Havel 1991: 34)

Since 1989, both the European Community (EC) decision-makers and the leaderships of the new Central European democracies have shared the idea that Western European managerial knowledge ought to be transferred to Poland, the Czech Republic, Slovakia, etc. to provide a skills basis for entrepreneurial activity in the new economic and political context. The proposed transaction has been between Western European suppliers of management knowledge and Central European consumers of that knowledge (management teachers and consultants, (future) entrepreneurs). But are the western sources really capable of playing any such (teaching) role? And if they are, will they increase or decrease independent thinking and action in Central Europe? All too often Western managers seem to prefer managerial 'ideas' which do not oblige them to think any further. How would the export of any such 'ideas' benefit the new democracies? The danger of realizing the prisoner's dream seems eminent: a free-market society wherein one chooses (buys) one's own incarceration.

THE LEARNERS

Managing has as its purpose the achievement of organizational adaptiveness and/or flexibility, the maintenance of (some form of) production, the pursuit of efficiency (most often via formalization and standardization) and the structuring of complexity (frequently via the coordinating of specializations). Managers create a structure of compliance in which they impose organization on themselves and their surroundings. Managing (supposedly) creates and maintains the patterns of behaviour needed to ensure organizational 'success'. Managers depend on a discourse of control to dominate organizational structure and influence performance. Managerial 'voice' supposedly determines organizational action. Managers achieve organizational obedience; activity (supposedly) suits their purposes. In the west their discourse of control mostly takes a rationalistic form wherein 'strategic choices' follow inimitably from market inevitabilitys. Consent is often achieved via the so-called TINA tendency (there is no alternative) (Clegg 1990: 578).

To be effective, a discourse of control must be contextually legitimized, i.e. it needs to achieve a 'seamless fit' with its social/political surroundings. In Poland one can, at present, differentiate between four fundamental discourses of control; each centres on an alternative set of core beliefs and leads to a disparate course of action. Managerial legitimacy is threatened by the lack of hegemony of any one discourse of control. No single rhetoric has achieved cultural dominance; any and all managerial initiatives may be challenged, opposed, frustrated. In contradistinction to its current ideological supremacy in Western Europe, managerialism remains an unstable and weak discourse in Central Europe.

THE CATHOLIC-NATIONALIST DISCOURSE

Two of the four managerial discourses currently heard in Poland, the Czech Republic and Slovakia echo the rhetoric of the 1920s and 1930s. The other two have a markedly 'new' sound to them. First, there is the Catholic-Nationalist discourse. This is an essentially 'moralist' discourse which refuses to accept the division between a secular economy and a spiritual society. The normal struggle of interests inherent in a market economy and in liberal democracy is fundamentally rejected. Faced by the difficulties of the transitional phase, voices refer back to a near-mystical national solidarity. Of course, the civil society of Central Europe is weak, there are no established political parties or other organizations (professional groups, labour unions, etc.) which represent the various social interests with any strength. Unlike in the west, many groups have no idea at all who to turn to in order to defend their interests. Flight from the economic threat takes the form of an anti-democratic totalitarianism. Aggressive nationalism and xenophobia fill the political vacuum. Democratic pluralism appears too threatening to many. The new market society provides opportunities for initiative and creativity, but it also threatens established bastions of power, hierarchy and stability. For the threatened, traditional values coupled with authoritarian politics may seem more attractive than does a pluralistic, dynamic and competitive society. The Utopian capitalism (which many believed, pre-1989) was not a severe meritocracy with losers as well as winners.

The realities of a market society have produced nostalgia for a less personally challenging system. Many are ill prepared for independent thinking and individual responsibility; they prefer a system of hierarchical authority with clearly defined 'rights' and 'wrongs'. Many feel themselves abandoned and betrayed by capitalism. Instead of gaining instant wealth and all the rewards of the consumer society, they are faced by a competitive labour market, including job insecurity and (often) criticism of their performance from their subordinates. The managerial myth, which they want to prevail over market economy complexity and democratic conflict, is one where society is organized so that everything is in order, where secular ideology is isomorphic to religious belief, where the distribution of social roles goes hand in hand with ideological justification, where God and social existence are one. The current tension between liberal democratic ideology and quotidian reality is experienced as unbearable.

Furthermore, because no Polish state existed from the end of the eighteenth century until 1918 (Poland was dismembered and split between Russia, Prussia and Austria) there is a strong tradition of opposition between society and the state. A similar problem exists in Slovakia, where congruence between the state and society has been singularly lacking. The church had already assumed the role of defending national identity in the nineteenth century and simply carried on this tradition during the Communist period. The Church defined a cultural space of relative liberty for believers and non-believers alike. Obviously the Church was crucial to *Solidarność*'s success. But some do not now want to accept the liberal separation between Church and state. Catholic nationalists retain the traditional Manichaean structure of dividing their world into 'us' (Polish, Catholic, good) and 'them' (Communist, cosmopolitan, bad). These fundamentalists seem to be embracing an authoritarian political tradition (Poland post-1926 under Piłsudski being a model) which would lead to an isolationist economy, in which the position of the managerial elite would be unquestioned and would be based upon ideological clout would count – not economic rationality or organizational efficiency. One totalitarian system would be exchanged for another. The political chaos of the present would be replaced by absolutist rigidity; the groping towards a new economic order would be superseded by iron-handed economic regimentation.

THE DISCOURSE OF POPULISM

Second, there is populism. In Poland there is a strong tradition of worker protest. Here the (mass) leader plays on the public's emotions. S/he does not try to convince the audience, but rather to move it. The mediatization of politics has led, everywhere, to soundbites, visual impressions, playing to the crowd. Politics has lost its pedagogic role; politicians try to please audiences not to educate them. In Central Europe, where there is little (or no) democratic tradition, an active engagement of the citizenry in politics has to be created. Under Communism, the first secretary of the party was a monarch, with absolute power unlimited by law. Between the government and the masses there was no reciprocal dialogue. Civil society – the intermediaries of free discussion, community organizations, political pluralism – was frustrated or even forbidden. Under Communism the role of the intellectual was pre-modern. The system did not acknowledge that the intellectuals should judge and criticize the politics they served. The Communist Party claimed absolute ideological supremacy.

In Poland, as long as the Party did not feel threatened in its political monopoly over power, extensive intellectual freedom was permitted. Independent thought existed in the universities. The clerks of the system (those who set up and maintain its administration) acted as auxiliaries to the powers that be. Their role was to get things done. The Utopian vision of Communism had disappeared into the ijskust (refrigerator) by 1956 (when the workers of Poznań revolted); and was replaced by a down-to-earth utilitarian effort to achieve a minimal level of prosperity. While the dissidents contested Communism's cultural supremacy, and thereby its political power, the clerks limited themselves to expressing occasional critical independence, in private, whilst allying themselves essentially with the system's pursuit of economic growth. Communism tried to prevent public opinion playing a role. Political policy was not supposed to be discussed and debated with the population. Governing was seen as a purely top-down affair. The masses were not supposed to follow the political system critically, but to blindly accept it. The rulers did not appeal for popular support; they tried not to depend on explaining themselves to the populace. Under Communism the gap between the logic of ruling and of being led became ever greater.

This heritage now leaves the masses unprepared to judge political discourse critically. Some leaders promise anything and everything the masses want. Such leaders claim that all demands will be met and that all needs will be fulfilled. A public unprepared for complex decision-making is promised simple solutions and magical results. Such demagogy gives the new democracy a bad name and endangers rational choice. But to be fair, one has to recognize that this same rhetoric played a different role in the recent past. The mass revolts (1953 DDR, 1956 Poland and Hungary, etc.) which so deeply marked the Communist period, coincided with moments of material crisis; for instance, rises in the prices of staple foods. In each case, including the 1980 strike at the Gdańsk shipyards, mass disappointment in the level of prosperity played a key role in the revolt. Populist leaders promised the masses that through revolt they could force the Communist elite to grant economic improvement. These popular leaders had no idea how prosperity really ought to be achieved. Resistance to Communism was (in part) a product of the system's economic ineffectiveness. The Communist monopoly on the political process drove its opponents into populist rhetoric, a rhetoric grounded in not having any (hope of) assuming concrete economic responsibility. This same de facto denial of responsibility now functions as a cancer within the young democracy, where commitment and accountability are supposed to be shared guiding principles.

THE DISSIDENTS' DISCOURSE

While the first two rhetorics seem to evoke demons of the European political past, the second two are more innovative and may well contain elements of a (common) political future. Third, there are the dissidents. There were very few Tadeusz Mazowiekis, Adam Michniks, and Bronislaw Geremeks. Not surprisingly one finds very few intellectuals today who admit to having been Communists, but surprisingly one also finds very few ex-dissidents! The dissidents experienced the Communist period (with its secret police, falsification(s) of history and authoritarian stupidities) with self-awareness. Most people stuck to sleepwalking. To quote a Polish aphorism: 'I dreamed this night of reality, what a relief when I got up!' (Stanislaw Jerzy Lec, *Mysli nieuczesane* 1957) Adam Michnik has called the Communist period the 'Auschwitz of the soul'. In the post-Communist period, the dissidents are not about to let one authoritarian discourse be succeeded by yet another:

> During the modern epoch, the characteristic tendency was to consider that nothing could co-exist with anything else which contradicted it, that the representation of the world ought to be complete and total. The notion of having *a view of world* is derived from these assumptions. For me, this is an idea which is debatable and in fact I do not really know what it means. Is the world really so simple that one point of view suffices to see

it in its entirety? I have thousands of parallel points of view which belong
to different things, to thousands of different opinions.

I think that after the modern period and its rational constructions,
created in the period of Descartes, a new era is debuting. Vaclav Bieloh-
radsky calls it postmodernist. This era will be dominated by a non-
doctrinaire and pluralist manner of thinking. In general I am persuaded
that it is more characteristic of humanity to reflect on each matter in a
different way, than to make use, each time, of the same way of thinking.

(Havel 1991: 32–33)

The dissidents refused to accept that, despite being under Communist rule,
their societies did not continue to belong to the social cultural space of
western Christianity. Europe represents for them the values of the Judeo-
Christian world, expressed through political, social, economic and cultural
liberty. Common values make political and economic cooperation possible.
It is asserted that there is a common metaphysical anchorage of the
European consciousness, wherein social responsibility and disinterested
commitment to the Other play a crucial role. Both Havel and Geremek
insist that the choice is between cynical demoralization and intimate
personal involvement (Duby and Geremek 1992: 114–125; Havel 1991:
37). The biggest danger is that some sort of fundamentalism will (try to)
destroy the individual nature of the choice of liberty and replace it with
dogma and ideology. The chief challenge to the end to ideology postulate is
that most people may be nearly incapable of self-definition. The role for the
intellectual is to support, facilitate and catalyse the process of liberty; i.e. to
be a spokesperson for the personal choice for shared, mutual commitment.
Geremek, in a passage in which he discusses the development of 'micro-
history' in postmodern discourse, ascribes to himself:

a passion for living humanity which one has to wrench from the process
of forgetting and from death. [As an intellectual (in my case a historian)
one] strives to present and understand [humanity] in a social context, in
the living body of interactions; in the very life of the society. Society –
for me the term signifies the lines of domination and dependence but
also the ways of living, thinking, feeling; . . . it embraces apparently
contradictory phenomena; [i.e.] exclusion and solidarity, [real] collective
behaviour and [mere] political strategy. . . . Societies are best defined and
understood by their condemnation or acceptance of *alterity*.

(Geremek 1993: 14–15)

For Geremek the best model of alterity is the *poète maudit*, i.e. the personal
voice marginal to all totalization, ideology, 'grand narrative', a role he
identifies with:

the dissident is, almost by definition, a being isolated and marginal,
condemned to exclusion. An heretic par excellence, sometimes a Jew,

risking to be locked up in a mental hospital – but history sometimes produces remarkable comings and goings. The opposition . . . [in Poland] had the support of society, suffered little from isolation and was exposed to a minimum of repression. . . . In the middle of the system, a movement was formed consisting of ten million members able to survive repression and ultimately to assume the role of an independent party capable of engaging in dialogue with those in power.

(Geremek 1993: 32)

In the 1960s and 1970s there were extremely few dissidents, but a very broad movement of support. In the 1980s the dissidents progressively gained hegemony over the civil society:

> The civil society is the vast space which extends between the intentions of the ruling group of a society and the everyday commonsensical, and routine behaviour of society's members; it is the space in which the joining together of the two into one relatively unified whole takes place. To be effective or, for that matter, to be of any consequence – at all for the way in which society is structured and 'works,' the dominant intentions of society must be sustained by the habituated behaviour of the multitude – be translated, so to speak, into their routine behavioural patterns. This condition of the dominant group's rule can be met by the civil society; if the civil society fails, the political state becomes the only alternative. In the first case we can speak of the 'hegemony' of the ruling group; in the second of its 'dominance.'

(Bauman 1976: 99)

The Communist bureaucrats attempted the 'conquest' of civil society, i.e. the coercion of popular thought. The technically oriented bureaucrats in power were set against accepting the free play of cultural production, common in the West (fuelled by competition between pluralist elites). Communism assumed Party dominance over the production and consumption of all cultural artefacts. But the ruling group did not produce concepts of the world which were rich and multifaceted enough to include everyone, or complex enough to generate creative debate and sustainable innovation.

The dissidents were the champions of critical discussion, social thought, personal artistic honesty. Instead of a society integrated via powerful beliefs and rich forms of expression, Communism led to a society dominated by political power with a weak and ineffective civil society. The dissidents were able to become important because they gained hegemony over people's beliefs. The dissidents produced the metaphors by which people lived, the symbols which really counted, the ideas which were valorized. Communism found itself reduced to a pure power confrontation with a civil society produced by its opponents. Communism, personified by bureaucrats dedicated to normality, was not imaginative, had no innovative fantasy and lacked charisma. The Communist rulers had little real control over events; in their managing, they spent more time 'putting out fires' than in creating effective strategies. The fundamental scenarios for potential futures all came from the dissidents. Communism had no legitimacy to produce ideas of the future; the dissidents were subversive because they possessed change, alterity, the possible. Popular culture progressively sided with the dissidents; the state gradually lost out to the civil society.

Thus the conflict wherein the dissidents destroyed the political legitimacy of Communism centred on the functioning of civil society. The dissidents were not, in the first place, social economic opponents, but rather social psychological or cultural ones. They conquered the Polish, Czech and Slovak civil society, prompting the Communists to withdraw from government. Post-1989 the state is up for grabs. Will the honours fall to the dissidents and to the civil society? Are they capable of defining effective economic policies? Can they maintain the support needed to rule; are they skilful at negotiating, compromising, communicating? The collapse of the then-dominant Communist power brokers was unexpected. The dissidents have continued post-1989 to defend liberty and to hunt for truth. But can the actions of the state be coordinated around a platform based on the dissidents' radical humanism? This would entail the development of new, very innovative political processes.

Communism had long left its Utopian phase behind it and entered a stage of pragmatic, instrumental or system management. Communism was concerned with getting things done and was dedicated to rational technocratic management. But the goal was self-defeating because the system was not able to deliver the promised goods. Will post-Communism entail different managerial politics or the same ones better implemented and/ or ideologically packaged? Whether espoused under capitalism or Communism, the ethos of managerial elites – the preference for order above risk, for prediction above guessing, for planning above creativity, for data above intuition – is the same. If post-Communism merely ushers in an intensified form of managerialism, then the dissidents will not have much of a role to play.

THE DISCOURSE OF THE NEW ENTREPRENEURS

Fourth, there are the new entrepreneurs. As already indicated there were relatively few dedicated Communists or dissidents. The new entrepreneurs come from the vast depoliticized mass characteristic of Communist society. During the period of opposition, in the 1980s, many of the new entrepreneurs were sympathetic to the newly emerging civil society. They sided with change, but were not activists either for or against Communism. Though they never fought Communism they have, up to now, gained the most from the post-Communist changes. They have occupied the economic space left vacant by the fall of Communism.

Some of new entrepreneurs have emerged from the old *nomenklatura*; they are ex-Communist managers who 'privatized' parts of the concerns they led, right into their own hands. Others have emerged from the artisan classes – shopkeepers, skilled workers (plumbers, carpenters, electricians, etc.), service providers (information technology, organization advisers, trainers). A few have started entirely new businesses. Almost the entire private sector is characterized by a lack of capital. Often the entrepreneur invests her/his limited savings, plus her/his own (as well as the family's) work and skills, into the new enterprise. The new entrepreneurs frequently have one foot in the traditional economy and the other in the newly emerging private one, i.e. they have retained their traditional job as well as created a new one. Most of the Polish, Czech or Slovak private sector is dedicated to trade and to service delivery, i.e. is small in scale and restricted in capital.

The apparatus of real market-economy capitalism is not in place; there is virtually no credit and little or no distribution system. Ownership structures, taxation and government controls are undefined. Accounting practices, legal frameworks and occupational training are nebulous. Specialisms are virtually unheard of: product development, finance, marketing, production are all one entrepreneurial act. The new entrepreneurs, in comparison to Western Europe, operate in a situation of radical de-differentiation. The characteristic that (ever since Adam Smith described the pin factory) has seemed to epitomize capitalism, the ever more extreme functional differentiation of labour, is weak in the Central European market sector. The new entrepreneurs take personal initiative, are directly responsible for results and work in direct proximity to the market.

The negative side to the picture is that there is considerable profiteering. Instead of lasting enterprises being built, the practices of the black economy are continued in 'fast-buck deals' designed to deliver a high return based on exploiting lacunae in the legal and/or market systems (Frybes 1992: 243–56). The new entrepreneurs (both the bona fide ones and the 'cowboys') are practitioners of postmodern organizing. The division of labour is informal and flexible, managing and non-management functions overlap, the whole is integrated with clanlike personalization, goals are eclectic and variable (Heydebrand 1989: 327).

I would argue that Fordism has long reached the limits of its effectiveness. Rationalised enterprises (based on forever increasing fragmentation of tasks, controlled by continually more elaborate systems of surveillance and ever more minutely planned a techno-managerial caste separated from the productive core) are running out of steam. Efficiency gains are being outstripped by the costs of surveillance and control. The progressive loss of flexibility; the lack of contact between management and the concern's internal or external environment; the inability to achieve cross functional creativity; all of these threaten Fordist organisation with obsolescence.

(Albertson 1988: 348)

Central Europe is unique in having a state enterprise sector which is rigidly Fordist and a private sector which is post-Fordist. The two sectors are not, and probably cannot be, successfully aligned. Herein lies the essential instability of the present economic situation. Inefficient machine bureaucracy faces innovative adhocracy.

STRUCTURES OF SOCIAL INFLUENCE

Each of the four discourses of control I have identified implies a structure of social influence. The Catholic nationalist rhetoric goes hand in hand with hierarchical organizations whose leaders legitimize their authoritarian dominance through an appeal to national homogeneity, religious conformism and obedience to 'permanent values'. The Catholic nationalists can agree with the new entrepreneurs that business leadership needs to be strong and with the populists that the masses have to be addressed in their own language. Conflict is the strongest with the dissidents, who are the champions of individual initiative, responsibility and judgement.

Populist rhetoric drives a wedge between the appeal made to the masses and actual political action. Since 1989, demagogic communication has often been attempted with the masses, while government action has been designed to stimulate modernization and economic restructuring. The balance between the leadership role as a catalyst for the outing of popular needs or frustrations and the actual practice of governing has often been unstable. When the leadership promises the masses whatever they want to hear but has to govern within actual economic and social contingencies mass disappointment and disillusion must be expected. An ever increasing charismatic contact with the masses will be needed to maintain the populist appeal. The dangers of provoking violent jealousies, irrational violence and the fuelling of social intolerance are considerable. The logic of populism displays many similarities to that of Catholic nationalism; both appeal to the masses' emotive reactions. Populism tends, like the Catholic nationalists, to create authoritarian leadership structures because it, like them, does not try to explain or rationally justify government action. The populists have a love–hate relationship with the dissidents. The two groups were bedfellows in opposition to Communism, and both espouse an emancipatory goal. But the populists do not believe in the dissidents' ability to be effective, and the dissidents do not believe that the populists really want to make an end to authoritarian rule.

The Dissidents support a radical democratization of society, with an emphasis on a humanist liberal approach to leadership. They most fear the fundamentalism of the Catholic nationalist camp, while sharing with the populists a commitment to the emancipation of the socially weak. The respect for individual creative action forms a bridge to the new entrepreneurs.

Finally, the new entrepreneurs value the dissidents' individualism but will make use of Catholic nationalist rhetoric when it allows them to increase their control over workers. Worker representation (populism/labour unions) are opposed. Worker populists are feared and thought to be a dangerous blockade to the managerial prerogatives needed to create a market economy. But populism's de facto disenfranchising of the masses (who are kept outside real political decision-making) is valued.

THE KNOWLEDGE

The Western providers of management knowledge convey their own discourse of control. If this is done self-consciously, the western teachers/trainers need to acknowledge the social structures in which their own expertise is embedded. There is never a guarantee that imparted knowledge will be used in the manner intended. In my experiences in Poland, the Czech Republic and Slovakia, I have encountered learners representative of all of the four categories described above. The Catholic nationalists have been the closest to the Communist old guard and had occupied elite positions pre-1989. Their role has seemed to be essentially conservative; they want to protect their social position(s). The new entrepreneurs have been far and away the largest group. In 1993 a Polish university lecturer needed a family income of around $850 per month to maintain a middle-class standard of life. Typically some $275 per month would be earnt by the husband at the university, $225 per month by the

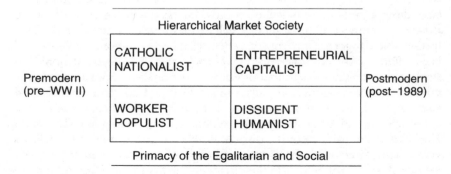

Figure 13.1 Matrix of political forces

wife in a skilled (white-collar) position and the husband would earn an additional $325 per month as an entrepreneur. A monthly deficit was not unusual. Persons who have thrown themselves entirely into the market economy gain their knowledge of business by becoming streetwise; they do not have time to follow management courses.

In Slovakia I have encountered more Worker Populism than in the Czech Republic or Poland. A grey area exists between Catholic nationalism and worker populism, where one encounters a mixture of them both. The dissidents, who are now (further) equipping themselves for managerial power, seem to be few and far between. Personally, I have chosen to teach postmodern management in Central Europe. The choice is whether or not one wishes to bring advanced Fordism to the Poles, Czechs and Slovaks. They are often eager to go on with the same Fordist system which failed under Communism by making it more powerful. Uni-directional managerial planning and one-sided top-down action have not been forsworn. While the Central Europeans are closer to direct, hands-on entrepreneurship than are many western managers, they still idealize IBM-like bureaucracy. Financial management wizardry, at the cost of production, appeals to them. Manipulating a fortune into existence seems much more attractive than earning it via production. Economic trickery sounds like much more powerful stuff than just plain hard work. Thus, the learners seem to call more for outdated manipulative knowledge leading to the further breakdown of production, confidence and efficiency, than for current insights stressing flexibility, reaction to customer needs, managerial accountability and high levels of trust in networked cooperation.

There is a tendency to strive for hyper-Communism, i.e. a system of intensified Fordism. Western management teachers are brought in to teach western control systems, which are much more tight, technologically sophisticated and manipulatively powerful than was the Communist administration. What is forgotten is that the 1989 collapse of Communist rule came from the breakdown in civil society. This very same process has been occurring in Western Europe, where it has been analysed by comparing European stagnation to Asian dynamism. The crisis in western civil society has attracted attention within the corporate culture movement, where the lack of motivation, leadership and creativity has been ascribed to a crisis in the quality of organizational cohesion. The symptoms of the Communist crisis in civil society – inefficient bureaucracies, ineffective and arrogant elites, cynical profiteering – sounds more familiar than we might like to admit. We thought that the fall of the Berlin Wall would lead to Central Europe's reforming its over-staffed, bureaucratically blocked, stagnant economies. We know that Western Europe is facing almost exactly the same crisis. Nonetheless we have been exporting to Central Europe the very same managerialism which got us into the crisis in the first place.

Obviously Poland, the Czech Republic and Slovakia can gain from many logistic, accounting, packaging, project management and production skills. But too few concrete, core business skills have been conveyed and too much Fordism, packaged as strategic management or marketing, has been on offer. Representatives of the Western European MBA culture of the 1980s can only tell Central Europeans how to destroy civil society. Not a very useful message. Representatives of bureaucratic management from the 1970s can only explain a form of organizing which has run out of steam. There's probably as much postmodern, innovative organizing going on in Central Europe as in western.

In the west we have not learnt to make technical skills function effectively in the service of genuinely client-centred strategies; in Central Europe many key skills are still underdeveloped. In Western Europe large concerns possess enormous wealth which they do not seem to be able to use creatively; Central Europe desperately lacks capital. The Western European economy has stagnated, unable to decide which risks are worth taking; Central Europe tends to be ineffectively driven forward from one emergency to the next. Western and Central European organizations remain too rigid, inefficient and populated by disaffected employees. Postmodern approaches to management strive to renew the civil society within organizations, making them into learning organizations capable of entrepreneurial creativity. For the Central Europeans, such approaches could lead to open organizations which marshal individual abilities, gain genuine commitment and maintain their creativity. There is no simple blueprint, no easy way of combining the dissident's feel for civil society with the new entrepreneurs' force of action.

A new discourse of control which combines communicative sensitivity and individual initiative and which links market effectiveness with social integration needs to be forged. For the western provider of management education, working in Central Europe offers the chance to be powerfully confronted with the crucial role civil society has to play in management. Both the rain of Central European change/innovation and that of Western European skills/experience will be washed into the gutter if the lessons of civil society's key role in managing are not learned.

REFERENCES

Albertson, N (1988) 'Postmodernism, post-Fordism and critical social theory', *Environment and Planning: Part D Society and Space*, 6, pp. 339–66.

Bauman, Z. (1976) 'The Party in system-management phase: change and continuity', in A.C. Janos (ed.) *Authoritarian Politics in Communist Europe*, Berkeley: Institute of International Studies.

Clegg, S. (1990) *Modern Organisations*, London: Sage.

Duby, G. and Geremek, B. (1992) *Passions communes*, Paris: Éditions du Seuil.

Frybes, M. (1992) 'Les Entrepreneurs privés d'Europe de l'Est', in G. Mink and J.-C. Szurek (1992) *Cet étrange Post-communisme*, Paris: Presses du CNRS/La Découverte.

Geremek, B. (1993) *Histoire sociale: exclusions et solidarité*, Leçon inaugurale, Paris: Collège de France.

Havel, V. (1991) interview with Adam Michnik in Warsaw *Gazeta Wyborcza* 279 (December 1991), translated and reprinted in G. Mink and J.-C. Szurek (1992) *Cet étrange Post-communisme*, Paris: Presses du CNRS/La Découverte.

Heydebrand, W.V. (1989) 'New organisational forms', *Work and Occupations* 16(3): 323–57.

Lec, S.J. (1957) *Mysli nieuczesane*, Warsaw.

Chapter 14

The manager's new clothes: on identity transfer in post-1989 Poland

Monika Kostera

This chapter examines some of the aspects of the changing identities of enterprises and managers in Poland. Since 1989, Polish enterprises have been participating in an intensive process of change. They are expected to undergo a more or less complete metamorphosis. Ownership forms are renegotiated and changed; structures, aims and social roles within the organizations change and the legitimacy of the old rules of the game is questioned daily. The manager becomes one of the central social roles associated with these changes.

But does it make sense to talk about 'organizational identity', or the identity of social roles? The term 'identity' is traditionally to be found in psychology, philosophy or ethics, where it relates to people ('sense of identity'). However, Barbara Czarniawska-Joerges (1994) assumes that identity, individual and organizational, is simply a modern institution, where institution is understood, after Berger and Luckmann (1966/1971) as the assumption that a given kind of action will be undertaken by a given kind of actor. I argue that individual identity is the result of interaction between the person and the environment. A similar process takes place between organizations and their environments. Modernity has norms about what is 'adequate', and within those there emerges a modern identity narrative, a kind of autobiography, where 'a person, an organisation and a text all become one' (Czarniawska-Joerges 1994: 199). Identities emerge from a continuous process of translation, where travelling ideas about what the identity might or ought to be like meet stationary ideas of what it already is. In this meeting friction is created, producing energy that makes translation possible (Latour 1986). Czarniawska-Joerges writes about the meeting of 'travelling ideas with a frame of reference, that is ideas in residence' (1994: 209). In order to accomplish a change of identity, it is not enough to make a decision on a high hierarchical level. Such decisions only make space for action.

In high modernity the mass media (primarily the TV, but also radio, the press, popular books, movies, etc.) are the medium of identity transfer. In Poland, managers are active readers of the press, daily and periodicals, therefore it is reasonable to explore the message of this medium in order to learn more about the process of identity transfer now taking place. My endeavour is not to depict the entire process of identity formation, but to picture two initial steps in this process: the image brought into fashion by the press, or the 'ideas given', and brief declared reactions to these ideas by the actors – the encounter with 'ideas in residence' (the latter I examine in more depth in Kostera).

METHOD

The analysis of identity transfer was carried out through a critical analysis of culture (cf. Denzin 1992). I chose three different titles, after having asked practising managers (students of two MBA-type programmes) which press titles they read. The most popular were *Businessman Magazine* (monthly), *Wprost* (weekly) and *Gazeta Wyborcza* (daily). I studied three complete volumes of *Businessman Magazine*, 1991–1993, and *Wprost* and *Gazeta Wyborcza* were subject to my studies from January 1993 until February 1994. I focused on the image of the enterprise and the managerial role that the papers conveyed.

Businessman Magazine is a monthly directed towards Polish business people. It contains professional articles about strategy, motivation, marketing, etc. authored by journalists but also by consultants and academics. The texts use a popular rhetoric, often employing metaphors and platitudes, frequently imported from business English. The journal publishes both Polish texts and reprints from western press. The monthly is quite expensive, is printed on high-quality paper and contains many pictures etc. The second paper I studied is the weekly *Wprost*. The weekly has the image of an ambitious socio-political journal. It contains regular business sections and is read by educated readers, among them managers. It publishes shorter stories, often about companies and managers, sometimes about abstract 'market economy phenomena' such as banking, finance, marketing, etc. The third paper, *Gazeta Wyborcza*, is the most popular Polish daily, founded by leading Polish oppositionists in 1989 as the first Polish free paper directed at the 'common reader'. Currently it reaches many different social groups, including managers. It contains a short business section every Wednesday, and its local supplement for the Warsaw region, *Gazeta Stoleczna*, often publishes texts about firms and business.

In addition, I carried out another critical cultural study, this time concerning the reactions of the readers, active managers and executive students of management of two different courses at Warsaw University. This was a window study, or, in Czarniawska-Joerges's words, a study where '[a] researcher opens an arbitrary time window and describes all that can be seen through it. Here it is the processes which are negotiated with the actors: what is central, important, new, routine, etc.' (1992b: 9).

The managers were asked to write essays-reviews of a chosen article in *Businessman Magazine*. I tried not to influence their writings, therefore they wrote these essays during the first class they had with me. I did not explain the detailed assumptions of my research, just asked them to review the article out of their experience and knowledge as managers, to focus on images of enterprises and managers, and to express their personal reactions. The respondents represented different types of enterprise: private, state-owned, privatized and from the public sector. Their age varied: the youngest was 28 and the oldest 56. The groups were predominately male: there were fifty-one men and eleven women. *Businessman Magazine* was a popular paper in both groups: a majority read the paper either regularly or relatively regularly.

EVERYDAY PRESS AND PERIODICALS: WHO IS THE HERO OF THE NEW MANAGEMENT NARRATIVE?

Enterprises: positive examples

There are many positive examples of enterprises to be found in the analysed volumes of *Businessman Magazine*. Most of them are of foreign (i.e. western) firms which are presented both generally and in the context of their operations on the Polish market. The firms are presented in the convention of promotional vignettes, with the emphasis on 'excellence', using panegyrical rhetoric. The titles of these articles say much about their content. For example, an article about McDonald's is entitled 'The big career of the little steak' (1992, 8: 8–10); Arthur Andersen is presented under the headline 'We invest in Poland's future' (1991, 4: 4–5); the functioning of Benckiser and Henkel on the Polish market is described in a story entitled 'The powder war' (1993, 5: 13–16); British Airways is portrayed in a text named 'The client is our master' (1992, 6: 56–59); a sweets producer is depicted in an article under the title 'The chocolate empire of Cadbury Ltd' (1992, 3: 4547).

The article about McDonald's starts with a narrative of founders' legend, which emphasizes the issue of 'intuition' and describes the firm as having a 'strong corporate culture', as being a firm where 'everybody' is committed to achieving the perfect quality product. The author thus introduces the firm's 'value system', for example 'The prominence of McDonald's is based on consequence. It is never forgotten what the true assets of the firm are. Quality, quickness, cleanliness, value! have been *knocked into each employee's head*. And these values are developed in the first hand' (1992, 8: 8, emphasis mine). The firm strives to achieve 'true perfection', which explains why the menu is not very diversified, or in the author's words: 'we will not be shocked by variety and luxury'. Instead, McDonald's hygienic standards are the highest possible, which we learn from the section entitled 'The hamburger is like a child'. The author acknowledges that 'work at McDonald's is no Sunday school'. However, in return the employees get 'satisfaction from working for a prestigious firm' (1992, 8: 8–9).

The positive examples of Polish enterprise are similar. The firms are not 'really' as perfect, but they achieve good results because they act similarly to western companies. They are described as focused exclusively on the economic sphere, even if a common trait of many Polish enterprises today is that they are active in both the economic and the political spheres (Kostera 1995). This second type of activity is either neglected in the examples or straightforwardly denied. An ostentatious disinterest in politics is often emphasized in the stories; for example, in a text about a radio station, Radio Kolor, the founder is quoted with approval expressing his contempt towards political games: 'In a word: your basic argument vis a vis the Council [the administrative political body giving concessions to radio stations the article was published when Radio Color was applying for concession] is the radio?', the reporter asks. The interviewee declares that he thinks exclusively in free-market terms (1993, 7: 8). Similarly, the owner of a clothing company is depicted as a person who was dreaming about freedom from political games, freedom from political slogans. In order to realize these dreams, he founded the company (1993, 7: 36).

Wprost also presents western companies, e.g. Procter & Gamble (1993, 17: 62–63), IBM (1993, 10: 67–68), Apple (1993, 23: 66–67), McDonald's and Burger King (1993, 30: 66–67), a ranking of American enterprises (1993, 22: 66–67). The style of presentation is less glorifying than that of *Businessman Magazine* and the stories are generally shorter. The categories of 'success' and 'innovativeness' appear probably as often (e.g. 1993, 23: 66–67). Employees' 'identification with the firm's goals' is emphasized as the western key to effectiveness (e.g. 1993, 23: 66–67). As for positive Polish examples, their presentation by *Wprost* is similar to that by *Businessman Magazine*, too. However, the language used for their description is different: adjectives are fewer, more often the authors narrate what the firm 'does', 'intends to do', or 'has done'.

A text about Zelmer, a household machinery producer, is entitled: 'Zelmer's success'. The article characterizes this firm as 'one of the few Polish enterprises whose products are more popular on our market than those of western competitors'. This is due to the fact that '[w]hile other enterprises just begin to adapt to the conditions of market economy, in Zelmer people already think and plan in a European way'. It means that the firm 'resign[s] from the traditional management model', to adopt 'full responsibility of the manager who makes strategic decisions and assumes own responsibility'. We also learn that the firm intends to mould a 'new kind of employee' (1993, 11: 68–69). Westerners are not only the passive ideal, but sometimes active helpers: a text presents Polish firms who, thanks to help from western consultants, managed to turn around. The author emphasizes the bad shape the firms were in and how the 'treatment' was undertaken, aimed at reorienting the firms to exclusive market focus. So, employment was reduced, funds were invested in marketing and advertising, new organizational structures were introduced, etc. (1994, 1: 66–68).

Gazeta Wyborcza presents vignettes of western companies and managers only occasionally. There are, however, many articles about Polish firms. These are often directed at the consumer, informing about products, their quality, consumers' rights, etc. Many articles compare products and services with each other. Sometimes the newspaper also presents examples of enterprises, mostly Polish, in an 'informative' tone, telling about how they managed to change. They typically use 'expert' language, with a certain inclination towards numbers. Thus, *Gazeta Stoleczna* published an article about a Polish enterprise under crisis management. The company is in bad shape, but a restructuring plan has been developed. It is seen as necessary to 'get an agreement with creditors' and/or to sell the company's attractively situated territory (1993, 248: 11).

Enterprises: negative examples

Discussion of non-western and non-'westernlike' Polish enterprises seldom appears on the pages of *Businessman Magazine*. Sometimes an author refers to them anonymously, to achieve an effect of contrast between what symbolizes the 'era that passed' and what is 'modern'. For example, in an article on architecture, Polish banks are criticized because they are 'an anachronism, not only because of their [unsatisfactory] financial operations. Their archaism exposes itself in their low architectonic standard and the obsolete security system [that they use] . . . (1992, 4: 27)'. Similarly, the firms did not know how to motivate employees: '[I]t sufficed to enter a 'communist' store, to come across with the shop-assistants complete antipathy towards the client, who feels he/she is an intruder, asks to be pardoned and politely begs to be given any information at all, with gratitude for even the most modest signs of interest [from the shop-assistant]' (1992, 5: 43). The answer is to introduce an appropriate western compensation system that 'ties' the employees' pay to their 'efficiency' (1992, 5: 43–45).

The above quotations are examples of the anonymous stereotyping of firms, which are merely episodes in texts dedicated to 'good' and 'excellent' firms or western management concepts. This way of presenting negative examples is typical of the volumes of *Businessman Magazine* I have studied. No more space is dedicated to them than a few sentences. The firms are never principal heroes (or, rather, villains), just secondary characters. What is more, the narrative about them is not even directed at them ('the firms of the past era'); its role is to be the contrasting background against which the presentation of good examples will be even more convincing.

Wprost publishes critical articles about enterprises, which are either introduced by name or presented anonymously. For example, an article relates the opinions of consultants, introduced as 'company doctors', who are diagnosing a Polish state-owned enterprise which they undertook to 'cure'. They detected 'a well progressed disease: employment three times as big as needed, the area four times as big as needed, three times as heavy energy use relative to the turnover as the competitors' (1994, 1: 66). A well-known state-owned enterprise from the machinery sector is criticized for its concentration on political games while its financial problems worsen. This firm is 'not famous because of tractor production', but for its 'everyday production of declarations, resolutions and political appeals' (1992, 31: 25). (This enterprise was in dire economic trouble, but recently started to secure its position. As far as I know, this can be seen as a consequence of its intensive political activity.)

An article about western fast-food bars begins with the following assertion (in bold print): 'Dirty, broken plates and the vile smell of milk bars will be replaced by the smile, freshness, youthfulness and cleanliness offered by McDonald's and Burger King' (1993, 30: 66). Note that the message does not say actually anything about milk bars (the cheap Polish fast-food bars, of varying standard and outlook, offering such dishes as dumplings, milk soups, pancakes, etc. which are regarded with affection by both Polish and foreign consumers). Instead, the text returns to milk bars only once more, and is otherwise dedicated to the 'excellent' McDonald's and Burger King: 'In Poland, thanks to the appearance of fast foods, the era of milk bars will end, the milk bars of broken plates, bent forks and knives, soiled aprons, fetor, and a big question mark on the plate' (1993, 30: 67).

Gazeta Wyborcza, in its local supplement *Gazeta Stoleczna*, sometimes also engages in negative labelling of firms, introducing them by name. For example, a food-producing enterprise is described in the following way: 'On the head quarter's roof still the old name . . . Around the buildings a smell that reminds of herring smokehouse. The impression is magnified even further by the clouds of smoke that flow in from behind the fence. The walls of the building are not plastered, they are grey from dirt' (1993, 242: 10). The article explains that this situation is caused by privatization that 'has been dawdling for two years now' and that the firm 'is afraid of foreign investors'. Its products sell well on the Polish market, 'for the time being', but 'strong competition has emerged'. The author narrates the internal political games going on in the enterprise. The story ends with a pessimistic statement by the director, who himself does not believe the market will 'opt for' such a second-rate firm. Critical articles in *Gazeta Stoleczna* follow a similar format: they depict the firm, state what its problems are and end in either pessimism or optimism about its future.

THE SET FOR IDENTITY CHANGE

All three papers, but most often *Businessman Magazine*, publish texts on management techniques and concepts – metaphors for change of management practice. The most popular issue is marketing and advertisement, presented almost exclusively as a useful and beneficial instrument. Motivation is also a popular topic. Many texts are concerned with 'how to motivate employees' and present western models, often together with western examples. Another preferred subject is strategy and strategic management. Here Polish concepts sometimes appear, but are most often illustrated with western examples. Otherwise the concepts are presented as 'imported' from the west, and it is explicitly advised that the Poles do not 'invent the wheel, but use the knowledge from the West' (1992/5: 19). A key word in *Businessman Magazine* and in *Wprost* is 'success'. Success is defined as a process and its constituents are listed in one article (*Businessman Magazine* 1991, 6: 25–27), but typically it appears as the magic end to all problems and the most desired state everybody wants to achieve.

THE MANAGER'S NEW CLOTHES

New roles for and images of managers are examined most often by *Businessman Magazine*. In the volumes I have studied, stories about managers were common and were typically written in a panegyrical tone, just as were the positive examples of firms. Both western and Polish managers were presented primarily in the categories of 'success' (e.g. 1992/5: 5). Success can be achieved through hard work, not political games. The Polish version of the American myth is often in use. Frequently the business person is presented as having had a tough start. For example, a well-known Polish manager is introduced as descending from a rather poor family. He started as a *Gastarbeiter* in the West, worked hard and studied simultaneously (1992, 2: 14). Similarly, Michael Dell 'started with a capital of $1000' (1992, 4: 7), an owner of a clothing producer sold jeans at a bazaar (1993/7: 36), a well-known female manager achieved her position through hard work, persistence and endurance (1992/1: 29), etc. The business person has to have 'new ideas', 'luck' and like 'adventure' (e.g. 1993/7: 37; 1992/4: 7; 1992/4: 21). 'Profits' are important, 'the enterprise must bring profit' (1992/1: 7), but 'profit is not all that business is about', there is also 'an inner need' (1991/4: 10–11). A modern manager is not intimidated by competition: 'it spurs him' (1993/8: 8). Politics is either not taken up at all or ridiculed and denied, even if the presented managers are famous for their skilful political games. There is one exception: an article about how to sell on the 'eastern' (Russian) market contains the advice to 'take care of the old boy network' (1993/7: 60–62).

The exemplary manager is sometimes characterized explicitly, often with the qualities of 'commitment to work hard', 'ability to overcome obstacles' and 'a strong drive to succeed' (1992/2: 59). The most popular traits throughout the volumes of *Businessman Magazine* I have studied are, perhaps, 'hard work' and 'profit making'. *Businessman Magazine* brings into fashion the lifestyle of the modern manager, including clothes, sports, travels. Advice is given on how to arrange the office, which car to choose, and which equipment is the best (most fashionable). Hagiographics about 'excellent' western managers are common in *Wprost*, e.g. Steve Wozniak (1993/23: 667), Bill Gates (1993/6: 68). These articles are, again, centred around the idea of 'success' (e.g. 1993/6: 68).

Articles about Polish managers also appear. In an article entitled 'In search of the Polish Iacocca: firms on cold turkey' (in which 'cold turkey' is a treatment for alcoholism), western consultants, 'company doctors', are quoted. The author states as an introduction that 'With firms as with life – mistakes are made from the moment of conception' (1994/1: 66) and suggests that Polish enterprises do poorly because 'the vast majority of contemporary managers, coming generally from the state sector, is not ready for 'healing' firms: *the intelligence level of 49% of the Polish managers is lower than the average*' (1994/1: 66; original emphasis). The source of this information is not mentioned. (I heard it quoted more than once by the media, likewise without any reference to the original source.) The reader is led to believe that a majority of Polish managers have 'problems with the attributes necessary for a manager: fast decision making, easy endurance of stress situations'. The managers do not have an adequate education, a majority of them can 'only boast of evening university diplomas' (note that this implies that a majority of the managers have higher education). 'Meanwhile the Polish economy badly needs a Polish Iacocca . . .' (1994/1: 66). Whenever Polish managers are mentioned in the text, the Polish word *kierownik* is used. When the author speaks of the desired image and of western managers, he uses the term *menedzer*. (To be a *kierownik* is old-fashioned, while it is modern to be a *menedzer*, even if the job is identical.)

GENDERED IMAGE

This section (based on texts published in *Businessman Magazine*) indicates that the image of the manager is strongly gendered. To be a manager is to be masculine. Men prevail among the presented managers. Female examples are seldom introduced, and then in branches considered to be 'female': an article about home decoration (1992/4: 21), an art gallery (1992/5: 58–59), a hotel (1991/4: 54–55). The owner of the hotel introduces herself as a 'housewife', because 'a hotel is a home too, just bigger'. The same person explains that she 'hates' the branch in which she started her career as a business person (stoneworks) because she dislikes 'using dirty language, shouting, being a man-woman'. She says that she is happy now because she is healthy, has a good husband and will be a mother soon. She presents her accomplishments at work as being of less importance (1991/4: 54–55).

Another female manager introduces herself in the following way: 'We are not beastly dames. Only a happy woman, happy with her life, confident about her home, can find time for doing something more' (1992/1: 30). The female reporter authoring this story adds that soroptimists, an organization in which the manager is a participant, 'firmly renounce ideas of emancipation, they reject the unhappy women-beasts fighting for who-knows-what'. The same heroine of a text almost totally dominated by issues of gender ('sex') believes that '[s]ex is of . . . no relevance', her cooperation with male colleagues is fine and she wants to be treated as a partner (1992/1: 30).

Female managers are often questioned about their family, home, marital status (I have not found a woman presented as unmarried in the articles studied); the reporters stress the priority of the traditional female role before all other roles, including the professional. A well-known female director is presented as 'perhaps in the first place, a happy housewife, mother of three children and a grandmother of two grandchildren'. The problems of splitting time between home and work are exposed, the same person admits that she '[o]ften believe[s], that [she] harm[s] the family' (1992/1: 29–30). The reporters address questions and statements to them that they would not address to a male manager, e.g. 'I believe that a woman who runs a construction site by herself, a renovation etc., must pay for it with her health' (1991/4: 54). There are exceptions: sometimes the woman manager is presented exclusively in her professional role. These articles are short and hard to find. Their tone is bland and matter of fact, with almost no metaphors; thus the otherwise so popular idea of success was not mentioned (1992/4: 21; 1992/6: 68).

Articles about male managers are quite different. Their family situation is not mentioned at all. The only allusion to a man's family situation in the sample is the following quotation from an article about a bank officer: 'As an epilogue, please tell us something about yourself. I'm 39 years old, I have a wife and two children . . . (1992, 2: 7)'. The manager then went on to talk about his hobbies. The form of lifestyle that is being brought into fashion is also addressed to men. The manager is shown as having traditional male hobbies, such as poker, golf, fishing. Pictures illustrating these texts display men almost exclusively. The front page of *Businessman Magazine* is typically a blow-up of a well-known manager's face. Of the volumes studied only one portrayed a woman: a manager who was also a minister in one of the post-1989 governments.

IDENTITY TRANSFER: FROM WHERE TO WHERE?

In Barbara Czarniawska-Joerges's (1994) essay on organizational identity, the author rewrites the story of the Swedish public sector as a tale about two sisters: one beautiful and the other ugly. The ugly sister, formerly the 'nice' one, is advised to imitate the beautiful sister by a doctor she consults. In this story, the private sector (the beautiful sister) is the author of the public sector's biography. The mass media's narrative can be told in a similar way.

Once upon a time there was a school with good pupils (Polish model enterprises) and bad pupils ('Communist enterprises', or state-owned enterprises that still are active in the political rather than the economic sphere). The good pupils were previously called 'bourgeois *Besserwissers*' and expelled from the school. The current bad pupils were not seen as such, but labelled 'athletic'. They did well and led a pleasant life, fighting and doing sports. Gym was the most important class, and they always achieved excellent grades. They still do well in sports, but gym is no longer on the school's curriculum. Their grades deteriorated almost overnight. The teachers see them as rather 'impossible' and give up on them. They like to remind the whole class of the situation of the bad pupils. They do not do this to encourage the bad pupils to start working, but to show the class that things have changed and that misbehaviour can end in expulsion. The pupils are also given a model to imitate: American students. The teachers talk about them in superlatives. Their own good pupils are praised as coming close to this ideal but never really accomplish perfection. They are, rather, the living proof that it is possible to try.

It is striking, however, that during inter-school contests, arranged every semester and crucial for the students' actual final results, sporting achievement is still a criterion for success. No wonder that the good pupils are not doing very well in practice. The bad ones do better, thanks to their proficiency in sports, old networks and sometimes brute force. But the true winners belong to neither of the two categories: they are silent students nobody talks about in the school, those who know how to combine a certain proficiency in sports with acceptable grades in other subjects.

In Barbara Czarniawska-Joerges's study the Swedish private sector is authoring the public sector's autobiography: the 'private sector usurps the role of the narrator and even the author, relegating the public administration to a side character in its own autobiography' (Czarniawska-Joerges 1994: 203). My analysis shows that the authors of the Polish state-owned enterprises are anonymous ghost-writers: journalists and consultants. In this autobiography the American firms are the main heroes, the ideal against which all other firms are measured. Some Polish firms, private or privatized, or at least undergoing restructuring, are approaching this ideal.

The Polish positive example is used as 'verisimilizer', proof that an advance toward the ideal is possible. This image is *maquillé* and one-sided: drawing attention exclusively to the firms' economic activity and withdrawing it from the political and even social activities many Polish enterprises engage in.

It is also important to mention language. Many new, foreign words are currently enriching the Polish language (even if not welcomed by all). And so, for example, the media often refer to *management* or *menedzment* (instead of *zarzldzanie*), *manager* or *menedzer* (instead of *kierownik*), *business* or *biznes*, *konsultant* (instead of *doradca*), etc. These words are either new (as *controlling*) or were formerly part of an elite expert language (as *marketing*). Now they are used by the 'common Pole', a part of everyday language. As noticed before, the use of these words has an emotional connotation: it is 'modern' to be a *menedzer* while it is passé to be a *kierownik*, even if the job is identical (more on Polish management-related words, their translations and meanings can be seen in Jankowicz 1994).

LABELS AND METAPHORS

Labels tell what 'reality is like', while metaphors point at 'how it might be' (Czarniawska-Joerges 1988). Labelling serves to characterize an identity that 'should be' changed. Metaphors help to accept the new identity. Labelling of enterprises in the press thus plays a diagnostic role. Labels refer to 'what is wrong', 'what should be changed'. The 'Communist enterprises' have poor motivation systems, too many employees, high costs, bad organization, irrational price policies, etc. These diagnostic labels are not the only ones given. Another kind ostentatiously condemn 'Communist enterprises', drawing the image in dark colours, and thus not describing them as 'ill' (and curable, or at least deserving of sympathy), but as inherently 'bad'. They are anachronisms, archaic, ugly, politicized, smelly, and cause regional tragedies. These labels are used as a background against which to compare the 'good identities', and I will here call them 'contrasting labels'. In order to understand their role it is helpful to consider the metaphors as generalized expressions of wish fulfilment. The metaphors brought into fashion by the press (the 'abstract' or 'theoretical' models and concepts) are almost identical to the images of American firms. 'Success' is the central metaphor in the narrative: a firm and a manager definitely 'should have it'. In the process of fashioning the identity image the press therefore makes use of contrasting labels as sticks and metaphors as carrots.

THE ENTERPRISE WITHOUT AN IDENTITY

In a study on differing managerial responses to change I concluded that the type of enterprises best suited to functioning in the current context in Poland are those which act simultaneously in two spheres: the economic and the political (Kostera 1995). I suggested that these firms prevail among large and medium-sized businesses in today's Poland. However, they are not allowed to have their own identity and their way of organizing is not mentioned by the press, nor is any activity other than economic. An exception is *Gazeta Wyborcza*, which, at least in one text, referred to an enterprise's social activity: its striving to preserve workplaces.

In contemporary Poland there is a tendency to see the mass media as the 'mirror of reality'. The myth has long since been outmoded in the West, where there is a tradition of freedom of speech. The press creates images by bringing into fashion certain ideas and identities and is thus a powerful active co-constructor of reality. But is the power of 'wording' perhaps weaker that the power of 'non-wording' (silence can be a puissant metaphor)? The social negotiations that shape identities are omitted by the media. Therefore some people and organizations might be forced into a normalizing (and streamlining) category, e.g. the politically active enterprises utilize the identity of the economically minded, women managers that of housewives. Silence can create greater discipline than can the shouting of commands.

POLISH AND FOREIGN EXAMPLES: WHAT IS THERE TO LEARN?

There are some noticeable differences between the images of Polish and foreign firms. First, in the volumes studied all foreign forms are western, and the firms most praised are those of the US. The stories about western firms are as one-sided as the contrasting Polish examples: they are simple and with a plain moral. The western recipe for success is – success; the definition of success is at the same time the recipe. Polish negative 'background' examples are, similarly, a failure because they are as they are. The Polish positive examples are different, because they are not the image of perfection, and very often they are problematized: they narrate stories of problems and how they were or are overcome.

What seem to be missing are such problematized stories about western firms: how they were in trouble and how they solved their problems. This would have several advantages: identification would be easier (the current combination is of the 'the king and the beggar' kind), and an emphasis would be put on the process and not upon effects already achieved. In organization theory, and particularly in theories of learning, a new specialization has appeared, of so-called 'risky organizations' (especially nuclear plants, but also airlines; see e.g. Weick 1987). For many years it has been believed that a safe and secure functioning of these organizations is just a derivative of the technical system (just as many Polish organization theorists and practitioners believe in 'organizational structures' that will solve all problems if implemented). Currently, after many tragic incidents, attention has been turned to the processes of organizing and management. It turned out that the most effective way of learning is through 'near-miss stories', i.e. stories about situations where the catastrophe has been averted. It is difficult to conclude what the most important causes of organizational effectiveness are ('the recipe for success is success'). Catastrophes have devastating emotional consequences, people are scared and avoid responsibility. The interest in a cool analysis is a characteristic of the analysers, not of the actors, who are directly and emotionally engaged in the situation. Near-miss stories have the advantage of not causing these ruinous emotional effects. They break through the surface of good functioning and uncover the mechanisms below, but do not go so far as to destroy the mechanism. It is these kinds of stories that are generally lacking in the media narratives about western firms and managers. My point is that they would be influential in the process of identity transfer, a point to which I shall return later in the chapter.

MANAGERIAL SYMBOLISM

Within the press titles I have studied, the new social role of the manager is brought into fashion mainly by *Businessman Magazine*. It is as one-sided as the image of the enterprises. The modern manager becomes a person preoccupied with the economic sphere, ostentatiously so. Further he (sic!) is a personification of the Polish version of the American myth. It is an idealized and romantic picture of 'Americanism', probably more Polish than American. In accordance with this romantic myth, the manager is a strong individualist, a powerful leader, a charismatic person, who also is resistant to stress and enjoys making money. At the same time, the manager symbolizes the change, personifies it, is a missionary of the new religion: the religion of economic rationality. The god of this religion is the free market, also known as the Invisible Hand who must be abided and trusted but can be pleased by the right-minded ones, the managers and business people 'of the new generation'.

It is important to note that the image brought into fashion by the press is consistent and simple and leaves little room for choice. The proposed identity is much more naive than the actual managerial responses to change, which are polyphonic and based on varying rationalities (Kostera 1995). Instead, the identity-image's one-sidedness is more reminiscent of the symbols transferred by the Communist Polish press: black and white, and always having a simple moral (see, e.g., Glowiński 1992). Choosing the 'wrong' identity is unthinkable: there is no acceptable image for 'dissidents', at least not in the press.

Even more one-sided and rigid is the image of the woman manager. She is not presented with an identity of her own, but with a remix of two others: that of the male manager and that of the traditional female social role.

Other press titles than those that I have studied confer more developed images, the identity of 'business woman' (usually spelt that way in Polish) is gaining growing popularity in non-conservative press titles. The daily *Rzeczpospolita* even had a steady column, 'Kobieta interesu' (business woman), and one of its monthly journals was dedicated to women in management (*Rzeczpospolita Magazyn* 1993: 3/1). The rhetoric of these texts is based on the 'feminine-in-management' trend. This apparently women-friendly rhetoric is deceptive, because it obscures what is important for women, appealing to them through an attractive 'package' (Calas and Smircich 1993). The 'feminine-in-management' trend emphasizes 'feminine' qualities, which are said to be crucial for management in the future. Women are needed as managers at local levels. At the same time, men become managers at the global levels, where 'feminine traits' are apparently not so necessary. The 'feminine-in-management' trend serves to cover up this tendency, which is similar to what happened to clerical jobs not so long ago (Calas and Smircich 1993).

It should be added, however, that the bringing into fashion of this image in Poland is more progressive than it is in the west. Polish managers, even men, generally lack the possibilities of a global career. The 'feminine-in-management' image is becoming a legitimate alternative for women not willing to adopt the abovementioned narrow role. It is, however, in my opinion not a radical solution for the Polish woman's situation. The image can contribute to enhancing the construction of traditional roles, closing the list of negotiable options for the future, as it remains based on a traditional set of values and stereotypes.

PRODUCTION OF ENERGY: REACTIONS TO THE IMAGES BROUGHT INTO FASHION

When travelling ideas meet with those in residence, energy is produced through friction (Czarniawska-Joerges 1994). Through this encounter, the process of transfer of ideas becomes creative: otherwise it runs in the colonization mode. From this point of view there is no reason to fear 'resistance to change', rather the contrary: energy is something valuable and makes action possible. My study of readers' reactions to the images brought into fashion by the Polish press shows that while the reactions were intense to some of them, others failed to produce any response.

Some of the respondents answered by summarizing the articles, with minimal personal comments. This 'escape from reaction' was, in my opinion, a way to express uncertainty, a delay in response. It was, however, not the most typical reaction. Typically, the reviews were quite personal. The readers reacted generally with a certain scepticism: they said they liked the articles, but considered them impossible to use in Poland, or in their own business practice. One of my respondents suggested a metaphor: the images were like a Parisian fashion show for a Polish viewer – he or she will use some of the ideas in ordering a new suit or dress from the local tailor, but will of course not buy any of the things presented.

IDEAS IN RESIDENCE MEET IDEAS ABOUT ENTERPRISES

Respondents were doubtful as to the feasibility of the proposed models. They often introduced alternative dimensions in their comments, notably the political. For example, a female manager considered the ideas of entrepreneurship in an article in *Businessman Magazine* as Utopian and remarked on the 'Polish reality': in order to raise capital one had to 'know the right people'. Managers reacted to the naiveté of the images, they often remarked that what the text says may be reasonable in the West but is just a 'fairy tale' in Poland. Sometimes they pointed out such differences as lack of reasons for optimism, low living standards, etc., but not always. There were many reactions of 'general mistrust' – we are 'obviously' different. Some respondents wrote whole essays explaining why they did not accept the proposed models. For example, a male manager for a state-owned enterprise wrote the following: '. . . [P]olish products were associated with ideally bad washing powder, but were the [Polish] powders really of bad quality? If state-owned plants did not invest in marketing, if the packages were not attractive, if there was a lack of suggestive and ingenious advertising: how could it be any different?'

Some of the respondents even proposed changes in the image so that it fitted reality better. 'Historical modifications' were common – 'Polish history should be taken into consideration' but there were other additions: educational, cultural, etc. Some respondents did not address their reactions to the authors of the texts but to some more or less well-defined 'authorities' – they should 'provide appropriate conditions', so that the western models applied better to Polish enterprises. Some of the respondents joined in a critique of Polish enterprises and elaborated on the authors' contrasting labelling. Typically, this kind of response was given by the MBA students. They either praised the ideas of the press or criticized them as being 'too old-fashioned', relating the latest US models and thus positioning the press' images as a kind of outmoded 'contrast'. Not all MBAs wrote reviews of this kind; some reacted in the way related above. However, none of the non-MBAs adopted the latter attitude.

Many of the reactions referred to politics, in one way or another, but often also to social problems. The managers added, sometimes sarcastically, a social dimension to the images brought into fashion. One respondent first wrote ironically about an article on western management models and the issue of 'excellence' introduced in it, and then remarked: 'no mention of unemployment, which certainly belongs to the current Polish reality, unemployment sometimes amounting to 30% . . .'. Another person mentioned the patronizing attitude to culture expressed by the business-centred articles: he wondered whether the real 'solution' to the problem was a 'collection into the hat', as (in his opinion) was suggested by the market model brought into fashion. One of the respondents criticized the motivation models 'it is not necessarily so that the group aims are more important than individuals' ones' and pointed out that employees are treated as small children in these texts.

MANAGERS WITH NO IDENTITY?

The role of the manager, made fashionable by the press, was commented upon with moderation, and much less often than the image of the enterprise. If it was addressed, it was typically a brief, slightly ironic remark, e.g. that the new manager enjoys elegant brands of alcohol but does not know much about them, or that s/he engages in negotiations but cannot see beyond stereotypes. While some respondents wrote lengthy essays on the image of the enterprise, they usually restrained from longer discussion of the managerial role, despite having been asked to comment upon this. This might be due to a lack of interest in this issue, but as the respondents were managers themselves I would rather opt for a different explanation. The topic seemed to be too emotionally laden for comments. A field too restricted for individual freedom, uncertainty and perhaps a resulting feeling of inadequacy may be some of the reasons for this prudence.

THE SILENCE OF THE WOMEN

Women are the immigrants in the organizational world (Czarniawska-Joerges 1992a). They are expected to 'adapt', i.e. to espouse the masculine identity (or an identity prepared for them by the male 'hosts'). They can from time to time bring some 'folklore' into organizational life: the immigrants can for example be asked to show their national costumes, and women can be asked to demonstrate some 'feminine management style'. They are allowed to be different, on condition that this difference is trivial (not quite serious) and not threatening to the culture of the 'hosts'. In other words, women must prove that they can behave as men do in order to be accepted (then it is said that 'women are as good as any man'). Simultaneously, the roles of 'immigrants', the 'guests' and women are subject to strong control; they cannot become a danger for the 'hosts'.

The transfer of organizational identity from west to east is carried out in its totality. The model is a highly idealized version of 'westernness' (no 'buts', no reservations are included in the message). There is, however, an exception to this totality: the western feminist debate. There are many models for women managers in the west and just one of them is taken up by the Polish press: the 'feminine-in-management' image. Otherwise the female role is defined patriarchally. What is more, the role is not subject to public discussion and has not even been addressed by my respondents: men and women alike. The problems of women 'do not exist' in the responses of my informants.

If the colonization of enterprises is taking place out loud, with a good deal of vociferous resistance, then the colonization of Polish women is silent, just as the courts of the Polish martial law pronounced their verdicts in silence, thus aiming not only at 'getting it over with' but also at depriving the trial of significance. It is more the transfer of 'ideas given' than a case of translation. In spite of its uni-directional character, the transfer of organizational identity may turn out to be creative: there seems to be some considerable potential in residence. The colonization of women is not creative at all: it is mundane, tedious, prosaic, and also it is kitsch:[1] similar to the past attempts at colonization by Communist totalitarian propaganda.

CONCLUSION: A FITTING IDENTITY

The identity image made fashionable by the press is a version of the myth about western, and perhaps particularly US, firms and managers. 'If we put on their clothes, the Polish enterprises will magically become as effective as the US' – seems to be the underlying belief. However, this ready-made idea of identity is not fully accepted by Polish managers themselves, who would perhaps prefer a tailor-made costume. They are assertive when they speak about their firms, and more reserved while talking of their own role.

One image was not commented on at all – that of the female manager. On this point all respondents, men and women alike, avoided comment. There seems, though, to be a certain energetic potential that can have a positive influence on identity negotiation. This does not apply to women managers, who wear whatever is handed out to them, as if hoping to be able to hide under the oversized clothes and continue to work shrouded from society's 'gaze'.

The black and white picture transferred does not seem appealing: the one-sided critique of the labels of background may evoke protest and rejection by managers who have lived long enough to be presented with various images of villains and 'enemies of the people' by the press.

The 'bringing into fashion' would perhaps be more effective if more near-miss stories were narrated, including those about western firms. The role that the images of western firms and managers play in the transfer further amplifies the associations with colonization. Polish managers, used to attempts to colonize them (under totalitarianism), have grown suspicious and sceptical about such endeavours. The totalitarian press was a spokes-institution for authorities disposing of a massive apparatus of enforcement of their expectations. The new press can engage and motivate; it can also manipulate, e.g. under the pretences of 'mirroring reality'. The UB (secret police) is gone, but other institutions may have a similar degrading role in society, especially if people are socialized to a reality in which the old realities are active. An open discussion is still needed as badly as ever.

NOTE

1 As Milan Kundera says, 'In the land of total kitsch the answers are known a priori and exclude any questions (1989: 172). Kitsch is, then, the obvious, the familiar and dear, the glue that holds us together. Kitsch is closely coupled with relations of power. Kitsch is acceptance: of being, of received ideas. It fails to surprise, it avoids amazement, it abhors the singular. Therefore, oppressive social constructions thrive on kitsch, among them stereotypes, prejudices and tight social roles.

REFERENCES AND FURTHER READING

Berger, P.L. and Luckmann, T. (1966/1971) *The Social Construction of Reality*, New York: Doubleday.
Calas, M.B. and Smircich, L. (1993) 'Dangerous liaisons: the feminine-in-management meets globalisation', *Business Horizons* (March–April), pp. 73–83.
Czarniawska-Joerges, B. (1988) *To Coin a Phrase*, Stockholm: Stockholm School of Economics.
Czarniawska-Joerges, B. (1992a) *Styrningens paradoxer. Scener ur den offentliga verksamheren*, Stockholm: Nordsteds Juridik.
Czarniawska-Joerges, B. (1992b) *Doing Interpretive Studies of Organisations*, working paper, Lund: Lunds Universitet, Institutet för Ekonomisk Forskning.
Czarniawska-Joerges, B. (1994) 'Narratives of individual and organisational identities', in S. Deetz (ed.) *Communication Yearbook* 17, London: Sage pp. 193–221.
Denzin, N.K. (1992) *Symbolic Interactionism and Cultural Studies: The Politics of Interpretation*, Oxford, UK: Blackwell.
Eco, U. (1990) *The Limits of Interpretation*, Cambridge: Cambridge University Press.
Glowiñski, M. (1992) *Rytual i demagogia: Trzynaście szkiców o sztuce zdegradowanej*, Warsaw: Open.
Hatch, M.J. and Ehrlich, S.B. (1993) 'Spontaneous humour as an indicator of paradox and ambiguity in organisations', *Organisation Studies* 14(4), pp. 505–26.
Jankowicz, A.D. (1994) 'The new journey to Jerusalem: mission and meaning in the managerial crusade to Eastern Europe', *Organisation Studies* 15(4), pp. 479–507.
Kostera, M. (1995) 'Differing managerial responses to change in Poland', *Organisation Studies* 16(4), pp. 693–7.
Kostera, M. (1996) *Postmodernism w zarządzaniu*. [Postmodernism and management], Warsaw: PWE.
Kundera, M. (1989) *Nieznosna lekkość bytu* [The unbearable lightness of being], translated from Czech into Polish by Agnieszka Holland, Wrocław: IWA.
Latour, B. (1986) 'The powers of association', in J.W. Law (ed.) *Power, Action and Belief: A New Sociology of Power?*, London: Routledge & Kegan Paul.
Weick, K.E. (1987) 'Organisational culture as a source of high reliability', *California Management Review* 24, pp. 112–27.

Chapter 15

Aid in trade: the dynamics of the post-Communist restructuring of management education

Slawomir Magala

The wave of restructuring processes in the post-Communist countries of Central and Eastern Europe has rolled over all institutions; economic, political and social as well as educational. The attitudes of EC countries towards these changes have been favourable, but the degree of willingness to assist in the transformation varies and so does the degree of understanding as to the forms of assistance most urgently needed. A general principle which emerged from the first five years of transformation is that an approach which stimulates partnership and the establishment of a working relationship produces more desirable effects than assistance modelled on 'aid for developing countries'.

It is argued here that it is not aid the post-Communist countries are looking for rather, increasing trade which will enable them to become true partners of their neighbours and competitors (i.e. those with market economies) so that they will be able to re-enter the global commercial traffic lanes (Soone 1993). In order for them to do this there needs to be a major restructuring of the economic system, the creation of new infrastructure and the development of a human resource capability. These are often seen as synonymous with the development of an entrepreneurial culture ('the making of the new entrepreneurs'). To do this requires a change in management education – hence the significance of the TEMPUS networks.

Through such schemes academic teachers like myself (whose teaching is linked to economic infrastructural change and to the shaping of new economic agents) are trying to provide the basics of business in a rapidly changing environment. The restructuring of business education in the Central and Eastern European countries should therefore reflect designs which aim to improve post-Communist trade. Does it? Did we succeed in bridging the gaps (between their business education and ours), smoothing the transitions (from economic education under planned state economy to business managerial education for a market economy) and facilitating true partnership in the future?

It is a question of interpretation and self-reflection. Have we accomplished what we planned by offering the Central European partners cooperation and networking programmes? Have we contributed to their increased chances in practising their trade and entering global trade networks? In other words, did we succeed in tutoring our future partners and competitors?

FROM PRISONS TO JUNGLES

In order to answer these questions we have to examine the present changes. There will be those which might be due to our temporary and limited influences. These we can safely claim credit for. There will be others which either happen by chance or result form the inner dynamics of the post-Communist academic institutions. Neither the chance events nor the results of the inner dynamics can be credited to our TEMPUS inputs. How can we distinguish between those we have contributed to and those we have not?

Let us begin with an analysis of the situation in most Central European post-Communist states. Amongst metaphors being used to describe the present situation in their academic institutions is the transition from a 'prison' to a 'jungle'.

The word 'prison' describes the expectations of economic education under Communist rule. With the limited role of the market there was little need for the potential managers of state enterprises to acquire business know-how. Their business lay at the whim of state economic plans as well as in the quality of cooperation with the experienced political authorities. These factors satisfactorily determined the priorities. The major economic universities therefore produced economists who dutifully studied the difference between a 'capitalist' market economy and a 'socialist' state economy. Intakes to these universities were also planned to produce economists to fill the 'slots' in a social division of labour designed and directly controlled by the political authorities. The choice of a specialization at a university (foreign trade, production, finances) was analogous to the selection of an employment vacancy. The university place was a 'slot' to be filled and the consequent employment and career were a series of positions in state-controlled enterprises and institutions.

There was no unemployment – there could be none – since all those who were taught and trained had to fill the slots which the state employer had already planned for them. If some graduates had no slots waiting for them, employment opportunities and careers were created – no market pressures limited the state planner in this system, although the notoriously low salaries of the professionals showed the vulnerability of this policy in the long run. I had the misfortune not to fill one of the designed slots: not because of the surplus of manpower but, I suspect, as a punishment for my lack of loyalty to the Communist authorities and a failure to conform! Generally speaking, potential mistakes in planning were easy to rectify – a relative overproduction of teachers or medical doctors in large cities resulted in lowering of their salaries, in increased numbers of women in the workforce (thus making the gender inequalities resurface in spite of the formal equality of employment opportunities) and in a gradual decline of the number of student places. A very rudimentary and slow mechanism of preserving job market balances was thus present 'in the margins'.

With the breakdown of the Communist system and of the planned economy, students and academic teachers found out that the constraints of a 'prison' were gone but were replaced by a new educational and job market – the 'jungle'.

CHARTING THE 'JUNGLES'

As the reforms of 1989/90 came and went bringing with them market reforms first to the Poles and the Hungarians, then to the Czechs, Slovaks, East Germans, Romanians and Bulgarians, the post-Soviet Balts, Ukrainians, Russians, White Russians and many others the academic institutions soon found they had to follow suit. They turned from being the 'prisons' where their students were kept before being released to these clearly defined jobs slots into 'jungles', where the teachers have to forecast the 'slots', design the curricula and attract the students; where students have to find their own paths and make their own choices and where the emerging businesses have to come looking for their employees.

The comparison of the post-Communist transition to a passage from a prison to a jungle reflects the relaxation of the strong state controls which, in turn, enables a 'jungle' of interests – heretofore kept in check – to clash freely. This change is not always psychologically easy to accept: 'New sets of values will replace the old ones imprinted on many generations by the old regime. Let us consider one example only. A Western reader may feel: why does this book say such trivial things as that people have the right to earn more than others if they are successful in business? But this truth, self-evident to an American, is not at all natural to a Pole or an East German' (Kornai 1990). Let us add that if a Pole, a Hungarian or an East German can at present be seen swallowing this principle, this is not necessarily the case in Russia, where the political parties promising an egalitarian distribution and an imperial autocracy are not at all unpopular (as testified by the electoral success of Zhirinovski).

The responses by the universities have been very different and can best be characterized by three different types of behaviour, exemplified by the Chinese, Russian and Central European cases.

THE CHINESE CASE

In the Chinese case (Magala *et al.* 1992) there was no change of the institution, and no major reshuffling of the top and middle management.

There existed limited individual staff mobility coupled with a reliance on formally approved contacts with broader international networks to modernize. However, all efforts to change the structure of a university were still being channelled through the established government contacts, and political discussion of power relations (both inside and outside of the university) was avoided.

There were many reformers in the post-Communist educational system and a relative ambiguity concerning the desirable approach for business education has not been easily removed from the initial forms of cooperation with EC partners. Among the obstacles which have been encountered by the reformers is the relative lack of business traditions that put a brake on a 'natural' form of cooperation which would resemble the 'filtering down' of the transformations through individual grass roots changes and improvements. The visiting professors and visiting programmes became an alternative to more symmetric exchange, making it easier for the Chinese academics to enjoy the company of the western visitors without either going abroad or having to initiate institutional changes as a result of more reciprocal and full-scale cooperation. The institutional order could have been preserved and contacts with the western academics limited to the 'slots' designed by the Communist bureaucrats without the 'spill-over' effect they might have had if returning Chinese academics had an impact upon their home institutions.

Moreover, the political conservatism went together with a genuine economic growth, thus opening a new structure of possibilities for the professionals and defusing their radical potential. The Chinese authorities have also manifested considerable skill in trying to attract career academic professionals back to China. By offering them better salaries and housing they have succeeded in reducing the defection rate. It remains to be seen if they have also succeeded in defusing their potential for becoming agents of transformation back in their home institutions.

THE RUSSIAN CASE

The Russian case (Magala 1992b) shows no change of the core institutional activities and only limited personnel reshuffling, reflecting power struggles within the middle and higher staff. In spite of the preservation of old courses (though not always under the old names), there is a gradual inclusion of commercial part-time educational services and an overall cosmetic change in the core activities; staff members are also increasingly motivated to carve out their 'semi-privatized' commercial niches in the overall structure of the educational services.

In Russia the political power of the Communist Party has either been broken or transformed through the economic privilege of the former *nomenklatura* and new entrepreneurs. The academics could not have remained neutral; neither could they freeze the status quo. However, while supplementing their traditional core curricula with a variety of part-time, executive and specialist courses on business management, bookkeeping, finance, legal and taxation advice for the entrepreneurs, they tried to preserve the personal, structural and institutional networks of the past. This was, for instance, the response of the Russian academics in Moscow: they have designed an MBA programme, but kept it inoperative as a full-time enterprise and offered its bits and pieces as brief educational courses for future entrepreneurs, charging fees and trying to finance the old full-time school according to the commercial principles applied in 'side activities'. A future inauguration of a full-time MBA programme was dependent on the proceeds from these extracurricular activities and on a number of western assistance projects which had been incorporated into it. They have renamed their courses and called themselves the International Business School (IBS), which is attached to the Moscow State Institute of International Relations (MGIMO). Under the Communists the school taught future diplomats and prepared them in international politics, languages and economic relations. The school's most valuable asset – excellent connections to the political elite – has slowly been supplemented by the emergent contacts with western educational institutions (leaflets for planned MBA classes announced teachers from Wake Forest University in the USA) and by the network of job openings in the emergent joint ventures (although it is very difficult to determine whether the jobs have been offered to the graduates because of the old reputation in languages and diplomacy and in the family background of students or because of the growing reputation of the 'managerial' reforms of the curriculum).

THE 'POLISH' CASE

This shows a change in the institutional and generational dynamics, a curriculum reform and a multiple response to the requirements of the market and political dynamics, resulting in a rapid restructuring, commercial initiatives and an intensified political struggle within academia.

Neither of the latter two cases (which must clearly be re-examined every year in view of the high rate of change in both countries in question) appears to me to present the real case of an institutional transformation with core activities and core personnel clearly involved. Neither allows for an open clash of different ideas on political environment, needs of the business community and interests of various groups among the staff. In order to find such cases we have to move to central eastern Europe, where the decline of Communist power was swift and the response of academics far-ranging. In other words, we have to examine the places where the shift from a prison to a jungle has been the most massive, most broadly supported, and best prepared by the alternative professional elites.

The three central-eastern European countries where this had been the case are Poland, the Czech and Slovak Republics and Hungary. The former East Germany is a specific case both because of the relatively late emergence of the social movement and professional elite dissent and because of the different post-Communist situation. Having become part of Germany the East German potential alternative elites did not face the disappearing *nomenklatura* but had to accept the elites of the former West Germany. What pressures did the educational institutions encounter after the non-Communist politicians came to power, privatization was introduced and entrepreneurs created a boom in non-state sectors of the economy?

The pressures were quite numerous and at the economic universities they have been felt most clearly in the following areas.

The new demand

The new demand for basic economic and business education for future new entrepreneurs and for the employees of the infrastructure of a market economy led to growing numbers of students and to a growing pressure to sell part-time and executive programmes. This growth of interest has been particularly visible since it came after a relative decline in the importance of higher education in the mid-1980s. Data on the relative decline of interest in university education in the period 1983–5 can be found in standard sources (e.g. statistical yearbook) if one compares the numbers of primary school graduates entering lycea (high schools whose primary function is to prepare a student for university study through general education) to the numbers before martial law was declared. Under the condition of a stagnating state-run economy higher education lost part of its allure (as testified by the decreasing numbers of candidates for the top middle-level schools preparing for an academic education). The emergence of the market economy increased the number of candidates for the economic, legal and other studies offering the status of 'professional' and preparing for business activities in the rapidly expanding non-state sector of the economy (or in the companies of a state sector trying to survive in a market environment).

The new competition

The new competition for the students and for the executive programmes led to a division into those staff members who represented old Marxian lore, were compromised by their Communist past and/or unwilling to meet the new demand and those who were eager to introduce elements of business management, managerial specializations and executive managerial programmes. The competition for university and extramural resources between these two groups has been reinforced by a new competitor on the educational market: private foundations and joint ventures of foreign consulting companies and foreign universities trying to create networks of professionals in the post-Communist countries. Prague International Business School, linked to the University of Economics in Prague, is one such institution situated in the Czech Republic. Similar examples can also be found in Warsaw and Budapest.

The new political vacuum

The new political vacuum was felt almost immediately after the most compromised Communist administrators left: the newly emergent lobbies and groups were unable to secure a clear majority in most elections to the offices of deans and rectors and had to enter a coalition which blurred the lines drawn by the new competition and prolonged the process of institutional transformation. Because of this blurring a generational factor began to play a very important role in determining the thrust and rate of reform.

The above mentioned pressures resulted in a number of initiatives being undertaken in order to upgrade the academic teachers (it is here that the role played by TEMPUS turned out to be quite substantial) and to facilitate their response to the new challenges. These pressures have also contributed to the search for more commercial programmes, either by turning open universities offering part-time programmes into profit centres (since the students now come to prepare themselves for self-employment, not to spend a few years enjoying the status of a student) or by designing or co-running various MBA or MBA-like programmes. The postgraduate MBA programme became the most popular form of business education both for the new educational entrepreneurs and for some academic teachers who decided to keep the security of their university jobs whilst also venturing into this lucrative sector of the educational market. Hence the proliferation of 'international MBAs' in Warsaw, Budapest and Prague in the very first period of restructuring (1990–1). The fact that MBA programmes are usually provided on a commercial basis also meant that both western and eastern academic teachers were motivated to calculate their fees outside the limitations imposed by public authorities regulating university education.

The struggle to reform the curriculum of economic universities thus had had a number of dimensions, outlined below.

The generational dimension

The younger generation had traditionally been less compromised by subservience to the Communist regime and much more open to a change towards business management education. However, the older generation had to fight for survival and became very inventive in closing alliances and digging in.

The political dimension

The existing political parties and the loyalties from the period of the Solidarity movement led to the political 'heroes' of the clandestine trade unions to form in 'clusters' around social consequences of radical educational reforms, thereby producing disturbing ambiguities. For example, imagine a proponent of radical reform of economic education who is willing to get rid of an old teacher of Marxian economic theory. He is willing to upgrade and modernize the curriculum, but can he, at the same time, sacrifice his colleague's job and claim that he defends the interests of the employees of the institution as a staunch member of Solidarity?.

The commercial dimension

Some clusters of academics opted for retaining a marginally reformed university alongside some private commercial venture. In the prison of a Communist state university, a commercial educational institution was not allowed. Once it had been allowed, some of the university teachers, especially the active ones with access to government liaisons and international contacts, discovered that through paying lip service to the reforms at their academic home they could reduce competition for their private, commercial 'international business schools'. They therefore preferred siding with the anti-reformers to prevent their universities from emerging as competitors of their own 'spare-time' ventures. This paradox actually illustrates very nicely the intricacies of democratic politics.

The international dimension

Lobbies of academic teachers differed with respect to their international networks, access to contacts and international assistance programmes such as TEMPUS. This difference in geographic distribution of contacts has played an active role in rallying support in the political struggle for power of a rector or a dean. If a western partner offered a complete personal computer workshop with up-to-date software and teaching possibilities, he might have increased the electoral chances of his Polish, Hungarian or Czech counterpart over the chances of someone who was only offered a library or a series of upgrading trips to the western universities. However, the exact structure of preference for various forms of assistance offered to the Central European economic universities by their western counterparts remains unknown and no studies have been available to date.

The last point deserves some attention. One should not assume that the influence of the 'western' counterparts on their Polish, Hungarian or Czech colleagues has been limited to showering them with 'gifts' in order to increase their relative power vis à vis their competitors for academic posts. First, there is an overall influence on the very willingness to visit various universities and to design a regular, systematic cooperation allowing Central European staff to 'shop' for books, ideas, curriculum designs, case and test materials, audio-visual aids, etc. This has been much more important in aiding the Central Europeans to form new, more regular and more 'normal' contacts with their western counterparts than any former types of less systematic and heavily controlled exchange could possibly ever be.

Second, the overall influence of the assistance projects – including the TEMPUS ones – has been most clearly perceived in the area of teaming-up and networking, primarily among the Central Europeans themselves. While it is possible that they would have teamed up and organized networks without TEMPUS projects, the availability of the latter has undoubtedly contributed to the acceleration of this process. In the very typical case of the Warsaw School of Economics (the former Main School for Planning and Statistics, which returned to the original name of the 'Main Commercial School' in Polish but opted for 'Warsaw School of Economics' in the English translation) a totally new network has been created. The reformers have now opened a new office which houses a team working both full time and part time on the ongoing reforms of the curriculum and the content of the courses as well as trying to consult all the other economic universities in the country.

The new demand, the new competition and the new political vacuum created favourable conditions for a profound institutional change. The new curricula reflect this change but have to be commented upon if the range and depth of reform are to be assessed.

In 1992 Warsaw School of Economics had entered the most important part of the processes of change: the curriculum war (in which the TEMPUS project played an important part by reinforcing the curriculum reform team clustered around one of the vice-presidents of the university and institutionalized around the Team for the Reform of Economic Education).

The composition of the university's top authorities reflected very clearly the new power struggle. The rector (university's president) had changed his political loyalties, but had been formed and had grown within the university bureaucracy under the Communists. Instead of lunching with the officials from the Central Committee of the Communist Party he had developed a habit of lunching with the bishops and the primate, but his attitude towards the curriculum changes was reserved and ambiguous. He managed to stay afloat by siding with the vice-president (pro-rector), whose support for curriculum reform was vital for its ultimate success a year later. The skills of the old-guard rector in playing the power game were displayed in the nomination of another vice-president (pro-rector), who had had extensive contacts with western academic counterparts and supported the reform but opted for a slower rate of change in order to spare some of the older and more conservative colleagues who might be 'phased out' within the new structure of the university. The power elite of the university was thus composed of the Rector (aged over 60), a Pro-rector for Change (aged over 40) and the second Pro-rector, who was a man of compromise as far as the scope and rate of change went (aged about 50).

The first and foremost element of reform was to remove the old structure of 'departments' and 'institutes' which reflected the economic specializations defined from the point of view of the state-controlled economy. The new structure (as can be seen in the Information Catalogue 1993/4, Warsaw, 1993) relied on the simple division of the 'basic core studies' and 'diploma courses' and offered seven specializations. The courses for both the basic and specialization (diploma) programmes were offered by the five colleges of the Warsaw School of Economics. For the students these changes meant not only a significant modernization and upgrading of their curriculum, but also a much greater liberty in selecting their own 'study path' through it. How have these changes been introduced? There are two major explanations of these changes: one has to do with the relatively strong tradition of the alternative sub-elites with rival programmes of change and the other has to do with generational loyalties.

ALTERNATIVE SUB-ELITES

The hypothesis about the role of alternative sub-elites is based on the theory of the role of elites in a democratic process. According to Etzioni-Halevy, the 'overtures' towards democracy have been much more advanced in Poland than in the former Soviet Union. The former has 'passed the threshold of full electoral democracy' while the latter 'has been in a near chaotic situation'. The explanation of these differences, according to the abovementioned sociologist, is linked to the different status of elites and sub-elites in these countries:

In line with this argument, it transpires that although neither in Poland nor in the Soviet Union did elites and sub-elites enjoy relative autonomy in the Western sense, nonetheless, from the end of the nineteenth century onwards, their autonomy was much more visible in Poland than it was in Soviet Union (. . .) In the Soviet Union, where elites and sub-elites did not develop a significant degree of autonomy, they were part of an autocratic regime's power structure and helped stabilise it through their complicity. Or else they were largely passive, and helped entrench and legitimise the regime through their very passivity, by default. By comparison, in Poland, where relative autonomy of elites was more highly developed, the relevant elites fulfilled an important role in furnishing symbols for, and crystallising centres of opposition to the regime, and in serving as an avant-garde in the battle for human rights and political liberties, and thus for democracy (. . .) The criteria for elite and sub-elite autonomy used are absence of its successful coercive repression, relative absence of control exerted on it through state and party administrative, material and symbolic resources, as well as lack of external control of its own administrative, material and symbolic resources. An elite and sub-elite's manifestation of autonomy by willingness to stand up to, as opposed to its submissiveness to the authorities will also be considered.

(Etzioni-Halevy 1993: 156–158)

The author explicitly states that she considers her explanations relevant for the power struggles at the universities by saying that: 'differences are surveyed below with respect to the elite (top leadership) and sub-elite (lower clergy) of the church, the leaders and activists of the trade unions, and the academic/intellectual elite and sub-elite both inside and outside universities' (p. 158).

In the elections to the top positions at the university held in June 1993, the president lost, the compromise vice-president was also forced out, and the vice-president who won asked a close collaborator of the pro-reform team to become a candidate for the president's office. She won. The president was not re-elected as he had hoped. The compromise vice-president was not even asked to become a candidate in the forthcoming elections. The vice-president whose programme won (and who had also been the most enthusiastic ally of the TEMPUS programmes) felt that he had achieved enough and that continuity of his policies would be guaranteed by his close collaborators in top positions at the university. Personally he felt that participating in power struggles diminished his chance for research development in his field (strategic management) and that he could safely withdraw from these struggles at this point. While this is not a classic happy ending, it clearly demonstrates the ability of an academic sub-elite focused on curriculum reform to oust the conservatives and compromisers from vital positions when change is at stake. The initiator of reforms did not intend to reap institutional benefits from his political victory, since a long march through the institutions had never been on his agenda. Should another issue arise and should he consider a political mobilization necessary to solve the problems, he might return to active university politics.

For the time being a new curriculum, newly upgraded facilities and newly retrained staff were clear signals that he had accomplished his goals and could return to his professional research interests. The sub-elite he had been a member of did not require full-time participation. They mobilized for issues rather than for institutional careers, for change rather than for the post-change retrenching and lobbying. This was made possible by the relative autonomy of the academic elite, making the struggle for power positions less vital in securing professional recognition and access to the institutional resources than would have been the case if there was no autonomy.

GENERATIONAL HYPOTHESIS

Another hypothesis which helps explain this behaviour is the generational one. Most of the members of the sub-elite at the Warsaw School of Economics which designed, implemented and institutionally secured the reform were below the age of 40–45. They succeeded against the generation which established their academic credentials and made their institutional careers under the Communists (those over 55) and they managed to break the unity of the generation caught between these two (c. 45–55). They did so by isolating those representatives of the 'middle' (aged 45–55) generation who had clearly been compromised by associating themselves with the former Communists or with the resistance against curriculum reforms and by attracting those who had previously been undecided.

The success of the youngest generation, which began its coming of age in the late 1960s and early 1970s, throws an interesting light on the generational hypothesis voiced by Polish sociologist Bronislaw Misztal (1993). According to Misztal, the Polish 'rebellious generation' was not as co-opted by the universities and institutions as its western counterparts were. The western 'angry young men and women of the 1960s' became vocal foci of social protest and new social movements. The Polish ones did not have this chance to march through the institutions ('frozen' by Communist control), so they simply joined the broader social movement in order to overthrow the Communists. By siding with the broader social movement they could emerge as an agent of change within the universities and begin their generational march through the institutions. Thus the radical theories of the 1970s and the 1980s voiced by the post-hippie and post-student-revolt sociologists were echoed in practice by the revolutionary overthrow of the Communist regimes and profound institutional reconstruction on the eastern side of the Elbe.

If Misztal is right, then the curriculum wars fought in Poland are a late equivalent of the radical (e.g. ecological) theories of the generational sub-elites, who theorized first and then started thinking about implementation (ecotheories followed by taxation of pollutants), while the eastern generational sub-elites fought first and started theorizing afterwards (first one had to abolish the Communist domination and then one could start rethinking the curriculum). If Misztal is wrong, then the curriculum wars fought in Poland are generationally non-specific. They are being fought by the younger generation because this is the generation whose members hope to achieve better positions in their march through the institutions, but they are an alliance of generations – including those who are 45, 35 and 25 (i.e. circa three generations) and their dynamics are totally different from the ones in western market societies.

I think that Misztal is right for three reasons. First, the impact of the 'former rebellious generation' on the current wave of changes, including curricular ones, has been the largest of all three sub-generations mentioned above. Those who 'came of age' in the anti-authoritarian period of the late 1960s and early 1970s clearly assumed leading positions in their generational clusters; they led their respective sub-elites.

Second, the fact that some Polish academic intellectuals (including, incidentally, Misztal and the undersigned) had to look for research opportunities outside Poland meant that both the transmission of critical theories in the social sciences and networking with western academic counterparts (including the TEMPUS projects) were considerably facilitated by their personal contacts and cultural skills; they were attracted – along with their international cooperation assistance projects – precisely to their own generation.

Third, having been less trained in institutional struggles than their co-opted western counterparts, the Polish generational reformers who had been ice-breakers in the period of overthrowing the Communist system failed to discern immediately the free-riders (of the generation of those aged 45–55) and the post-Communists (of the generation aged 55–65) in their alliances within the academic communities. However, by 1993 the process of retrenching and realignment had advanced very considerably (although it was much swifter at the economic universities than elsewhere) and the Polish counterparts of the western co-opted radicals also acquired basic political skills for political struggles under democracy.

The case is very significant from the point of the western strategies of aiding educational trade in the post-Communist countries. It shows that these strategies work best in partnership with wider initiatives. Let us hope that through the analysis of these dynamics of change we can contribute to the transformation process without frustrating expectations on the one hand and without creating 'learnt helplessness' on the other. A gradual evolution of the formal requirements of the TEMPUS programme clearly indicates that this is the interpretation which has been gaining ground. The fact that under the new rules an academic institution in Central/Eastern Europe can assume the role of a coordinator and actually manage the administration of the projects is a step forward compared to the initial lodging of this responsibility on the western side. Let us hope that the networks created through the TEMPUS projects will continue to play a significant role in bridging the gaps between two parts of Europe separated until very recently by the 'iron curtain'.

REFERENCES

Etzioni-Halevy, E. (1993) *The Elite Connection: Problems and Potential of Western Democracy*, London: Polity Press.

Kornai, J. (1990) *The Road to a Free Economy. Shifting From a Socialist System: The Example of Hungary*, New York: Norton.

Magala, S. 1992 (ed.) *Dismantling the Dinosaur, Business As Unusual in Moscow and St Petersburg*, Delft: Eburon.

Magala, S. *et al.* 1992 (eds) *Opening New Doors: A Business Survey in the People's Republic of China*, Delft: Eburon.

Misztal, B. (1993) 'New times, new social movements and new sociological theories. Legacy of the rebellious generation of the sixties', *World Congress of Sociology*, Bielefeld: Fort Wayne.

Soone, S. (1993) 'Business as Unusual in the Baltic Republics', paper presented at *Rotterdam's World Trade Centre*, organized by S. Magala.

Chapter 16

The flying university: institutional transformation in Poland

Kristina Genell and Monika Kostera

This chapter is about the relationship between the past and the present in the context of institutional transformation in Poland. The case in question is a department within one of the major universities in Poland. The changes that have occurred in this organization during the last few years may, at first sight, appear quite radical. We believe, however, that, in the light of past experiences, it is possible to interpret these changes in other ways.

TRANSFER OF KNOWLEDGE IN EDUCATIONAL ORGANIZATIONS

In order to be able to change, it is important to obtain knowledge about what is to be changed and the condition that one is aiming for. Some transfer of knowledge must therefore take place. This transfer of knowledge is easily visible, and, perhaps, especially difficult, in organizations that themselves are dealing with the transfer of knowledge, e.g. universities. In all the Eastern European countries, education is considered an important part of the change process and consequently major changes within the education systems have been announced. By changing the content and structure of the education system, the overall transition process is supposed be facilitated. And most important in this respect is higher education dealing with political and economical issues.

According to Ramirez and Boli (1987), the institutionalization of education takes place at the world level, not at local levels. If this is so, the situation becomes more complicated when considering the possibility of locally introduced radical changes in those types of organizations. In 1990 a change programme concerning economic education in Poland was ordered by the then Minister of Finance, Leszek Balcerowicz. According to this programme, many of the changes hitherto made were merely cosmetic and were made in order to save the *anciens régimes* at the universities. In 1990 the key roles in all areas in economic schools in Poland were played by 'a generation of professors and assistant professors, who owed their advancements and careers to party pacts . . .'. In the programme it is, thus, heavily emphasized that economic education in Poland is in need of radical reform (Beksiak *et al.* 1990: 14). We therefore consider universities and business schools that are dealing with education in economic subjects, and accordingly the teachers and researchers working there, as a relevant example of a group affected by the changes that are going on in Poland.

And there are changes going on within universities. Or at least people say that there are. An interesting development has been observed in one of the case organizations included in an empirical study of changes in higher economic education in Poland in which a paradoxical picture seems to emerge. The building of the department stands empty while there is frenetic teaching activity in many dispersed places under many names and forms. Several new organizations have been created, all by the same people, originating from the same department. This situation is, some may claim, not paradoxical or puzzling at all. The simple explanation is that the extremely low salaries of university teachers in Poland forces them to have extra, more well-paid, jobs on the side; or that the bureaucratic structure of the university, with conservative people in top positions, encourages those who want changes to realize them outside the original organization.

Complaints about low salaries and unwieldy bureaucracies are, however, in no way unique to the Polish situation. In Sweden, university teachers claim that their salaries are extremely low when compared to the standards of other European countries. As in the Polish case, it is rather common to have extra jobs and assignments on the side. The extent of these extra activities appears, however, to be somewhat more modest than in Poland. When it comes to the possibilities of making different kinds of changes in the universities, the Polish situation does not seem very different either. Of course, the change processes that are going on in Polish society at large are hard to compare to anything else, but one should bear in mind that universities on the whole are not normally looked upon as especially inclined to change. On the contrary, universities and colleges are often used as examples of a thorough institutionalization of rules and structures (see, e.g., Meyer and Rowan 1992; Boli 1989) and therefore, to say the least, considered difficult to change. The complaint about universities being rigid bureaucracies is probably as old as the institution of university itself.

Thus, although the two explanations above are strong and convincing, we think that there is something more or something else to it. Otherwise, as an outsider one would simply react to the Polish picture with 'the same as at home, but more'. But this picture did surprise us somewhat, and we therefore believe that there are also other ways to look at this phenomenon, i.e. the 'new' economic education in Poland. Perhaps, as is often the case in puzzling situations when one encounters something unknown, the first step is to think by analogy instead of by logic.

When studying the activities of the people at this department we came to think about the 'flying university'. This phenomenon originates in the

Polish history of occupation, when universities were closed by occupation forces and education in politically controversial subjects was prohibited. There has been a tradition in the history of higher education in Poland, during periods of different types of occupation, to pursue underground activities at the universities. These activities were, however, located in many different places, e.g. people's apartments, in order to escape the police, hence the denomination 'flying'. These activities started in the end of the nineteenth century and went on, in various forms, into the late 1980s. The flying university as an institution thus turned out to be durable.

No longer underground, the organization of education at the above-mentioned department strongly resembles the flying university, since a lot of the activities are going on somewhere else. But is it not an attempt to romanticize what is currently going on at Polish universities? In this chapter we are trying to analyse the phenomenon in the light of the historical institution, in order to establish whether it is just an analogy, or else some kind of institutional continuity, and which consequences for organizing it may entail.

In the next section we will discuss our basic assumptions and some theoretical foundations that we will refer to in this chapter. In the third section of the text we will give some examples of flying universities from the Polish history of occupation, military and otherwise, in order to shed some light on the present development. In section four, an account of the case of the contemporary flying university will be presented, based on field material from the study mentioned above. Finally, we will analyse and discuss the relevance of the metaphor of the flying university.

IDEAS, INSTITUTIONS AND IDENTITY

The transition process going on in all kinds of organizations in Eastern Europe is, at all levels and in all matters, a question of getting people to think and act in new ways. A major part of what used to be taken for granted is now called into question. One could look upon this process as a transfer of knowledge, or as a transfer of ideas. It is important to mention that we regard knowledge as something that is temporally and locally agreed upon (Rorty 1987). The universities in Eastern Europe are good examples in this respect. What used to be taught and considered 'good knowledge' before 1989 is now in many cases looked upon as completely useless. Nowadays, new ideas are becoming fashionable and will soon be, or in many cases already are, regarded as legitimate knowledge.

Where do the new ideas come from? Ideas emerge from a perpetual process, which we see as translation – not diffusion, as has been tradition-ally conceived (Latour 1986). The metaphor of diffusion, as many other metaphors used in this context, is rather mechanistic in implying a focus on the idea in question and giving no importance whatsoever to the receiving organization. The receiver plays a very passive role in this model (Sahlin-Andersson 1994a: 173). But, according to the translation model, 'the spread of time and space of anything – claims, orders, artefacts, goods – is in the hands of people; each of these people may act in many different ways, letting the token drop, or modifying it, or deflecting it, or betraying it, or adding to it, or appropriating it' (Latour 1986: 267).

Travelling ideas meet stationary ideas, i.e. a frame of reference, and it is in this encounter that friction is created, as there is no initial impetus: all energy is produced within the process, through friction (Latour 1986; Czarniawska and Joerges 1995). Thus, ideas do not 'diffuse'. They are passed on by people and each one translates them according to her/his own frame of reference. 'Insofar as one can speak about inertia of social life, that is, habits, routines, and institutional behaviour, it is this inertia that stops the movement of ideas. Without friction there is no translation; at best, it is the case of *received ideas*. Friction can be seen as the energizing clash between ideas in residence and travelling ideas, which leads to the transformation of both' (Czarniawska-Joerges 1994: 208–209).

And this is, indeed, what is going on in Poland today. New, travelling, ideas meet the old, solid, stationary, ones. Almost everything, even the ideas most taken for granted, is called into question. The changes going on in Poland are, thus, from many points of view so radical that the process could be looked upon as a case of, or several cases of, institutional transformation (see, e.g., Sahlin-Andersson 1994a: 170). The old, solid, ideas that now are being challenged could then be regarded as institutions. By institutions we understand, together with Jacobsson (1994: 39), the ideas which create specific activities and unities and fit them into a wider context. Institutionalization is the process by which ideas and patterns of behaviour are coming to be taken for granted by people in organizations. They come to be taken for granted because they are regulated according to the law, or because they become established by habits or professional norms.

This process of reality-construction is not necessarily intentional, not always at any rate. An important part of it is unintentional and unconscious, as much of what we call norms and values is taken for granted. If we return to the subject of this paper, i.e. Polish economic education, it is obvious that many of the 'rules of the game', i.e. the most important definitions of 'what an organization really is', 'who a manager is', 'what a teacher should be like', 'what should be taught to business and management students', etc. are particularly enduring and solid. They are taken for granted, and often unquestioned or even 'unquestionable'. In other words, they could be regarded as institutions, and we choose to call them that. Another suitable denomination is Callon and Latour's (1981: 285) concept of black boxes, taken from the field of aviation and applied in an institutional context for the first time by Whitley (1972). The black boxes contain something that is no longer considered; they are things whose contents have become a matter of indifference. The more elements one can put into the black box, the broader a construction one can raise, and in this way one can become a so-called macro-actor. Callon and Latour compare these black boxes to Leviathan, a monster impossible to control. 'The Leviathan is such a monster that its essential being cannot be stabilised in any of the great metaphors we usually employ. It is at the same time machine, market, code, body and war' (1981: 294).

This description fits rather well with the political and economic situation in the former Eastern Europe. A lot of actions and structures existed because they were taken for granted and forgotten. If somebody mentioned them, it was, nevertheless, prohibited to criticize, let alone try to change them. They are the institutions, or black boxes, which are supposed to be changed now.

As is probably well known to most observers, this is not an easy task. Most institutions are slow to change, especially those which involve the most vital social agreements, those necessary to make sense of reality. This holds true particularly for those cultural constructs that are not subject to conscious societal discussion and negotiation. Among them are the institutions of enterprise, organizing, education, gender, etc. People are more or less unwilling to modify them. In other words, we tend to believe that the less we talk about something, the greater the possibility that it will remain unchanged. This is the case of unchallenged traditions: often they are considered as non-negotiable, essential and fundamental truths. But, this is also the case with issues of 'lesser interest'. How do social phenomena acquire that status? It can happen in many different ways. One obvious explanation is that during important societal events one group of problems or actors gains the main role, while others remain in the shadow. These side roles tend to remain unchanged. We believe that this is what is happening in Poland today. In the sphere of business administration the obvious central characters are the manager and the enterprise. Other actors play side roles in the change process. For the moment, university teachers seem to be playing a side role in the economic change process which clearly has a focus on company managers. This somewhat 'hidden' position of the university teachers does not mean, however, that their role is unimportant. Rather, the different roles complement each other and become important on different occasions (Czarniawska-Joerges and Wolff 1991: 530–531). Right now, Polish university teacher appears to be in the shadow. But, as we will show later in this paper, their role as educators of future managers is not to be underestimated.

What characterizes, then, the role of these educators? Has it changed over the last few years, and, if so, how? We have already described the ongoing transition process in Poland as a case of institutional transformation. Another, but related, way to look upon such radical changes is as a change of identity (see, e.g., Sahlin-Andersson 1994a: 170). We will argue that the professional identity of Polish academic teachers, as well as the identity of other groups involved in the transition processes (see Chapter 14), is changing. According to Sahlin-Andersson (1994b), one can regard institutionally based group identities as the building blocks of which organizations are constructed. Identity formation is a process of structuration based on the expectations of the actors involved and of other actors with whom they are interacting. The process of identity construction is thus affected by the actor in question as well as by other related actors. Czarniawska-Joerges (1994) argues that it is relevant to treat identity construction as a continuous process of narration. This process is then compared to the writing of an autobiography with several authors. In this paper we will try to put together a narrative fitting the Polish academic management teachers.

THE HISTORICAL ROOTS OF THE FLYING UNIVERSITY

As should be evident from the first section of this paper, higher education is often regarded as an institution whose shape is similar across the world. Nevertheless, there is always a tradition: *Grandes Écoles* in France, Oxbridge in England, and flying universities in Poland. Since the beginning of the 1880s, flying universities have existed in Poland in one way or another. In this section of the paper we will give some fairly short examples from the Polish history of occupation; examples from periods of Russian, German and 'Communist' occupation. Our idea is that the present development at some Polish universities will be placed in a different light when displayed against these historical events.

The flying university

The first flying university started its activities in 1882 or 1883 when Poland was under Russian occupation, and the Czar's persecution against Polish history and culture was at its strongest. However, it was not only a question of difficulties experienced by people at the universities trying to pursue their teaching activities the way they wanted when under occupation, it was also a matter of gender and equality (Cywinski 1984). During the 1870s and 1880s the opportunities for women to achieve education had increased but, as in many other European countries, the universities were still closed to women. The possibilities for women to obtain higher education were very small.

It is also important to mention that there was an extensive dissatisfaction, among scientists as well as students, with what the official university education had to offer when it came to 'contact with a true science of international status' (Cywinski 1984). Many study circles were established, and the people who were most active in this respect were women. The first systematic attempts to organize these activities were made in the academic year 1882/3. In 1885/86 the work within those study circles became more systematized and organized. The initiator and organizer was called Jadwiga Szczawinska (who later married Jan Wladyslaw Dawid, the first experimental psychologist in Poland). She started courses for young women in Polish language and literature, with an obvious aim of educating future school teachers. Later her aim became to obtain a complete curriculum, by systematizing and standardizing the organizational forms of the study circles. A coordinating board, which defined the curriculum and decided about exams, was established. It took also care of the fees paid by the students. In this way a clandestine university, the flying university, was created.

The university was called 'flying' because the students and the teachers had to move between different locations in order to escape from the police (Lifton 1988). There is not much material about the activities of the flying university left from this period, since all written accounts were avoided in order to keep everything connected with the flying university as secret as possible. There are, however, some documents from the police files (Cywinski 1984), which contain the curriculum for the first two years of studies at the flying university. The programme consisted of all kinds of subjects, social as well as natural sciences, mathematics, humanities, and one 'faculty' was pedagogic.

Because of the clandestine character of the university, it is hard to evaluate its programmes. It is always easy to overestimate such heroic activities, pursued under difficult circumstances. According to Cywinski, however, when compared to the programmes of the then Warsaw University, the flying university represented a much higher level of education. Many highly renowned scientists like Chlebowski, who taught Polish literature, Maria Weryho in philosophy, Ludwik Krzywicki, professor in sociology, and others were involved in the activities of the flying university, which offered social as well as academic opportunities. Obviously, the professors who taught at the flying university did so at great risk. They did, however, earn quite a lot of money from this venture. In fact, the system of the flying university was much more profitable for those involved than the one that was to follow (the Association of Scientific Courses) during liberalization. Many of the professors at the flying university therefore did not join the activities of this new, and officially sanctioned, association.

The flying university continued its activities from 1885/86 until 1905. At the beginning only women were included, but from about 1890 men who were looking for knowledge of a social and humanistic kind joined the students. In the academic year 1889/1890 the number of registered students was about 1000, many of whom later became known for their scientific, educational, social or political activity. The most famous was probably Marie Sklodowska, later known as Marie Curie.

In 1889/1990 a discussion about how the money collected for entrance tickets should be spent led to a conflict between the apparently dominant Jadwiga Dawid, who was accused of despotism, and the rest of the members of the board. The result of this conflict was that the flying university was divided, and a new 'republican' one was created. This new university lasted, in the form of loosely connected courses, until 1905, when liberalization allowed its transformation into an official association of scientific courses, in 1920 replaced by the Free Polish University (Cywinski 1984).

World War II: underground education continues

During the period of German occupation the universities were closed. The only form of 'higher' education that was allowed to exist was in some technical vocational training schools. But, just as during earlier periods of occupation, the Polish institutions of higher education pursued underground activities. During the whole period of war there were underground senior high-schools that supplied the universities with students (Czeslaw 1964). In 1941 all these underground university activities were coordinated by the physicist Stefan Pienkowski.

The underground activities during the war were mostly concentrated in Warsaw (with a total of 9,000 students), but they went on in some other Polish cities as well, e.g. Lwów and Wilno (leading to an overall total of slightly more than 10,000 students). In Kraków, most of the university professors had ended up in concentration camps. The most extensive activities were pursued at the Warsaw university, within law, medicine and many other subjects. The technical university was actively engaged in underground education, as well as the school of economics and several other schools. An organization called Uniwersytet Ziem Zachodnich (the University of Western Territories) was established by professors expelled from the university in Poznań. In spite of the difficulties and dangers, a lot of research took place during the war, and the contribution in the form of research reports, textbooks and teaching materials was substantial.

Flying universities during Communism

As the result of the Yalta agreement after World War II, Poland again lost much of its independence. As with other Eastern and Central European countries, Poland was assigned the role of Soviet satellite, and although it kept its political status as a state, its real sovereignty was limited. Under Soviet control, Communism was introduced, political parties liquidated or merged into one monopolist Communist Party and the Polish Workers' United Party.

During the first years after the war, the universities and schools often employed pre-war professors as teachers of 'traditional' subjects, e.g. the natural sciences. Communist activists were appointed 'chief pedagogues', i.e. directors and teachers of subjects of political interest, such as the history of the Soviet Communist Party, 'social sciences', etc. Political terror was acute until two years after the death of Stalin, and there were scarcely any clandestine academic institutions. Students from that time, with whom we have spoken, say that the pre-war teachers often openly risked their freedom and perhaps even their lives, when they refused to teach in accordance with Soviet propaganda. In spite of the political situation, the students received quite a competent education alongside the propaganda. The possibility of a functioning flying university was limited.

After the relative liberalization of 1956, the Polish flying university started to work again. Well-known professors, such as the philosopher Leszek Kolakowski, the poet Antoni Slonimski, and many less famous, took up the risky business of giving illegal lectures. Most of the lectures concerned topics which were officially banned (e.g. the non-Soviet version of World War II, non-Stalinist philosophy, etc.) or distorted in the approved curriculum. During the more liberal periods, e.g. 1956–1958, the early 1970s, 1980–1981, many flying-university lectures were given at the universities. The rest of the time, the work was more conspiratorial. Lectures took place in private apartments, and as Jacek Kuron (1991) recalls, the police either waited outside to arrest and beat up the students and lecturers or entered the apartment and interrupted the lecture. Besides the more conventional lectures there were also a great deal of self-studies and study circles. These were popular during the 1980s and could also be very risky. The students often invited famous scientists and dissidents to such meetings.

The activities and directions of the various kinds of flying universities seem to have been different. During the two first periods of occupation, the important matter was not what subjects to teach, but to make the best use of the possibilities to offer any kind of higher education, since the universities were closed by the occupation forces and, accordingly, almost all higher education activities were forbidden. During these periods there seem to have been no viable alternatives. When looking at the period of Communism, the situation was somewhat different. The underground activities during this period were concentrated on subjects that could be regarded as politically controversial, subjects within which interpretations not concordant with the official ones were possible. During this period official university education was extensive but selective. This means that the underground activities had other roles, namely as alternatives or supplements to the official education programmes. Now it was no longer the teaching activities per se that were dangerous to engage in, but rather their content. It is hard to tell if this new situation implied any differences concerning the risks involved or the engagement from the participants.

The identity of the underground teachers was, however, relatively stable during all the periods we have outlined. They were people taking considerable risks, sacrificing their career, personal security or even freedom in the service of society. This identity is closer to that of the missionary than that of the ordinary teacher. Even if the clandestine teachers were quite well paid on occasion (although sometimes they performed their lectures for free), they did not consider it as payment for the job done, but rather as a humble offering not recompensing their contribution. The dignity and social prestige attached to the role of the flying university teacher was, naturally, emphasized more than the pecuniary interest involved.

We will now turn to what we regard as the present flying university, and here we will be able to discern yet another picture. The flying actors from this organization are dealing with subjects that now, generally, are looked upon as official and very useful.

THE MODERN FLYING UNIVERSITY

About the faculty

This is a story about a Faculty of Management at one of the major Polish universities and it is said to be one of the first university departments in Poland that dealt with issues of management. The faculty was founded in 1972, and educational as well as research activities are carried out. The main goal is to educate specialists working in private- as well as public-sector organizations. The management group of the faculty consisted, at the time of the study, of one dean and three vice-deans (responsible for the areas of teaching, research and foreign relations). The highest governing body is the Faculty Council, which has forty-four members from different categories. The faculty has seven departments divided into sections, and 137 people are employed.

There are five different types of programmes at the faculty: full-time studies (five years) with two directions, business administration and public administration; part-time evening studies; a practically oriented bachelor programme (three years); and master's studies for students who already have a diploma. There are two versions of the master's programme: a one-year (for managers from different types of organizations) and a two-year programme. Financing the education programmes is a big problem since less and less money comes from the state budget. At present the part-time students and the master's students pay for their education, while 'ordinary' full-time studies, up to now, are free of charge.

An explosion of new schools

During the last five years there have been a lot of changes in economic education in Poland, and this faculty, as well as other organizations, has been influenced in different ways. In this paper we will concentrate on one of these changes, one that is very conspicuous and important to all Polish organizations that are dealing with economic education. It is also highly relevant for the concept of the flying university.

This very extensive change is the explosion of private and 'semi-private' schools offering programmes, courses and seminars in management. Education in management and business administration is thus offered not only at the established universities, but also at polytechnical schools, private business schools and consulting firms. In some cases the activities are based on cooperation with American or Western European universities. In any case, there is a huge demand for education in business and economics and, accordingly, a large market for skilled lecturers with some knowledge in business administration and management. There is a lack of good lecturers so it is possible to earn several times one's ordinary salary by teaching a few hours at a private school or working as a consultant.

A new flying university?

The faculty described above could be looked upon as a solid and established institution, almost a model bureaucracy. And yet, looking at it, we come to think of a flying university. Why is that? Let us explain our way of seeing things. First, for somebody who decides to spend some time in the faculty's main building observing it, it seems to be rather ephemeral and shifting. People are not there: they come in at a great haste and leave in the same way. They move fast between lectures. This is so because most people working or studying at this faculty have other jobs on the side. Second, and this is an issue we will return to later in this paper, the teachers sometimes seem to look upon themselves as missionaries.

The teachers lecture at other organizations that pay better, or work in private companies or joint ventures. The result of this is that they spend very little time at the faculty and in some cases they don't spend much time preparing their lectures either. Those who suffer most from this arrangement are the students at the university, who are not in a position to make demands concerning the quality of the education since they, in most cases, do not pay any fees (in contrast to the MBA students). However, many of the students also have jobs on the side and therefore do not spend very much time at the university either. So, to a great extent, many of the teachers, as well as the students, are 'flying':

> They work in companies. We have some big guys here, who are CEOs at big joint ventures between Polish and American companies. Then, of course, they work at banks and consulting firms. And they have some lectures that they sell in town, that are rather well paid.(1)[1]

All the students work. All better students work, starting more or less after the second or third year at the university. They work in consulting companies, they work in stockbrokers offices . . . they have learned 150 new things, the way it is in real life, and they come to the lectures with a different knowledge and this is something I like. . . . This does not mean that they study. They have less and less time for their studies.(2)

The situation at this faculty is in no way unique, either for Polish universities or for universities in other countries. One thing that is interesting is that some of the flying teachers and researchers have created four new organizations themselves, organizations that in some cases are connected to the faculty and the university. When one tries to understand those organizations and how they are related to each other a complex picture emerges, which most of the respondents involved had difficulties explaining. What is evident, however, is a relationship between the different organizations through the people working within them:

> So this is a very complex picture from the institutional point of view, but at the same time all these institutions are using the same pool of professors whose home institutions are schools, departments in the universities like this one. These people are employed part time in many different institutions.(3)

It is important to have in mind, and it is also apparent from the quotations above, that these new organizations are not the only places that the teachers are flying to; but we consider them a relevant example of the flying activities that are going on at this department. But why are four different organizations needed? One answer we got to this question was that it has to do with the legal system in Poland. After the 'revolution' in 1989, some people at the faculty decided that it would be a challenge to form a new and independent academic organization, and they wanted to do it as a part of the university, in the legal form of a foundation. But for some reason the Ministry of Education did not approve of this.

> So this is why we had to start a company. Because for the company we did not need any approvals.(4)

The new business school was established the same year as a limited liability company, owned by some Polish enterprises and a few individual investors. Of course, for the people involved there are advantages and disadvantages with this arrangement. A private firm is more flexible and independent and resolves the financial situation, but, on the other hand, a diploma from the university carries more prestige for the students than one from an independent private school.

A few years later there were some initiatives at the university concerning cooperation with Western European and American business schools, and there was a possibility of starting a joint MBA programme with a French management school and an American university. This cooperation was supposed to be with the business school. It was, however, impossible for the foreign universities to start a joint programme with a limited liability company. Therefore a new organization had to be created in 1991, a management centre within the university, and the students that graduate also get a university diploma.

> The centre is a part of the university and has been set by the senate. It is an institution to carry out the programmes together with foreign universities. The business school, in other words a joint stock company, a private firm to make money, to train managers.(2)

This centre was formally separated from the business school, but consisted of exactly the same people:

> We are the same people in different organizational shapes.(5)

The third organization was founded in order to get money for this joint MBA programme. According to some of the people involved, domestic and foreign sponsors preferred to give the money directly to the MBA programme rather than the university. In order to avoid the university getting hold of the money, a foundation was established, the task of which was exclusively to collect money. After 1990 many new business schools were established at different locations in Poland. Some of them achieved the status of a higher education institution, i.e. they were approved by the Ministry of Education. The people at the business school started to think about opening a formal higher education institution (formal according to Polish law). Their first idea was to transform the already existing business school into a university. This, according to the Ministry of Education, was not possible for legal reasons. A new school therefore had to be created.

The initiators of these activities thus ended up with four different organizations, three of which are pursuing educational activities and one of which is collecting money. The same people are working within all these organizations, They also work at the faculty of management at the university and have their own consulting firms, plus some other assignments as well.

ORGANIZED CONFUSION

What, then, are the consequences of this situation? One is perhaps not chaos, but some kind of organized confusion, at least to an outside observer. It was almost impossible to make an appointment to see any of these people, and if that did finally succeed it was almost impossible to conduct an interview. It is extremely difficult to interview somebody who is running in and out of his (most of them are men!) room at the same time he is talking to you, gets interrupted at least ten times during half an hour by the telephone, and five times by his secretary and five times by some of his students whom he has promised to meet at the same time as the interview. And all the time someone is drilling in the wall in the next room, so it will be impossible to hear what you have recorded on the tape. This pace of work will probably lead to serious stress. But somehow they seem to manage and to keep it all sorted out.

Another consequence is that the building of the faculty of management at the university stands almost empty. Perhaps it is an exaggeration to say that nobody is there, because the students are there and so are the teachers who are giving lectures at the moment. But as soon as they have finished they leave for another of their other jobs. The activities at the university are, for most people, given least priority. There are few standards which are really followed. In some cases it opens up the possibility for individual creativity; in others – perhaps indolence. People can do as they wish.

One problem connected with this situation is that very few people are doing research. ('Nobody does any thinking there.'(2)) However, not everybody has disappeared. It is possible to divide the people at the faculty into different categories. First, there were those who have definitely left. They were the people who left the faculty in 1989, mostly for the Ministry of Privatization, but also for other organizations. According to one of the respondents, those people belonged to the younger generation, which could have transformed and restructured the faculty. They have, however, disappeared completely. At the most, they visit the faculty on rare occasions as guest lecturers. Because of this, the average age of the faculty is rather high. The second category is 'the old boys' power club'. They are the ones still left. They do not want change, and they are doing quite well. The third category is made up of the 'multifunctionals', the flying ones (to some extent this also includes the students) described above who are at many different places in the same time – or try to be. Why are they doing this, what are they driven by and how will it end?

Obviously, one possible explanation is money. The average salary for a university teacher is extremely low and, accordingly, not possible to live on. Most of the teachers and researchers therefore are more or less compelled to hold other, better-paid, jobs. For the moment there are many opportunities to find such jobs. The market for people with some knowledge about different areas within business and economics is enormous. As we mentioned earlier – there has been an explosion of new schools and institutes offering courses and programmes in management, which also means that there is a great need for teachers and lecturers at these organizations. Other ways to earn this extra money are to work for private companies, one's own or somebody else's, or as some kind of business consultant. That reminds us of the fact mentioned earlier that many of the professors involved in the underground activities of the former flying universities earnt quite substantial money for taking the risk that this involvement entailed. The people involved in the present flying universities do not take that kind of risk, since their activities in no way are prohibited but in most cases looked upon as very useful, necessary, fashionable, official and without alternatives. Instead they face the risk of overworking themselves.

For many of those people, the matter of prestige is probably as important as the money involved. It is very flattering to get so many offers from so many people within different organizations. It could be regarded as confirmation that what they are doing is extremely important, which is what they strongly believe themselves. Most of the 'flying' teachers do think that their work is very useful and important to individuals and also to the economic development of their country. They have a mission. The new situation means that what they are teaching now is something that will, or already does, exist in Polish society a market economy:

> Before, they used to say that 'we were talking about the moon', about something that didn't exist, that nobody needed. But right now it has, kind of, turned around. What we are doing is very popular and it is very useful. We feel that we are needed, that is fantastic.(1)

Although they probably would not like the religious association, but would rather be looked upon as experts, the parallel to missionaries does seem pertinent (Kostera 1993). Many of those people really do believe in what they are doing and think that the best will come out of it. But they are not the only ones who believe in the blessings of the market, something that we will discuss in the final section. If we return to the historical flying universities there are obvious similarities. Those involved in the then underground educational activities also had a mission. They wanted to spread the kind of knowledge that they believed was true, but which was for various reasons prohibited by the occupational forces. In short, they believed that there were other ways of looking upon what is or is not considered as knowledge and other ways to construct the world than those officially sanctioned.

Finally, the present flying university could be looked upon as a way of escaping the established structures, or institutions, in order to be able to do what one wants, because this was the way things had to be done before, under different forms of occupation, when one's activities were prohibited and very risky to engage in. Even though this is not the case nowadays, people more or less automatically continue to act in the same way no longer underground, but still outside the formal, original organization.

We think that the concept of occupation is relevant in this respect. During long periods, Poland has been under Russian as well as German occupation. For an even longer period it was, if not formally, then more or less in reality, occupied by the Soviet Union. Another way to see it is as occupation by Communism. Is Poland occupied nowadays, and, if so, by whom or what? One possible interpretation is that Poland is partly occupied by its past and that people therefore continue to act as though flying universities are still a necessity, even though what they are teaching now is considered as official and necessary knowledge that very soon will probably be taken for granted. One way of expressing this phenomenon is that it has become institutionalized and that one must escape the established institutions when trying to change something or do something differently. Reforming from within does not seem possible. In this case it is, of course, not a question of occupation in the concrete sense of the word, i.e. taking possession of a country or a town, but rather some kind of spiritual occupation by the institutions emerging from the past.

Another way of looking at the present state of occupation is to regard Poland as occupied by the market, or by ideas about the market, and accordingly by the USA and Western Europe. Parallel to the explosion of new business schools and management courses, there has been an invasion of people from western universities as well as consulting firms, who want to 'help' the Poles to become 'marketized' as quickly as possible. We will return to this kind of occupation in the last section.

SOME FINAL COMMENTS

A new identity narrative – the authors

One way of looking at the state of the present university is, thus, as a consequence of a meeting of ideas from past times of occupation with those emanating from the present process of democratization and marketization. People continue to act in partly similar ways, even though it is not necessary for them to do so, at least not for the same reasons as before. The old institutions are, as could be expected, slow to change. But it is also obvious that something has happened. Ironically, the actors who are very active within the current process of professional identity transformation in Poland – the academic teachers – are not themselves the object of this process. When considering their own change of identity, they could, as we have mentioned earlier, be looked upon rather as side characters. They do not seem to have an identity 'in stock' for their own use. They contribute to the shaping of the identity of managers and enterprises (Kostera 1996), but nobody – not even they themselves – seems to be interested in writing an identity narrative for them. No wonder that the stationary ideas are so important in the construction of their actual social role today. Nevertheless, there seem to be changes going on. Who are the potential authors of a possible new identity narrative?

Alexandersson and Trossmark (1994) discuss the role of history in the creation of identity. People look back at history in order to achieve a feeling of togetherness and belonging; they seek their collective identity. In this sense the concept of identity is connected to social institutions. The contemporary identity narrative of Polish academic management teachers is thus written by the past (history), and to a certain degree it emerges as a side product of their writing the script for company managers. The teachers, aware of their role in the identity-shaping process for managers, take on the romantic identity of flying-university members – they feel they perform something important, even if society is not focusing on them for the moment.

We thus consider history as the first author of this narrative. The second author of the narrative is the identity negotiators i.e. the teachers, students, employers, managers, etc. taking part in the process of identity bargaining for the new managers. The teachers borrow some of the images; like the new manager, they think in terms of profit, they are 'dynamic', 'active', 'on the move' all these traits fit well the flying-university lifestyle and a male lifestyle. It is now forgotten that the first flying university was formed by women and primarily for women. The teachers take on the male identity of the manager. In this way the present edits the past.

The present ideas about desirable identities in the 'new' Polish society emanate, to a great extent, from non-Polish sources. During the last five years the invasion of foreign people and organizations dealing with business education has been enormous. This development can be looked upon as a mixed blessing. On the one hand, competence within certain areas is lacking, and if cooperation with the Polish teachers is working well the advantages outweigh the disadvantages, especially as, in many cases, the 'invaders' have a very high level of ambition. They learn a lot about Poland and Polish history in advance and they are very interested in achieving good contacts with the students and in adapting themselves to Polish needs and requirements.

But on the other hand, this is not always the case. It is not uncommon for foreigners to come to Poland without the slightest idea about what the Polish students already know and what they do not. Their approach is that the whole of Eastern and Central Europe is a cognitive desert, where nobody knows anything about business administration and management. They come and tell the students something that is absolutely basic knowledge to their own American or British students, as well as to the Polish students in question.

They are using 'plantation syndrome' stereotypes that these (*the Poles!*) are completely wild people who don't know anything about anything.(3)

And, obviously, this is not worth paying for. The problem seems to be how to achieve the partnership relationship between 'donor' and 'recipient'. In many cases the donors are dominating the relationship and try to sell something that they could not sell elsewhere, at least not at that price. It is also common for the recipients not to know what it is they need and how to negotiate it.

> I think we probably need some form of institutional development which would enable us to use this foreign help. And to ask for certain things instead of being completely dominated by foreign partners who are using their government funds to finance themselves.(3)

One of us (Kostera 1993) has compared the foreign teachers and consultants to the medieval crusaders. Western involvement in the transition in Poland, and other countries as well, is thus not a process of conversation, but a monologue or, if we extending the religious metaphor, a sermon. It is a question of one-way communication. In modern society one can also regard the mass media as an important medium of identity transfer (Fiske 1987; Kostera, Chapter 14). We are primarily thinking about television, but also about radio, the press, popular books, movies, etc. The propensity to keep up with what is discussed in the press is quite high among Polish managers, and television and radio are also very popular (Falkowska 1992; Koprowska 1992). The media bring ideas of identity into fashion. The whole process of identity formation encompasses several phases of translation, and it can be seen as social negotiations in which the actors take part. The role of the media in Poland can be regarded as involving the initial step in this process. Thus, the authors of the present identity narrative are history, the teachers themselves, the mass media, as well as foreign consultants and teachers – the crusaders.

Persistence of the old institutions

Considering that the work conditions of all these different actors have changed dramatically during the last few years, one would also expect a dramatically reconstructed identity for Polish academic management teachers. But is it so? As we have shown earlier in the paper, there are many similarities between the various periods of flying universities and the present situation. People continue to act as if they are still under occupation, which, in one sense, they are.

What is clear is that the institution of higher education in Poland has acquired a peculiar shape during the last two hundred years (as compared to Western European standards). A major part of university education had to be kept secret and underground. It is hard to dispute that, in spite of radically changed circumstances, these conditions must make a lasting impression on future development. We find it interesting and relevant to discuss some possible reasons for this persistence.

The most obvious one is institutional inertia. The concept of institution implies something that persists and is slow to change, and we have shown earlier that education is often used as an example in this respect. In this particular case it is important to have in mind that the people presently working at the 'new flying university' were never socialized into working at what Western Europeans or Americans would call a 'normal' university. The institution of the flying university is as persistent and indisposed to change as any other educational institution. Furthermore, some conditions which obstruct the possibilities for change are persistent as well. We have already mentioned the image of the university as a typical bureaucracy that is holding on to the old power structures, with conservative people in positions from which the most important decisions are made.

Another, not very romantic but nevertheless obvious, reason is money. The salaries paid at the university compare very badly to the remuneration paid by private business schools, consultancy firms, etc. No wonder that the underpaid university teachers seize every opportunity to increase their earnings. If we return to the previous flying universities, money was important there also, even though other more glorious reasons came to the forefront.

Finally, and most importantly, the flying university provides a source for the professional identity of management teachers, and so plays an important role in the transition process. During the various periods of flying universities, the source of professional identity was not the 'home' organization, i.e. the official university. The source of professional identity was rather the teaching activities per se, since they implied something that was considered very important and highly prestigious. In a way the situation is similar today, in that the many commitments made by the teachers make them feel as if they are doing something useful and important. The 'official' university is, however, also an important source of their professional identity when it comes to the question of legitimacy. Even though the teachers in many cases do not look upon their activities at the university as important, belonging to an established university makes them part of an international scientific network.

The unintended consequence of all this is that the present flying teachers help to reproduce the institutions that they want to change. When the people who want the changes go somewhere else to realize their ambitions as they do now and as they did during the previous periods of flying universities the ones in charge of the original organization can keep on doing what they always have done. In this way the flying teachers themselves obstruct the change processes at the university, even though their intention is probably the opposite.

NOTE

1   The numbers in parentheses refer to the interviews conducted.

REFERENCES AND FURTHER READING

Abrahamson, E. (1996) 'Technical and aesthetic fashion', in B. Czarniawska and G. Sevón (eds) *Translating Organisational Change*, Berlin: de Gruyter.

Alexandersson, O. and Trossmark, P. (1994) 'En fotnot om förnyelseprocesser: hur hårt stövlarna sitter fast i det historiska träsket märker man först när man försöker springa!' (A note on renewal processes), research proposal, Lund, Lund University, Department of Business Administration.

Beksiak, J. (1987) 'Enterprise and reform: the Polish experience', *European Economic Review* 31, pp. 118–24.

Beksiak, J. Chmiolecha, E., Grzelońska, U., Muller, A., and Winiecki, J. (1990) *Higher Economic Education in Poland – its present state and proposals for immediate change*, Economic Research Program for Central and Eastern Europe, Warsaw.

Bolesta-Kukulka, K. (1992) *Gra o wladze a gospodarka polska 1944–1991* [The game for control and the Polish economy 1944–1991], Warsaw: PWE.

Boli, J. (1989) *New Citizens For a New Society – The Institutional Origins of Mass Schooling in Sweden*, Oxford: Pergamon Press.

Callon, M. and Latour, B. (1981) 'Unscrewing the big Leviathan: how actors macro-structure reality and how sociologists help them to do so', in K. Knorr-Cetina and A. Cicourel (eds) *Advances in Social Theory and Methodology*, London: Routledge & Kegan Paul.

Connor, W.D. and Ploszajski, P. (eds) (1992) *Escape from Socialism: The Polish Route*. Warsaw: IFIS.

Cywinski, B. (1984) *Rodowody niepokornych* [Genealogies of the unsubdued], Warsaw: Wydawnictwo Krag.

Czarniawska-Joerges, B. (1994) 'Narratives of individual and organisational identities', in S. Deetz (ed.) *Communication Yearbook* 17, Newbury Park, CA: Sage.

Czarniawska-Joerges, B. (forthcoming) *Managing Warsaw in the 1990s: A Field Study*.

Czarniawska, B. and Joerges, B. (1995) 'Winds of organisational change: how ideas translate into objects and actions', in S. Bacharach, P. Gagliardi and B. Mundell (eds) *Research in Organisation Sociology*, vol. 13: pp. 171–209. Connecticut, NJ: JAI Press.

Czarniawska-Joerges, B. and Wolff, R. (1991) 'Leaders, managers, entrepreneurs on and off the organisational stage', *Organisation Studies* 12(4), pp. 529–46.

Czeslaw, W. (1964) *Z dziejow tajnej oswiaty w latach okupacji 1939–1944* [The history of clandestine education during the occupation of 1939–1944], Warsaw: Nasza Ksiegarnia.

Davies, B. and Harré, R. (1991) 'Positioning: the discursive production of selves', *Journal for the Theory of Social Behaviour* 20(1), pp. 43–63.

Falkowska, M. (1992) 'Zarys zmian w zyciu kulturalnym Polakow' [A sketch of changes in the cultural lives of the Poles], in M. Grabowska (ed.) *Barometr Kultury* [The cultural barometer], Warsaw: Instytut Kultury.

Fiske, J. (1987) *Television Culture*, London and New York: Routledge.

Jacobsson, B. (1994) 'Reformer och organisatorisk identitet' [Reforms and organisational identity], in B. Jacobsson (ed.) *Organisationsexperiment i kommuner och landsting* [Organisational experiments in municipalities and county councils], Stockholm: Nerenius & Santérus förlag AB.

Koprowska, T. (1992) 'Rola telewizji w spolecznym obiegu literatury' [The role of television in the social scope of literature], in M. Grabowska (ed.) *Barometr Kultury* [The cultural barometer], Warsaw: Institut Kultury.

Kostera, M. (1993) 'The modern crusade: the missionaries of management come to Eastern Europe' working paper, School of Management, Warsaw University.

Kostera, M. (1996) *Postmodernizm e zarządzania* (Postmodernism in management), Warszawa: PWE.
Kozminiski, A.K. (1993) *Catching Up? Organisational and Management Change in the Ex-Socialist Block*, New York: SUNY Press.
Kuron, J. (1991) *Gwiezdy czas* [The time of the stars], London: ANEKS.
Latour, B. (1986) 'The powers of association', in J. Law (ed.) *Power, Action and Belief*, London: Routledge & Kegan Paul.
Lifton, B.J. (1988) *The King of Children: A Biography of Janusz Korczak*, New York: Schocken Books.
Meyer, J.W. (1987) 'Self and life course: institutionalisation and its effects', in Thomas, G.W., Meyer, J.W., Ramirez, F.O., and Boli, J. (eds) *Institutional Structure: Constituting State, Society, and the Individual*, Newbury Park, CA: Sage.
Meyer, J.W. and Rowan, B. (1992) 'The structure of educational organisations', in J.W. Meyer and W.R. Scott (eds) *Organisational Environments: Ritual and Rationality*, Newbury Park, CA: Sage.
Ramirez, F.O. and Boli, J. (1987) 'Global patterns of educational institutionalisation', in Thomas, G.M., Meyer, J.W., Ramirez, F.O., and Boli, J. (Eds) *Institutional Structure: Constituting State, Society, and the Individual*, Newbury Park, CA: Sage.
Rorty, R. (1987) 'Scientific rationality as solidarity', in J. Nelson, A. Megill and D. McCloskey (eds) *The Rhetoric of the Human Sciences*, Madison: University of Wisconsin Press.
Røvik, K.-A. (1996) 'Deinstitutionalization and the logic of fashion', in B. Czarniawska and G. Sevón (eds) *Translating Organisational Change*, Berlin: de Gruyter.
Sachs, J. (1994) *Polens väg tillbaka* [Poland's jump to the market economy], Stockholm: SNS förlag.
Sahlin-Andersson, K. (1994a) 'Varför låter sig organisationer omvandlas?', [Why do organisations let themselves change?], in B. Jacobsson (ed.) *Organisationsexperiment i kommuner och landsting* [Organisational experiments in municipalities and county councils], Stockholm: Nerenius & Santérus förlag AB.
Sahlin-Andersson, K. (1994b) 'Group identities as the building blocks of organisations: a story about nurses' daily work', *Scandinavian Journal of Management* 10(2), pp. 131–45.
Whitley, R.D. (1972) 'Black boxism and the sociology of science', *Sociological Review Monograph* 18, pp. 61–92.

Part III

Educating for entrepreneurship: breaking down the boundaries

Chapter 17

Holistic learning in the new Central Europe

Monica Lee

The quaternity is an archetype of almost universal occurrence. It forms the logical basis for any whole judgement. There are always four elements, four primal qualities, four colours, four castes, four ways of spiritual development etc. So too, there are four aspects of psychological orientation in order to orientate ourselves, we must have a function which ascertains that something is there (sensation); a second function which establishes what it is (thinking); a third function which states whether it suits us or not, whether we wish to accept it or no (feeling), and a fourth function which indicates where it came from and where it is going (intuition). The ideal completeness is a circle or sphere, but its natural minimal division is a quaternity.

(Jung 1961)

Elsewhere in this book the dominant form of formal education and learning in Central Europe has been termed 'ex cathedra' – an approach by which the professor passes on received wisdom, normally through lectures and in a way that removes 'power' from the individual and her/his circumstances and deifies the subject matter. German management education is typified by 'in-house' provision, such that managers are trained on the job and for particular jobs; French management education by formalized provision, such that they might learn 'facts' about group development without reflecting upon the development of their own educational group; and UK management education by variety – any of the above (and many more approaches) are on offer – providing a wide element of individual choice and great difficulty in making accurate comparisons between 'products'.

In this chapter I suggest that there are four main approaches to learning; that these approaches offer different views of the world; that the functioning of 'reality' occurs in such a way that each of us normally operates within one approach or another; and that these differences help account for macro – (national) differences as well as micro-tensions between academe and organizations. I suggest that these differences in approach have differing implications for educational provision. If differing forms of education are socially determined, and in turn act as a form of social engineering, then 'educators' (whatever their nationality) need to consider the emergent forms of society that their activities are colluding with (see Chapter 8 for a more detailed discussion of this). If the various approaches to education are seen as complementary, then combined they offer a view of holistic learning which might reflect future societal needs.

I am, for the sake of discussion, presenting these ideas quite categorically, but I would like to start by qualifying or moderating this by acknowledging that whilst conceptual separation is necessary for exploratory purposes, it does impose false constraints on the interlinking of micro and macro variables, and potentially on the relationship between theory and practice. As Mangham (1990: 105) notes, 'Imposing any frame . . . has consequences, since a way of seeing is simultaneously and necessarily a way of not seeing; metaphors, models and frames illuminate some features at the expense of others'.

FORMS OF LEARNING

There are many different schools of learning theory. Historically, behaviourism, cognitive learning and humanism have each held sway; and each has its 'believers'. In this section I posit four, theoretically derived, 'types' of learning, as shown in Figure 17.1. In each case, I will give a brief description of the theoretical approach involved followed by examples. Before doing this, however, it is worth making a distinction between the conscious, subconscious and unconscious. These three categories can be seen as stages of accessibility or awareness. Conscious awareness is directable and reportable; the subconscious is accessible upon introspection, and, thus, is able to be made conscious. Regardless of the depth of introspection, however, the unconscious remains inaccessible – it is equivalent to the deeper primal urges and/or the physical level of nerve impulses and cognitive-motor coordination. The making conscious of 'unconscious' learning (by explaining the physical stages and strategies that are undertaken in skilled behaviour) can result in an apparent de-skilling (Englekamp and Zimmer 1995). Similarly, an individual can feel 'stuck' when s/he comes to the realization that repetitive aspects of her/himself are rooted in previously unacknowledged (and perhaps unwelcome) aspects of her/his psyche.

Behaviourists see learning as directly linked to behavioural outcomes. Learning is moulded and reinforced by a series of linked steps that, at each stage, associate reward with appropriate behaviour. In the example of learning to drive, the reward might be the pleasure felt at being able to change gear proficiently. The learners are probably aware (and conscious) that they can shift gears whereas previously they had been unable to do so. Subconscious learning that is also taking place (for example, about the

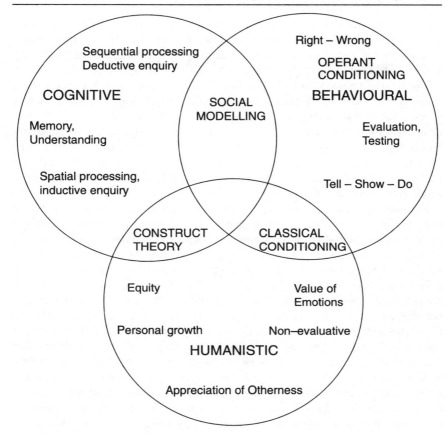

Figure 17.1 A typology of theories of learning

relationship between engine noise and the need to shift) can be made accessible via introspection. Regardless of the depth of introspection, however, there is some learning that remains inaccessible. For instance, in this case, at the physical level of nerve impulses and cognitive-motor coordination. Behavioural learning focuses on rewards for meeting externally defined criteria for 'appropriate' behaviour. In societal terms this approach can be likened to military training, which can be viewed as those at the top of a hierarchy being given power to define and enforce behavioural expectations in terms of 'right' or 'wrong', with no regard for individual preference, motivation or belief.

Cognitivists stress potential behaviour. The person who is learning to drive might improve her/his gear-shifting by learning more about how the gearbox operates through reading a manual, or a forgotten conversation with a friend about problems encountered when in a similar position might help. The learner knows much that is not translated immediately into action and often is not aware of her/his knowledge (Social Learning Theory and Observational Learning – see, e.g., Bandura 1977). Cognitivists study the ability of learners to transfer learning from one situation to another. 'Maps' of understanding of the relationships between events and concepts are constructed. Learning appears to be cumulative and linked to memory and perception (Howe 1980). Socially, this approach is characteristic of traditional academe, in which there is a search for knowledge and understanding based on the assumption that truth can be identified if there is sufficient intellectual understanding. Accepted theory can be challenged through the power of argument, and supremacy is achievable by those with the most acute cognitive faculties.

Humanists stress perception, arguing that each individual creates her/his own version of 'reality' based upon the way in which s/he structures (or map) her/his individual perceptions and memories, unique experiences and anticipations of the future (see, for example, Construct Theory – Kelly 1955). Cultural differences in mapped concepts are linked to how groups of individuals share 'identity' (Jankowicz 1994). 'Learning' is the gaining of deeper insight into the individual's view of her/himself as located within her/his perception of the world. For example, whilst going through the frustrations of perfecting the skill of gear-changing, the learner might gain deeper insight into her/his reactions to frustration. The social match for this approach could be the non-hierarchical community that values individualism and supports the individual in her/his search for self-definition.

In more common parlance, these three approaches could be styled as learning with the hands, the head or the heart. During a traditional university lecture students and lecturer concentrate upon learning at the head level (the academic content). They collude with a variety of behavioural norms at the hands level (those that sometimes cause problems when dealing with 'experienced managers' who refuse to collude with the traditional educational norms), such as when to question and how to take notes. Learning at the heart level could take the form of an increasing dislike of sitting still and being talked down to.

Experiential Learning is derived from reasoning which takes the other three into account and is the fourth archetype I will discuss here. It is perhaps more a model than a theory. It can be seen as a 'cognitive' account that links behaviourism and humanism. Honey and Mumford (1989) suggest that 'experience' plays a part in any learning, regardless of whether or not it is acknowledged within the educational process. Any 'experience' is an opportunity for learning. One of the best-known models of experiential learning is that of Kolb (1974, 1984), who suggests that the process of learning is cyclical, revolving through experience, reflection, theorizing and planning. In Figure 17.2 this is represented by the large (arrowed) circle.

There has been criticism of Kolb's model. Burgoyne (1992) argues that in

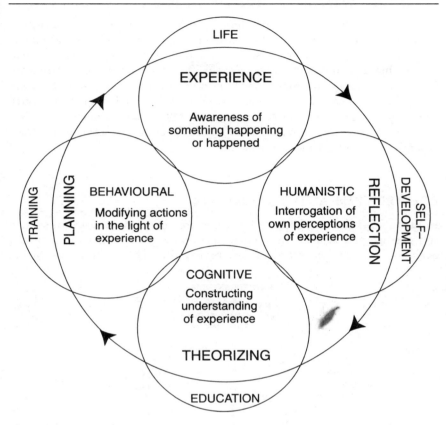

Figure 17.2 Mapping learning

bringing out some important aspects of the learning process it obscures those that deal with the emotional aspects of learning. By not making explicit the potential difference between effective and ineffective learning Kolb comes close to relativism. If people only 'see what they want or expect to see' in their experiences they are blocked from effective learning. These points are (partially) addressed by recognizing the role that subconscious learning plays, even in, for example, the direct transference of knowledge. A process, either internal or externally facilitated, is needed that enables critical observation and evaluation of experience. The learner is then able to distance her/himself from her/his experience rather than just 'replaying' it. The ability to translate the experience into potentially actionable, and realistically testable, future experience is crucial. An extension of the model is to suggest that each individual has a preferred type of learning style (Kolb 1976) and that development in learning is linked to strengthening the non-preferred approaches.

These notions question the degree to which traditional educational provision recognizes the learning preferences of both students and educators. The extent to which provision is designed to utilize prior experience in a way that maximizes effective learning is also questionable (Beckwith 1991). The design of much short non-qualification provision focusing upon the enhancement of managerial efficacy is based upon this model. The social correlate of this focus might be Winch and Schneider's (1993) 'knowledge-based organizations' providing specialized services or Mintzberg's (1979) operating adhocracies.

ARCHETYPES AND LEARNING

In Figure 17.3 the four 'types' of learning are linked to the form of society and are mapped against the Jungian quaternity given in the quote at the beginning of the chapter (and interpreted through the work of Myers

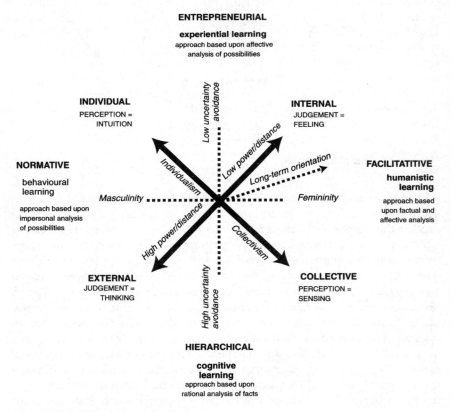

Figure 17.3 Mapping of typologies

(1962)) and against Hofstede's (1991) dimensions of culture. It could be argued that this form of joint mapping is inappropriate. One referent describes micro-parameters of an individual's approach to life whilst the other represents macro- (national) parameters. The first referent deals with an individual's view of life as extrapolated from 'types' of personal preference in perceiving and judging her/his world, the extent to which individuals prefer to rely on sensing or intuition when making meaning of their world (perceiving) and the extent to which individuals prefer to rely upon thought or feelings when coming to conclusions about the import of the meaning that they have made (judging).

In contrast, the second referent describes national culture in terms of its position along five dimensions: those of individualism v. collectivism; low v. high power distance; masculinity v. femininity; low v. high uncertainty avoidance; and short- v. long-term orientation. The positivistic nature of Hofstede's initial work (from which these dimensions are derived) has led to the 'categorization' of national culture in a misleadingly broad and potentially exclusive manner. For example, the Netherlands are described as having a 'feminine' culture, yet the man normally retains leadership in Dutch families. Similarly, France is categorized as high power distance, in which 'Salary systems show wide gaps between top and bottom in the organisation. Workers are relatively uneducated and manual work has a much lower status than office work. Superiors are entitled to privileges . . . Visible signs of status in large power distance countries contribute to the authority of bosses . . .' (Hofstede 1991: 35–6). The UK is categorized as low power distance, in which the reverse is held to occur!

Hofstede makes it clear that many organizations illustrate a mix of these basic trends; however, categorization can impede a more complex discussion of the issues. For example, Poland is classed, alongside Sweden and Germany, as almost centrally balanced between long- and short-term orientation. Yet, as illustrated elsewhere in this book, Poland (as a nation) is a compromise of relatively extreme and disparate tendencies towards either long- or short-term orientation, whilst both Sweden and Germany show less polarization.

Despite the problems associated with the categorization of nations, Hofstede's dimensions are illuminative if viewed as relativistic indicators of preference and as an attempt to describe archetypes rather than 'reality'. This also minimizes the tension between the adoption of individual and national referents in Figure 17.3. We are left with a pattern by which one 'preference' is interpreted through the extent to which its opposite is realized; in which exploration of the unit under investigation is independent of the 'size' of the unit and is, instead, linked to the unit's relationship to its wider context. In other words, the 'categories' presented in Figure 17.3 as archetypal are applicable to any size of grouping (to individuals, organizations and nations). It is not necessary for all components of a 'unit' to be 'located' within the same archetype. For example, it might be that organizations need the stability of a hierarchical national structure in order to be truly innovative, or that individuals need the safety net of centralized social support in order to be able to be highly entrepreneurial.

In Figure 17.3 the 'Hierarchical' quarter is characterized by a system of high leader control in a rationalized environment, in which independent thought, action and the ability to cope with ambiguity are minimized. The archetypal hierarchical person is sensitive to the requirements of those in power and to the analytic nature of 'acceptable' contributions. Questioning is allowed, so long as it occurs within the recognized hierarchical structure and conforms to the 'scientific' investigative format.

The 'Normative' archetype is characterized by a particularly strong focus upon the creation and maintenance of behavioural norms supporting a leader-defined vision of the future. Rules of the predominant culture are imposed, under the assumption that without such imposition individuals would have little 'self control'. Appropriate behaviour is seen to evidence belief in the leader's vision. Ultimate power is awarded to those who can convert others to their view of existence. Thus questioning of these norms is anarchic or heretical behaviour; however, the coercive environment encourages such rebellion.

The archetypal 'entrepreneur' views externally imposed values and codes of behaviour as non-mandatory, and preserves the freedom to question and choose. S/he responds rapidly in a changing environment and is able to be anticipatorily proactive. However, as 'individualists', archetypal entrepreneurs, whilst able to lead others, have difficulty working as equals with others or as subordinates, potentially falling into a damaging pattern of impotence and rivalry (Stacey 1991).

The facilitative archetype is characterized by cooperative social responsibility within a flexible power structure. This requires the ability to understand the machinations of the external world whilst maintaining integrity and lack of 'game-playing' (Baddeley and James 1987; Berne 1964; Harris 1973). Lack of uni-directional leadership challenges the group decision-making processes, such that the organization's political system might result in power vacuum and drift (Stacey 1991).

There is empirical evidence of correlation between the form of parenting and the child's life stance (Baumrind 1973; Bee 1985), and between career and family history (Cromie et al. 1992). Similarly, there is evidence that choice of curricula, methodological approach and course design is partially governed by the value base of the providers and thus perpetuates that value base (Ashton 1988). The notion of co-regulated social development might help describe how archetypes become 'reality'.

LEARNING AND CO-REGULATED SOCIAL DEVELOPMENT

Co-regulated social development picks up the notion of 'identity formation', as discussed by Kostera and by Genell and Kostera elsewhere in this book (see Chapters 14 and 16), and by Lee (1995a). It assumes that 'society' is a mutually negotiated (albeit normally subconsciously and often through collusion; see Lee 1994) but ephemeral construction that comes into 'being' through the collusive perceptions of those who are both within and without that community. In other words, to know what you are you also have to know what you are not. 'Society' exists in so far as people agree to its existence and could be a family unit or a nation. In some way (whether by being born into and thus socialized within it, as in a family or nation; through meeting likeminded people and thus forming friendship groups; or formally through induction into an organization) individuals come to identify (and be identified by others) as part of a community. In doing so they help create and collude with underlying values and norms. Together, individuals co-regulate the community, and the community, collectively, influences the individual's development. In adopting a particular approach to learning the community is also adopting assumptions about societal form and about the roles and characteristics of those who contribute to it.

Figure 17.4 links approaches to learning with aspects of 'culture'. The 'cognitive' environment carries with it group norms about received wisdom and the value of qualifications. Power is vested in those who have achieved qualifications and those who can give them. Cogent argument carries more importance than does applicability or individual difference. The archetypal 'problem' student (or heretic, Harshbarger 1973) would be someone who lacked sufficient intelligence to master the required concepts. The 'behavioural' environment focuses upon activity, functionalism and the importance of the end result. Norms are about identifying competence and filling the 'training gap' to achieve appropriate levels of competence. The heretic is someone unable to demonstrate the required competence. The 'humanistic' environment focuses upon difference and equality. Received wisdom (in so far as it epitomizes a particular view of reality) is inappropriate, as are identifiable and assessable 'competencies' (in so far as they epitomize a 'right' way of doing things). The problem participant is unwilling to explore and share her/his affective and attitudinal aspects. In the 'experiential' environment the focus is on actionable outcomes – the end justifies the means. The heretic is someone who questions the route or prefers inactivity ('The confidence to act is a prerequisite for learning', Blackler 1993). By comparison, the focus in the 'holistic' environment (discussed below) is upon balance – the acceptance

	BEHAVIOURAL LEARNING	COGNITIVE LEARNING	HUMANISTIC LEARNING	EXPERIENTIAL LEARNING	HOLISTIC DEVELOPMENT
FOCUS	Demonstration of appropriate behaviour	Accretion of conventional wisdom	Exploration of affective aspects of self	Utilization of skilled practice	Integration of all aspects of self, and of self with surroundings
CATCH PHRASE	Normative: functionalism	Hierarchical: rigorous thought	Facilitative: authenticity	Entrepreneurial: pragmatism	Synergetic: managing boundaries
ARENA	Transmission of craft and skills through practice and feedback	Development of conceptual ability, understanding and memory	Deepening sense of self through the making conscious of emotions, attitudes and value bases	Increasing ability to apply action appropriate to specific circumstances	Perception of self as complex, balancing dark and light sides of inner self, skills and conceptual ability
ROOTS OF POWER	Proven ability to achieve pre-stated goals	Expertise and knowledge, as recognized by external criteria	Personal power based upon self belief and direction	Proactive ability to influence the situation	Empowerment by reflective and ethical management of own and others' agendas
IMPLICIT NORMS OF MICRO-CULTURE	Defer to experts view of the 'right way' in which to do things; the transmission of skills	Defer to experts, the transmission and passive reception of knowledge; searching for the 'correct' answer	Multiple realities, irrelevance of expertise and external evaluative criteria, though others' perceptions of self provide an important mirror	Individual approach to interpreting the environment and 'solving' the problems it presents	Multiple realities, expertise given due value, seeking equitable balance between interests of self and others

COMMON LOCATION	Generally the product of the professional body as stakeholder; competency-based accreditation against progressively harder 'craft' standards	Generally the product of academe as stakeholder;; progressive levels of theoretically based qualifications; academe and traditional education	Generally the product of the individual as stakeholder; facilitated non-evaluative exploration of affective self, normally through sharing with others	Generally the product of the individual as stakeholder; short course, non-qualification 'life skills' provision designed to enhance proactivity	Generally the product of multiple stakeholders; interdisciplinary, broad-based collaborative provision meeting individual and self-defined needs
COMMON METHODS	Apprenticeship, guided practice, mentoring, 'tell–show–do', 'systematic approach to training'	Ex cathedra = lecture, tutorials, exams and tests of knowledge, sometimes of understanding	Encounter groups, outdoor development, self-development groups, confrontation and support	Updating, guided practice, skills surgeries	Experiential learning, action learning, lifelong/open learning; multicultural managing diversity

Figure 17.4 Correlates to archetypal views of learning

and valuing of difference. The heretic is someone attempting control over, or denial of, others.

This offers a framework for understanding the different approaches taken by academe, organizations and individuals as stakeholders in the educational process. It also provides a framework for understanding national difference in approach to learning and development (Easterby-Smith and Lee 1992), and the problems and potential when attempting to work cross-culturally using alternative methodologies, such as action learning in a society that values the ex-cathedra approach (Jankowicz 1994; Stead and Lee 1996).

HOLISTIC LEARNING

The point is, however, that this is a framework – a mapping. The four approaches to learning have been presented as if they are mutually exclusive; however, dictatorships tend to request absolute belief as well as behaviour (cf. religious wars); academe is concerned with appropriate behaviour and belief as well as the search for ultimate truth (cf. the initial rejection of Darwinism); self-development entails evaluation (cf. equity theory); and learning from experience is greater than the act of experiencing (Burgoyne 1992). As Dewey (1938) pointed out, 'It is not enough to insist upon the necessity of experience, nor even of activity in experience. Everything depends upon the quality of experience which is had . . . every experience lives in further experiences.' Learning is not restricted to what is being taught – individuals make sense of their experiences holistically (combining the 'learning' from head, hands and heart). Their perception of their history and anticipation of the future will influence their current learning (Lee 1994). Whilst educators often focus upon the product of learning as if it were the learning itself (Gross 1987), if there are forty people experiencing the same educational process, each will approach it from different directions and 'learn' different things from it, and, given that learning can (and often does) occur below the level of conscious awareness, much of the learning will not be easily accessible to interrogative measures of assessment.

The holistic approach has some similarity to 'action theory' proposed within a knowledge worker/postmodern perspective and inspired by the information explosion (Blackler 1993; Clegg 1994; Willmott 1987). The field of knowledge work highlights individuals and organizations as contextualized activity systems within power-based networks, involving non-linear processes of multiple translation in areas of crucial uncertainty (Blackler *et al.* 1993; Knights *et al.* 1993). Alvesson (1993) argues that the traditional view of knowledge as a function of cognition is tightly bounded, but that the wider view of 'knowledge' adopted in this field involves a mix of knowledge-intensive and subjective-intuitive rhetoric that leads to ambiguity. Thus, whilst some of the underlying themes presented here could be reframed as those offered by 'knowledge-work' theorists, I have chosen to retain a more traditional terminology for the sake of clarity. It is worth noting, however, that these ideas are not new. They are implicit in Confucianism (Lin and Lee 1996) and have long held sway (ideologically, if not always in practice) in the East.

This line of thought recognizes, and assumes, that learning occurs to the 'whole' person. The more the whole person is engaged in learning, the more relevance and impact it has on that person's existence. For example, in Figure 17.2, cumulative learning (more of the same) could be characterized by an increase in the size of the relevant circle, whilst developmental learning would involve learning across the circles and necessitate the inclusion of a third axis, with individual development represented as a spiral extending along that axis. All aspects of the person would be involved in that 'learning' and we could imagine that the learning would be likely to have a transformative effect upon the person, such that the person no longer views life in exactly the same way as s/he did previously.

Figure 17.3 can be understood in the same way. No national or organizational form can exist in isolation – its profile is necessarily understood through comparison with others. Without that comparison the community cannot know what it is not, and therefore cannot know what it is. This is, for example, the reason why an international placement is mandatory in a globally focused Master's Programme (in strategic human resource development and organizational change) that I direct – how can we talk about ways of changing our own organizational cultures when we are so firmly rooted in them that we cannot understand them in comparative terms?

Bateson (1973) suggests that there exists a hierarchy of learning, in which one level provides the context for the level below. The structures and mechanisms for this are debatable (Burgoyne and Hodgson 1983; Klein 1989) however, there appears to be general agreement about the existence of two principle levels of learning (Fiol and Lyles 1985). The lower level is characterized by repetition of past behaviours, whilst the higher level entails the development of complex rules and associations in order to facilitate new actions. This can be seen in the light of Bartunek and Moch's (1987) description of second- and third-order change, in which second-order change attempts are designed to phase in particular frameworks in which events are understood (schemata) and phase out others, whereas third-order change attempts aim to help learners develop the capacity to identify and change their own schemata as they see fit.

Similar notions of shift can be seen in double/triple-loop learning (Garratt 1987; Hawkins 1991) and the Rogerian approach, in which a facilitator helps others to help themselves (Rogers 1951, 1959). Thus, movement from second- to third-order change involves a transformative shift in approach – experiencing becomes a way of restoring meaning to life (Vasilyuk 1984). Holistic development suggests a move towards the non-rigid integration of self, reflection and experience, alongside the ability to translate the inte-grative experience into potentially actionable, and realistically testable, future experience.

Many communities are adopting the rhetoric of 'working with diversity', yet the principles of this are, in practice, likely to be an anathema to the community. As described above, the community is likely to gain its sense of self (or identity) by reaching common views of what is not acceptable – what is heresy and thus what needs to be 'controlled' – what is 'right' and what is 'wrong'. Development would entail a shifting of these boundaries (while maintaining the basal assumptions), while transformation would entail a fundamental shift in the basic assumptions. For example, several of the chapters in this book (cf. Kristina Gennell and Monika Kostera: The Flying University) document how Central Europe has developed but question the extent to which it has really undergone transformation.

In contrast, the notion of holism is one of relativity – of the sense of self as located within a wider dynamic and relativistic arena. It entails accep-tance of the heretic as a valued Other, and recognizes that individuals and organizations (despite their 'presenting approach') contain hidden elements of their opposites. It is the conflict between these or with the environment (Emery and Trist, 1965) that generates creative tension and transformation (Pascale 1990). Transformation (rather than change) entails the adoption of elements of alternative approaches (a change in 'life stance' rather than 'more of the same') and thus the abandonment of previous mechanisms by which the community maintained its sense of self.

HOLISTIC LEARNING AND THE FUTURE

Changes across Europe are encouraging each cultural element to disaggre-gate in a search for its unique identity (often looking to its history to help in that search). These identities are most easily co-created by agreeing what they are not (with an attendant rise in Nationalism). I am suggesting that a way forward for each community (wherever located) might be through a transformative route of holism!

Let us, however, forget for the minute the potentially evangelical nature of the last few paragraphs and turn instead to practicalities. I have suggested that education is a form of social determinism. As educators (whether teachers, parents or friends) we normally offer the form of educational provision we are used to – it seems 'right' to us as it is part of our heritage. In doing so we promulgate that heritage. We might do so deliber-ately, in order to 'socialize' those we are educating towards particular ends (as, for example, by encouraging students to value rigorous thought and extensive knowledge over the attainment of practical skills, or by designing in-house provision for a corporate client that encourages managers to support the corporate mission), or we might do so inadvertently, passing along our prejudices with our education.

Possibly the only way we might side-step this would be by letting the recipient be the master of the educative process – as in action learning. However, as I argue elsewhere (Lee 1995b), the rhetoric often outstrips practice. Any educational methodology carries with it its value base and assumptions about the learning process, including those that might be seen to facilitate a holistic approach to life. Moreover, as Hugo Letiche suggests in Chapter 19, the more potentially holistic the methodology, the more the provision is likely to be swayed by the personal preferences of educators and recipients. The more it is swayed, the less it is likely to challenge participants in a transformative manner and the more it is likely to reinforce (or at least collude with) existing educational assumptions and mores.

The vision therefore becomes less one of bravely trying to create a wonderful new future and more one of trying to minimize the re-creation of existing blindnesses. A sort of damage limitation exercise. So what might these existing blindnesses be?

I suggest that the adoption of any form of unitary vision of existence entails blindnesses. This is unlikely to cause a problem in an unchanging environment. Individuals, organizations and nations continue to uphold 'traditional' values, as they have been proved (by their very existence) to be following a successful strategy. As we each strive to adjust to the myriad daily challenges that thrust themselves at us, it becomes clear that Marshall and Stewart's (1981a, b) contented middle managers (secure in their positions, working steadily and with no need ever to achieve more) are now a thing of the past. These challenges increasingly require us to address them through all the facilities at our disposal. We need to 'switch hats' as necessary, to involve ourselves in reflection, conceptualization, planning and action, whilst attempting to maintain some sense of wholeness. In other words, we are being forced to draw upon the gamut of our quaternaries and exist in a holistic manner.

The rise in demand for alternative forms of educational provision in Central Europe, documented throughout this book, indicates the desire for a wide range of educational provision that supports aspects of 'learning' that were previously neglected. If asked to speculate about whether holistic learning will ever reach any prominence, I would reply that I think it is already doing so. Not as a planned and carefully integrated form of educational methodology, but in a haphazard, often badly regulated, and exciting way. It is emerging through customer demand. Life itself is providing the action learning, and educational provision (of all forms) is running to catch up with the wide range of requests it receives. Provision that ignores experience is losing favour and the providers can either modify their offerings or lose students. There is no middle ground.

If asked to speculate further, I might even go so far as to suggest that, as technology improves and transnational interdependence grows, it is likely that individuals, organizations and nations will increasingly see their relationships with others as symbiotic (see Lee 1995c for a discussion of this), and themselves as (of necessity) contextualized within a web of difference and similarity.

In conclusion, therefore, I suggest that we have always learnt holistically, but that educational provision has not traditionally recognized this. However, as individuals, organizations and nations become increasingly challenged by the changing environment they become vocal in their need to develop their full range of abilities. The profile of provision is changing to meet these demands and will do so – whether planned or not.

REFERENCES

Alvesson, M. (1993) 'Organisations as rhetoric: knowledge-intensive firms and the struggle with ambiguity', *Journal of Management Studies* 30, pp. 997–1,015.

Ashton, D.J.L. (1988) 'Are business schools good learning organisations?: institutional values and their effects in management education', *Personnel Review* 17(4), pp. 6–14.

Baddeley, S. and James, K. (1987) 'Owl, fox, donkey or sheep: political skills for managers', *Management Education and Development* 18, pp. 3–19.

Bandura, A. (1977) *Social Learning Theory*, New Jersey: Prentice Hall.

Bartunek, J.M. and Moch, M.K. (1987) 'First-order, second-order, and third-order change and organisation development interventions: a cognitive approach', *Journal of Applied Behavioural Science* 23, pp. 483–500.

Bateson, G. (1973) *Steps to an Ecology of the Mind*, London: Palladin.

Baumrind, D. (1973) 'The development of instrumental competence through socialisation', in A.D. Pick (ed.) *Minnesota Symposium on Child Psychology*, vol. 7, Minneapolis: University of Minnesota Press.

Bee, H. (1985) *The Developing Child*, New York: Harper & Row.

Beckwith, J. (1991) 'Approaches to learning, their context and relationship to assessment performance', *Higher Education* 22, pp. 17–30.

Berne, E. (1964) *Games People Play: The Psychology of Human Relationships*, London: Penguin.

Blackler, F. (1993) 'Knowledge and the theory of organisations: organisations as activity systems and the reframing of management', *Journal of Management Studies* 30, pp. 863–884.

Blackler, F., Reed, M. and Whitaker, A. (1993) 'Editorial introduction: knowledge workers and contemporary organisations', *Journal of Management Studies* 30, pp. 851–62.

Burgoyne, J.G. (1992) 'Frameworks for understanding individual and collective professional development'. *Education and Child Psychology* 9(2), pp. 45–52.

Burgoyne J.G. and Hodgson V.E. (1983) 'Natural learning and managerial action: a phenomenological study in the field setting', *Journal of Management Studies* 20(1), pp. 387–99.

Clegg, C. (1994) 'Psychology and information technology: the study of cognition in organisations', *British Journal of Psychology* 85, pp. 449–77.

Cromie, S., Callaghan, I. and Jansen, M. (1992) 'The entrepreneurial tendencies of managers: a research note', *British Journal of Management* 3, pp. 1–5.

Dewey, J. (1938) *Experience and Education*, New York: Collier.

Easterby-Smith, M. and Lee, M. (1992) *United Kingdom Management Education in the '90's: Policies and Priorities*, unpublished report commissioned by Institute for Public Policy Research, available from Lancaster University, UK.

Emery, F.E. and Trist, E.L. (1965) 'The causal texture of organisational environments', *Human Relations* 18, pp. 21–32.

Engelkamp, J. and Zimmer, H.D. (1995) 'Similarity of movement in recognition of self-performed tasks and of verbal tasks', *British Journal of Psychology* 86, pp. 241–52.

Fiol, C.M. and Lyles, M.A. (1985) 'Organisational learning', *Academy of Management Review* 10(4), pp. 803–13.

Garratt, B. (1987) *The Learning Organisation*, London: Fontana.

Gross, R. (1987) *Psychology: The Science of Mind and Behaviour*, London: Arnold.

Harris, T. (1973) *I'm OK – You're OK*, London: Pan Books.

Harshbarger, D. (1973) 'The individual and the social order: notes on the management of heresy and deviance in complex organisations', *Human Relations* 26(2), pp. 251–69.

Hawkins, P. (1991) 'The spiritual dimension of the learning organisation', *Management Education and Development* 22, pp. 172–87.

Hofstede, G. (1991) *Cultures and Organisations, Software of the Mind: Intercultural Cooperation and its Importance for Survival*, London: McGraw-Hill.

Honey, P. and Mumford, A. (19890 *The Manual of Learning Opportunities*, Maidenhead: Peter Honey.

Howe, M. (1980) *The Psychology of Human Learning*, London: Harper & Row.

Jankowicz, A.D. (1994) 'Parcels from abroad: the transfer of meaning to Eastern Europe', *Journal of European Business Education* 3(2) pp. 1–19.

Jung, C.G. (1961) 'Psychology and religion: west and east', *Collected Works*, vol. II, p. 167, cited in C.G. Jung (1961) *Memories, Dreams and Reflections*, London: Flamingo.

Kelly, G. (1955) *A Theory of Personality: The Psychology of Personal Constructs*, New York: Norton.

Klein J.I. (1989) 'Parenthetic learning in organisations: toward the unlearning of the unlearning model', *Journal of Management Studies* 26(3), pp. 291–308.

Knights, D., Murray, F. and Willmott, H. (1993) 'Networking as knowledge work: a study of strategic interorganisational development in the finance services industry, *Journal of Management Studies* 30, pp. 975–95.

Kolb, D. (1974) 'On management and the learning process', in D.A. Kolb, I.M. Rubin and J.M. McIntyre (eds) *Organisational Psychology*, 2nd edn, Englewood Cliffs, N.J: Prentice-Hall.

Kolb, D. (1976) *Learning Style Inventory: Technical Manual*, Boston, MA: Mcber.

Kolb, D. (1984) *Experiential Learning*, Englewood Cliffs, NJ: Prentice-Hall.

Lee, M.M. (1994) 'Clothing and collusion', *Proceedings of the SCOS Conference*, Calgary.

Lee, M.M. (1995a) 'The opposing self: the truth is there is no truth', *Proceedings of the SCOS Conference*, Turku.

Lee, M.M. (1995b) 'Working with freedom of choice in Central Europe', *Management Learning* 26(2): pp. 215–30.

Lee, M.M. (1995c) 'Gender and future realities', *Proceedings of the Aesthetics in Organisations Conference*, Bolton.

Lin, J. and Lee, M.M. (1996) 'An integration of Industry Internationalisation and

Human Resources Development' in *Proceedings of Chinese American Academic and Professional* Convention, Ottawa, Canada. (in press; in Chinese).

Mangham, I. (1990) 'Managing as a performing art', *British Journal of Management* 1, pp. 105–15.

Marshall, J. and Stewart, R. (1981a) 'Managers' job perceptions: part 1 – Their overall frameworks and working strategies', *Journal of Management Studies* 18, pp. 177–89.

Marshall, J. and Stewart, R. (1981b) 'Managers' job perceptions: part 2 – Opportunities for and attitudes to choice', *Journal Of Management Studies* 18, pp. 263–75.

Mintzberg, H. (1979) *The Structuring of Organisations*, Englewood Cliffs, NJ: Prentice-Hall.

Myers, I. (1962). *The Myers-Briggs Type Indicator*, Palo Alto, CA: Consulting Psychologists Press.

Pascale, R.T. (1978) 'Zen and the art of management', *Harvard Business Review* (March–April).

Pascale, R.T. (1990) *Managing on the edge*. London: Penguin.

Rogers, C.R. (1951) *Client Centred Therapy*, Boston, MA: Houghton Mifflin.

Rogers, C.R. (1959) 'A theory of therapy, personality, and interpersonal relationships as developed in the client-centred framework', in S. Koch (ed.) *Psychology: A Study of a Science*, vol. 3, New York: McGraw-Hill.

Stacey, R. (1991) *The Chaos Frontier: Creative Strategic Control for Business*, Oxford: Butterworth-Heinemann.

Stead, V. and Lee, M.M. (1996) 'Intercultural perspectives on HRD' in Stewart, J. and McGoldrick, J. (eds.) *Human Resource Development: Perspectives, Strategies and Practice*, London: Pitman. pp. 47–70.

Vasilyuk, F. (1984) *The Psychology of Experiencing: The Resolution of Life's Critical Situations*, English translation 1991, Hemel Hempstead: Harvester Wheatsheaf.

Willmott, H. (1987) 'Studying managerial work: a critique and a proposal', *Journal of Management Studies* 24. pp. 249–70.

Winch, G. and Schneider, E. (1993) 'Managing the knowledge-based organisation: the case of architectural practice', *Journal of Management Studies* 30, pp. 923–37.

Chapter 18

Uses of case studies in Central Europe

Hugo Letiche

THE BACKGROUND

It seems evident that in a situation where management education cannot be prescriptive it has to be descriptive. It would be culturally arrogant and historically naive for western academics (and/or consultants) to pretend that they know what should be done in Central Europe. The transformation of monopoly state economies into market societies is unprecedented, and is occurring in cultural contexts which have been more or less ignored by mainstream western scholarship for fifty years. Furthermore, while levels of industrialization and consumption might warrant it, the Western Europe experience of the 1950s cannot be transposed on to the current Central European situation without distorting political, international, economic and technological factors, etc. Also, the generation of academics now active in the west do not really know much about their own national development during the 1950s. Nor, one discovers in dialogue with Central Europeans, do we really know very much about the advanced capitalist institutions within which our societies are embedded (Law 1991).

The problem is that the socio-technical systems upon which our economies are based are inherently implicit. The tremendous efficiency of our economies is made possible by a successful process of not thinking about most things. The worker, line manager, member of staff does not, most of the time, create her/his very own way of doing things. They follow, (often implicit) protocols of action, as does everyone from senior manager to the CEO. We have built much of our managerial knowledge into our (physical and social) technology, varying from very primitive technologies such as that of the textbook/cook book/machine manual, up to very sophisticated ones such as business strategies/robotology/expert systems/CAD-CAM. Most of the time we do no think our actions through, but rather, having chosen a culturally accepted goal, we follow prescribed procedures. We cook the meal without understanding nutrition or being a creative judge of spices or cooking methods. We have little or no depth-level insight into the procedures we follow ('Where did they come from?' 'Why do they work?'

'What were the alternatives?'). In fact, it is just this unburdening of ourselves of most awareness that permits us to be enormously efficient. By forgetting most of our 'knowledge' and limiting ourselves to a few key 'action points' we enable ourselves to act quickly and effectively, unencumbered by an almost limitless number of potential issues and problems. Thus, by not knowing, by embedding most knowledge and skills in the forgotten, we achieve 'performativity'. When Central Europeans start to ask us how we really do things, we either have to admit that we do not know or we have to bring all our forgotten assumptions back into consciousness. Neither option actually brings the Central European into our sphere of operation. If we want to let Central Europeans see us in action, we have to choose to suppress explanation and to be task and activity directed. Only by way of a prohibition on the prescriptive and normative which favours problem solving and *performativity*, do we approximate 'normal' activity. The case method is probably the best way to demonstrate the 'not knowing' (i.e. key attitudes, skills and cognition of capitalist *performativity* are implicit) of 'market economy success.'

THE CASE

Cases are potentially 'open texts' permitting western scholars and Central Europeans to project their mindsets on to the material and to talk about the results. But what will such a use of text produce qua learning? Harvard Business School constructs managerial consciousness with these texts (case studies), i.e. produces managers who feel confident that they know what to do in real decision-making situations. But Harvard cases tutored in Central Europe with western tutors and western methods will inevitably be deconstructed by polyphonic results. Instead of revealing action grounded on common shared assumptions, the cases will demonstrate the lack of commonality between the western tutors and Central European managers. One can see the differences, in my experience, by examining the function of the 'shifters'; i.e. the uses of 'Is', 'mes' and 'yous'. The shifters, I submit, mean fundamentally different things to a Pole than to a western MBA student/lecturer. Running cases in Poland reveals an 'I' which is either a voice out to please smoothing troubled waters and in possession of manifold social skills or a voice which is aggressively dismissive and nearly violently commanding. Criticism of (Communist) institutions and practices evokes (fairly easily) the second voice, as does the demand that the individual be judged (i.e. take responsibility) for the collective (group) result. The 'me' rarely has the self-analytical undertones, linked to an assumption of deep psychological drives rooted in childhood development, fairly common in the west. And the 'you' is not task-driven but out to avoid conflict and responsibility, permitting both parties to profit from the situation as much as possible. Likewise, closure occurs differently.

Discussion ends not with a solution but with ritualized community (a person in authority makes a speech, the group goes drinking and ends up singing together, some form of formalized discourse is produced). Problems or conflicts on a content level are not 'solved'; rather, conversation is led back to a harmonious ceremonial level. The unobservant western tutor might think that agreement has been achieved, while in fact the process of talking has simply been stopped. The Polish definitions of the shifters are re-imposed and western managerial practices do not advance. In so far as western 'experts' accept serving the cause of the Polish identity, as briefly discussed above, they can run capitalist cases for Polish consumption. But the 'I' being developed is not that of the Harvard Business School but that of the post-Communist entrepreneur. In effect, the cases will be used to strengthen the background assumptions of the Polish shifters, i.e. clientelism, strengthened (traditional) power relations and the defence of the (existing) political-industrial complex; all of which are in opposition to the creation of an open market society.

THE ANALYSIS

Cases are an effective form of management education just as long as one leaves most political and economic assumptions implicit; the case maximizes performativity within a stable political/social context. For most managerial tasks there is '*almost* one best way' of action which students are to internalize. Since management is such a very inexact activity, the '*almost* one best way' does permit considerable variation and 'sufficing'. But implicit agreement exists on the political and social assumptions which are to remain hidden. Only rarely do questions of 'sustainable economic growth' or 'business ethics' disturb the casework. In all my experience in western business schools, I have never had the political/power/social assumptions of managing questioned by the students during a case exercise. But do we wish in Central Europe to take the political/social structures as much for granted as we do in the west? Is capitalist performativity achievable on the basis of typical Central Europe social assumptions? Casework makes the politics of management education almost invisible. It embeds power relations in the managerial technology of everyday action, making them implicit and depoliticizing the exercise of control. But should we propagate these effects in the current circumstances of Central Europe? Should the hidden assumptions, inherent in western managerial performativity remain hidden in the Central European context? Do we want to give support to the Polish, Czech, Slovak, etc. managerial elites?

Western managerialism is a form of political sleight of hand; it embeds political power in inherent structures of economic activity, in order to create an apolitical performative society. Are we ready to perform the same ideological function for the Central European (ex-Communist) elites? Only if we answer 'yes' to these questions does the case method seem appropriate. We can deconstruct cases, which means problematizing all the things which are meant to remain implicit. This teaching tactic does not intend to produce self-confident managers ready to take control, but questioning doubting individuals confronted by a fundamental crisis in their political/social assumptions. Do we want to run cases as they are supposed to be run or to frustrate the process (and probably frustrate the learners at the same time) by running anti-cases? One can pretend that the choice is not there by claiming that the case involves a really thorough examination of the economic/social/political/cultural context within which action has to take place. But no one who has experienced working with cases will really believe this claim. The power of the case if not in its *potential* intellectual inclusiveness, but in its *actual* (quasi) reproduction of the exclusion of all the factors which can be made irrelevant to action. But the pursuit of action for action's sake (i.e. of performativity) seems even more monstrous in Central Europe than at home. But if we go off to Central Europe to deconstruct performativity we invite the criticism 'Why didn't we first do that at home?'

REFERENCE

Law, J. (ed.) (1991) *A Sociology of Monsters: Essays on Power, Technology and Domination*, London: Routledge.

Chapter 19

Doing action research in the new Central Europe

Hugo Letiche

The use of Action Research/Action Learning in post-Communist Central Europe seems logical enough. There is an urgent need (i) to explore a rapidly changing context, (ii) to take informed action and (iii) to facilitate change. Action Research/Action Learning are attractive because they seem to provide metalevel procedures of intervention without prejudging which action shall emerge. External facilitators, such as myself, can help Central European colleagues to follow a pattern of diagnosis – dialogue – action steps – evaluation. My 'foreignness' helps me, during the first two phases of the action research/learning cycle, to question current practice and to open up discussion. Since the Central Europeans progressively 'own' the research as it evolves they become 'internal change agents' in the latter phases of the research cycle. This seemingly 'neat' division of labour breaks down (at least somewhat) in practice, because action research/action learning raise as many questions about how to proceed as they provide answers. Our multinational team (British, Dutch, Austrian, Canadian, Danish, Polish, American) of 'external facilitators' had to navigate our way through a minefield of social assumptions about change and many questions about the degree of structure needed or desired in the actual research setting. These are put schematically in Figure 19.1, and I shall clarify and comment on these differences in this chapter.

SOCIAL ASSUMPTIONS

Since 1990, western management school academics have been faced with the challenge of bringing their expertise to bear in post-Communist settings. I believe that post-Communist Europe has dramatically confronted us with the end of enlightenment certainties. No doctrine or political movement embraced the enlightenment principles of social rationality, faith in human progress, political perfectibility so radically as did Communism. Its collapse has left a group of European countries – Poland, the Czech Republic, Hungary, Slovakia which have lost (nearly) all faith in the enlightenment tradition. But what sort of management can

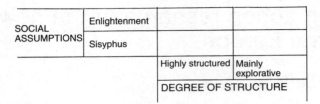

SOCIAL ASSUMPTIONS	Enlightenment		
	Sisyphus		
		Highly structured	Mainly explorative
		DEGREE OF STRUCTURE	

Figure 19.1 Assumptions and structure: a research matrix

emerge without the ideological support of the enlightenment assumptions? In the west it is fairly deviant intellectually to embrace postmodern assumptions and to reject the managerial doctrines of enlightenment rationality which managers use to assume that there is one best way to manage and that (some sort of) *management by objectives* is possible. In Central Europe, non-reflective entrepreneurship takes the place of rules of procedure and orthodoxy of practice. In Central Europe postmodernism is not a radical alternative to common practice, it is the order of the day. Central Europe has no use for research into unchanging permanence ('laws'). Normal (social) science has little to offer in this extremely unstable environment.

Action learning/Research, with their emphasis on the dynamics of change, offer our best jumping-off point to facilitate managerial action in the new Central Europe. On the one hand there exists within management learning a tradition of action learning/research focused on developing managerial awareness and activity, and, on the other hand, there exists in pedagogics (i.e. teacher training) a reflective practitioner movement. Reg Revans is the spiritual father of the former; learning organization theory can be thought of as a powerful update. The second tradition has John Stenhouse, Chris Argyris and David Schoen as forefathers; it has become (virtually) the mainstream trend in teacher training (Zeichner 1993). The two traditions do not share the same common basic assumptions about social change. Revans is a radical pessimist in the tradition of Nietzsche; Schoen and Argyris are progressive reformers in the line of the humanist enlightenment. Action research assumes that learning demands change and that by trying to change practice to meet posited goals one discovers one's own fundamental characteristics, as well as those of circumstance; all of which seems relevant enough to the post-Communist context.

But do we assume that action research leads to the discovery of rational solutions or that it reveals permanent problems? Revans grounded his concept of learning in the dialectical tension between human resistance to learning and the need to find (in some sense) an adequate response to life's challenges/opportunities/problems. Revans asserted that school learning (training, university education, etc.) stressed questions and answers. Schooling is, he argues, based on a strategy of assign and correct. Teachers/trainers tell learners what to 'learn' and thereafter control learner 'results'. Learning is defined in terms of (some sort of) mastery of predetermined (cognitive, technical, practical) behaviour(s). Learning thus is a neverending chain of mastering answers to teachers' questions, learning the causes to preselected effects and reacting to someone else's actions. Revans accepted that 'standard learning' has its place but argued that real managerial problems were of a different nature. The problems of organizing are characterized by problems, i.e. recurrent dilemmas which can never be 'solved'. Tensions for instance, in large organizations between, on the one hand, individuality or creativity and, on the other hand, order or efficiency will never go away. There is no right answer or universal formula to be applied. Organization strives, at the same time, to achieve optimum levels of operation, intrinsic motivation, organizational renewal and unpredictable flashes of talent, and to maintain predictability, routine and authority. Such managerial 'shopping lists' form permanent quandaries for managerial action.

The myth of Sisyphus provides an apt metaphor: Sisyphus rolls the stone up the hill (for instance, the manager finds an effective combination for R&D of creativity and control), only to have it roll back down again when he approaches the summit (for instance, production and marketing enter the scene) (Camus 1942). The challenge reappears of finding appropriate balance. Management's basic tasks form a dynamic field of problems: the tensions between research and development, production, finance, marketing, logistics, etc. are inherently Sisyphus-like. Action research is futile if it promises to find definitive or final answers to such problems. The process of investigation has value, as long as one realizes that the results are tentative contextual responses to complex problems. If research connotes generalizable results, i.e. claims to transcend the unique, then Revans rejects (on ontological grounds) the appropriateness of any such activity in management practice. Human social existence can, via a process of mutual support and criticism, lead to reflection and renewed insight/practice. Richer and better-informed responses to problems are possible. But 'reality' is not linear. The paradoxes and complexities of organizing cannot be resolved. Learners can deepen their experience. More complete reflection on practice can replace more simplistic monodisciplinary response. Records of experience can lead to insights, they can provoke reflection and stimulate creativity, but they do not lead to general principles or validated theories. Heightened awareness of managerial problems will not produce universalizable rules of behaviour. The more that one knows, the less one will try to generalize. The more learning that takes place, the more the learners will accept the ontological priority of their problems.

Human social existence is inherently problematic – knowledge of existence must respect this fundamental characteristic. Revans rejects, in this manner, what we have come to call the *grand narratives* of social thought.

Only the specific observation, true to circumstance, remains loyal to occurrence. Thus Revans's ontology is postmodern *avant la lettre*. His social ontology rejects abstract generalizable thought for specific experiential problem-solving. Revans prioritizes the social organizing of discussion, investigation and reflection above any reification of 'organization', or the generalizations of business gurus, or the 'truth' of (whatever) theory. For Revans the process of investigation is more important than the 'models' of rational practice. Revans' Action Learning, with its stress on the learner 'with a problem' and a facilitation process balancing between support and critique, is potentially an important impulse to cooperative investigation between Central Europeans and ourselves.

In contradistinction, the 'reflective practitioner movement' has assumed that learning can lead to a more just and humane society. In its origins the reflective practitioner movement stressed the value of knowledge, gained in practice, via direct professional activity. Knowledge rooted in concrete practice was prioritized – above results from the psychological laboratory, or those derived from experimental testing of theoretical propositions. The assertion was that real-life learning was not improved via traditional research; only practitioner-based investigation, guided by actual in-service problems, addressed itself to veritable practical issues. Teaching/training/learning are activities which need facilitation grounded in the *tacit* awareness of professionals. Not research articles or textbook 'facts', but practitioner-implicit skills – i.e. ways of doing things form the backbone to practice. The goal of the reflective practitioner movement has been to make tacit knowledge more accessible. Therefore this movement sought to valorize the teacher/trainer/manager, who all too often was dismissed in the academic status game to the 'unscientific' junk heap. It was claimed that practitioner skills and not scientific research were the basis for improvement. Better education (management) could only be achieved by passing through the portals of the school (company). Practitioner in-practice knowledge (i.e. professional cognitive and behavioural repertoires) were seen as the key to improved results. Not only did practitioner research highlight the real crux of professional action (i.e. the skills, creativity and behavioural resources required) but also influenced professionals to be more active towards their practice.

The practitioner-researcher is much more than a passive funnel through which preset models of action flow. By studying their tacit skills, professionals will (supposedly) become more aware of how they contextualize knowledge, empower clients and make energy flow via their interactive craft. Context-bound knowledge can then form the crux to an expanded professionalism. The reflexive practitioner movement has become a tree with many branches. In a recent survey article Kenneth Zeichner (1993) identifies five: the academic (i.e. emphasis on subject matter and the translation of subject matter knowledge to situations of practice), the social efficiency (i.e., research-based knowledge of the social sciences is used to create a dynamic process of practitioner self-examination), developmentalist (i.e., emphasis on growth and understanding), social reconstructionist (i.e., the pursuit of a more humane and just society) and the generic (i.e., reflection for reflection's sake). All of these presuppose basic modernist assumptions. Rational analysis and planning are tools of incremental self-improvement. Progress occurs via improved insight. The professions are firmly (though implicitly) rooted in their role of guaranteeing social enlightenment. The strategy of the French republicans (the so-called 'radicals' of classical French liberalism) is reconfirmed. The professions, via the power of the state, 'civilize' mankind to democratic principles which lead to a progressively more liberal society.

Nowhere outside France is the choice for enlightenment-based liberal democracy quite so strong. Anglo-Saxon conservatism and German/Italian Christian Democracy prioritize tradition above individual rational analysis. Thus, British action research struggles to reverse common priorities and to assert a professional mission statement wherein growth in analytic ability is crucial to social development. Not tradition but growth in rationality supposedly leads to informed behaviour and to a normally unspecified 'good' result. German and Italian action research have often been identified with (neo-)Marxism. The 'truth of reflection' was identified with changing the circumstance of the 'downtrodden' or 'oppressed'. The crux of the matter was change in power and/or wealth differentials, leading to equality. The enlightenment tradition, whether embodied in French 'radicalism', British 'growth of awareness' or continental 'neo-Marxism', is long in social optimism but short in concrete social analysis.

Will improvement in 'expert' action based on growth in rational awareness lead to sustainable economic development and/or democratization? What proof is there that social change can really be rationally driven? What specific and tangible projects are actually being proposed, or, even better, have been successful? Can we be certain that the enlightenment agenda, where growth of rationality leads to morally worthy results, is more credible than Foucault's (1966) prediction that the increasing encroachment of 'rationality' into human existence will only imprison humanity in an ever tighter straitjacket of rules and conformity, and that this will be accompanied by ever more encompassing norms and increasing numbers of transgressors who will have to be banished? Naive faith in rationality seems strange in the late twentieth century. Which rationality, after all, are we referring to – that of economic growth leading to pollution and environmental crisis or that of social engineering leading to bureaucratic hegemony? The enlightenment agenda seems viable only when unquestioned.

Finally, on the political level, what certainties could be used to ground action research (i.e. reflection on practice) to a 'just' relationship to Others? Since the 1970s, social democracy and neo-Marxism have lost (nearly) all their self-confidence; previous safe points of orientation have fallen away and have not been replaced by new ones. The old division of research into (i) a positivism which politically reaffirmed the *status quo*, (ii) a (psychological) humanism which fosters social reform without challenging dominant social relationships and (iii) an emancipatory or radical paradigm which, through conflict, ferments fundamentally alternative social arrangements is a mirror of the political divisions of the west during the Cold War (Burrell and Morgan 1979).

The conservative block cooperated on and off with a fairly large reformist coalition, while they both, most of the time, opposed the fairly small radical opposition. But these political divisions have run out of steam. Since 1989 they no longer define the political landscape. The radicals have disappeared; the reformers have lost their clarity. Positivism has lost much of its purity. The research landscape needs to be redefined by new commitments and forms of engagement. Absolute trust in scientific progress, whether (neo-)Positivist or (neo-)Marxist, may have disappeared but it has not been replaced by the 'tragic-comic' image of *Sisyphus*. Do Western European academics who cooperate with colleagues in post-Communist Central Europe actually believe in 'enlightenment progress' or do they really see themselves as part of a 'tragic-comic' script? However inconsistent it may be, my recollection is that the answer was both at once.

DEGREE OF STRUCTURE

When undertaking action research should one's research steps be highly prestructured or primarily contextually guided? And if research is to be contextually constituted what should be the role of the 'reflective practitioner'? The call for reflective professionalism has been attacked, with claims that it is grounded on assumptions which cannot support close examination. What exactly is 'reflective practice'? What do action researchers really do and why is it worth the effort? Realizing the necessity of giving answers to these fundamental questions, academic champions of action research have increasingly become involved in the analysis of the concept of 'reflection'. Paradoxically this has led to a form of 'reflection' on the practice of 'reflective practitioners' in which actual practitioners do not participate. 'Reflection' has been thematized as a theoretical issue, one discussed by academics in a debate largely closed off to practitioners. The old divide between reflective professionals (academics, researchers) and practitioners has been reconstituted around the theme of reflection.

An essentially intuitive concept like reflection, can perhaps be replaced by 'rigorous' research procedures; but action research then becomes a socially engaged fieldwork version of the normal empirical research cycle (i.e., orientation – theory – hypothesis – data collection – analysis – conclusion). Applied evaluation research answering the question Did professional action lead to desired results? and project planning leading to Producing knowledge-based products and services, can lend themselves to such a script. A short statement on the 'context of the problem' (summarized from interviews held at Gdansk University) highlights the social and professional significance:

> During the Communist period didactic experimentation in university teaching stood still for forty years. The transference of knowledge occurred via lecturing; students were periodically controlled in work groups. Case-based, inquiry and discussion methods were unknown; projects, field work and internships were unheard of.
>
> To support the conversion to a market economy, university educators need to develop didactic expertise permitting students to model the key social-cognitive skills of the market economy. Mastery of case-based teaching has been identified as a potentially important step in this direction.

The purpose of the research is further clarified via a statement of the research problem; such as:

> To be able to teach cases effectively, faculty have to learn to research and write state-of-the-art business cases. In this project, via cooperative business case development, we have identified the in-practice needs for development of Polish and Slovak university management teachers. An effective programme of intervention, leading to case development and implementation in the curriculum with local faculty providing powerful role models; has, on the basis of the co-research, been identified.

Hereafter, a literature review would be needed to detail: the didactic situation in management teaching in Central Europe; the emerging political support in Poland, and the Czech Republic and Slovakia for case-based curriculum; the characteristics of case-based teaching and the methods of case development currently practised in the west. Thereafter, would come the statement of the hypothesis: 'by writing and teaching business cases Polish and Slovak lecturers gain in the skills characteristic to management practice in a market economy, and are enabled to function as successful role models for their students.' Further rationale in support of the hypothesis would then be followed by operational definitions of the variables. This project model is obviously highly structured, and because it assumes that practice can progress via growth in knowledge, I categorize it as illustrative of 'enlightenment' thinking. Projects can be (fairly) tightly structured, and assume that their results lead to (social) progress without becoming quite as archetypically 'normal (social) science' as has been described. Nonaka (1994) has received a lot of attention by stressing the conversion from *tacit knowledge* to *explicit knowledge* within corporate knowledge creation. He leaves, in theory, more room for the unstructured cultural and subjective factors of learning than occurred in the example above.

The leap of faith from reflection to planned action made possible by explicating tacit knowledge, wears very thin when the social (historical) value of increased rationality comes under doubt. This is exactly what has happened in Central Europe. It has led to what I term 'mainly explorative' work. Projects and ensuing texts explore a theme without claiming to have their subject matter 'under control'. The research is often born of participant observation, but the researcher does not have the ambition of achieving clear thematization leading to uni-directional conclusions. Practice no longer means any *one* thing. It is acknowledged that the research is more descriptive than prescriptive, and that one researcher's description may not be another's. Tsoukas (1994) and Kelly (1994) are champions of the new 'unstructured' approach. Tsoukas argues that organizational behaviour is undergoing a paradigm shift from *social engineering*, which is highly structured and enlightenment-based, to *reflective practice*, which is mainly explorative and, at least in part, 'Sisyphus-ian'. Kelly stresses self-replicating, self-repairing learning structures with control from the bottom up (i.e. priority of the parts over the 'whole', governance is *not* by any central command), growth by chunking (i.e., complexity is a product of simple modules working more and more closely together) and the honouring of your errors (i.e., development via trial and error can only work if 'error' is permissible). Not rational control but the workings of *vivisystems* (i.e. life itself) are championed. Kelly's biological paradigm pits the entropy inherent in all nature against the vivisystem's creativity (i.e. life's characteristic of dynamic development, balanced on the edge of chaos but sufficiently stable to prevail). Innovation, for Kelly, is a product of co-evolution – of complex processes of competition and cooperation which do not follow any plan, break down regularly, but have over time achieved ever greater levels of complexity.

Poststructuralist thought has also fuelled the current attack on the primacy of 'structure'. Difference has become acknowledged as a key ontological quality of human existence. We have learnt from (post)structuralism that language (i.e., communication, cooperation, economic organization) is dependent on the play of 'difference' and that personal identity, likewise, is a product of self/other, I/me, memory/perception difference(s). Difference thinking teaches us that 'organization' exists in relationship to 'disorganization' and that 'control' can only be significant in relationship to what is 'out of control'. Control has far too long been identified with 'distal' (i.e. at a distance, uninvolved, rational, abstract) to the detriment of 'proximal' (i.e. experiential, committed, personal) (Cooper and Law 1994). Difference thinking clarifies that the 'distal' can only exist thanks to the 'proximal', and vice versa. Pure abstraction without an experiential base is meaningless, and the purely individual without shared structures of speech and thought is inexpressible. Thus, the effort to let 'structure' (i.e.

the 'distal') predominate is misguided – the co-evolution of the 'distal' and 'proximal' needs to be the order of the day. 'Meaning' is an unstable effort to balance the 'distal' and 'proximal' which leapfrogs from one 'text' to the other without ever achieving lasting stability. Thus, the effort to 'know', i.e., to let a research 'text' mean, is only partially structurable and Sisyphus-ian.

DOING ACTION RESEARCH IN POLAND AND SLOVAKIA

Social assumptions

What are the social assumptions of our research practice when assisting action learning/research projects in Poland and Slovakia? Looking back on the five years of action-research interventions with which I have already been involved (via TEMPUS and ACE) in Central Europe (1990–1995) and those that I am currently engaged in (via TEMPUS in the Slovak Republic (1995–1998) I see a fundamental political difference between an 'enlightenment' and a 'Sisyphus' camp. The one group wants to facilitate a rebirth of individualism and the other has been dedicated to the improvement of existing practice. The logic of the Polish Tadeusz Mazowiecki government symbolizes the latter, and Timothy Garton Ash's vision of Central Europe the former. Ash has, at least since 1983, posed as the voice of the Central European *inteligent*:

> the *inteligencja* has had a mission to uphold the spirit and culture of the nation against the political powers that be. This romantic version of noblesse oblige is at the heart of the traditional Polish definition of what it is to be an intellectual or, more broadly, a member of the educated class – an *inteligent*. It is a subjective, idealistic self-definition in which the idea takes absolute precedence over reality and consciousness determines being. In the condition of unfreedom, it proclaims the principle of As If. Try to live *as if* you live in a free country.
>
> (Ash 1990: 105–6)

Now it really is *as if* Poles live in a free country. Communist totalitarianism, however mitigated, has been replaced by democratic elections; the planned economy has been supplanted by an attenuated form of a market economy. The double life of Communism, where one said and did one thing in public but had another opinion in private, has been disbanded. It is *as if* the 'true facts' of economic and political existence are slowly coming out in the open. But will a 'hypermarket' of western ideas, publications and research take over? Will intellectual zapping – wherein ideas do not really matter but excitement and fashion predominate become the order of the day? Will ideas cease to count; will intellectuals no longer matter? The KOR (Committee for Social self-defence) and Solidarity oppositions made intellectuals like Adam Michnik into heroes. For Ash, the commitment to thought, the engagement to ideas, was the positive use of adversity which distinguished the Central European opposition to Communism. (Ash 1989)

But now that freedom is no longer a form of intellectual as if, but has become a concrete daily problem, what will happen to the intellectuals? Ash describes the fall of Communism as the victory of as if thinking (Ash 1990). The intellectuals, who via their own creativity and effort had – despite severe government pressure and against all the odds experienced freedom) brought Communist totalitarianism to its fall. Ash describes the Czechoslovakian Velvet Revolution as an intellectual happening where creativity came to power. Not careful planning, economic analysis and realistic deliberation, but freedom, passion and emotive integrity overcame forty years of Communism. Volunteerism – the freed spirit prevailed over police force; ethical honesty won over totalitarianism; spontaneity and solidarity were more powerful than calculating cynicism.

In contradistinction, the Tadeusz Mazowiecki government never assumed that the effects of Communism were, in any real sense, over and done with. Political leadership in Central Europe remains a very fragile thing. The state is very weak; it is corrupt, inefficient, technically incompetent and invested with little legitimacy. The apparatchik of yesterday has become the capitalist of today: then, local party official; now, owner of benzine stations. The abrogation of Communist power occurred when the Communist governments/parties had no idea what to do next; nor any ability to generate new programmes, proposals or solutions. The (ex-) Communists are the technical cadre who have kept society running, though not running very well. If forced to choose between an economy that runs badly and one that does not run at all, any sane government will embrace the former. The dilemma of the Tadeusz Mazowiecki government was that it had to get on with things as best it could. Economic logistics could be improved (i.e. more and better goods in the stores), the right to travel restored, fear of totalitarianism reduced, but a new internationally competitive economy could not be imagined into existence. Post-Communist Poland may have lost the Communist system, but it has not gained much in its place. A citizenry used to profiteering, clientelism and a lackadaisical work ethic couldn't be changed instantly. Notwithstanding the idealism of the few dissidents, everyday life became more confused, competitive and uncertain. The old heavy-handed mechanisms of control (secret police, indoctrination, censorship) have been abandoned, but western consumer society's techniques of control (everything is available but no one has enough money to buy what they'd want to) have replaced them. An enormous, and for many very threatening, growth in complexity has occurred. A controlling system where one had precious little to choose has been replaced by more choices than many can understand or manage.

Post-Communism is confusing, paradoxical and complex. In these circumstances, the old concept of the intellectual ['Persons active in public life, officially or clandestinely, who create or diffuse ideas, opinions and models of behaviour, conscious of their social mission'] is out of date (Jerzy Jedlicki 1993). That concept of the Polish intellectual's mission was focused on preserving the national memory and character from government (censorship) distortions. In so far as Poland has now become a normal democratic country, 'the intellectuals as a particular social group and mission is done with' (Jedlicki 1993); Poland is living the *fin de l'intelligentsia*. Many Polish intellectuals are painfully aware of their weakness in comparison to the up-to-date meritocracies of the 'first world'. A contemporary, problem-solving, concrete, highly skilled middle class is what is needed. Hands-on experts, applied specialists and qualified practitioners produce the wealth upon which democracy and the welfare state are based.

When I look back on the action research projects in Poland and Slovakia (and just a little bit in the Czech Republic) in which I participated, I see an initial period of idealization, quickly followed by realism. In 1989–90 the fantasy of radical democracy was prevalent: what we had failed to achieve in 1968 was now supposedly within hand's reach in Warsaw and Prague. Our old (enlightenment) idealisms resurfaced despite everything that we had supposedly learnt in the last twenty years about the consumer society (i.e., hyper-capitalism and performativity). But very quickly we realized that Mazowiecki was right: the real challenge was to achieve a modicum of freedom while struggling to keep one's economic head above water. In effect, Poland (and Slovakia) entered into the world-wide competition of the market system with outdated and inefficient economies. Whatever gains in freedom we might help to facilitate within the universities, the prison of ineffective cadres and management would determine society more strongly. Our efforts could not begin to counterbalance the dead weight of *clientelism* and the history of bureaucratic hegemony. Thus we were back to Sisyphus – however hard we might try to support emergent entrepreneurial activity, the economic and political limits of Polish (or Slovak) society would inevitably catch up with us.

Degree of structure

I worked in central Europe in a tutor team which did not try to 'control' the Fellows' learning (the western staff were called tutors and the Central Europeans fellows – there were around six of the former and each year thirty of the latter). De facto we rejected the reflective practitioner approach, because we were not committed, in the Polish and Slovak contexts, to the externalization of existing tacit knowledge, but rather to the socialization of the Fellows in the ethos of explorative discussion and innovative problem-solving. The tutors' intervention strategy was unstructured, in the sense that we did not predefine cognitive contents or skills to be mastered but did have clear attitudinal goals. We wanted the Fellows to learn to deal with complexity, to accept multiplicity, to feel comfortable with emergent strategies. We championed the Revans point of view: (i) the subject has to genuinely bring her/his problem(s) to discussion for real learning to occur and (ii) one cannot change an organization if one cannot change oneself. Thus, we entered into joint problem-solving with the Fellows. In small nationally heterogeneous groups, interdisciplinary teams examined the problems encountered in trying to achieve more effective management education in post-Communist Central Europe.

The cooperation was problem-focused and concrete. The tutors did not present blueprints for management education but worked collaboratively to try to achieve change. Together we worked on course design, general curriculum reform, creating learning materials, developing didactic repertoires, initiating company–university cooperation (internships, in-company projects, company-sponsored consulting). The key process characteristic to the approach was small-group collaboration where we criticized and gave support to one another. The western tutors did not play the role of being 'better informed' and 'more knowledgeable'. Working together inevitably confronted us with suspense, humour, intelligence, pleasure, vivacity, wisdom but also with pretensions, boredom, irritation, anger and antipathy. Because we championed no political 'truth' and did not define clear working procedures, there were moments when we feared our Fellows 'might be drowning'. Was our approach too unstructured; did our social assumptions demand too much tolerance of frustration? But we could be honest to ourselves and to the Fellows only by acting as we did.

The tension between structure ('distal') and exploration ('proximal') was continually present. Obviously exploration is a form of structure; and if there is no exploration, nothing remains to be structured. 'Proximal' investigation of the *self*, via group dynamic exercises, took place in the workshops, while fieldwork, centring on changing work structures, confronted the Fellows with the 'distal'. The group dynamic exercises were designed to intensify the Fellows' contact with their self and to stimulate them to display their self's desires/hopes/freedom to others. Training occurred to master feedback and debriefing in order to improve the quality of communication and to strengthen more open and constructive interaction by diminishing judgemental, inhibiting exchanges. A learning-by-doing introduction to case studies, stressing here-and-now engagement with the new post-Communist society, was held. Fellows were encouraged to keep professional diaries to: (i) identify practice which met/did not meet the self's criteria for excellence and (ii) to examine the differences between what the *self* wants, believes, aspires to, and what happens on a daily basis. Process evaluation was organized to explore openness, learner–tutor cooperation and directness of expression.

Value-setting exercises, modelled on Polish (Slovak) circumstances, examined how Fellows reacted when the time demands of professional improvement, preparing one's lectures, keeping up to date, consulting opportunities, research and private life {family} were all in conflict. Staff–student dialogue was modelled by letting western graduate students, in pairs, discuss their purposes, motivation and learning with Central European lecturers, who compared and contrasted the attitudes of the Western European students to their own. By opening up staff–student dialogue, we tried to get the Fellows to examine higher education from the students' point of view and to explore the possibilities of staff–student co-research and cooperative problem-solving. These interventions tried to reveal the potential of constructive, participatory faculty–student interaction which could slowly replace the unilateral, authoritarian teaching models now in place. Evaluation and feedback sessions were used to examine the tutors' work, to reveal differences between us and to acknowledge openly the complexity we faced working in new, fairly unknown circumstances.

In general, we emphasized *perspectivism* in the debriefing of the exercises: often there were many differing points of view expressed. By solving and writing (short) cases in set groups, we explored the dynamic tension between critical dialogue and trust when the Other challenges as well as supports us. The longest activity, requiring the most work and commitment, was the in-service project, where the Fellows, preferably in small groups, pursued a Diagnosis – Dialogue – Action Step – Evaluation change cycle in their own work situation. These action-learning projects allowed us to work through the micro-politics of change, confront the complexity of motivation, examine the rapidly changing circumstances, and develop in-practice skills. In the project, small group cooperation focused around a single theme for action, such as writing Polish cases for (future) HRM specialists or designing a computer game around the logistic problems of a (Slovak) company. These real-life problems produced powerful teamwork. Thus, on a process level our programme was very structured, in the sense that we had an arsenal of exercises and activities which we used with the Fellows.

Our programme was more problem than individual centred. The workshop curriculum and project supervision could have focused more on the individual participants. Each person's educational biography could have served as a basis for further reflection. The Fellows could have been encouraged to enter a creative reflective process by understanding what they do, why they do it and what they want to achieve in the future. Such a strategy could have begun by taking a good long look at the personal educational biography (identify good and bad learning experiences, both as learner and as teacher) and been followed by identifying preferences and professional commitments (for instance by maintaining and analysing a personal professional diary) in order, finally, to generate change plans and action steps. The group significance and institutional import of the activity would have emerged spontaneously as others responded to one's (attempted) initiatives.

Western tutors can encourage Central Europeans to write their own educational biographies, to keep professional diaries and to analyse their practice as steps towards change. But this strategy seems to assume a culture of self-examination and self-criticism where personal effectiveness is highly valued. Most of the Fellows had only recently been introduced to the management skills and behavioural repertoires needed in capitalist society; they needed time and 'psychic space' to internalize these new practices. We chose for a less threatening learning environment than personal effectiveness (PE) provides. Furthermore, PE assumes that, at least to some degree, one right pattern of behaviour exists, i.e. the 'effective' one. We did not want to posit any such (enlightenment) assumption, or to claim (however implicitly) that we, the tutors, knew what 'was best for' Central Europe.

MIXING THE MODELS

On the one hand we have been strongly influenced by Revans, who has a highly structured Sisyphus-ian model of action learning; and on the other hand we have embraced new paradigm co-research, which is much less structured in its role definitions and learning goals (Reason and Rowan 1981). The new Central Europe is most definitely out of control; work there cannot be effectively planned or prestructured. Central Europe is a very dynamic vivisystem; which, right now, is evolving every which way. The rate of change may have slowed a bit since 1991, but when we began there was a sense of radical indeterminacy. Contradictory demands seemed to be made of practice, making it very difficult to set performance standards and rendering the definition of achievement ambivalent. At once: (i) we strove for improvement in practice by emphasizing openness, dialogue, cooperation, inquiry, reflection; and (ii) attempted to facilitate and encourage the Fellows to deal with the heightened levels of ambiguity born of competing knowledge claims, working with stakeholders at cross-purposes and all the ambiguity of post-Communist society.

Our programme centred on developing open social interactions as if they were the social psychological building blocks of a democratic society and inherently worthwhile, and we also stressed the limits of social rationality/planning/control, acknowledging that post-Communism is a situation of social ambiguity and human complexity which reveals the lack of discernible *telos* in society. Nothing indicated to us a clear model for action. While we rejected the rather facile social optimism of Schoen and Argyris (i.e. enlightenment/exploratory action learning), we practised nonetheless much of what they preached. Though we come from a culture of zapping – where TV remote control is employed to achieve the rapid, frenzied change of channels and the subject is everywhere and nowhere, i.e. attends to all channels [worlds, universes, sources of information] and none, we still championed 'understanding', 'dialogue' and 'interaction.' Though our society does not attach itself to any coherence, support any single reading of history, but rather zaps its way from the most attractive image to the most seductive fragment, we defended intellectual discussion and reflective practice. (Pivot 1990)

Action learning, in effect, demands the rejection of zapping for commitment, involvement, engagement. Instead of instantaneous change of zapping, we called for a rather long, slow effort at modifying practice. Instead of a pattern of flight/return/re-departure, we demanded project involvement lasting months. We assumed that education should lead to learning and freedom and were amazed when real learning, discussion or thought occurred in anything as institutionalized as our own programme. The university is for us a huge mass of offices connected only by the central heating pipes; and yet it is also (potentially) a centre of cooperation and reflection.

ON BALANCE

It is quite easy to see that it is a waste of money to send western university lecturers, at great cost, to Central Europe to go on a lecture tour, especially when the ideas lectured can be found in books; but active, hands-on professional cooperation can potentially stimulate the development of Central European management education. Such a process of joint professional cooperation can aptly be called Action Learning/Research because it undertakes to study practice and to understand it in the perspective of change. But, as explored in this chapter, the social assumptions of Action Learning/Research are ambivalent. On the one hand they imply, at a minimum, a logic of personal growth through dialogue, commitment and openness if not, more extremely, the achieving of personal effectiveness. On the other hand, they are sensitive to contextual (historical/cultural) factors which severely limit any assumption of individual agency. After five years of working in Central Europe, I would still approach facilitating improvement of professional training with an action research mindset; but I am now more uncertain about what this means and what I am really assuming.

Central Europeans are in a great hurry to achieve minimal competence in market-economy skills; they often do not want to be bothered with fundamental discussions about purpose. For the Fellows, the crux of the matter was to get quickly down to work, and to get something done which furthered their own performativity. Those who insist on believing in the quick fix (i.e. give me the solutions, I don't need to know the theories behind them) rejected the learning route we'd set out for them. For those who accept that there are no ready-made answers, concrete attention to practice offers a pragmatic approach to change. Nonetheless, one can get the cart before the horse. Action Learning/Research can overemphasize reflection to the detriment of the change process. The facilitators need to understand their own goals: are they offering an apprenticeship in complexity and multiplicity; are they transferring skills leading to freedom and wealth; or are they offering a (consistent/inconsistent) combination of the two?

On the pragmatic level, we facilitated the production of case studies, computer simulations, course designs, new curriculum and the development of interactive teaching methods and materials, including in-company projects and internships. The products were the sort of things which are desperately needed, though obviously lots more is needed than our project could produce. But the crisis in Central European management education is not only caused by a shortage of market-economy skills (though the skills level does desperately need developing); the crisis is also one of educational purpose and identity. What vision of learning and thought will prevail in Central European universities? Action learning/research is obviously not a sufficient answer to such a question. But action learning/research is a pragmatic point of departure for concrete cooperation, beyond which we all have to define our contextual principles and in-practice goals.

REFERENCES

Argyris, C. and Schoen D.A. (1978) *Organizational Learning*, Reading, MA: Addison-Wesley.

Ash, T.G. (1989) *The Uses of Adversity*, New York: Random House.

Ash, T.G. (1990) *The Magic Lantern*. New York: Random House.

Ash, T.G. (1993) *In Europe's Name: Germany and the Divided Continent*, New York: Random House.

Burrell, G. and Morgan, G. (1979) *Sociological paradigms and organisational analysis*, London: Heinemann.

Camus, A. (1942) *Le Mythe de Sisyphe* (the myth of Sisyphus), Paris: Éditions Gallimard.

Checkland, P. (1991) *From Framework through Experience to Learning: The Essential Nature of Action Research*. Manuscript: Department of Systems and Information, Lancaster University.

Cooper, R. and Law, J. (1994) 'Organisation: Distal and proximal views' in Bacharach, S. (ed.) *The Sociology of Organisations*, Greenwich, Conn.: JAI.

van Dongen, H.J. (1993) 'The end of great narratives on organizational theory', in H. van Driel (ed.) *Ontwikkeling van bedrijfskundig denken en doen* (Developments in management thinking and doing), Delft: Eburon.

Foucault, M. (1966) *Les Mots et les choses* (The order of things), Paris: Éditions Gallimard.

Jedlicki, J. (1993) 'Pologne: l'intelligentsia au tournant de l'histoire', *Le Débat* 76 (September–October), pp. 32–39.

Kelly, K. (1994) *Out of Control*, Reading, Mass: Addison-Wesley.

Nonaka, I. (1991) 'The knowledge creating company', *Harvard Business Review* 96 (November–December). pp. 96–104.

Nonaka, I. (1994) 'A dynamic theory of organizational knowledge creation', *Organizational Science* 5(1), pp. 14–37.

Pivot, B. (1990) *Le Métier de lire*, Paris: le débat allimand.

Polanyi, M. (1966) *The Tacit Dimension*, London: Routledge & Kegan Paul.

Reason, P. and Rowan, J. (1981) *Human Inquiry, A Sourcebook of new paradigm research*, Chichester: John Wiley.

Schoen, D.A. (1983) *The Reflective Practitioner*, New York: Basic Books.

Tsoukas, H. (1994) *New thinking in Organisational Behaviour*, London: Heinemann.

Zeichner, K. (1993) 'Research on Teacher Thinking and different views of reflective practice', Keynote address, *ISATT conference*, Götenberg, Sweden.

Chapter 20

Some thoughts on the future of Polish MBA courses

Michael J. Thomas

Having been involved with Polish management education since 1980, and having had the opportunity of helping build four institutions, I would like to use this opportunity to reflect on the problems facing those engaged in management education and training in 1996, particularly at the MBA level in Poland. The Pierson Report, published in the United States in 1959, and which undoubtedly had a profound impact on the development of MBA programmes in America, stated:

> The diversity and complexity of purposes served by business schools put chief responsibility on the individual institution to meet its own obligations in its own way. Each school should accordingly approach its work in a bold and independent spirit, demonstrating the same qualities of vigorous, imaginative leadership which its graduates will be increasingly called on to display.
>
> (Pierson: 122, 3)

That is my philosophical starting point. I want to see a diversity of MBA programmes in Poland, and I want to see each 'school' displaying boldness and independence, characteristics not generally associated with Polish higher education, certainly pre-1989!

No single set of precepts exists in the field of business education – the world of management is complex and education and training for it reflects that complexity. For Poland, and for all the countries of Eastern and Central Europe, complexity is compounded and confounded by the advice which is being offered, and in some cases even forced upon one. I am always forcibly struck by the fact that the bureaucrats at the World Bank in Washington, who enjoy tax-free salaries and inflation-proofed pensions, argue vigorously for flexible labour markets as a means to reducing unemployment and for completely unfettered markets as a means to economic recovery and growth. A strong whiff of hypocrisy can be detected.

As my Polish colleagues develop their MBA programmes, to whom should they listen? They know what the challenge is: business of all types requires more and more managers who have the depth of business expertise to operate the complex mechanisms that make up the modern company, and the depth of knowledge to do so wisely and ethically, to meet the demands and expectations of society for greater wealth and influence within the wider world community.

Depth and breadth are themes that will occur. For Poland at this time, that wider community immediately embraces the European Community, to whose ranks Poland aspires. Poles would be quite less than human if they were not confused by the advice they are receiving.

First, you will be aware that there are four distinct models of European (University) business education:

1 British
2 French *grandes écoles*
3 NW European (Nordic, German, Benelux)
4 S European (including French Universities).

These traditions are distinct from one another, and some diversity exists within each group. As the consensus within the European Union grows, there is huge pressure on (Western) European business education to reflect the reality faced by European managers, namely to transcend the limits of their own national culture and to immerse themselves in other (European) cultures. European integration is a force for convergence, hence business educators must seek what I will call proactive diversity. By this term I mean to encourage each business school to be different and distinct, but to be aware of the necessity to harmonize around the demands of the European Union.

I should perhaps explain why I have placed emphasis on the European Union. If we do not cooperate in Europe we will be defeated competitively by the Americans. The Americans have already influenced management education in Europe, not always to good effect. I happen to believe that American capitalism (more correctly Anglo-American capitalism) should not be imported into Europe. I am a strong advocate of Rhenish capitalism, or Nordic capitalism (which my Polish friends may prefer). The European market and the European value system together represent a force for good which we collectively have a responsibility to nurture and help grow. From a strong European base we will be able to compete globally (as Unilever, Siemens, ABB, Mercedes-Benz, Airbus Industries, Phillips, Thomson, etc. have demonstrated). I believe that American capitalism has some major structural flaws that will weaken it in the twenty-first century, flaws that are not as yet present in European capitalism.

My plea is for harmonization and proactive diversity in Polish MBA programmes. The MBA is a preparation for business leadership, and in this short paper I want to present a short menu of issues that need to be addressed. I shall address in greater depth only the last item on my menu.

1 The Curriculum. I have already mentioned the issue of breadth v. depth. I think that handling this conflict is one of the great problems for management educators. It is clearly related to the nature of the students recruited to a course – do we educate for the short, medium or long term?

2 The Students. For an MBA you must recruit students with high intellectual aptitude and proven leadership ability.

3 The Faculty. Sometimes said to be the most precious resource a business school possesses, though few faculty would recognize that the pricing mechanism reflects this! The management of faculty time is critical and the ability to manage the teaching/administration/consulting mix is a much greater challenge at the present time in Eastern Europe than it is in Western Europe (where it remains a difficult problem).

4 Teaching Methods. The lecture method, so entrenched in the traditions of Eastern Europe university education, is probably the least effective method of instruction in higher management education. Proactivity, participation, decision-making, presentation skills as a means to learning are what should characterize instruction methods in MBA programmes. Polish business schools must urgently develop case materials, utilizing indigenous Polish experience since 1990, and of course incorporating greater utilization of foreign case-study material where it is relevant and not too overburdened with local cultural baggage.

5 Research. The question of research within business schools is a subject of great controversy. I will merely observe that my own philosophy is reflected in the Pierson Report:

> The broad purpose of business research may be said to increase the fund of scientific knowledge about the operations of the individual firm. To this end business schools need to concentrate on developing a body of widely applicable generalisations which have been scientifically tested and can be used in developing still further knowledge of area . . . Research in an applied field, as in any field, must consider why, not simply how, events occur.
>
> (Pierson ibid.)

The acid test of the advice is whether businessmen find the research accessible and useful. Too frequently, particularly in America, much business school research serves the purpose of influencing academic peer groups (for purposes of promotion) and too rarely serves the needs of the business community.

6 Institutional Relationships. The typical (Polish) business school should serve three publics:

- The community within which the business school is housed. Many business schools are housed within universities (in America and Western Europe the great majority are thus linked), hence their culture is linked to that of the larger university community. In Poland at the present time that is not always helpful, partly because of the competition for resources in an environment that is starved of resources, partly because management education in its post-1990 setting is philosophically so different from its university progenitors as to require a high degree of separation and independence. Other business schools, the so-called independent business schools, operate either totally divorced from the university sector or at arm's length from it. I regard the board of directors of such schools as a very critical 'public', perhaps more likely to reflect the community's concerns than a typical university senate.

- The business community. As MBAs become part of the Polish landscape, there is a critical need to establish firm links with the business community. That community may not immediately see the need for MBA-qualified employees – in the short term, multinational companies are picking up the best Polish MBA graduates. But Poland's ability to survive and compete both within the European Union and in the global market may be greatly influenced by the availability of well-trained Polish MBA graduates. Thus, the Polish business community must be sold on the value of an MBA degree. Indeed they must be sold on the need to invest in MBA education, for in the future it must be hoped that many more company-sponsored candidates will be forthcoming. Be sure that the novelty value of the MBA designation will soon wear off. Business schools must be able to demonstrate that their own graduates have track records in industry and commerce that already demonstrate the value and relevance of the qualification.

- The management professions. The third public is one in which I am particularly interested. I have just demitted office as Chairman of the Chartered Institute of Marketing, the largest body of professional marketing managers in the world. I was proud to be only the second academic elected to the chairmanship in the Institute's history. I regarded my election as some evidence of the business community's judgement about the relevance of my contribution to the field of marketing practice. In Poland pre-1989, professionalism in management was impossible since managers had to serve Party and plan. In the west the management professions – accounting, finance, human resources management, marketing, operations research, market research,

research and development, engineering – are widely acknowledged, organized and indeed valued.

What do professions profess?

- That they have mastered an esoteric body of knowledge based on systematic theory;
- its acquisition is by way of formal advanced education;
- that that knowledge is useful and valuable in solving clients' problems;
- by virtue of superior knowledge, professionals can, if they choose, exercise power over their clients;
- because of this power, professionals are governed by a code of ethics;
- it is the responsibility of professionals to avoid conflicts of interest in serving their clients;
- in exchange for status, authority and autonomy (reinforced by self-regulation), a social contract must exist between society and a profession;
- the ultimate client for a profession is society and its need.

I conclude by urging my Polish colleagues to support, through their MBA programmes, the development of the management professions and indeed to be proactive in their support of the development of professional management associations.

I wish to argue that the ultimate criterion of success of an MBA programme is that its graduates regard themselves as management professionals in exactly the same way as graduates of medical or legal courses regard themselves as professionals. MBAs themselves must encourage and nurture the development of professional associations in Poland so that, through these associations, they may address society and its concerns.

> What will happen next? Does the victory of the multi-party system in the countries of Central and Eastern Europe mean the end of their estrangement from the West? Will they, by introducing the classical division of powers – a legislature, executive and judiciary – recognise the supremacy of all Western values? Will the years of suffering under totalitarian rule be obliterated, erased and the people start from scratch? Should the thinkers, poets and artists join their Western colleagues in the somewhat marginal role assigned to them in societies busy with selling and buying?

Czesław Milosz wrote this in 1990 (Milosz 1990: 164), it resonates with concern about the future. It continues with these final thoughts:

> I hope that the turmoil in those countries [he was referring to Poland, the Baltic States, and the then Czechoslovakia] has *not* been a temporary phase, a passage to an ordinary society of earners and consumers, but rather the birth of a new form of human interaction, of a non-utopian style and vision.

(Milosz 1990: 165)

That is the challenge facing professional MBAs. Can Poland become an extraordinary society?

REFERENCES

Milosz, C. (1990) *The State of Europe, Christmas Eve 1989*, Granta 30 (Winter), London.
Pierson, F.C. (1959) *The Education of American Businessmen*, New York: McGraw-Hill.

Chapter 21

Case 3: Łódź Fabrics

Hugo Letiche and Grzegorz Urbanck

INTRODUCTION

The case describes a Polish company facing the uncertainty of the trans-formation process from a state-dominated and planned economy to a market one. However, the company is confronted with the paradox that the market economy, during this phase of the transition, is being imposed, top-down, by the state. Thus, just as before, government policy and action are central to all economic planning and action. What is new is that management is slowly asserting its control over local, in-company issues – and foreign markets and financiers are western.

Students can study and analyse the case individually or, if one wishes to make use of the proposed role game, in (four) groups. Groups examine the case from the point of view of one of the key stakeholders:

- the management of Łódź Fabrics
- the workers council of Łódź Fabrics
- representatives of the Polish government (national as well as provincial)
- a (western) consulting group hired by the Bank for Reconstruction and Development of Post-Communist Central Europe to facilitate the reor-ganization of Łódź Fabrics to make it creditworthy.

In the role play each group is represented by two people. The task is to draft a common plan for restructuring Łódź Fabrics. The Bank is only willing to grant a loan to finance a plan of restructuring if (1) all parties agree to the plan and (2) the bank is convinced that the company has a real chance of success. In at least two rounds of negotiation, the representatives meet to make initial proposals for restructuring and to negotiate a com-promise plan. Negotiation can best take place under time pressure. In each subgroup (or individually) students need to ask themselves:

- How should Łódź Fabrics foster its change capacity: what resources does it possess/lack to adjust to new economic, social, organizational demands?
- How should Łódź Fabrics help itself to change? What sort of change

process is needed? Does change of organizational process or structure need to be prioritized? Why?

- What are the opportunities and threats involved in the American offer? Is it a good idea for Łódź Fabrics to enter into this cooperation?
- What programme of automatization would be appropriate? Examine the socio-technical implications of automatization. Would it achieve greater efficiency or merely lead to bottlenecks?
- What intercultural problems (between Poles: experts/workers, managers/labour union, business/government; or between different nationalities: Poles/foreign investors or customers) would you anticipate? Are they solvable? How?
- How could one best motivate Łódź managers and workers?

THE CASE

Łódź Fabrics is a state-owned manufacturer of fabrics. It is located in Łódź, Poland's second largest city. Łódź is the centre of the Polish fabric industry. It also has a very high unemployment level: approximately 18 per cent of the workforce is unemployed (against a national average of 12%). The textile industry in general (and including Łódź Fabrics) has suffered terribly from a severe depression caused by the decrease in domestic demand and the drying up of the most important export market (ex-USSR).

The company

The Łódź Fabrics plant covers an area of 80 hectares. There are considerable unproductive fixed assets such as unused old buildings and two ponds which cannot be sold (at present) because of legal barriers, but upon which property taxes have to be paid.

The product line includes a broad range of textiles, including linen and flannel. Their products are considered to be the best or amongst the best in Poland. Production is taking place with relatively old equipment, i.e. on average twenty-five years old. Management believes that the high quality in most product lines is achieved thanks to the enormous commitment of the qualified labour. To improve quality further it is necessary to invest in new technology. It will be necessary to invest US$10 million in the next three years (for example, 1995 to 1998) to maintain/improve the quality level.

Management sees the reduction of the time needed to go from product design (planning) to production from six months to three weeks as its most important single success in the last years.

Currently the mill is being under-utilized. Significant worker layoff has occurred. Production capacity is about 50 million square metres a year; plant utilization is at approximately the 40 per cent level. In the last year, company revenue was US$20 million.

The people

The management of Łódź Fabrics includes a mixture of youth and maturity. The Managing Director is a 36-year-old textile engineer. He is said to be the guiding light behind current reforms. He has worked at Łódź Fabrics since his graduation from the Institute of Technology. He has climbed his way up the management ladder, beginning as a foreman.

There are four Vice-Directors. The Vice-Director of Production is 58 and a textile engineer. He is said to be a very conservative, production-oriented manager. But he seems to be turning around and adjusting to new circumstances.

The Vice-Director of Finance is 33; she is a woman with an MBA specializing in finance from the Erasmus University in Rotterdam. She belongs to the so-called new wave of managers. She has been working with Łódź Fabrics for two years. She has been seeking financial support for Łódź Fabrics from both national and foreign sources. She is considered to be 'a person who never gives up'.

The Vice-Director of Marketing is 30 with an MA in Foreign Trade. Before starting at Łódź Fabrics two years ago, he had spent two years working for Siemens (consumer electronics marketing division) in Germany. He is very marketing oriented, with lots of ideas about how to sell Łódź Fabrics' output. He often complains about the limited budget for his department. It is commonly accepted that he and the Production Director have different opinions concerning corporate priorities.

The Vice-Director of Information Systems is 35 with a master's in Computer Sciences. Before joining Łódź Fabrics he had run his own computer software company. He was appointed to a newly created position at Łódź Fabrics to organize corporate computerization. He will have to apply computerization to the following areas:

- inventory control (there are two warehouses for fabrics and two show-rooms where samples of all fabrics produced in the last five years are on display. Currently they do not know how much of each fabric they have in stock)
- credit and debits (Łódź Fabrics sells on credit to many customers; they do not know whether or when clients have paid.
- financial records (up-to-date records of accounts payable and receivable, payrolls and financial performance all have to be developed)
- production management (production scheduling, CAD/CAM). Because of a limited budget he will have to conduct computerization gradually, starting with the highest-priority areas.

Top management salaries are at present approximately US$600 per month, which is around five times those of production workers.

The company employs 2,500 people. During the last year more than

1,000 people have been laid off. Management believes that optimum efficiency would be achieved by laying off another 1,000 people, but a proposal to do so has been rejected by the labour unions and the Workers' Council. The Workers' Council is a powerful organ in this state-owned company; it has the right to veto management decisions.

Privatization

The company is not planning to privatize immediately. This is because of a lack of potential new owners, as well as because management does not believe that the company's results would make it an attractive object for sale. Management is seriously considering so-called commercialization which would make Łódź Fabrics into a joint stock company with all shares in the hands of the state. Commercialization would change the legal status of the firm, giving more power to management and weakening the position of the Workers' Council. It would also open Łódź Fabrics up for foreign participation in its capital and/or for joint ventures.

Markets

In 1988 Polish citizens consumed on average 30 metres of fabrics annually. Current consumption has decreased to 11 metres a year.

The total number of Polish fabric retailers and wholesalers is unknown. It is estimated that there are between 20,000 and 25,000. There are around 2,250 big clothing manufacturers who buy directly from the producers. Much consumption takes place by small or medium-sized private clothing producers. Łódź Fabrics has approximately 1,200 regular customers. In addition, it sells per month to approximately 1,000 (often quite small orders) unregistered customers. The customer profile is as follows: large customers 50; medium customers 200; small customers 950. Because of the lack of an adequate computer system, Łódź Fabrics cannot adequately keep track of its customers.

Thirty percent of sales go abroad. In the 1980s (before the collapse of the USSR market) the company exported 60% of production, especially to the Soviet Republics. Currently foreign sales go (in order of importance) to the USA, Germany, Italy, France, Canada, England and Spain. The company wants to develop new customer contacts in Western Europe. It sells abroad mainly through its own sales representatives (in the USA and in Germany) or via the Polish foreign trade agency FabricsImpex. It wants to increase sales through its own sales network and to become independent of expensive trade agency representation.

Domestic sales and marketing

Ten sales people are currently employed. Łódź Fabrics is looking for wholesalers to increase penetration into the market of smaller customers. At present 10% of sales goes via wholesalers and the rest is via their own sales people. The sales people call the potential customer's fabrics purchaser directly (in person or by phone).

Łódź Fabrics participates in two branch trade fairs each year and is considering participating in foreign trade fairs. It took part in a trade fair in Johannesburg last year but considers the experiment to have failed because of a lack of experience in such events.

Recently it has developed a catalogue containing information about the company and some samples. It is going to distribute it among potential domestic and foreign customers.

In order to better motivate its sales staff it has developed a commission system, based on a basic salary, dependent on the sales staff meeting its overall monthly quota and providing for individual bonuses linked to yet better results. It is considering switching to individual quotas and bonuses.

Competition

Łódź Fabrics has a 5% market share in Poland in cottons. Its market share has been increasing (last year it was 3.5%). It is the fourth or fifth largest fabric producer in Poland (in terms of sales). There exist around seven companies with a market share between 5–7%; all others are smaller.

Łódź Fabrics are not afraid of domestic competition, since all the companies are roughly in the same situation; but they are very concerned about foreign competition, especially from the Far East. Importers could flood the market with low-quality, cheap Asian fabrics (China, Taiwan, Indonesia). In the long run inferior fabrics probably couldn't maintain a significant market share, but the short-term effect could be disastrous. The fabric manufacturers lobby is seeking government tariff protection from 'dumping'.

Free trade with the EU is also a potential threat. EU productivity is some eight times that of the Polish. But the difference in wages more than offsets the difference in productivity. Also, free trade with the EU is not expected soon; a significant period of adjustment seems assured.

Proposition for cooperation

During a recent visit to the USA the Marketing Director made contact with the President of a medium-sized American fabric producer, Dyersburg Fabrics. Dyersburg has a comparable product range to Łódź. It produces cotton and cotton/polyester fabrics. The company employs 1,200 people and its revenue was US$100 million last year. It is seeking a partnership in

Eastern Europe. It intends, in the beginning, to sell Dyersburg products in Eastern Europe, with the possibility, later, of joint production. In the long run, Dyersburg wants a Polish partner as a bridgehead to eventual penetration of the Russian market.

THE ROLE PLAY

Each group (see above) is represented by two people. Because the meeting is so important it is chaired by the regional governor (a possible role for the lecturer). Each team is asked to introduce itself *briefly* (who are you and what can you offer Łódź Fabrics?). Then the participants discuss the future strategy of Łódź Fabrics.

The future strategy of Łódź Fabrics

Each group makes a short presentation (maximum 5 minutes) including concrete proposals taking the issues into account. After introduction and initial presentations, the meeting is adjourned. Each group has 30 minutes to discuss its response to the other groups' positions. A second round of discussion follows, where the representatives respond to each other's proposals. Every effort should be made to agree a joint plan to gain (bank) funding. At the end of the exercise one evaluates the results on content and process levels.

AFTERWORD

In the opinion of the case's authors the American proposal is a red herring. The case was initially drafted to be tried out with Polish participants. The American offer was introduced to test their sense of dependence or weakness. Would they recognize that the American firm only wants to (mis-)use Łódź Fabrics, as a bridge to selling its own goods in Central Europe and Russia? Or would their sense of western superiority be so large that they would want to enter into any joint venture with an American partner, no matter how limited the (apparent) gains? When we tested the case on Polish academics they chose in large majorities to enter into the joint venture. When we have run the case with Western European students the results have been mixed, mostly favouring going-it-alone.

Part IV

Concluding Section

Chapter 22

Boundaries, complexities and futures

Monica Lee and Hugo Letiche

This book can be read on several levels. At one level it is clearly a book about the tensions and possibilities arising from the changes in Central Europe. The contributors to this volume bring together an unusually wide range of national and discipline-based backgrounds. They bring with their particular viewpoints a plethora of insights and interpretations, providing background information that a uni-disciplinary or monocultural focus could not match. This book can therefore be seen as a wide-ranging source of information for anyone generally interested in the problems and potentials of the transitional situation in a rapidly changing Europe.

At a second level, this book is about the role that management and managers play in 'free-market' economies. Such economies rely upon the efficacy of management; yet, as this book illustrates profusely, 'management' is not a unitary concept. There is no clear, single or unquestioned definition of 'management'. Instead, management appears to be a situated and complex phenomenon – one that relies upon the context within which it is placed for the clarity of a localized definition. Many of the contributors, particularly in Part II, focus on ways of understanding the local situation as a necessary first step in appreciating the context-specific role that 'management' plays within the circumstances. It follows from this that the role of the manager (and success or failure in this role) can also only be understood in terms of localized circumstance. This book offers a range of interpretative frameworks and models – of management and the managerial role as played out empirically in Central Europe. The import of these interpretations, however, is not geographically limited. They are of relevance to recent discussions of the global/local nature of the managerial role, and are useful reading for anyone engaged in this debate.

At a third level, the book is about the ways in which the full gamut of management educational provision creates, supports or hinders 'effective' management. As is made evident throughout the book, this is a complex statement. It depends upon some agreement about what 'effective' management is, whilst the parameters of 'management education' (and thus its provision) are interdependent and wide-ranging. The book is about management education yet includes chapters that focus on politics, economics, history, psychology, culture and identity, as well as the more normally recognized foci of educational philosophy and methodology. Such eclecticism mirrors the editors' view that the remit of 'management education' extends from national politics (and thus national structures and resources), through educational establishments (whether mainstream or alternative including their structures, politics and resources), through the preferences, philosophy and politics of individual 'educators', to the actual, realized, 'educational provision', including curricula, resources and methods.

A holistic approach is adopted in the belief that each area effects each of the others and thus cannot be taken alone without seriously distorting the picture. All areas are thus interdependent. For example, a national drive for cost-effectiveness and reduction in the educational budget, with associated lack of human and teaching resources, might force providers (against their educational preferences) to adopt methods associated with mass education, i.e. low status (and thus cheap) staff who are reading from specialist texts to a large auditorium filled with students, all of whom are busy transcribing the spoken word. This might lead to mass examinations and to the assumption (by both staff and students) that the effective transfer of knowledge is the ultimate goal. This, in turn, might lead to the establishment of systems that increasingly value the transfer of knowledge at the expense of wisdom or applicability of that knowledge. The chosen educational method might be an entirely appropriate response to wider circumstances.

At a time when educational budgets are being cut across Europe, awareness of such interdependence is very pertinent to management education. Urgency is hereby leant to the need to discuss what is really meant by 'education'? Is it a cyclical amplification of existing societal norms? Is it a way of encouraging debate and openness? Is it about reviewing practice in the light of theory? Does it enhance practice? Is it a way of examining societal aspiration? Is it a way of working towards new and different futures?

The contributors to this book adopt different stances to answering these questions. For some, education should find the best way to transfer received wisdom; for others, it ought to link theory and practice. For some, education occurs as classroom practice; for others, education occurs outside the traditional classroom situation (e.g. through the media). For some, education is about retroactively meeting students' wants; for others, it is about proactively meeting society's needs. For some, education is a driver of change; for others, 'changes' in education offer no more than appearances of change. And so on. These differences of opinion are central to this book, impact upon us all and will not go away.

BOUNDARIES AND COMPLEXITY

The book also stresses that the management of change is an open systems phenomenon; but if this is so, can it occur within the political stance of cultural relativism? This is the fourth level at which this book can be read, and it is the one that we wish to focus on here. Despite the different themes mentioned above, the book is essentially about the dilemmas of change.

The book has been split into three parts, each of which offers an alternative approach to change. In Part I the authors appear to approach change from a fairly 'tightly' bounded position. One way of operating is presented as superior to others and carries the expectation (hope) that others will agree to or accept this apparently inevitable superiority. Each author in this section presents her/his case as if there were a 'right' way of doing things – and that the key challenge is to establish what that 'right' way might be. The authors suggest that particular models of management education ought to be the most appropriate for the Central Europeans to adopt – whether the clarity of the American approach (Francis Aguilar; Edward Cyrson and Urszula Ornarowicz); the diversity of the Western European approach (Gordon Shenton); or particular preferred methods, such as case study (Michael Thomas). Each of these approaches is rooted in a particular political understanding and educational philosophy. These are also explicitly addressed within Part I. Jerzy Dietl, and Marianna Strzy-zewska-Kaminska and Bogdan Wawrzyniak both identify their political and economic boundaries, whilst Monica Lee presents her philosophical preferences as a central factor.

In presenting pictures, the authors have, of necessity, also presented the boundaries within which they operate. There are clear delineations to their areas of concern and they present their picture as a coherent whole. In general, these delineations or boundaries remain unstated. The boundaries to each world-view are sufficiently clear (to those who share that world-view) to make the statement of them assumed, and thus irrelevant or almost impossible. How can one know the parameters of one's own world-view without knowing what alternative views might look like?

The second section of the book exemplifies a 'loosely' bound logic of change – this was called 'patterned' logic in the introduction, and is, in essence, a stance of cultural relativity. There is no one 'right' view that has dominance over others; instead, all views are equal but each holds different implications. Contributors to Part II map different views and offer frameworks by which to understand them. They are explicit about their boundaries and identify where these boundaries are transgressed or how they shift, creating new patterns. They explore the differing implications of their multiple and interconnected 'loosely' bound logic(s). Essentially, the authors are standing back and presenting their values as open to interpretation. Obviously, none of the accounts is value-free – they are inevitably derived from the author's value base and present 'life' as understood by the author from that perspective. Some of these chapters (such as that by Hugo Letiche) are argued passionately. In general, however, the values that are transmitted are those of respect for understanding and of valuing difference. The individual's role within this is to make sense of, and thus 'rational' judgements about, the complexity of world-views on offer. 'Loosely' bounded logic demands that readers understand and accommodate themselves to the perspective of others.

The section explores shifting political (Steve Crawshaw) and economic boundaries (Andrzej Kozminski); shifting views of 'management' as a situated concept (Hugo Letiche, Monika Kostera); the forms of 'aid' that might be entailed (Slawomir Magala); and the implications this holds for shifting forms of management education (Kozminski). All these contributions are reflexive – they question their own assumptions and those of others. Other contributions question, as well, the values underlying 'resistance to change' (Devi Jankowicz), asking to what extent change is really occuring in Central Europe (Kristina Genell and Monika Kostera) and in what sort of timescales this is or is not happening (Steve Crawshaw). Taken together, these contributions explore complexity and relativity. They introduce the complexity of working cross-culturally, including the need to understand the situation from the other's point of view, the need to withhold value judgement until one's own boundaries are understood, the need to see the situation as a pattern in which all elements hold meaning only in so far as they relate to other elements. Meaning and 'culture' are relative in these 'loosely' bound rationalities.

Few would deny that, globally, nations and large enterprises are either willingly embracing (or being forced into) an awareness of other cultures. In some cases such awareness is based upon competition and feelings of threat, leading to a need to understand the 'other' in order to be able to compete. In other cases the different parties seek cross-cultural cooperation. Few would deny that cooperative cross-cultural working is much more successful, in both task outcomes and in minimized personal cost, if those involved attempt to understand each other's world-views, try to be aware of their own prejudices, and aspire to reach compromise through the valuing of the different strengths that the other parties bring to the situation. Similarly, few would deny that current political and social rhetoric increasingly describes multiculturalism, a lack of racism or sexism, and the reduction of hierarchy as desirable.

There appears to be a general societal move towards the acknowledgement, if not acceptance, of diversity and of globalism. It is becoming impossible to live in one culture. Almost all cultures touch one another through international business, and 'relativize' each other in the process. This move is accompanied by the increasing vocalism of 'postmodernists'. They are lumped together here as a unity to emphasize their world-view of 'multiple realities' and complexity, despite a correlated tenet of postmodernism which denies the unitary, anticipating the lack of stable core beliefs in their work. Slowly, everyone is exposed to everyone else's 'voyeuristic' gaze, in which the distinction between the 'centre' and the 'researcher' is lost. Cultural relativism is becoming the economically consistent perspective from which to view existence – for managers, politicians, organizations, educationalists and academics alike.

Taken together, the first two sections of this book might be seen to indicate some sort of statement about the processes of change and, thus, about the contributors' 'reflexivity'. These parts could be read to indicate that change occurs through confrontation between 'tightly' bounded positions, which then 'loosen' as the boundaries are questioned, a process which forces the parties to acknowledge cultural relativism which, within this scenario, is the 'best' way of being – and is thus not a particularly culturally relativistic point of view at all. Parts I and II could be seen as the modernist tradition of absolute truth and cultural imperialism v. postmodernist assertion of shifting boundaries, flexibility, complexity and relativism. This simplistic analysis, however, is belied by Part III.

In essence, the third section questions the role of 'agents of change' and thus the nature of change. The very existence of the concept of 'change agents' implies that for many people change can be catalysed and is subject to human volition. The rhetoric of the 'free market' clearly stresses deliberately changing one's circumstances for the betterment of one's chosen reference group. It sings of success through entrepreneurship, motivation, dedication and well-judged choices that inspire 'beneficial' change. Working within the 'free market' entails the individualistic search for the magic formula, the niche, the clarity of 'identity', at the expense of the collectivistic subsuming of self within social structures that provide support for all (cf. Slawomir Magala). The logic of the 'free market' and entrepreneurship can be 'tightly' or 'loosely' bounded. We assert that because it is about individualistic striving, which by its very nature promotes one view, aspiration, achievement over and above others and at the expense of others – thus it is inherently 'tightly' bounded. However, it is culturally ruinous to let it overwhelm the social system. Bounding the civil society tightly to such a narrow logic destroys the dynamism of the liberal society to pursue creativity, cultural renewal, social innovation and organizational experimentation.

The third section, therefore, builds upon both of the other sections. The contributions within Part III focus upon ways of educating for entrepreneurship. They suggest that successful entrepreneurs need to be able to step back and see the patterns of cultural relativism. They argue that in order to promote this, alternative (less tightly bounded, less prescriptive and more complex) educational methods need to be employed. They present a view of education that is essentially 'Postmodern' – one in which the 'learner' is presented with (and helped to work through) the complexity of the situation and is encouraged to define her/his own 'reality'. The underlying message, however, is that the 'learner' is, or has the potential to be, an active agent of change, that in defining their own reality learners have a responsibility to themselves to follow through on their own logics and to work for their realization. The 'successful' entrepreneur needs to maintain a balance between seeing the multiplicity of the realities around her/him and cutting through all this complexity in order to establish her/his own proactive (commercially viable) reality.

FUTURES

The first two sections of the book, therefore, do not present stages of change so much as two different sides (or foci) of the processes of change. The questions underlying every single contribution to the book are 'What would be the best form of reality to adopt?' and 'What form of future are we aspiring to?' It is these fundamental questions that we wish to focus on in our conclusions. We shall do this in two ways. First by overviewing possible world trends, and then by exploring aspects of societal aspiration.

World trends

Gazing into the crystal ball appears to be complex and unpredictable, yet some forecasts, such as those offered by Godet and Barre (1988) and Jouvenel (1988) appear, with hindsight, to be close to reality. A generalist view of the impact of new technology (Toffler 1980) might be that the increasing use of electronics will lead to global communications and power will shift from nation state to transnational organization. Within this is forecast the development of post-economic value-systems (Toffler 1985). Psychological, moral, social and aesthetic values will come to the fore, accompanied by highly differentiated social structures, in which men and women will need to be capable of making complex value-based decisions, to learn rapidly and to develop their imagination. Other writers reinforce the notion of culture-specific national and regional variations (Hofstede 1979; 1980; Nasif et al. 1991; Senker 1992), leading to views of the increasing stratification of society and nations. One's power and prosperity become directly linked to the availability and use of new technologies (Moenaert et al. 1993).

Problems in prediction, however, are linked to the dynamic nature of the open systems with which we have been dealing throughout. Take, for example, Ashton and Perica's (1993) suggestion that the longer-term impact of forecasting is cyclically related to the way in which threats presented to the environment from hyper-industrialization, the over-exploitation of resources and the dematerialization of production via new technologies are met. An alternative way of working is to look to a desired future and then outline a path towards it. 'This approach differs from a traditional long-range planning approach based upon a single set of environmental assumptions about the future in recognizing that, although the future is a continuation of existing trends, it is subject to modification by events that have some probability of occurrence' (Morrison 1990: 23). Futurists argue for sustainable economic growth in which real gross national product per capita is increasing over time without threat of feedback from biophysical (pollution or resource problems) or social impacts (social disruption) (Pearce *et al.* 1989); sustainable development, in which 'the needs of the present (are met) without compromising the ability of future generations to meet their own needs' (Bruntland 1987); and a scenario of creative advantage in which each nation concentrates on its unique qualities and offers these to others (Gorz 1989; Henderson 1989; Stuke 1990), as opposed to Porter's (1990) view of competitive advantage. However, it is worth noting that Slaughter (1993) has called for individuals and organizations to create their own models and derive their own views of the dynamics of change rather than rely on utilizing off-the-shelf accounts of the future.

Wierzbicki (1991) has summarized a prognostic report of the Poland 2000 Committee of the Polish Academy of Sciences, which analyses the potential impact of three forms of societal aspiration in Poland. He concludes that informed educational reform in which students are prepared for a broad professional life in a way that stimulates adaptability and entrepreneurial attitudes, and which supports closer research and development links with industry and enterprise, alongside a scepticism about a wholesale reliance upon market forces is of critical importance. He sees educational reform as contributing to a redressing of environmental damage and a radical decrease in energy and material consumption rates. He also considers, however, that the recent focus upon short-term free-market mechanisms is likely to hinder the development of the necessary infrastructure. He therefore calls for the creation of a structural development policy that is not only realized by the government but is perceived and pursued by the entire society. Support for this view can be found in Northcott (1991: 348). This report sketches general scenarios with regard to the way that government policies might affect business and management in the UK, possible economic implications of each having been tested with the use of the Cambridge Econometrics model. As with Wierzbicki, the report is nation-specific. However, the similarity between the two reports is notable, and the delineation and predictive testing of what could be seen as archetypal futures merit further discussion.

The first scenario addressed is that of a market-oriented approach, with lower income tax, reduced government spending and supply-side changes to improve the efficiency of the market and raise labour productivity. This would be likely to give a fast rise in consumers' expenditure, a slow fall in unemployment and an early improvement in the balance of payments. The second scenario illustrates an interventionist approach, with higher income tax, higher government spending on social services, and expansion of R&D as well as training schemes to increase productivity. This would be likely to give a slow rise in consumers' expenditure, a fast fall in unemployment and an early improvement in the balance of payments. The third scenario is an environment-oriented approach, with higher prices for water, electricity, petrol, gas and coal, but lower prices for many other categories of expenditure. Less energy-dependent services, such as health, education and most recreational services, would benefit. These price changes would bring major shifts in demand and output. Structural shifts would be considerable; the deflationary effect of the carbon tax would be broadly offset by reductions in value added tax. Declines in the energy-intensive sectors would be offset by increases elsewhere. Total economic growth, therefore, would be much the same as with the other forecasts.

Despite the different political and ideological principles upon which they are based, the projected consequences of the three approaches are similar in economic terms. This conclusion is supported by Meadows *et al.* (1992) and by the World Development Report (1992: 178), which finds a 'growing consensus that policies for economic efficiency and for environmental management are complementary'. It can be argued, therefore, that choice of future is linked more to societal (political) aspiration than 'scientific' criteria.

SOCIETAL ASPIRATION

Management education in the new Europe is, inherently, a marriage of western (European) cognitive building blocks and the local culture. The 'ideas to be mastered', 'skills to be learnt', 'attitudes to be developed' are all drawn from a discourse developed in the industrialized capitalist countries during the last fifty years. That discourse can be 'evangelized' or 'relativized', 'persuasively asserted' or 'actively debunked', 'accepted' or 'deconstructed', but in some form or fashion it is going to be presented. Slowly the managerial discourse will adopt local garb; it will find its way into Central European cases, textbooks adapted for indigenous circumstances and books (ghost-written) by local business heroes. Eventually the Central Europeans will forget that capitalist managerialism is an imported discourse; they will find it just as 'normal' as the Spanish or Dutch find it today. But at present 'managerialism' is a foreign discourse. It is mistrusted by some and highly valued by others, understood by a few and feared by many. How do we think the marriage will develop between the foreign text of 'business education' and the local processes of societal change; what possible scenarios do we envision for business education in the new Europe?

Scenarios are based upon modelling primary driving forces to understand the dynamics shaping a probable future. Basically these forces fall roughly into four categories: (1) the social (norms, values, lifestyles), (2) the economic (micro- and macro-economics as well as inter-company relations), (3) the political (government policy and action) and (4) the technological (production processes, research & development). To develop scenarios we must identify uncertainties crucial to the possible development of the primary driving forces. Such forces will normally cut across several (if not all) of the categories. Scenarios are evolved by reducing a great number of (possible) uncertainties to a limited number of factors. Normally two axes are defined, allowing the scenario writers to define four quadrants, each of which defines a possible future.

Since our question focuses on economic change and culture, one possible quadrant would be based on a comparison of Centralized (one authority/power) versus Decentralized (authority/power spread through the organization) with Informal (personal power) versus Formal (role power) forms of interaction. The resulting quadrant would look like Figure 22.1.

There exist differing discourses of management suited to each quadrant: human resource development and virtual organization best fit the first; American textbooks from Mintzberg to Porter give support to the second; 'the-right-person-in-the-right-position-at-the-right-time' thinking, as well as business process re-engineering, fits the third; and 'walk-the-talk' literature stressing

Figure 22.1 Mapping futures through approach to power

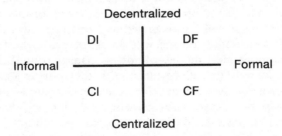

DI: The Decentralized/Informal organization stresses improvisation, growth, and 'win–win' relationships; it is a world of highly motivated creative people who seek personal fulfilment through their work.

DF: The Decentralized/Formal organization is problem- and goal-oriented; expertise is highly valued as long as it can 'deliver the goods', end results (profits) are paramount. Managing is more 'task-' than 'position-'directed; matrix organization is likely.

CF: The Centralized/Formal organization is highly rational and structured; there is a 'right way' to do things (rules and procedures) which is believed to be logical and efficient.

CI: The Centralized/Informal organization is paternalistic; powerful leaders create a micro-political field about them in which 'favourites' are rewarded.

highly personal entrepreneurial leadership reaffirms the fourth. Communism seems to have explicitly asserted Centralized/Formal organizing whilst implicitly condoning 'clientism' (i.e. Centralized/Informal organizing). Polish capitalism has embraced Informalized/Central action, whilst the rhetoric of most western business discourse is Decentralized/Formal. The 'relativism' of this book reflects a prejudice to Decentralized/Informal managing.

Because of the availability of data on Poland, we will explore these issues using Poland as the exemplar. Trompenaars' data (published in 1993) shows Polish managers as having minimal trust in 'roles' (i.e. Weberian 'bureaucracy') and a strong commitment to 'individualized authority' (even more than Spanish or Swedish managers). For the Poles (more than other Central Europeans), managers are people who get the job done (but Brits, Dutch, Americans are even stronger in this conviction). In Trompenaars' data, the Poles are less accepting of paternalistic power than those in the other post-Communist societies. More than most other nationalities, they stress that organizational success depends on the manager's personality. Nonetheless the defeatism of fifty years of Communism has not disappeared: Polish managers believe, much less than Western European ones, that 'what happens to them is their own doing'.

Centralized Informal organization will embrace extreme 'liberalism' and the 'market economy'; there is little or no resistance to the successful businessman. But the law of the marketplace can reward some while it impoverishes many others. Managers feel themselves responsible for their fiefdoms but not for society at large. Management education, if it stresses competitive advantage and provides tools for making profits, will be highly valued — otherwise it will be dismissed as 'academic' or 'irrelevant'. The multinationals which enter Poland will almost inevitably be formally organized. If they impose clear models of how to manage from their home base, they practice Central-Formal organization. If they pursue local differentiation within their global strategy, they will be Decentral-Formal in their organization. In both cases management education will be needed and valued in order to impose a Formal organizational culture. Thus, the role of management education is likely to legitimize multinational formalization.

The chance that postmodern thinking, leading to the informalization of management, will be effective in the new Europe is remote. Postmodernism accompanies post-industrialism. It is a reaction to a social situation which has reached the limits of effective formalization and needs to withdraw from the brink of self-destructive over-rationalization. At best, the postmodernists can discover in the new Europe what informal managing looks like, but the analysis of excessive rationalization will not be of much interest to Central Europeans. In Trompenaars' terms, Polish management education is endangered by: (i) the political backlash engendered by the extreme partiality of the Central/Informal model of organizing and/or (ii) the resentment evoked by being seen as merely a legitimating discourse for a formalization process initiated by foreign businesses. Both problems are already observable.

If we turn to Hofstede's frame of reference we see that Poland scored about the same in 'uncertainty avoidance' as do the Northwestern Europeans (Dutch or Norwegians) (ITIM 1995). The Brits and Danes accept the risks of 'winning and losing' in the marketplace more than do the Poles. The Brits and Danes are much less concerned with rules and order and are much more willing to take risks than are the Poles. But those in the Latin countries (the French, the Spanish, Italians) as well as the Germans are all much more threatened by the unexpected and uncertain than are the Poles. Risk-taking, economic stress, acceptance of dissent are all ambivalent matters for the Poles – they are all somewhat accepted, but also feared. On the other hand, Poles are very clear on the 'masculinity' scale. Poland is rated as having one of the most 'masculine' cultures in Europe (at the same level as the Swiss and Italian cultures). The culture highly values the 'achiever' and is dedicated to 'success'. Symbols of power, such as fast cars and luxury purchases, are lionized. This factor holds little sympathy or support for the economically weak and underprivileged.

Power distance in Poland has been determined to be significantly less than in France, slightly less than in Spain and the same as in Italy. Hungary and the Czech Republic, as well as the Northwest European countries, such as the UK and Holland, are all much lower on this scale. Thus, Poles accept more inequality in power than do the other Central European post-Ccommunist societies. Though the power distance differential is not extreme (as in the case of Russia), one would not expect a strong movement to egalitarianism or social levelling in Poland. The score for 'individualism' is the same as for the Czechs, higher than for the Hungarians and near that of the Finns or Austrians, but much lower than for the Dutch or the Brits. The combination of factors reveals a fairly strong need for rules and order ('uncertainty avoidance') coupled with a very strong need for individual ambition and success ('masculinity') that is unhindered by a strong demand for equality ('power distance') and is without the sense of self which tempers action through a strong moral sense or facilitates innovation and creativity ('individualism'). Thus Poland seems to be a very success-oriented culture with a weak social consciousness and which is not very likely to innovate new products or services. According to this, management education will be an uphill battle. Managers will want to exploit knowledge to become wealthy, but not to pay attention to the environment, needs of clients or social development. There is a large danger that management education will feed a rather narrow form of egoism and thereby gain the reputation of serving a socially destructive pattern of managerialism.

The most common scenarios for the next ten years have often compared Fragmentation/Coherence to Individual/Community, see Figure 22.2.

If we examine Poland within this framework we discover a society

Figure 22.2 Mapping futures through approach to social cohesion

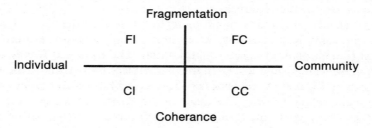

FI: Fragmentation/Individual is a social circumstance in which economic rationality has prevailed over other social/political norms; very few people have permanent jobs; competition for work, wealth and status is very strong. The individual has to be assertive and to focus on the individual 'I' to survive. Globalization has made the world economy extremely extremely competitive; there are no safe havens from international competition.

CI: Coherence/Individual is a situation in which the limits of the consumer society have led to increased social awareness. A society of informed self-interest has organized itself around self-help groups and effective ways of meso-social action. Norms of 'win–win' relationships, pursuit of community and achievement of consensus are strong, though organized social existence (such as government) is very weak. Many 'lifestyles' and forms of merchandise are available; groups of people have learnt to cooperate and make choices together, which has led to them defining their own local sense of purpose and harmony.

CC: Coherence/Community offers a society which has returned to regulation and government intervention in economic existence as the only effective way to achieve and maintain social stability. Only strong government can channel capitalism in a socially constructive direction. Pure market economy proved unable to deliver either freedom or wealth. New governmentalism can marginalize the power of the large corporations and achieve a stable, and reasonably just, world order.

FC: Fragmentation/Community is a circumstance in which market supremacy has led to (near) permanent recession and economic malaise. The social stress which continuous declining wealth produces forces the powerful to re-embrace strong government. Society lacks strong cultural cement society threatens to unravel. But since there is no real alternative, one has to try to make the best of an unsatisfactory situation.

emerging from Community/Coherence and currently moving towards Fragmentation/Individual. Will the current trend to FI be maintained? Presidential and legislative elections have seemed to indicate that the FC (Fragmentation/Community) option is setting in. This is more a defensive strategy than a proactive one. The FI trend can only be maintained, we believe, as long as the possibilities for growth, innovation and renewal (which it signals) outstrip the dangers of marginalization, unemployment and declining welfare. Wealthy over-controlled nations can reduce the power of cartels, free themselves from the stranglehold of inefficiency and attack a record of entrepreneurial stagnation. Poland does not have the economic slack to be able to permit very much 'creative destruction'. A CI strategy (Coherence/Individual) is not realistic in the new Europe. What this amounts to is the (near) victory of civil society over capitalist logic. This is a society wherein consumerization has been mastered by meso-level cooperation. Instead of market relations conquering all social interaction, new social forms of cooperation are able to make use of the market to their own advantage. Freely chosen fairly small social groups are in control of their own community/destiny. The logic of the civil society prevails; the choice of cooperation and the forces of group adhesion are stronger than the forces of world capitalism. There is no sign at all that the Polish citizenry can achieve such economic and cultural self-determination in the near future. This scenario sounds rather Utopian even for the richest of societies.

A return to a government-guided economic policy, but with developing welfare and market competition sounds like the most positive possibility. The CC (Coherence/Community) stratagem is rather undramatic. In it one re-creates government control without abandoning market economics. One tries to facilitate catch-up economic development to achieve the quality of product and service provision which makes one competitive. Poland is trying to develop a market niche for herself within international capitalism, probably centring on agriculture and the low-wage production of industrial goods. Management has to focus on the control function: the Polish economy will seek survival through increased efficiency. There is little room for managerial innovation in this scenario. What Poland will need to do is to train a competent echelon of middle managers who can achieve qualitatively competitive production. Strategy will be determined within controlling foreign multinationals which own Polish production facilities and/or buy Polish goods. Domestic management will need to focus on quality and price. Within this scenario Poland will enjoy little economic independence and will not have the wealth needed to develop really new products or services. The core economies of countries like Germany and France will orchestrate European economic development; Poland's concern will be not to miss the boat altogether. Illusions of fundamental experimentation, held by many in 1989–90, will be abandoned through fear of an FC (Fragmentation/Community) pattern of development, in which Poland would decline into a poor backwater of Western Europe which does not profit from Western European economic growth.

END WORD

Having explored both cultural and social-economic scenarios for Poland, we are left, as we started, with questions. Some are relatively straight forward – though still hard to answer. They question the validity, reliability and generalizability of the data we have used, and whether we have interpreted these data appropriately. Is it really possible to reduce a culture to a few basic criteria, and, if so, are these the 'right' ones? Is it really possible to examine a single country and extrapolate from that? In order to look at the future of one nation, do we not have to look at the interdependencies and possible futures of all nations?

Another sort of question focuses upon the assumptions behind these analyses. Are the bases of 'culture' fixed, or do they change? If they change, can they do so quickly – as with (hysterical) adherence to charismatic leaders, such as pop stars or Hitler-figures? What of the unexpected technological advance that might irrevocably change our existence? What of unprecedented natural or man-made disasters that have a global influence?

Further questions relate to the activities of individuals (you and I) and the extent of our influence upon these scenarios. Everyone involved in the work described throughout this book is, in some way or another, an agent of change. How do we balance our feelings of individual agency with those of impotence in the face of social structure and historical inevitability? Surely we have to believe that we have some effect, otherwise why do we act in the ways we do? In other words – we return to the start and ask 'What are we doing here?'

REFERENCES AND FURTHER READING

Ashton, D.J.L. and Perica, L. (1993) 'The future of management education: the impact of new paradigms', working paper, Lancaster University, UK.

Bruntland, G.H. (1987) *Our Common Future. Report for the World Commission on Environment and Development*, Oxford: Oxford University Press.

Featherstone, M. (1990) *Global Culture*, London: Sage.

Featherstone, M., Lash, S. and Robertson, R. (1995) *Global Modernities*, London: Sage.

Godet, M. and Barre, R. (1988) 'Into the next decade: major trends and uncertainties', *Futures* 20(4), pp. 410–23.

Gorz, A. (1989) *Critique of Economic Reason*, London: Verso.

Henderson, H. (1989) 'Mutual development: towards new criteria and indicators', *Futures* 21(6), pp. 571–84.

Hofstede, G. (1979) 'Hierarchical power difference in 40 countries', in C. Lammers and D. Hickson (eds) *Organisations Alike and Unlike*, London: Routledge.

Hofstede, G. (1980) *Culture's Consequences: International Differences in Work-related Values*, Beverley Hills: Sage.

ITIM (1995) *5-D Pocket Guide. Country Scores and Definitions*, The Hague: ITIM.

Jouvenel, H. de (1988) 'Europe at the dawn of the third millennium', *Futures* 20(5), pp. 505–18.

Meadows, D.H., Meadows, D.L. and Randers, J. (1992) *Beyond the Limits: Global Collapse or a Sustainable Future*, London: Earthscan Publications Ltd.

Moenaert, R., De Meyer, A. and Clarysee, B. (1994) 'Understanding international differences in the management of technology and innovation', in Wm E. Souder and J.D. Sherman (eds) *Managing New Technology Development*, New York: McGraw Hill.

Morrison, J.L. (1990) *The Alternative Futures Approach to Strategic Planning: A Handbook for Planners in Higher Education*, paper presented at Global change: implications for the future of higher education, international strategic planning seminar, Scotland: St Andrews University.

Nasif, E.G., Al-Daeaj, H., Ebrahimi, B. and Thiboudeaux, M.S. (1991) 'Methodological problems in cross-cultural research: an updated review', *Management International Review* 31, pp. 79–91.

Northcott, J. (1991) *Britain in 2010*, Policy Studies Institute Report, London: PSI Publishing.

Pearce, D., Markandaya, A. and Barbier, B. (1989) *Blueprint for a Green Economy*, Report for the Department of the Environment, UK, London: Earthscan Publications Ltd.

Porter, M.E. (1990) 'The competitive advantage of nations', *Harvard Business Review* (March–April), pp. 73–93.

Senker, P. (1992) 'Technological change and the future of work', *Futures* 24(4), pp. 351–64.

Slaughter, R. (1993) 'Looking for the real "megatrends"', *Futures* 25(8), pp. 351–64.

Stuke, L. (1990) *Signs of Hope: Working Towards our Common Future*, Oxford: Oxford University Press.

Toffler, A. (1980) *The Third Wave*, London: Pan Books.

Toffler, A. (1985) *The Adaptive Corporation*, London: Pan Books.

Trompenaars, F. (1993) *Riding the Waves of Culture*, London: Nicholas Brealey.

Urry, J. (1990) *The Tourist Gaze*, London: Sage.

Wierzbicki, A.P. (1991) 'Poland's development dilemmas on the verge of the 21st Century', *Futures* 23(4), pp. 392–401.

Wilkinson, L. (1995) 'How to build scenarios', *Scenarios* 3(11), pp. 74–81 (special wired edition).

World Development Report (1992) *Development and the Environment: World Development Indicators*, Oxford: Oxford University Press/World Bank.

Index